Humanistic Studies in the Communication Arts

EROTIC COMMUNICATIONS

Studies in Sex, Sin and Censorship

A TAXONOMY OF
CONCEPTS IN COMMUNICATION
by Reed H. Blake and Edwin O. Haroldsen

COMMUNICATIONS AND MEDIA
Constructing a Cross Discipline
by George N. Gordon

ETHICS AND THE PRESS
Readings in Mass Media Morality
Edited by John C. Merrill and Ralph D. Barney

DRAMA IN LIFE
The Uses of Communication in Society
Edited by James E. Combs and Michael W. Mansfield

INTERNATIONAL AND INTERCULTURAL COMMUNICATION
Edited by Heinz-Dietrich Fischer and John C. Merrill

EXISTENTIAL JOURNALISM
by John C. Merrill

THE COMMUNICATIONS REVOLUTION
A History of Mass Media in the United States
by George N. Gordon

COMMUNICATION ARTS IN THE ANCIENT WORLD
Edited by Eric A. Havelock and Jackson P. Hershbell

EDITORIAL AND PERSUASIVE WRITING
by Harry W. Stonecipher

ENTERTAINMENT
A Cross-Cultural Examination
Edited by Heinz-Dietrich Fischer and Stefan R. Melnik

COMMUNICATION THEORIES
Origins, Methods, Uses
by Werner J. Severin and James W. Tankard

CRITICIZING THE CRITICS
by John W. English

EROTIC COMMUNICATIONS
Studies in Sex, Sin and Censorship
by George N. Gordon

Humanistic Studies in | H S / C A | The Communication Arts

Erotic Communications:

Studies in Sex, Sin and Censorship

by GEORGE N. GORDON

COMMUNICATION ARTS BOOKS

HASTINGS HOUSE, PUBLISHERS

New York 10016

For my wife Nancy (aka Bobbie),
the original Australian mouse,
who has for nearly three decades
put up with all of this.

Library of Congress Cataloging in Publication Data

Gordon, George N   Erotic communications.

   (Humanistic studies in the communication arts)
(Communication arts books)
  Bibliography: p.
  Includes index.
  1. Erotica.   2. Communication in sex.
3. Pornography—Social aspects.   4. Censorship.
I. Title.
HQ460.G67   1980   301.2'1   79-24944
ISBN 0-8038-1959-5
ISBN 0-8038-1960-9 pbk.

Published simultaneously in Canada by
Copp Clark Ltd., Toronto
Designed by Al Lichtenberg
Printed in the United States of America

CONTENTS

Part Three: THE FUTURE

INTRODUCTION

In facing up to reality, we can rise above reality.
—Eugene Ionesco

BY THE TIME that I was old enough to write this book, I discovered that I was too old to write it. I wrote it anyway.

I believe it was A. N. Whitehead who lamented the irony that the young are gifted with imagination but lack experience and that the old have plenty of experience but are short of imagination, or words to this effect. I do not think Whitehead meant his aphorism to apply directly to erotic communications but, because eroticism calls to mind so many analogies to various other sorts of human enterprises, particularly intellectual ones, the shoe indeed fits. Or so it does in my case.

The impetus for the document that follows was generated by experience, not necessarily my own erotic experience, a matter that I shall get to before many pages pass. For many years I have followed with interest the heated discussions, experimentation and learned literary production that concerns types of human communication that probably *do not exist,* until I had eventually collected quite an extensive library of books and articles concerning them. I mean such equivocal (and admittedly arguable) arcana as Extrasensory Perception, Subliminal Persuasion (sexual and non-sexual), Psychokinesis, and the entire storehouse of demiurges that have sprung like Minerva from Dr. H. M. McLuhan's peculiar frontal lobes such as "hot" and "cold" and "oral" and "tactile" and "linear" and "non-linear" media.

Having once and long ago dabbled in conjuring, especially so-called "mentalism" and stage hypnosis, I remained—and remain to this day—fascinated by the deep thirst of so many people, particularly many who fancy themselves intellectuals, for trickery and illusion dressed up as enlightenment and/or experiment.

I also find revealing the generalization that I have often heard from professional magicians: The more educated an audience, the easier it is to fool them, an entirely logical axiom when one thinks about it a bit. Even the most clever conjurer has difficulty deceiving a fairly smart dog. Children are a tricky audience, not knowing the rules of causality and uncertain of the invariable laws of nature, they often see right through extremely clever deceptions. The perfect audience for the stage magician consists entirely of MENSA members, providing that most of them are professional people such as physicians, scientists, psychologists, lawyers or professors of anything. These individuals are usually credulous, simply because they tend to pursue quite rational and logical trains of thought. They trust their senses, distrust their feelings, intuition and common sense, know precisely what is possible and what is impossible and exactly why it is and is not.

Staring at my considerable but somewhat useless collection of volumes concerning the subjects noted above, I was one day struck by the fact that thousands, possibly millions of dollars and God knows how many man hours of labor had been spent intensively studying these matters that, as far as I was able to tell, probably, as I say, do *not* exist. For some reason, I then thought of the human sexual urge and the many ways it is obviously mediated between human beings. It occurred to me that, also to the best of my knowledge, erotic communications *do* and *must* exist. "How much money, time, energy or wisdom had been spent in their study?" I asked, not quite aloud. The question has remained with me.

For the next few years I tried to remain alert to any and all articles and books, responsible and irresponsible, that, first, accepted as a discreet aspect of the human condition the transfer or process of interchange of erotic feeling from one person to another and, second, tried to explain any but the most obvious aspects of these phenomena. Aside from a few paragraphs in a few execrable pornographic novels, some psychological studies and occasional conjectures, my cupboard was relatively bare. I had stumbled, it seemed, upon a more or less unexplored subject!

My next step was to search out people who considered themselves—or were considered by others—experts in the field of erotic interchange either in the flesh, on tape, film or in print. My Candidian adventures make up some of the observations that fill this book, so I shall not dilate upon them in this prefatory section. The sum and substance of what I found was that in erotic transactions, expertise and insight do not necessarily travel together. In fact, quite the contrary is true, in that some of the most profound observations I discovered about heterosexual communications came from homosexuals, and celibates of various kinds seemed quite often unusually sensitive to nuances of sexuality that active participants do not notice.

I cannot claim that my next step was to organize my findings into a systematic investigation of erotica or sexual behavior of any kind. My problem was methodological, knowing full well that I was dealing with a fragile subject indeed and that the rough fingers of quantification or any other inappropriate scientific yardstick might destroy the fabric of my interest. I also concluded that subjective criticism alone would merely yield an interesting but undistinguished autobiography or one or another sort of pyrotechnical display illustrating supposed "tensions" between art, culture and pornography. These tensions, incidentally, have been demonstrated to be more illusory than real by Morse Peckham in his brilliant (and highly subjective) book on the subject published about ten years ago and to which I owe a larger debt than I am inclined to admit here. Without *Art and Pornography,* I would neither have had the nerve nor sustained the impulse to attempt this volume and, although Dr. Peckham and I do not see our common subject (where and when it converges) in quite the same light, my admiration for his erudition and courage, particularly the latter, is boundless.

My methodology is therefore more journalistic than analytic, more critical than scientific, more tentative than confirmatory and often more anecdotal than categorical. At one point, after I had been working on these essays for some years, my well-meaning publisher asked me one day at lunch what my "conclusions" were. The best I could do was stare at him while he buttered a soft roll and ate it.

Whatever I conclude, I fear that it is either terribly trite or terribly complex or sometimes both. Sexual communications are unquestionably the most *important* communications in which human beings indulge, both objectively and subjectively. This is trite. Sexual communications are often mistaken for creative acts and are easily politicized in certain instances because of the inherent sense of rebellion and individuality that they seem to provide for certain people in certain cultures at certain times. This is complex. And so it goes through most of this volume. Let me merely note here that I hope I have avoided excesses of triteness and explained relatively clearly some of the frightening complexities of mind into which this adventure has taken me.

Adventure indeed it has been, a journey that I am delighted to see the end of—for the time being, at least! One reason concerns the issue of language that I discuss in the first chapter but to which I had better also refer to briefly here, before the unwary reader plunges ahead unwarned.

To say what I want to say in the manner that I want to say it, I have found it impossible to pretend to extensive academic objectivity whenever this pretense itself raises a smoke screen between myself and the full meanings I hope to clarify and use. So-called "vulgarisms" and the fine old Anglo-Saxon terms (as well as colorful neologisms) in which we often choose to discuss in no-nonsense fashion the actual data of our sexual experiences as we live them are absolutely germane to even an elementary understanding of erotic human transactions. I have used these words quite freely for the precise purposes that they are also used in culture: to invest a term with nuances of meaning it would otherwise lack, to shock or engender affective responses, to clarify the contexts of otherwise hazy ideas or to invest the writer or a speaker with character. Being a creature inordinately interested in words, I made up my mind at the outset of my work to speak to my reader as candidly, as directly and as relevantly as I found necessary, rather than pussy-foot in circles like the sycophants of Charles II, translating perfectly direct, simple and colorful English words and phrases into sterile Latinate refinements in order to set themselves apart from the man in the street.

One is only free of the mysticism of language, as I shall discuss shortly, when one comprehends clearly the relationships of words to reality, an objective not too difficult to pursue but one that does require a certain amount of determination—particularly in church or in the groves of academe. The temptation to euphemize in most serious works on sex and culture is unfortunately enormous, especially when one writes in a role of scholar, teacher or savant. I have not euphemized! And I hope both my publisher and readers will understand the reasons before they have read far or long.

Let me also aver firmly that this volume is not for everyone—certainly not for children, entirely because it is too complex for them and not because I consider one word of it corruptive! (Children are far more difficult to corrupt than is generally believed, just as they are also much more difficult to educate than they are supposed to be!)

Should my prospective readers hope to find in this book a systematic approach to erotic communications in the sociological or social-psychological manner of a Schramm, Laswell, Lazarsfeld, Newcomb, de Sola Pool or any other social and behavioral scientist who has nibbled in the colorful garden of so-called "communications theory" for the past generation, let me advise them to shut this volume right here and now and place it back on their library, bookstore, colleague's or neighbor's shelf immediately and unread. The sort of facile theory articulation and model constructions that these approaches permit are not what I have been up to at all, nor do I think erotica lends itself to interesting heurisms of this sort in any shape, manner or form—with a few minor exceptions.

Should any other potential customer confuse this volume with the enormous pseudo-library (published mostly in California) credited to real or fictional "Doctors" and "Ph.D.'s" concerning various aspects of sexology—some astounding, amazing and bizarre, written under the pretense of "scientific" investigation that turn out after a quasi-scholarly introduction to be covers for "kink" and poorly written pornography (frequently so-called detailed "case-studies" of fanciful deviants)—he or she is in for a disappointment of major proportions. His or her money might better be spent on other erotic diversions, books included, or which I have found no shortage in the English-speaking world.

As I have noted, the preparation of this volume has been for many reasons a difficult enterprise. I have spent far longer at it than I had originally intended, spoiled as I had been by a deceptive enjoyment of English composition and ignorant of the challenges awaiting me in this particular adventure—as I have called it—much less of the continual necessity for painful self-analysis and personal tests of my own prejudices and values that it demanded. Without considerable help, I would have had to stop at the end of this Introduction.

Some of this help was provided by individuals who, for one reason or another, have requested anonymity. I am diffident, also, about mentioning the names of some others. They know who they are and they have my gratitude. Among those I think that I may thank directly for aid and comfort entirely without trepidation or embarrassment to them are the following, all of whom contributed much directly or indirectly to *Erotic Communications*. In alphabetical order, they are: Les and Micki Baker, Christine Young Callahan, Sharon Carabine, Werner Freitag, Beverlee Galli, Andrea Giles, Al Goldstein, Harry C. Gordon, Gordon Hitchens, Stephen Ross, the late William Sears, Stephen Shapiro, Elsa Spector, Robert Sumner, Robert Vogt, Frank Wekerle, Armand Weston and Stephen Ziplow. My friend and editor Russell F. Neale, as always, stoked the engine whenever it started losing steam and must assume some of the blame or praise for either the creative or the foolhardy act that produced this particular book in the first place.

For better or worse, however, this is my own legitimate offspring, and all dissent, criticisms and/or horse laughs should be directed to me and not to the people above, nor to any other friend, relative, associate, student or acquaintance—all of whom were in every instance simply trying to help.

November 1979   George N. Gordon
                                       Forest Hills, New York
                                       Whitehall, Pennsylvania

PART ONE

:: THE PAST

The Erotic Enigma

Science and sex exist, in some measure, in contexts antipathetic to each other.

Garry Wills

THE SERIOUS STUDY of eroticism—or the frivolous study of it—is more and more becoming a problem of language. Not semantics, linguistics or English positivistic philosophy but simply language and the symbol system for which it stands.

Here we have a blessing and a curse. On one side, new freedoms of discourse in America (and elsewhere) have opened apparent avenues of candor previously shut tightly since, roughly, the pre-Victorian period. Partly as a result, I think, of the spread of mass communications and partly because of the infinitely complicated changes we call "social evolution," the contemporary psychologist, sociologist, author or playwright is permitted a degree of candor in erotic matters that have been closed to him for a long time. What the author of the play *Equus* was able to say on a stage employing an affective vocabulary of two totally nude actors, male and female, attempting—and failing—to copulate, no other playwright in the Western world that I know of since Rome has been able to communicate theatrically in *quite the same terms*. When I, as a social scientist, culture critic or what have you, write seriously in the second paragraph of a volume on eroticism (under the imprimatur of a well-regarded publisher

2

of entertainments for children and cookbooks) that the copulation attempted in *Equus* was an effective dramatic display of a failed fuck, I am indulging in a type of literary freedom that few writers of generally distributed books have had since the eighteenth century. Note also that I chose neither italics nor quote marks to set off the word "fuck." This linguistic freedom is strange to nearly all contemporary social science and to most cultural criticism in England and the United States, being a product of the past decade or so.

Good for it, say I, but candor of this sort has always been equivocal, mainly because the words "fuck" and "copulate," while supposedly meaning exactly the same thing, are *heard* differently by different listeners and readers according to any number of personal variables: age, sex, religion, personal psycho-history, education and all the rest of those cultural determinants that go into the interpretation of words. In our period of open discourse, *both* words *may*, however, also mean different things to different people and even to the same people at different times.

Considerable damage has been and is being done to a once-common vocabulary of those matters that effect erotic communications centrally—matters that most societies envelop in an unbelievably rich and complicated fabric (or cat's cradle) of taboo words—a vocabulary that we in the West have certainly not thrown into the ash can but are simply in the process of redesigning—with unusual haste.

After a recent and often tedious journey through the major literature of eroticism and commentary upon it, one thing, at least, is clear to me. The most uncomfortable participants in what I hope I shall presently show is a *demimonde* of mysticism—possibly even a schizoid metaphysic—are those who attempt to analyze and parse its history, nature and peculiarities, not those writers and artists who make eroticism the object of their scrutiny. Even such unflappable authorities as Kronhausen[1] sometimes seem bewildered concerning the appropriate terminologies for their inquiries, especially when dealing with directly pornographic writing past and present. Masters and Johnson[2] were in a similar fix, arguing, in fact, for a supposedly "new" type of sexual permissiveness, while finding themselves, at the same time, constrained by the vocabulary of popularized medicine and psychology, which is denied (by virtue of its still active taboo system) that very permissive atmosphere of discourse. Pseudo-pornography (a term that I think does not require definition) like *The Hite Report*[3] displays amusing but unsettling ambivalence. In this volume, we find a rigid and censored vocabulary reporting ultra-candid statements made and supposedly written by 3,019 respondents to the author's questionnaires! Even literary critic Morse Peckham,[4] author of (by far) the best analysis of the dynamics of artistic eroticism to date, is extremely uncomfortable in a literary way with his subject. He is scrupulous never to allow the mask of

---

[1] Footnotes are arranged by chapter at the end of the book.

a detached gentleman of letters and scholar fall from his face, but he twists into linguistic gymnastics in order to describe the same pornographic communications that he is, when all is said, defending brilliantly.

A paradox? Possibly. An anomaly? Maybe. Certainly these are all contradictions of symbology, linguistic blind alleys or solipsisms of some kind, and not without their funny side.

The circumstances in which all of these writers find themselves (as did, in some measure, the author and director of *Equus,* by fabricating a shocking climax that was missing from the plot of the story) were caused, I feel, by the notion that our time and place is simply and in many respects out of joint. For example, various linguistic traditions that still haunt the English language probably were born before the Roman occupation of Britain. They were exacerbated among common men by Charles II's Restoration French cronies (who refused to use them) and doctrinized by the person, and later the ghost, of Queen Victoria (who anathematized them). How shocked we seemed to be to hear, on the Watergate tapes, that Richard Nixon and his cronies spoke together in private in the way that men in our society of their station generally speak to one another in private! At least, anti-Nixonians were shocked—about as much as right-wing politicos were shocked by the news (long known to many) that President Kennedy liked to dally more than occasionally with pretty women of dubious reputations. That Nixon said "shit" in company and that Kennedy, although married, took to bed an occasional "piece of tail" (an acceptable Harvard locution) I find neither remarkable, funny, shocking or noteworthy—until the news is communicated to the public. Suddenly, considering its time and place, it becomes slightly anachronistic, a good deal more so than the news, for instance, that our revered Abraham Lincoln cussed like a Trojan or that Aimee Semple McPherson was (or behaved like) a nymphomaniac.

Where, I now ask, does this leave the contemporary analyst of erotic communications?

It leaves him or her with the first of many puzzles and problems that will make up the substance of the inquiry to follow. Fortune favors us in some measure, because the times, with respect to erotic language at least, are turning less and less "out of joint" as the years roll rapidly by. It was, for instance, by no oversight that psychiatrist Jurgen Ruesch did *not* include erotic communications in his inventory of the many modes and varieties of human communication written over a decade ago.[5] He was writing both in a time and for a public where this subject, even among intellectuals, was beneath notice or irrelevant, considering the nature of his intent. To consider eroticism, sex or lascivious arousal a means of communication seemed then to be mixing apples with oranges, mainly because the domain of sexuality was regarded as a discrete form of human activity cut off in large part from other communications, which were understood to be largely matters of cognition or the transaction of so-called "information." That the information might include the fact that psychiatrists often become sexually aroused by their patients was neither proper nor relevant to the topic.

It is precisely as improper and irrelevant to the study of communication of information (and only information) *today,* of course, as is the fact that male and female college professors are often stimulated sexually by their students—irrelevant at least to most administrators of our institutions of higher learning. (Freud candidly discussed the former issue, as have many psychiatrists since, and many college administrators are forever worrying about teachers and students who actually *do* crawl into bed with one another. I am concerned here mainly with the propriety of matters like these in the domain of the study of human communications.)

My temporary solution to this problem will entail, I fear, the idea of the *homme moyen sensuel,* that Gallic concept almost beaten to death, as we shall see, in our statutes, courts and classrooms but which manages to create a standard to which to repair when none other exists. In no way does this compromise solution (if compromise it is) in value judgments *solve* the enigmas of language to which I have referred above, nor does it accomplish anything more for us than to facilitate the inquiry to follow. Few of us like to think of ourselves as average, even in the matter of vocabulary and especially in the matter of sensuality. But a mean must exist, and the chances are that you and I are not far away from it—or we are closer to it than we think.

Because the language used in any analytic attempt delimits to some degree the boundaries and depths of my inquiry, I must allow myself the privileges of age and status—whatever they may be—by interpreting that golden mean for my reader, caring not one bit if I offend him or her in doing so. Neither do I care that many of my colleagues in academia might find cause to snicker at my scrupulous linguistic behavior in matters, say, of a scatological sort or acts of a highly perverse nature, if and when I reach my own limits of candor and language, and the taboos of *today* come marching in. Nor shall I call Blacks "niggers" or Jews "kikes," because these words, and their silent emotional impedimenta, are "no-no's" of the present taboo system in which I live—although I may be acquainted with some Blacks and/or Jews that I might indeed best describe linguistically with these *verboten* terms. On the other hand, pricks, balls, cunts, hardons and similar fine old Anglo-Saxon terms need not, I think, bother us more than cursorily as we examine them from logical and psychological perspectives past, present and future of communication, blessed—and cursed—by Eros.

No, I have not solved the enigma of erotic language, nor shall I by the time we reach the final page of this volume. I have made a treaty with a paradox, the first of many to come. Some will be contained solely within the empire of language, and some, as we shall see, are, as of the moment, almost entirely sorrowfully indescribable—even in our lexicon of words, plump with voodoo and taboo.

Detachment

The reader will note that the problem of language for any writer boils down to a personal problem. It is, especially for the sociocultural analyst, closely related to an ancient question in both art and science concerning how objective or uninvolved in his so-called "subject matter" a theoretically wise or enlightened investigator should be when sharing his wisdom or light with somebody else. In the sciences (the natural sciences, at any rate), we usually enjoy pretending to *total* objectivity. But the anti-deterministic principles of Heisenberg do not—and cannot—resist extrapolation even into data that have been gathered for us by robots and processed by computers. The fundamental instrument of human observation still remains the human sensory apparatus, and knowledge, to the best of our knowledge, cannot exist independently of man if it is scientifically viable. Nor is a moratorium drawn upon this near-mathematical paradox when human and social fields are under scrutiny nor—and especially—is language, in any manner and however used, exempt from it.

What I have said in the previous section about language is therefore but one special case of a general principle in regard to the relationship between any worker and his tools. A hammer does not drive in a nail; a carpenter does, even if the procedure is automated. (Automation, like the use of written language or book publishing, simply removes the immediate physical presence of one rascal among many from the mischief he intentionally or unintentionally produces!)

Garry Wills' observation at the start of this chapter applies *especially* to sex but, due to his care in phrasing, it probably applies to every other human enterprise undertaken in the name of science, art, utility, social progress, altruism, God, mother and country. Sensuality, eroticism, sex—or any profound human emotion—tends to exacerbate nearly everything in one's field of perception. How does one pretend to objectivity with bullets whizzing around one's head? Dr. Kinsey, Dr. Peckham and Dr. Masters have all been tempered by the same experience. At one point or another, the fiction of detachment must be discarded. Even, I have discovered, most of the cold-blooded operators who are involved in such commercial sex as pornography and prostitution almost invariably experience their own personal breaking points, as hardened to the effluvia, taste and commercial aspects of eroticism as many of them seem to be. Or so we shall discover.

I have never known an expert professional magician who did not, somewhere in his psyche, believe in black magic. Nor have I met a performing mind reader who did not cosset a secret bias toward the existence of ESP. Professionals like these, we might assume, should be quite "detached" from the mysticism of magic and unorthodox psychic phenomena. Similarly, actors and playwrights and directors and set designers (and even stage hands) openly admit that they, more than the average man, believe in the fairyland of theatre in their heart of hearts. Most of them are proud of it. Why not?

Possibly creative artists are more honest or candid than most of us who pretend to cool phenomenology or talk blandly about "normative" studies of behaviors we personally find attractive or repellent. Consult, for instance, any book on the current state of education as an institution in the West, especially a liberal arts education. I wonder why it is that so many of us pretend not to notice the "frivolous inertia" with which education is treated in our time and place. In the words of A. N. Whitehead, "It is difficult to restrain within oneself a savage rage." So wrote the gentle mathematician-philosopher[6] who knew, better than many men of lesser wisdom who argue to the contrary, the futility of detachment—or worse, the *pretense* of detachment.

The invitation to a detached stance is particularly keen, however, when the subjects of an investigation involve fundamental human processes before which the strongest of us are *inevitably* subject. Two matters of such concern (among many) are sexuality and death, the latter transmuted these days into the quasi-science of "thanatology" and objectified in journal articles and books by writers who, one assumes, are convinced (or wish to appear convinced) that they will never die. To a genuinely sensitive observer, say Ernest Becker, who forced himself to face his own mortality in his classic, *The Denial of Death,* the charade of objectivity and detachment is discarded almost from the outset. His book yields, by the time one puts it down, the shock treatment of sharing company with a scientist of wisdom at the same time that one is thrown into intimacy with a dying man. This much cannot be said (with the exception possibly, of some of the work of Havelock Ellis) of most analytic writers who have recently turned their attention to eroticism.

In this respect, I much prefer Xaviera Hollander as a sexologist to Albert Ellis, mindful of the fact that the former madame and whore is a pseudonym for various slick paper magazine writers who, at least, allow themselves literary and psychological freedom forbidden by Dr. Ellis' superficial propriety. Were Xaviera (I hope she will forgive the intimacy!) given a Ph.D., no doubt she would detach herself from the pop image of super-cunt, which is an entirely honest image, I believe. In its place, we would find a "detached" Dr. Hollander, capable, like the garden-variety sexologist, of Vulcanizing the soft stuff of eroticism into the unchewable rubber of mere titular "phenomena" and therefore remaining untouched by it or its consequences.

My personal concern at the moment with death is tangential, largely because I am so terribly frightened of it. Eroticism has become another matter, my interest possibly being the prelude to an impending truce with the loss of my own mortality, in that I think I am at last quite *incapable* of detached pretense when it comes to fundamental postulates of my own—or anyone else's—sexual *persona.* This feat is by no means heroic, and in its way must, I think, be repeated as standard procedure by mature gynecologists, proctologists, undertakers and coroners day in and day out. My interest, however, is much less in physical mechanics than social behavior. So, possibly, I may claim just a *bit* more heroism than my medical and pathologist brethren, but not nearly as much as that of good playwrights, novelists, poets and artists I have known (and read), who have performed the same sort of bloodless surgery I shall attempt in this volume.

While I cannot pretend to total equanimity if I had to face or relive all (or even most) of the approximately 14,000 orgasms I have experienced so far in life, let me note that they have occurred under a fairly wide variety of socio-cultural and psychologically oriented circumstances. (Nor am I bragging. The total is naturally a pretty rough statistical count, based upon what I remember to be an average per week since the age of twelve. That it may or may not differ from any other man's or woman's is entirely irrelevant to me. I am also unconcerned with its relationship to normative sexual behavior.) Just as Becker, in choosing to write about death, clearly and openly decided to write about himself and the onset of death in tandem—because he was both brilliant and honest—I think that I owe it to my reader at least to be honest.

The principle here is a large one and it extends into the domains of the behavioral and social sciences and goes well beyond eroticism and/or death in that all so called "meanings" that we impute to our data are, in both the first and last analysis (but not necessarily in-between), man-made artifacts. Literary critic I. A. Richards long ago clarified this concept in his books on meaning, particularly in *The Meaning of Meaning,* written with C. K. Ogden, the father of the objective test or parlor game (as you prefer), The Semantic Differential.[7] That Richards followed the "engaged" path of literary criticism to articulate his explanations into the cultural invention of meaning and that Ogden followed a road of greater apparent "detachment" is indeed interesting, but what else would one expect at the time of the publication of *Meaning* (1923)?

Social psychology—that is, the psychology of collective behavior—has staked out territory in the domain of the quantitative investigation of language in general and behavioral psychology in particular. It therefore depends upon instruments like the Semantic Differential to translate phenomena in the natural world into behavior-like quantities that may be scaled and compared. For better or worse, leave it to the test constructors of the world to detach themselves as fully from the very concept of *involvement* as they can so that they may construct an objective measuring device like the Differential in order to determine the subjective meanings of certain words set in a triad of categories (all open to semantic reservations) in order to objectify (or detach) this same sort of involvement for purposes of objective study!

(Please do not try to figure out the preceding sentence, because, like the Semantic Differential itself, its power is greatest if it remains an impressionistic statement examined only in outline rather than in implication. Both are similar to an impressionistic painting that falls apart into blobs of color upon close scrutiny, and that is exactly what they *should* be and what, I think, both Ogden and I intend. I feel, frankly, a kinship to people who invent and use instruments like the Semantic Differential and the Q-Sort in order to study human attitudes, as well as to the people who invent opinionnaires and questionnaires that aim to detach from individuals their involvement with certain aspects of their environment. I have used some of these instruments in the past, and will use some others—original, stolen and borrowed—in this volume, along with whatever equivocal data they reveal for the same reason that others do: I prefer, in *certain* instances concerning *certain* matters, a questionable detachment on my part to a blatantly biased and shakily held involvement in and toward certain aspects of the world around me.)

To return to the late Ernest Becker, I am thankful that he has warned us how difficult and frustrating is this flight from detachment regarding so much of the data we "process." "How can one trust any meanings that are not man-made?" he writes. "These are the only meanings that we can securely know; nature seems unconcerned, even viciously antagonistic to human meanings; and we fight by *trying* to bring our own dependable meanings into the world. But human meanings are fragile, ephemeral; they are constantly being discredited by historical events and natural calamities."[8] One result is that we often give up the fight to remain involved and integrated in what we ourselves know (or intuit) from the experience of living, and, in our terror (Becker's word) of the consequences of living, we abstractify a universe that is *not* man-made. It may well be God's—the point Becker is making—but it may also be Koestler's "god in the machine," that is, some sort of order in the universe, mathematical dependability, technological magic or those useful pseudo-gods for which art, poetry, music or science stand for many of us.

Here, we think, we have at last something that is *not* ephemeral, not transcendent and evanescent! It was there before we were born, will be there after we die and operates outside the capsule of self and our own personalities. To live in such a way is, in every sense of the word, *human,* bringing art, poetry, science, technology, mathematics, history and most other meaning destroyers and makers into the ambit of the *human*ities. They are the qualities upon which many of us base our primary affections, and nothing is clearer or more human than our claim that their pursuit "takes us out of ourselves."

So Becker, the dying behavioral scientist, tells us that most of us eventually arrive at a point in life when there is no way any longer to hide from the merciless facts of existence, and we must come at last to the confrontation with human meaning. Neither our pencils, typewriters, editors, printers, publishers, colleagues, friends or relatives can any longer help to detach us from our fundamental loneliness, a concern not unknown to the ancients and complex fellow citizens who live in today's world in what we ironically call "primitive" or "undeveloped" societies.

Whether or not we keep listening to the breath of our particular gods until our own respiration fails, much the same phenomenon is part and parcel—and a corollary of—our sensual selves: that aspect of our personalities which is erotic by virtue of its sensitivity to pain and pleasure and that permits us temporary anesthesia from man-made meanings via the distractions of fear and self-involvement on one hand, the quasi-orgasmic distractions of pleasure or euphoria on the other.

There is more than poetic conceit to the cliché that one dies a little in pleasure at the act of love, and probably most of us have experienced in fucking what I can only describe as "a small death." Some of us feel this sensation profoundly and frequently for the best of reasons. Eroticism (like intense sustained pain), to one degree or another, detaches us from our flight from involvement in *knowing* ourselves. At one point or another, we lose cognitive control over our social, cultural and psychological anchors: thus is the language of fucking (since first it was recorded) hurled beyond the limits of decorum and social restraints. Modern literary pornographers must even utilize non-language, such as "Aaahhh, oooh, My God! Oooh . . . No . . . Nooo . . . HHH . . . Goooddd . . . I'm cuuuummmm-miiiiinnnnng! Oooooo! Oooooo!" and so on, to make this point, really quite a serious and telling one.[9]

In eroticism we therefore discard meanings that are made by man's super-agencies like Becker's "historical events and natural calamities" and find ourselves considerably engaged in subjective meanings that we ourselves have experienced in the wind tunnel of consciousness. I grant that a woman experiencing orgasm (the character in the novel, for instance, from which I have quoted above) is hardly at the extremity of lost individuality that many dying people are. But the sources and potentials for the deviation from meaning in existence are similar for both. They are considerably detached from the pretext of social or intellectual involvements and are left more or less to their own semantic and emotional resources. How they therefore perceive and experience both their orgasms and their deaths, temporary or final, is largely a private matter.

The world of eroticism lies, for the most part, behind this green door, which was expertly symbolized in the recent pornographic film that used this symbol in its title. The film displayed (better than most such movies) the surface psychodynamics of such a private world, as when (as has happened in history) privacy is exploited in a social or theatrical arena to provide the jaded with a glimpse of a forbidden world.[10] For, sexual hygienists to the contrary, some measure of eroticism must be "forbidden" from social sharing in much the same way as both the fear of death and death itself are, no matter how fancifully thanatological therapy develops. This is not to say that in love-making, fucking or whatever you want to call it, we may not cosset wide illusions of sharing. But the degree and nature of this dynamic remains, I think, a mystery, particularly when it results largely from the stimulation of an *individual's* imagination.

I have known prostitutes, for instance, who have claimed near sexual anesthesia at the same time that their partners (they say) were convinced of sharing an emotion with them. Their stylized sex play was (and continues to be) more charged with eroticism than the sex encounters their customers had with less skilled partners—sex encounters that were consummated in the name of "love" or "sharing" rather than "commerce." (These whores, incidentally, are behaving not unlike the good and faithful Victorian wife of a century ago, who was not *supposed* to find sex particularly erotic—*if* she was a lady. I have, however, learned in my researches for this book, first, never to trust completely the testimony of a whore regarding her sexual experiences and, second, not to trust what I read in Victorian literature about women.)

What then *is* shared eroticism? Some Freudians claim that whores so eroticize the money they are paid that a sort of sharing takes place: a magnificent orgasm on one side and a hefty fee on the other. But one requires a sense of humor meaner than mine to accept this sort of sophistry.

All of which is a long-winded way of illustrating, I hope, that the detached study of eroticism, like the detached study of death, is indeed possible, probably scientifically desirable for certain ends and within certain teleologies, both of which we find in considerable supply today. Both are also subject to many and specific delimitations, most of which are obvious except to individuals trained to respect too religiously certain American (and now British) positivistic traditions in the social and behavioral sciences. Within these traditions they are the *only* meaningful data concerning the subject. All the rest may as well be poetry or—heaven forbid—graphic art, drama or storytelling. Their worship presents a fundamental teleological question concerning ends, however, that is answered in a roundabout manner in the famous normative argument for sexual morality as practiced as espoused by Kinsey in his second volume of research into sexual behavior. His was the naive but solemn plea that morality should bend to custom, if that custom could be scientifically demonstrated to constitute either normal (or even average) human behavior.[11]

The fact that this sort of defense can also be made for the morality of lying, cheating at cards or preparing false income tax statements was obviously too subtle a point to bother deeply either Kinsey the entomologist or his behaviorally oriented associates. Insects, after all, do little *except* behave. They certainly do not lie or cheat at cards or prepare bogus statements of income for the IRS. And Kinsey's moralizing has already gone through meat grinders of criticism bigger and sharper than I can invent.

The principle of this criticism applies, however, to a wider and more important range of quasi-scientific sex studies than Kinsey's alone and extends directly to the morality implicit in today's so-called "sex therapy" that has emerged from the studies, mainly via, I suppose, the various works of Masters and Johnson. The transition of the latter team from laboratory clinicians and scientists to moral philosophers has been less elegant than Kinsey's leap from bug collector to moralist, but it employs the same sort of loose teleology based on assumptions of "sexual adjustment" that may or may not be groundless and depends upon a construction of eroticism itself that reduces sexuality to a therapeutic tool in obtaining that philosophical will-o'-the-wisp—the good life. I say "reduces," because any rationale for eroticism other than the one nature has obviously provided for our race, the continuation of our species, must resort to some type of revelation or mysticism for its justification. In no manner, however, do I wish to demean a well-meaning search for the bluebird of happiness through eroticism—or in any other socially harmless way—but I do question the assumptions that underlie the supposedly scientific (or moral) bases for such a search, unless they reflect the laws and theories of *some* science, as reproduction of the species does for the biology of evolution.

In sum, I cannot demean or deny the search for "detachment" by students of eroticism or death or laughter or altruism and/or other similar matters, but I cannot share anyone's enthusiasm for such a stance. I am especially skeptical when and if the search concerns apparent transactions of erotic feelings. A clever laboratory instrument may indeed measure the rate at which I achieve an erection when stimulated by a picture of a sexy chipmunk. But I *hope* the reader has some questions for me after he discovers the rate at which my penile tissue engorges whenever I see *this* particular rodent in this particular pose! The news that I do *not* react the same way to hamsters may also be measured with scientific precision, but there is absolutely no way that I am able to report, as a "detached" investigator of myself, either what is happening or why. You may wish to listen to my version of the etiology of this state of affairs, but the value of what I have to say will depend, in the end, upon *my* degree of self-insight and upon the general acuity of *your* perceptions of me and *your* ability to empathize and sympathize with the unique creature that I am.

Love and Infantilism

One peculiarity of eroticism is the way in which the concept of "love" is so often segregated from sexual feeling. At times, contemporary sexologists talk about love almost as if it is a different class of experience from eroticism. Love is sometimes—but not necessarily—found in the candy box of sensual pleasure with less sureness than but as much serendipity as I remember feeling on finding a joyful prize in a red, white and blue box of Crackerjacks when I was a youngster. Or, if you wish, love is similar to American public education in the South prior to the famous Supreme Court decision of the nineteen-fifties: separate from sensuality but equal to it in importance and personal fulfillment. Sex without love is simply a possibility, or an unfortunate but sometimes inevitable possibility and/or an unhappy probability. It all depends, as a British novelist once observed, on "what you mean by love."

This may be a well-deserved confusion because of the sloppiness of a language that allows one four-letter word to describe such a plethora of human relationships! Love has also been intertwined with almost every literary facet of our Judaic tradition after Christianity innoculated it with Greek and Oriental mysticism and set it wandering into the Middle Ages. The latter mischief is usually blamed on St. Paul, but secular and religious love had already been hopelessly manhandled and confused in the four Gospels before him, and the chief culprit in Christian tradition is probably Jesus Himself. Religion aside, however, love is still what makes our world go 'round. We love our wives, parents, children, countries, favorite recipes, cats and dogs, gods, possessions, hobbies, currency and selves with indiscriminate passion (probably quite genuine) that, compared to the narrow focus of our erotic feelings, is, in Freudian terms, nothing less than "polymorph perverse."

Tracing the ormolu history of love in our tradition, therefore, depends first on how you define it and second on where you look. There is so much of it in our heritage that has been translated into contemporary cultural language that you are probably going to find it everywhere. I favor the type of search exemplified by Denis deRougemont's essentially religious characterizations of love as myth in literature, a technique of investigation employed with urbanity and sophistication in *Love in the Western World* and *Love Declared,* or that by Johan Huizinga in his journey into the sources of romance in medieval literature.

A literary-historical perspective is, for the most part, I think, the conventional heuristic approach to "love" as defined in today's humanitarian tradition. It is a painfully small purview and may just as well lean upon the Old Testament as upon Goethe. If it *is* largely a literary conceit, love as we know it may have been born (or died) at any moment in our Western tradition up to the present century. It has ebbed and flowed, been lionized and damned, through all poetic periods of romanticism: the worlds, for instance, of Wordsworth, Byron, Keats and Shelley and that of Edna Ferber, Faith Baldwin, Daphne DuMaurier as well as by all our contemporary covens of romantic writers of prose and film melodrama, to say nothing of the people (or machines) who write the sludge we see on television.

Love in our society is a self-fulfilling prophesy! Having articulated its parameters, dimensions, outlines and color scheme and described its force and power, we educate each generation into its ambiguous labyrinths, expecting from it a patchwork of love delivered through life, educating most young people by means of a multitude of institutions that they are, at best, *crazy* if they cannot and do not love the things and people that their times and mores dictate. Thus, an unnatural (or psychotic) parent does not *love* his child. An ungrateful (or psychotic) child does not *love* his parents. A life of sex without *love* is a sign of a deep characterological defect (or psychosis), and so forth. Into love's channels, deep emotions seem to flow into the human race, and man's culture seems endlessly inventive in finding places for it to run.

I cannot question the emotional validity of love—even in the many amorphous forms we have come to know it in the New World in our time. More than once in more than half a century of living, one or another version of love's dislocations has nearly killed me—or, at least, I thought it did, which amounts to the same thing. An individual forced by love's disorientation to banal suicide, psychogenic illness, alcoholism or merely careless driving ends up just as dead as someone seething with metastasis—and often just as painfully. If he or she is driven to these extremes by love's lost labors, so be it, but I happen to think the damage may occur as frequently from love's labors gained!

Let me reaffirm, however, the wisdom of the many, many sages who, starting with Voltaire, have hurled a perfectly fair challenge at society: How many of us would ever have fallen in love had we never heard the word spoken, had we never been trained to love by tradition? (The answer is necessarily complex, because there appears to be a psychological basis to certain kinds of petting and stroking behaviors that may or may not be merely instincts extrapolated out to loving behavior. Does a mother cat, for instance, *love* her kittens?) Psychobiology aside, however, both our literary and spiritual traditions have orchestrated for our culture(s) a complex symphony in the management of our proclivities for love, an orchestration that is similar, I shall hope to show before I retire my pencil, to what we have done to the erotic emotions that center upon activities of our erogenous sensors, particularly those between our legs; the latter have been also ramified into proportions that may be called—in order to keep the metaphor straight—"operatic." Two quick examples: the "love" of devout Nazis for blood and soil and the love of our own public for the *persona* of the late Bing Crosby, Elvis Presley or John Kennedy.

In a book on the cultural bases of persuasion I wrote eight or nine years ago (its original draft), I was reasonably convinced, following ideas of Rollo May, Erich Fromm and other analysts popular at the time, that love in the West had been seized from its best settings, as had family life, religion and art, and had been turned into an integument of social adjustment and therapy. Following other writers at the time, I called modern love, as was then preached by the young and sung about by fast-fading rock groups and practiced by faddist group therapists, "the new Puritanism." [12]

In some ways I was right, I think, but in others I was dreadfully wrong. Indeed, we still prescribe "tender loving care" for infants, but all the infant seems to give a damn about is how "tender" his or her care is!

The phrase "He (she) needs a lot of love" is still dispensed by morons with medicine-show abandon, but, to most of us who are faced daily with problems of dealing with the discontents and troubles of others, the phrase is meaningless. Probably legalized abortions and the great bedroom game of contraception has also, in recent years, shifted the center of gravity of marriage or connubiality as a contemporary institution.

The result is that love is rapidly becoming a highly ephemeral quality that may or may not be thrown into the achievement of successful cohabitation—even if the partnership lasts for a lifetime. And it has fallen into decreasing importance in song and story, at least in its older, romantic constructions. A symptom of all of this can be discovered in the fact that the popular love lyrics we used to take somewhat seriously thirty or more years ago sound today as though they have sunk into the swampy sentimental substructure upon which they once comfortably rested. They are not even slick expressions of sentiment any longer; they are merely self-defeating sentimentality made of the same antiquarian fluff that female Victorian melodramas and novels once were. Sorry to say, they are even funny. (So, of course, is the more recent anthem of Nixon years, Vietnam and gay and women's liberation:*What the World Needs Now Is Love*.)

I was a victim of the love cults of the time in my role as social auditor eight years ago, and I am probably equally victimized at the moment, although I cannot, like the people in Socrates' cave, rightly tell the shadows from reality. Nor do I think I need to. For the present, and especially for purposes of this volume, I am ready, like most of us, to join the dying Sigmund Freud in his identification of love, particularly in its "purest" form (be this human or godly), with neurosis and infantilism, and to leave it there with a middle-European shrug.[13]

As Abraham Franzblau cheerfully reminds us, Cupid is invariably depicted as an infant, and this may well be our ubiquitous non-conscious guide in our journey from cradle love to the multifarious versions of adult love. He writes:

> The infant wants the exclusive love of his mother; the lover wants the exclusive love of his beloved. The infant tremendously overvalues his love object; so do lovers. The infant fantasizes of omnipotence; so has the man who has won a girl and sets out to lay the world at her feet. The infant sees the commonplace as exciting; so do lovers—in each sunset, opening bud and bird's song.[14]

Just as, in Franzblau's words, "the roots of romantic love stem from the cradle and have a long and complex developmental history," so the pathway *from* socialized, acculturated love leads one down an already worn path *to* the cradle—and not only romantic love, but its other incarnations as well. The Christ is (to me) at his most spiritually powerful when he is painted as an infant in his mother's arms—powerful enough to create cults of mother-worship that have plagued Christianity since the Arian heresy and serve today as the rallying cry of womens' libbers among nuns and the growing female clergy. Every evangelist asks that we come to him or her "as a child;" so do non-religious or spiritual movements like Alcoholics Anonymous and its many imitators. Most of them work amazingly well—to the consternation of behavioral Puritans who want to rationalize *all* psychotherapy, especially that which deals with addictions, because they are convinced that their inchoate, metaphorical constructions of the central nervous system hath power to conquer all things.

When we come as children for peace of mind or body or whatever else, we accept as given the infantile nature of love and, like the aged Freud, recognize that our chances for reading meaning or happiness into our lives depend upon the acceptance of neurosis. We then shrug our shoulders and opt for the lesser of many evils—the benign neurosis or Freud's "illusion." If we are smart, we know exactly what we are doing, but, regardless of which way we wear our true colors, we choose that particular solution to our problems because we really have so little choice. That choice invariably involves love! We have followed the prescriptive advice of the psychiatrist in T. S. Elliot's remarkable play, *The Cocktail Party,* which, thirty years ago, was regarded as a gloomy directive to personal resignation. Today it is merely realistic and sounds more modern than when it was written. (So, incidentally, does O'Neill's *The Iceman Cometh,* first produced a few years before Elliot's play.)

Are we who love happy? Who cares? The oldest psychiatric joke I know is the response to that question: "No, he only *thinks* he is happy." This is a lover's answer.

I am, I suppose simply reassuring my reader that I do not intend to try to damage any of his or her beloved constructions of love in my examination of erotic communications. Nor do I think I need to be too concerned about romantic love as an unseen variable in most erotic exchanges in our particular time and place. For good or bad, our infantilism, on display in collective dimensions via countless conduits—and the fact that we are now *living* in the future of Freud's grand illusion—protects love's health and welfare far beyond my tiny abilities to do it damage. Love is safe—even from the new Puritans I needlessly disparaged eight years ago, and of whom I breathlessly warned my readers to beware. I overestimated the contemporary thrust and potency of therapeutic psychology, mental health campaigns and the zeal of most of the do-gooders who surrounded me, just as I underestimated the sticking power of the ubiquitous manifestations of neurotic and delusive love to which we, the weak, the vulnerable and the unconvinced, *must* cling in order to survive. Freud was wiser in his old age than I had thought, and common men and women like you and me were a little more hesitant to fall for this particular cultural con game during the unsettled period of recent history than I had imagined.

What Is Erotic?

I wish this were a foolish question.

I also wish it could be answered by using the same mechanical devices on a sample population that Masters and Johnson were able to employ to measure vaginal lubrication, rate of erections and other intimate matters.

I wish, in other words, that it might be answered either by recourse to biology, science or special expertise. Even my favorite scholars of eroticism, the Drs. Phyllis and Eberhard Kronhausen, who are, I suppose, as close as we arrive to experts in the matter, defer to public consensus in the last analysis of their analyses of pornography of various kinds in history.[15] In other words, something is or was erotic because, at one time or another, there was a community of agreement that it was erotic. And this agreement was, or is, history and part of the record.

I cannot criticize the Kronhausens for this intellectual dodge, because, frankly, for all its semantic and tautological traps, it is probably about the best that today's scholarly mind can do. It is the same sort of kitty-chasing-tail game that jurists get into when they attempt to define "pornography" or "obscenity," and one cannot fault the uses of ambiguity if they are somehow productive. The Kronhausens may well have been, to date, *more* productive with their *implied* notion of eroticism than all our judges and lawmakers have been in their *specific* struggles to pin down the terms "pornography" and "obscenity" for statutory purposes.

The Freudian answer to the question of where, when and how to hunt for eroticism is too broad and generalized to serve as anything but a psychoanalytic tool. The association of libido, gratification and pleasure with eroticism takes us from the cradle to the grave and follows us, awake and asleep, through everything we do from point A to Z in life's alphabet. Suck we must when we are born, just as shit and pee we must to stay alive. A trip through an institution for dilapidated psychotics or an old folks' home reminds us—as biographer-novelist Ann Pinchot once observed—that, *in extremis,* we clutch our genitals when all other reliable sources of human gratification fail because of age or derangement or both. (Modified and subtle instances of this phenomenon are common in everyday life and quite visible to the trained observer of non-verbal communications.)

In addition, we puff cigarettes, hoard our symbolic feces in the guise of bank accounts and stamp collections, expel rage in pseudo-orgasms and verbal diarrhea—and masturbate in bizarre ways beyond imagining as we jog, walk, swim, dance, watch morning sunrises, exault in good or bad weather, listen to symphony orchestras and bounce babies on our knees. The non-eroticized life, in libidinal terms, is not only not worth living, it is impossible to live! Freud to the contrary, a cigar is *never* only a cigar but invariably an instrument of homeostasis or pleasure: an erotic joy of boundless pleasure when compared to *not* smoking a cigar when you want one—unless, of course, one craves the strange masochistic route of denial that provides its own peculiar and commonplace versions of pleasure, as any reformed smoker, drinker, nail biter or previously fat person will almost invariably tell you. Exquisite pleasure neatly eroticized!

I cannot fault this freewheeling psychoanalytic construction of eroticism, because it does have its uses apparently—both in therapy and in literature. More than this, it explains well much behavior that must otherwise be called "human nature." I am also convinced that the absence of the omni-erotic in living is pure boredom. This is a valuable concept taken alone (to which I shall return in the last part of this book), but one also that is worth considering before we reject (for our purposes) neo-Freudian constructions of eroticism. Juvenile hoods eroticize the excitement of what appears to most of us to be "senseless" vandalism because of sheer boredom. It is not senseless. It is, in fact, as sensible as a visit to an exhibition of paintings. How else can one explain the glut of elaborate, artless graffiti that covers so much of what is left of our urban jungles, subways and outdoor advertising?

When such eroticism runs amuck, history hands us Leopolds and Loebs (bored intellectuals) or Charles Mansons (bored institutional personalities)—and possibly Hitlers as well. In a study of counterfeiting years ago, I was amazed to discover the enormous erotic content of this high-degree-*specialist* criminal's desire to *"make* money" (for *"make"* read *"shit"*). In a long study of acting, theatre, professional magic and mind reading, I have yet to clarify the gorgeous tangle of sensualities that accompany both the urge to deceive one's fellow man with clever manipulation and lies and why it *is* fun to be fooled, even if the fooling involves utterly transparent nonsense that, at times, is accomplished by gross and infantile exhibitionists. Similarly, when a clever person eroticizes the fact of *power* and the trappings of power, as many analysts have suggested, he is led through history by a sophisticated Machiavelli indeed, ending where? In the Watergate complex of Washington D.C.? In the Kremlin? Or in the local political club house? Take your choice.

No, I am not, like Dr. Skinner and/or many academic psychologists today, eager to destroy or even so much as injure what amounts to a fascinating epistemology that has, for the past seventy or so years, been artfully structured for us by the psychoanalytic fraternity and sorority. Too much of value has been accomplished by it, if not on analysts' couches then indeed on canvas, in marble and metal, in literature, the drama, ballet, films and music.

The unfortunate aspect of the neo-Freudian view of eroticism is mainly that it offers us a bewildering embarrassment of riches, little of which holds more than semiotic power. Its value is that it helps us to *explain*. But explanation alone does not necessarily take us far in understanding anything. Pan-eroticism provides a wonderful unifying principle built on faith for a godless, deductive science. It is certainly also a product of its time and place in history. It is, was and remains consonant with the shattering impact of Darwinism upon biology (and sociology) and adds up to a proper thumb in the nose at Victorianism as well as nineteenth- and twentieth-century logical positivism. It remains today an acute modifier of the latter's intellectual stepson: psychological and sociological behaviorism. How I wish it were not so much beside the point of the descriptive study of sex, sin and censorship, which are the concerns of this book!

Ours will therefore be a *selective* construction of eroticism, I fear, the eroticism of the Drs. Kronhausen and others which has to do with the kind of reactions that we may not be able to pin down in the behavior of others but can invariably locate in ourselves. Nor do I wish to reduce this concept to the mere term "genital commotion," as certain legal minds have. I mean far more by eroticism, and so do the Kronhausens. The apparent focus of our common concerns have to do with *specific* sexual pleasure in human beings that do not *always* relate to genitalia.

(I grant that the term "sexual" is poorly used here, but I do not know how better to describe the parameters of the emotions or feelings I am discussing. I might use the legalist's word "prurient," which is not bad, because it is entirely a metaphor that compares sexual emotion with itching, and itching of many kinds is more real than the entirely nebulous term "sexual feeling." "Lust" is a hopelessly loaded word, connoting Victorian and Biblical associations. What indeed *is* the factor that unites the sensation that produces a hard-on in a male, a wet pussy in a female and an ambiguous chill in a pre-pubescent youngster? Certainly not the functions of genitalia taken alone! One may as well ask what the sensation caused by the color green is—and this has frequently and futilely been asked by people who should know better. No, the stimulus and subsequent gratification—I cannot imagine what—in the individual who likes to smell old shoes is only "sexual" for purposes of conversation. It falls, however, into the same class as the strange but extraordinary sensuality of a sweet young thing I once courted who adored having her ear chewed by males—adored it, distressingly to me, in preference to any other kind of erotic play. I have always liked the word "horny," but it is severely limited by its derivation, the British "horn," another word for "hard-on" and strictly male. "Randy" is a good adjective but produces no noun and is also almost exclusively British. I might do better in French, but to what end? I am stuck with "sex" as my context, when I do not always and entirely refer to matters that deal with concerns of gender, invariably implied by the word "sex.")

This "sexual" pleasure must, of course, be felt as a biologically *possible* function of the certain individual to which it refers. Exactly *what* it is, let us say, to the average seven-year old girl is difficult to describe precisely, but it appears to be there. What it may be to a Roman Catholic priest is, I imagine, somewhat less difficult to imagine, depending of course on the priest (or nun), but it is also there—probably motivating some kind of conscious sublimation, if this is possible. In most men and women, regardless of gender, education, class or such, it is, for most of their adult life at any rate, apparently quite a clear and identifiable emotion.

To regard it as exclusively or fundamentally genital, as I say, is absurd. It is in part a learned response, independent in some of its aspects to cock and cunt and allied equipment. On the other hand, it is impossible *not* to associate eroticism with our endocrine systems, human preceptors and the central nervous system—all of which are apparently necessary for the transmission of a given stimulus, internal or external, to a felt response. The nature, precise function and many interactions of systems as well as the organs associated with them remains at present, however, largely cloaked in mystery. What happens when these systems or organs *mal*function (hyperfunction, hypofunction or quit altogether) is *not* nearly as obscure. In most instances with which I am familiar, however, induced malfunctions—say a barrage of erotic stimuli over a long period of time—often produce different results in different people and seem not to occur in simplistic fashion: that is, they give us every sign of simply being parts of a total perceptive system that may recognize the malfunction, attempt to compensate for it or, possibly, exacerbate it.[16]

While I am happiest leaving problems of human biology to biologists (although not necessarily to physicians), I am afraid that it is only in biology that we can locate our jumping-off place for an analysis of eroticism in human culture, past and present. Instrumentation does indeed exist that allows us to infer—but only infer—that eroticism as a *felt* state is usually accompanied by biological changes in the central nervous and endocrine systems that are a good deal more *specific,* say, than many other kinds of affective changes. I mean that all thought and feeling is probably accompanied by (or possibly caused by) psychological changes in the human nervous system, but some of it, most of it, is so slight or subtle that it can be measured (if it can be measured at all) only by means of amplified electrical signals of an encephalogram. Eroticism is usually more specific (and dramatic) than, say, the emotion of frustration engendered by a difficult crossword puzzle. Our present instruments of biological measurement seem able to give us a *fair* idea of when it is or is not present in many instances. (I think that the coordination of this instrumentation and its use on multiple subjects is the major contribution of Masters and Johnson to the science of the classification of human behavior.)

In terms of communication, however, we are still left with a tautology: Whatever stimulus that is evoked in B by A (whatever A is) is an erotic stimulus if it produces psychobiological results that can be identified, one way or another, as producing erotic feelings! I am back with my chipmunk.

Can we do better than this? We had better.

We can, if we put aside psychobiology (and Freudianism too) long enough to accept a homogeneous cultural field of symbols and convergences of meanings which allows us to say that a poem is "sad" or that certain music is "happy" or that certain visual images on film or a canvas are "menacing." I grant that all of these adjectives are to some degree mere critical observations and that they are also manners of speaking. But they are also precisely those psychological factors related to meaning that Ogden and Richards centered on when they searched for the cultural coherence of all meanings in *The Meaning of Meaning*.

Without such a communality of agreed symbols as an integument of society, language would be impossible. Eroticism would not be, but it would not exist in human terms any more elegantly than it exists—except solely as anthromorphism—in other animal species. A doctoral dissertation analyzing eroticism in horses is, I am afraid, therefore a possibility for tomorrow's scholar. It may have been written already. Although it would center on horse behaviors, these behaviors would have to depend for meanings entirely upon analogies to a human semantic. Semantics are puzzling constructions of culture that may themselves be parsed, but let us leave theories of their origins to Noam Chomsky and other structuralists. I mean that, at present, their etiology remains entirely speculative to some, theoretical to others and established fact or law to nobody, with all my respect to the remarkable accomplishments of Dr. Chomsky.

Our erotic tautology is therefore no less tautology than it was three paragraphs ago. But now it is at least a tautology that may help us to articulate certain kinds of assumptions about the communication of feelings. At worst, it is no less vague than similar semantics used by say, political scientists ("revolutionary fervor"), psychologists ("claustrophobia"), sociologists ("class structure"), psychiatrists ("depression") or even physicians ("pain") or interior decorators ("warm colors"). In all these examples, *something* occurs when the items in parentheses are present in human consciousness, and they all boil down to a common consensus about certain symbols that are part of a specific semantic relevant to each type of observation. *In no instance* is any one of them an observable, measurable phenomenon much different from what students of philosophy call "constructs." (Everything does not fall into the category of a construct with ease. When I bleed, my blood runs from me. When I die, I am no longer alive, and so on. These phenomena are categorized by language, naturally, and their images are communicated by means of it, but they are not tautologies *given* meaning by language in the same sense that felt observed phenomena are.)

Ah, you say, what an elaborate defense of the simple notion that, when all is said and done, everything that is erotic (according to a vague definition) is indeed erotic. Back to the same old tautology!

Not so. What I am doing, I hope, is referring eroticism (and the idea of it) first, to culture, second, to individuals similarly acculturated to respond in certain ways to common cultural stimuli and, third, to an implied but nevertheless subjectively *real feeling of response* that is apparently shared by human beings reared in similar ways in the same society. I am also now permitting that which may be erotic to you to be a stimulus different from what is erotic to me—naturally within certain fairly narrow margins prescribed by our different natures and nurturing. What I can expect of you, however, is that you will, in all probability, share enough common cultural factors with me so that you will at least have *some* perception of the possibility of my response when I say to you that I am stimulated erotically by that which is repulsive to you. Or by a chipmunk. Whatever else you may think of me is irrelevant! It is only important that you understand what I am talking about if I tell you, for instance, that I may find a high colonic enema an exquisite erotic experience. (I do not, or, better still, have not up to now. I cannot predict the future.) That is, these are my legitimate expectations, if you are not an enema freak and I am.

Talk and Action

Upon these assumptions, therefore, erotic communications may be regarded as a specific type of communications, certainly as specific as, for instance, humorous communications or the communications of much so-called "information." Communicated information usually takes the form of a semantic code and is much less elaborate, most of the time, than either eroticism or humor. Both of the latter would require highly complex coding (so complex that it has not yet been invented) provided by the symbology of discursive language and resisting translation into most—but not all—types of analogies made possible by various mathematics for coding purposes.

Recent linguistic freedoms in print in the West, to which I have previously referred, have at least rendered such inquiry not only possible but possibly profitable. Here we have a change that is not as specifically centered on philological or semiotic concerns as it appears at first glance, although I grant that the thrust of law and social constraint is usually first and foremost upon the semiotic aspects of the evils they confront: semantics, syntactics and pragmatics of what people *communicate* rather than what people *do*.

Semiotics are, however, like the bottles or glasses in which we must place our booze before we can drink it, being indispensable elements in the distribution of liquor but having little to do with the consumption of alcohol, drunkenness and subsequent hangovers. Studying bottles and glasses tells us little about the nature of drinking as a hobby, addiction to it—or anything else related to this hoary culture trait. What matters is the source of the semiotic which, like the Scotch in a pinch-bottle, is indeed a culture trait, a custom, a complex recipe and the end product of much trial and error experiment over a long period of time.

When certain social critics claim that we cannot legislate against (or regulate) morals, this semiotic curiosity is usually what they are talking about. Prohibitionists in the United States eventually discovered that legislation against commerce in *bottles* and *glasses* was nearly impossible, just as our legalists are finding out today that laws against the semiotics of eroticism are difficult to write and more difficult to enforce. (The tangle of legislative problems presented by the enormous commerce in marijuana today is another example.) Were the force of law—meaning police power—directed specifically against *drinking* and/or the *behaviors* associated with sexual morals, the result would be the kind of bogus social purity once achieved to a remarkable degree by Hitler in Germany and is, to some degree, at work in most Communist nations today.

(In certain Communist-bloc nations, for instance, alcoholism is an enormous, expensive and debilitating problem. But little is done—and it could be—to modify traditional values in regard to drinking. It is here a sign of virility, there a sign of good health, elsewhere a symbol of the good life. Governmental oligarchs, however, are naturally deeply concerned about the distribution of bottles and glasses for, it seems to me, good reasons. Cheap, plentiful supplies of potent alcoholic drinks may be employed, in some of these countries, as a manipulative political weapon in that alcoholism tends to dampen the reformist zeal in many people. Modern Poland is one example.)

The Whorf-Sapir hypothesis, for all its weaknesses, has achieved, more or less, the status of an axiom in the social and behavioral sciences. Most of us are agreed, temporarily at least, that language seems to follow custom. The semiotic within which I am therefore bound is a sum total of the abstractions of values from the culture in which I live. Until someone can prove otherwise, I am both the victim and the honored guest of the words I use and symbols I have in my power to evoke meanings. When I note, as I did at the beginning of this chapter, that language has today given me new freedoms as a writer in a conceptual sense, I am also saying much more than this. My freedom is a function of the lifestyles of our time and place, lifestyles that are always in the process of psychological transition: that is, they are preparing to change somehow, in a manner that will be, if not revolutionary at the extreme, then at least unsettling to those social institutions that do not change with them.

Just as I began this discussion with talk about talk, let me end it with talk about action.

Not so long ago, Vance Packard, a sensitive reporter, surveyed from his journalist's perspective the erotic environment of our nation and wrote:

There have been suggestions that we are in the midst of a "sexual revolution." What in fact is occurring seems too chaotic and variable to be described best as a revolution. A revolution implies a clear movement in an understood and generally supported direction. As I have examined my evidence, the phrase that kept springing to mind as more appropriately descriptive of the state of male-female relationships in the late 1960s is "sexual wilderness." [17]

Recent analysts of revolution, from Whitehead to Lenin to Chalmers Johnson, remind us that the establishment's view of most impending changes—whatever they are—is that of coming chaos. To the orderly mind, particularly one like Packard's, chaos and wilderness are congruent—if not often identical—terms. This is because, on semiotic grounds, a reordering of priorities waits invariably in the wings along with a change in symbol structures, new semantic relationships between words and reality, and new laws, moral codes and ethics. These changes enter with a good deal of noise and fanfare onto the social stage, and I admit that they are, to many, frightening to behold.

What this apparent "chaos"—or even the *threat* of chaos—does is spotlight an advance guard of change in the civil order that may indeed herald the *possibility* of revolution of one sort or another: the all-too-perceptible Chekhovian diminution of an old aristocracy and keepers of the flame into impotent fools and clowns, the sound of the axe razing the trees in the forest or the raging rhetoric of a Che Guevera (another physician, like Chekhov) off somewhere in the hills promising rationality in place of medievalism. One also hears the flurry of accompanying inconsistencies and insecurities on the part of bureaucrats who know that all governments, in the end, require certain people to stamp passports, issue licenses, keep records and translate common language into inscrutable instructions on tax forms. All this is the panic before the panic, and to the objective observer it provides the illusion of a wilderness.

We are, at present, immersed in an unsettling, apparently quiet period of erotic enigma that Packard calls a "sexual revolution," but which I would prefer to call nothing until I see how it works out. The ground rules for some human relationships are certainly changing. The integuments of present relationships are also changing. Thus, the overall configurations of communications are changing—in nature, style, scope and content—and these changes are being felt in all the institutions of culture that are affected by what men and women regard today as "erotic." I can think of few institutions that are immune: not the church, not the university, not industry, not commerce, and certainly not our patriotic zeal, as I hope to demonstrate.

What I propose to do in the coming chapters, and what I hope I have done so far, is to take advantage of the illusion of comparative quiet in this bewildering moment to concentrate upon the semiotics of eroticism as we have come to know them through the multiple ways they have been and are communicated in the Western World and upon the forces that either facilitate or hinder these transactions. My point here, however, is that the study of the current erotic enigma is a matter of seizing a unique opportunity. This is the moment. If the job is not at least attempted now, the enigma may regrow its old carapace that, at the present instant, seems to have lost much of its usual protective hardness.

How well I am suited for the task I presume the reader has already judged. My direction, I think, is quite clear and my delimitations obvious. Our next inquiry will therefore be in large part historical: along various paths of culture that we have come. It is a less unsettling trip, as we shall see, than into any possible future. It is also more cozy than the present.

A Hurried Peek at Early Erotica

What art history seems finally to prove is that the more consciously a man sits down to Create a Work of Art, the more surely he will fail to produce anything like one.

—Alan Gowans

ALTHOUGH IT IS frequently the sort of speculation one regrets, I am inclined to believe that what we today in the West (and in parts of the East, particularly in Japan) tend to regard as functional "erotic communications" may well be phenomena of fairly recent origins. By this I mean, of course, neither sexual activity in any gross form *nor* cultural aspects of it that may (or may not) have been blended with art and/or religion in history or in pre-history, but the idea of "eroticism" as understood in the moral tradition of, largely, today's Judeo-Christian cultures.

The actual survival of our specialized, vulnerable species is a remarkable testament, in fact, to the tenacity of man as a fucking animal (or animal who fucks), considering the elaborate and sometimes devastating inhibitory mechanisms that have insulated him—and continue to separate him—from the rest of the sexual creatures on the planet, present and extinct.[1] What these mechanisms are remains a mystery. They have been placed physiologically by the gods of evolution somewhere in the frontal lobes of the cerebellum, although *exactly* where only these gods know. They make their presence felt by means of an elaborate semiotic of metaphors—symbols and rituals mostly—that do indeed infuse both art and religion with certain prescriptive aspects. But they are also enfolded into

26

nearly every other facet of culture as well. Whatever they are, they are distinctively human, although they are also a part of the continuum from primate apes to man. In this particular transition, the secret of their birth and development is locked in obscurity. Here is one history that it is safe to say we shall *never* uncover, because it must have been almost entirely behavioral and lacked tools—artifacts that remained, that did not perish with that behavior as hundreds of thousands of years passed.

Our-so-called "Puritan heritage" may be motive enough for the observation that the peculiar nature of human self-consciousness (as opposed to its apparent absence in all other vertebrates) was probably the most dangerous risk that *nature* took in the development of our race, not necessarily because of our physical vulnerability to the ravages of nature—in spite of a wily brain that gave and is giving the natural world a run for its money—but because of man's psychological vulnerability to his novel and, I suppose, untested sense of his own being. Whenever and wherever man's first gods were made, this particular resolution of the inevitable deadly tension between that part of human behavior that was analogous to the animals (who seem to pee, shit, fuck and even die with an apparent disregard of the values of their acts) and the complex structure of human semiotics thrust upon the earliest members of our species with *these new born gods watching* was probably the most dangerous challenge *mankind* has to date overcome in the continuation of the species. Certainly it was more perilous than the present threat of nuclear energy.

Put more simply, at one point in man's evolution he had to handle a new and unanswerable problem that life had presented to him in its evolutionary process: Was he an animal or a god? The Egyptian answer, given quite recently as the history of *homo sapiens* is told, that we are *both* could not, I think (and here my Puritan gorge may be rising), satisfy the philosophical curiosity of a somewhat feral (but no less intelligent than you or me) so-called "primitive man" any more then it satisfies today's vestigial "primitive" cultures, none of which is quite as pristine as romantic folk like to think.[2]

Had this seesaw answer dipped in enough places often enough in the godly direction, an era of tranquillity might have spread through the land, but, little by little, most likely, mankind's frontal lobes—or the images they allowed him to create of his divinity—would have doomed his species to extinction so many millennia ago that there is no sense speculating when. Nor is this primal peril a conceit I have brewed for literary purposes. It remains the overarching theme of the Garden of Eden Biblical tale—neatly complicated by late apocryphists employing a gorgeous cluster of symbols—and is repeated in spirit if not in letter by all myths of man's creation that I have ever heard of, including some devised in this century. *Vide* William James and company.

Worse, mankind today may still maintain such a power of extinction, born of self-consciousness and emotional dispositions (wishes?) to play the role of his own god—that is, not to pee, shit, fuck and die but to *transcend*. Transcend what? Peeing, shitting and fucking for the most part and, of course, corporeal death. But do not be deceived by apparent similarities in this transcendentalism to the multitude of current Eastern philosophies in which man the animal and man the god abrade all too little against one another in the modern world, leaving stasis and poverty in their wake. No, this transcendentalism is as Western as the thick chocolate shake and the Big Mac.

I mean the same gods who, in their moodiest days, bothered O'Neill and Shaw, among others—gods of birth control, sterilization, abortion, and psychoactive drugs to start, and ending with more sophisticated gods who now manipulate—and will eventually control—genetic codes in germ plasma and/or crack the riddles of our central nervous system's communication mechanisms. The latter trends in biological science can (and must) reach but one end: reduction to nil of the tensions and abrasions that have existed since Eden between man the self-conscious auditor of his fate, exploiter of his senses and coward of his death, and man the peeing, shitting, fucking future cadaver who, for reasons he does not wish to parse, invariably burns, buries and/or embalms his dead in order to remind himself of the limits of mortality.

That the seesaw of choice made eons ago may one day swing in the other direction is certainly possible. Our decision, if decision it was, to survive as a species coeval with other animal life on this planet was by no means a binding contract between our progenitors and their descendants. Nor could it be. As history rolls, it was made but a moment ago, and enough evidence is now filling our notebooks (or computers) to speculate that the next swing on the fulcrum of time is simply the second motion of the seesaw, continuous and with hardly a bump on the ground.

The Roots of Eroticism

Against this background, it is fair to call the term "eroticism" a "culture trait" with all the tentative relativism that this latter term implies, the political result of its overuse today. From the comfort of such a position, we may then rest assured by the archaeologists and anthropologists that certain limestone and other sorts of Ice Age bric-a-brac found during this century in Europe are "fertility symbols." Some of these items are quite exquisite, interesting and ingenious: an ivory figurine, for instance, I take to be the representation *both* of an apparently pregnant woman *and* a penis, the buttocks of the female serving as the scrotum and balls of what may, in its time, have served, for all anyone knows, as a representation of a fertility god or a dildo or both.[3] (See Figure 1.)

If I am right about the hermaphrodite nature of this particular object, it must have served prehistoric man as a sexual communication, but chances are that I (and most archaeologists and anthropologists) are dead

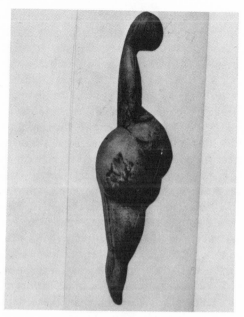

Figure 1: Prehistoric Ivory "Fertility Symbol"

wrong, because we know next to nothing about the "culture" from which this "trait" or symbol has been extracted. It is, in truth, a crude projective test for the twentieth-century eye and mind, and reminds me of an old joke about the psychiatric patient who accuses a therapist administering an ink blot test of having a dirty mind because the latter drew "these damn filthy pictures!" Nothing—not even the similarity of this strange ancient "Venus" to later ones, or to those found in contemporary titular "primitive" societies—provides us with reliable missing information that might, for instance, tell us whether the object was part of a game, a cooking implement, a funeral icon or merely the aberration of one lunatic child's mind, buried and somehow protected from the ravages of time because it was *outside* the domain of "culture traits."

What I am getting at is that considerable humility is necessary before what appears to our eyes to be an ancient sexual communication can be accurately taxonomized as "erotic" once it is removed from its original cultural setting. A safe guess is that half of such material labeled in our books and museums as erotic—that is, designed to *arouse* sexual feelings— is simply illustrating biological functions such as pregnancy, intercourse, breast feeding and so on for purposes we cannot even begin to speculate about or even imagine today. Although we have kept fair track of many of the gods men in our historical tradition have worshiped for the past four thousand years or so, of migrations and wars (and their attendant technologies), the record shows more gaps than substance. All keepers of our history, from Heroditus and Plutarch to Toynbee have been forced to assume that they serve scholarship best by playing gods rather than mortals themselves. What they have told us about their past worlds has therefore been inordinately pre-frontal, cerebral and objective, with a few exceptions. The latter are usually individuals who do not cast themselves in the role of historian but satirists or gossips or diarists like Petronius Arbiter, Juvenal or—closer to home—Samuel Pepys and the Victorian gentleman who wrote *My Secret Life,* to which I shall return in the next chapter.

The historian as god is not an unfamiliar contemporary notion; it has been chewed over by modern scholars as different as Gottschalk from Barzun. A fine argument may be made that, be he ever so humble, no historian can be anything *but* a god, since he's capable of destroying the fiscal reputation of George Washington with one hand while turning a rascal like William Marcy Tweed into a saint with the other. More than this, he can revise and recreate culture: Feed some statistics into the proper computer, for instance, and it is possible objectively (and, it is claimed, scientifically) to vindicate or celebrate the institution of *pre-bellum* slavery in Georgia, if this be the historian's whim. Here is a magic obviously reserved for gods, not men! So turns the world, as most historians must turn it! These miracles are often no less startling than those derived from technologies that are less complex than historical scholarship, but, for all that, no more or less wonderful are the keepers of history's works to behold.[4]

My purpose here is not to excoriate historians for doing what culture has always demanded of them but only to somewhat revise our sense of perspective concerning all historical artifacts—be they religious symbols, arrowheads, paintings, statues, buildings, poems or plays—that are so frequently and facilely related to non-existent "culture traits" by museum keepers and people who write (or put together) coffeetable books. Guessing is fine as long as one recognizes the frivolity of a guess.

For instance, the considerable expertise that I bring to European porcelain of the past two centuries deserts me in large part (but not entirely) when I consider the cultural role of a rare Christmas Plate fired in Denmark as recently as 1908 for numerous reasons that I would happily include in a book on porcelain were I writing one. I know *what* the plate *is;* I can describe it, cite its rarity, its method of production, and so on. But I am unable to affirm that I know *why* it is and what the circumstances of affective motivation critical to its obvious emotional tone were when it was made. I know what it means to *me,* but when I tell you that, I am talking like an historian or teacher of philosophy or art whose best skill is that of autobiography.

If this problem bewitches a porcelain collector, one can easily imagine its implications for the student of eroticism, simply because porcelain art, like all art, must survive through time in the domains of thought and material substance as well as that of feeling. Only in this latter way are art and eroticism similar: They are both characterized largely by feeling states that are functions of a cultural consensus and therefore frequently non-transmittable socially from era to era or place to place. Many histories of eroticism have been put together with loving care, but they cannot avoid our ancient problems of the meaning of meaning.[5]

Ancient Attic vases and clay objects provide us with all sorts of sexual representations that we are assured are "erotic" or designed for sexual arousal. I suppose, for instance, that a Greek woman, naked, carrying a phallus shaped like an enormous fish is *somewhat* erotic to me and possibly even conjures up symbolic, sensual and linguistic relations of genitalia to fish, but this erotic quality of the picture is, for the most part, my own projection. Neither does my modest study of Greek theatre and philosophy expose its affective nature to me in any but the most vague and shadowy way. While I think I also know something about Roman life—and its classical language—I recall a youthful visit to the Vitti house in Pompeii shortly after World War II. It was an historical disaster for me. Despite the graphic nature of the frescos and the famous symbolic painting of a man weighing his prick on a scale balanced with gold, I knew that this childishly obvious pornography had no erotic value to me. As for the Romans, the functions it served for them remained total mystery, mainly because I could choose from so many possibilities. I required another couple of decades to understand the apparent obscurity of Roman eroticism, and that I would not even discover it hiding somewhere in the verses of Catullus. (The latter blow, I must admit, was a disappointment of some magnitude, because I was assured by others that the dynamics of Latin eroticism would indeed come clear if I translated the poems myself. I did, up to the point at which I discovered that I was on a fool's errand.)

The argument of many authors of the coffeetable books, however, is that eroticism is a universal instinct and that the emotions it generates are identical at all times and places, hypotheses that cannot, I think, be disproved. To illustrate, let me compare erotic emotion itself to the tragic sense of purgation that was apparently generated in the first audiences of great Greek Tragedies. Fear of nature, fear of death, cowardice, false pride (and, to the Greeks in their most somber attitudes, all pride was apparently false by definition)—all are universal human emotions, as far as we know. Possibly they are by-products of instinct. What characterizes the "pity and fear," however, to which Greek audiences were aroused by the theatrical occasions—I cannot even call them "plays" or "dramas"—of Sophocles and Aeschylus, I can only imagine in the same faint light with which I still view Roman eroticism or "pornography." (Even the latter word is confusing, because the erotic content of what one might want to write or read about whores in Greece—and why—remains speculative, and I am forced to categorize poor romantic Cattulus as a "pornographer" because of the wanton appetites of his pseudonymous "Lesbia.")

The honest classicist, teacher of drama or actor (Olivier as Oedipus comes immediately to mind) knows that he cannot—and therefore does not attempt—to replicate ancient catharsis when he introduces these plays to the modern public and the modern mind. I have heard theatre-going in ancient Greece described by classicists as "rather like a religious ceremony, possibly the Catholic High Mass." But then I have also heard Japanese Noh drama described exactly this way by experts, and both analogies are obviously ludicrous except, possibly, for purposes of roughly categorizing human experiences. Of this I am sure: The Greek and Roman "theatre" and "drama," both comic and tragic, had precious little to do with what either of these words *connote* to any man or woman (even Olivier) who has been acculturated in twentieth-century theatrical and dramatic traditions. That they *denote* certain Greek and Roman rituals that have counterparts in modern experience goes without saying, but so do gladitorial contests, feeding Christians and slaves to lions and the deadly militant extravaganzas produced by the Emperor Nero in the large (and original) arena called the "Colosseum."

Certainly we know with some clarity what the ancients laughed at, what they cried at and what they cringed at. We may even know what kind of vicarious experiences gave their men hard-ons, if, as is probable, this was one function of satyr plays, Aristophonic sex comedies and the wonderful comedies of Plautus—as well as of a vulgar street theatre, that existed certainly in Rome and probably also in Greece but was apparently never written down. What we do not know is *why* these people laughed, cried, cringed *or* (most difficult for one to imagine) why these experiences caused erections—if indeed they did.

A person who has, for instance, had the opportunity to live in a culture where the female face has been seen as erotic but the cunt has not (at least to the same degree) may empathize with these unsolvable puzzles. Watching rural modern Sicilian youths literally "come" in their trousers (with minimum manual stimulation) when a fair-to-passing-pretty (to my eyes) *genuine* blonde girl (in so far as the eye can see) walks down a street is indeed a tempering experience for those of us raised in cooler Anglo-Saxon environments. So is the (apparently) ancient Mediterranean adoration of hairy female legs and enormous tufts of hair growing in women's armpits, both of which I personally find revolting but remediable. One may as well question the nature of erotic content in an Eskimo kiss, and no end of speculation has centered with good reason upon the Eskimo proboscis as an erotic symbol by the sort of psychologists who are interested in this kind of thing. The one answer that does *not* suffice for psychologist or layman, when considering any of these questions, is *"chacun a' son gout."*

What we find in our history books are mere clues to the sensual roots of eroticism, phenomena that, I submit, must move through time and space before they become amenable to more than description and/or appreciation as art and/or a fanciful reincarnation of spirit and style, as in the film *Fellini's Satyricon.* In this movie, analogies and metaphors of what may or may not have been erotic in antiquity are translated into an erotic vocabulary of, in fact, a minority of the world's population, but it is a vocabulary clear enough to communicate its largely satirical objectives to its audience with some success.[6]

The roots of contemporary eroticism are found, therefore, only in relatively crude physical and neurological sensations that men and women everywhere share with one another. They are not, as many art historians, anthropologists, archaeologists, drama critics and others may have us believe, forever on display in one or another series of cultural events. On the other hand, with the eventual expansion of surrogate means of communication in the West (like the printing press), followed by multiple means of mass communication (like motion pictures and broadcasting), something of a continuum of erotic value could be created within limited geographical domains, first, by preserving cultural values and spreading them widely and, second, by educating the erotic senses of wider populations than had heretofore been available for training.

As we shall see in the next section, wide ranging institutions like the Roman Empire, the Christian Church and certain artistic traditions developed intricate and apparently powerful vocabularies of eroticism limited to those populations privy to their vocabularies. What almost all of them lacked for a long time was a strong enough thrust of communication to spread them to large, accessible populations as well as sufficient permanent media either to hand them from generation to generation or to reorganize them, rewrite them, redraw them and bring them up to date as various societies changed, no matter how slowly.

The avidity with which eroticism was devoured by the technologies of communication that might allow people to accomplish these ends is confirmed by one startling (to me) fact: *Each and every instrument of communication that has been devised to date by man (including television) has been almost immediately turned to the service of what the culture in which it was invented called "pornography,"* not on a limited basis but to whatever extent that technology—and the inventive mind of man—could contrive, regardless of so-called "public attitudes" at the time or of the law.[7]

Eroticism Comes of Age

How inevitable, then, that the history of eroticism is neither more nor less than a reflection, however dim, of the history of art—or the arts—in any tradition or culture. Here we have the outcome of an historical inevitability or, to be more precise, the equipment with which history is made to unfold. This is equipment in technology—or "technique" to some—by which impressions of a social order are preserved in words, pictures, statues or what have you. Like every other academic endeavor—or any social science—history is only as reliable as the technology out of which it is made, the techniques by which it is kept. How much of this technology (a record, I suppose, of what men did in the past important or fortunate enough to be preserved beyond its own time) might be fairly called "art," I cannot guess.

The fashion of the moment I write has currently filled our museums' exhibition cases with Egyptian statuary, artifacts, goldwork, diadems, jewels and similar fascinating manifestations of a fraction of the genius of a culture long dead. To our eyes, these items are homage to the arts. And well they should be, although a little more selectivity might be exercised by museum keepers and modern artisans who copy or reproduce them. God knows what most of them were in their own time, and that particular god—or house of gods—is unfortunately long dead. Trapped in desert tombs for centuries, religious technologies combined with nobody knows how many other kinds of techniques (including pictograph of manifests that inventory the riches of dead kings)—all come out of the time machine as art, just as relics of most of the recording techniques of the distant past do.[8]

Here in New York City, a movement is today afoot to preserve what was once a monument to railroad technology, Grand Central Station. The reasons, which are largely supposed to be artistic, make some sense to me here and now. That we destroyed our old Pennsylvania Station, a nineteenth-century monument to railroading which insanely and beautifully imitated one of the greatest Roman technologies, that of plumbing and public baths, was considered by many, including me, a sacrilege. But technology does not—nor does it ever—turn automatically into art so quickly and indomitably more than superficially.

When thinking in less elephantine terms than railroad stations and over shorter periods of time, technology, both sacred and profane, becomes first what we call an "antique" and then, by a process of selection, a work of art. Within shorter time frames, certain specific technologies may add a step: from *collector's item* to antique to work of art. The relatively recent technology of postal stamps is an excellent example; ancient and modern coins are a bit more ambiguous. Eventually, however, many of us have a strong sense that some of the world's coins and stamps will, in a half-millenium or so, end up as objects of art. This, I suppose, is one of the reasons so many of us collect them—no greater folly, I think, than making out a will and/or purchasing a "permanent" gravesite, and no smarter.

Mainly, most erotica of the past survives, as noted above, under the rubric of "art." Whether or not a contemporary pubic vibrator will end up in this category, I shudder to conjecture. Merkins and dildos that have survived from the Renaissance certainly have (more the latter than the former), and I have seen them exhibited with suitable reverence many times, usually along with medieval chastity belts. That exactly the same reverence *may* be shown in a few hundred years to a pornographic film sequence in full color and sound (that I have also seen) illustrating the use of a vibrator for masturbatory purposes by an attractive nude young lady is, accordingly, far from unlikely. Just such an eventuality was depicted, a little too soon, I think, in the film, *A Clockwork Orange.* Earliest drawings of dildoes actually being *used* that I find in our pictorial artistic tradition appear in the eighteenth century, although I believe chronologically earlier examples exist in the Orient. Written discussion of the relationship of dildo to cunt is ancient. But how and by what criteria does one compare such writing, say, to a contemporary porno film? I fear that eventually we shall have to try to answer this question, but not at this point.

Ambiguities of art aside, certain points must necessarily be remade here to be made at all. The history of eroticism, like most history, skims the nitty-gritty of personal reality and, one way or another, leans heavily upon what the historian has no choice but to use as primary data: the arts of time that has passed. The arts, on the other hand, serve the historian as fundamental techniques for recreating images of the collective nerves, sinews, muscles and brains of the past. This is just *one* of the many cultural functions of what any group of people at any time call "art," and it is not my purpose here to compare this particular function to any other ones. What is important is only that certain kinds of cultural values—some of them pretty abstract—are only amenable to the present via the technology of yesterday's art, and it seems reasonable to assume that the greater the emotional (or non-cognitive) content of whatever historical quality is being observed, the greater the dependence upon art will be. Once again, my observation that erotica as we know it in the West seems to be a relatively *recent* phenomenon calls to attention the degree to which all history is at the mercy of surviving samples of former technologies—what historians call their "sources." I think it important, also, to observe here that this impression of recency *may* very well be false. But I know of little history, even relatively contemporary history, that cannot be told without the identical *caveat,* if it is told well.

Because of this relationship between those means of communication that have survived as art and the impression we receive from them of what was considered erotic yesterday, some sort of crude lexicon of relics may be roughly sketched. From antiquity, the bulk of the material that has survived comprises an amazing hodge-podge of statuary, pictures (found mostly on household artifacts), poems (like those of Sappho and Ovid that make up a small part of a much greater lost universe), plays (many of those most interesting to the historian of eroticism also lost or not recorded in print) and biographies, the closest documents we find to what we would like to believe are authentic history. Social and religious commentary also contain erotic materials: Martial and Juvenal were poets—and much more; Apeleius was a teller of classic stories, but he also showed us the evil side of Cupid's nature (or the dark underworld of sexuality) in clear metaphors, granting that all the godly references in his works were intended to perform metaphorical service.

In Judaism and the Old Testament, one finds a sort of mixture of erotic tonality and socio-legal significance that is inevitable in a document that apparently evolved the way the Bible did. Wakefield Poole, a modern pornographic filmmaker, attempted to produce a pornographic version of the early part of the Bible. It failed miserably, just as John Huston's pompous but "square" version did, and as nearly all dramatic recreations attempted in the past century (even of the Garden of Eden story) have failed—unless they have been played for comedy or contemporary carnival shows in the manner of C. B. DeMille.

The Bible, possibly, illustrates as well as any other historical document the degree of erotic entropy that exists between the past and the present. The nomadic Hebrews were at least sensual enough for Saint Paul to recognize a need to modify their traditions of licentiousness (detailed most clearly for modern scrutiny in *The Song of Solomon*) by describing the power of eroticism to corrupt men's souls in many ways. So Onan spills his seed upon the ground to curb his lust. Moses shatters his tablets before the goings-on around a golden calf, and the Mosaic code itself harshly treats that ancient, inevitable corollary of marriage: adultery.

The later Gospels of Christ seem then to create, apparently for the first time in history, the erotic enigma of a God who, in effect, screws or rapes a virgin, who remains intact yet bears the Christ, son of God, mortal Messiah and holy spirit. This is only one of the many mystical triads that gave—and gives—Christianity its enormous multifarious fascination and appeal. But cohabitation of gods with mortals was not unknown in Greek mythology, and every (or almost every) culture's myths contain one or another version of the famous Amphitryon myth: god fucks a mortal to produce a demi-god, Hercules in the case of Alcmena, Amphitryon's wife and Jupiter's lover.[9]

The gospels are fraught with potential erotic content, and so might be Christianity today were it not for the remainder of the New Testament. Despite the (inevitable?) infusion of Greek comedy into the events involving Christ's birth, this god of the Hebrews is not, in our time at least, a god given to strong emotions. (Jupiter, Alcmena's lover, has the self-control of a tom cat!) He does not take Mary in lust—or even in adultery, strictly speaking—and his son himself becomes, most notably at the hands of St. Paul, a god of *love,* in large measure *because* of Jesus' non-sexual creation. With and after Paul, Jesus stands as the ultimate symbol of the sort of human affection that involves the *least* quantum of erotic emotion, and he played this role until the coming of the Freudian period of the Christian era.

How simple it is, therefore, to see the seeds of the "love versus lust" polarity through which every man, born in sin, now had to walk on his personal path during the long and dramatic spread and growth of Christianity in the West! And how difficult is this path, even when we are guided by as eloquent a sufferer from tormenting, conflicting passions as St. Augustine! In the ontology of Christianity, we begin to limn the psychological tensions that would, at various times in the years to come, make deadly enemies out of the man of God and the man of art. The same tension sowed the seeds of the archangel Lucifer's expulsion to hell and the mushrooming here and there, to the present day, of covens of witches and diabolists and black cats, as well as the institutionalization of devil worship and the Black Mass. In the latter, naturally, Christ was (and is) profaned (in ways we shall eventually have to examine) so that the devil's omni-erotic touch might now have power to turn Christian love inside out. The cross is returned to its (probably) phallic origins and is used accordingly much of the time.

Simple? Certainly, but possibly wrong and beside the point of our modest objectives. For much of the period we call "the Middle Ages" in Europe, the Church was the major agent of intra- and intercultural communications. It trained the scribes who copied books in the scriptoria, and there was little purpose in learning to read at all if not to serve the ends of God—true for Hebrews and Moslems as well as for Christians. The agonies, religious and secular, that therefore inevitably beset population after population born into sin and condemned them, probably by popular consensus, to an ambiguous eternity was but an extension of the ambiguities of a continent and a millennium of ironies. The populace of the continent survived hundreds of years of the poetic inspiration of Christian mysticism and beauty on one hand, and of the filth of daily life, plagues, venal clergymen, countless pointless crusades, poverty and stupidities that are legion on the other. Here is a paradox I think I should leave to the cameras of an Ingmar Bergman. (Has it ever been told more dramatically than in *The Seventh Seal* or *The Virgin Spring*? Yes. I suppose it has—many times, but Bergman's genius in these movies is notable and remarkable.) If it is fair to say that "secular man" existed at all in the Middle Ages, his cultural viability became increasingly important as the era ended. Christian love was secularized to some degree in the romance of knighthood and was encapsulated into the songs and poems of minstrels, troubadours and their ballads. The eroticism we think we find in *Tristan und Isolde* or *Le Roman de la Rose* or, for that matter, *The Divine Comedy* was all created for a communication system that spread its messages to a growing semi-secular elite, at the same time that it had to satisfy conflicting passions of an enormous and schismatized church—a church becoming more and more torn apart as the centuries wore on toward the Reformation.

Pinning down the eroticism or sexual function of these late medieval songs and stories cannot, I fear, be done, because they themselves have parsed eroticism so freely and cleverly that different eyes will behold different things each time they are read. The poet himself may have become an erotic symbol (viz: Dante), and, for some, so did the minstrels as well as the so-called "Goliardi," that strange wenching, drinking and singing order of peripatetic scholars and quasi-monks, so often disowned by established churchmen. The verses they sang and the stories they made up centered on love, but it was a love so fashioned that the adoration of

Christ (and Christian love with Pauline emphasis) could not easily be severed from romantic, often asexual, love and, especially for the "Goliardi," even carnal love or lust, which they did not regard as the devil's work.

No doubt this same sort of erotic equivocation could be found in much theatre—largely unrecorded—or pre-Renaissance Europe. Strolling players there were aplenty, and of various kinds: clowns, acrobats, dancers, comedians, animal trainers and singers, among others. The legitimate theatre of the sixteenth century was given its form and some of its substance hundreds of years earlier, when the church literally exploded its territorial limits and brought its miracle and mystery plays out into town squares, and eventually into open playhouses built for dramatic purposes. Despite the fact that the miracles and mysteries had to retell either Biblical stories or the adventures of saints, I doubt that even the most devout passion play did not, somehow, take advantage of and stimulate a wide range of man's passions, wider, at least, than those generally activated by church ceremonies. If not, why bother with the plays?

Miracle plays evolved into various fanciful morality dramas, and these, while suitably reverential, tended to be a good deal more secular, lasted longer and dealt with a broader range of interests than their religious counterparts for the best of reasons. Because they centered upon morals, or the triumph of good over evil, they had at the same time to portray the evil over which good indeed triumphed. This little trick was continued well into and beyond the age of D. W. Griffith and any number of film directors who followed him, and it remains, I suppose, a wrinkle still employed by film and television producers. It has always been easy enough to understand, despite recent confusions created by calling it a "theory of compensatory values." (sic) Nor is it even absent today from a good number of pornographic films that, in the last analysis, take the side of virtue against sin, although the sin indicted has been portrayed with delight and obvious relish. (*The Devil in Miss Jones* is an excellent and explicit example, but it is only one of many, many others.) The few scripts of the morality plays that have come down to us give us only tiny glimpses of this broadening emotional spectrum, and they constitute but a fraction of many thousands of lost dramas. Nor was the eroticism of their pious, church-going audience in the thirteenth century more than vaguely consonant with our eroticism today.

In this spirit—the spirit, I think, of the so-called "morality tale"— were the best known secular documents written during the three or four centuries after the end of the first millennium A.D. We think of them today as somewhat bawdy and lascivious, but set in their own time frameworks, they are both *more* and *less* "racy" than they seem to the modern reader. I mean Boccaccio's *Decameron*, Chaucer's *Canterbury Tales* and the writing of François Villon. One illustration helps clarify a host of problems.

The *Decameron* scandalized many church fathers in the fourteenth century, when it was written. Exactly how much and why, we are not sure, but some two hundred or more years after it was published, Rome produced an updated list of books prohibited for Christians (by then, increasingly, Catholics), and, sure enough, Boccaccio was on the list. Using criteria of the time, it met the church's assumptive ukase that books of a depraved nature of any sort tend to corrupt the pious and therefore should be censored. What was *not* on the list—and sold briskly in countries and lands under Rome's hegemony—was a version of the *Decameron* in which the erotic parts (or those parts we would *today* call "erotic") were *not* expurgated, but in which the priests, nuns, monks and other churchmen (and women) who sport so merrily in the original edition were changed into lawyers, doctors, tradesmen and other secular folks. (We must also remember that the Anglo-Saxon vulgarities that cause college freshmen to titter at Chaucerian verse were the *only* words available at the time to describe arses, cunts, farts and similar phenomena. Circumlocution in referring to these functions did not influence letters to a notable degree until Charles II brought back Latinized euphemisims for these terms in the seventeenth century after his exile in France. Post-Restoration English is the language that gave us the erotic vocabulary we use today, as well as new functions, expletives like "fuck" and "shit" that currently are used more, I think, for non-erotic than erotic purposes by both men and women.)

That the classic revivalism of the Renaissance, especially in Italy and England, gave new energy to the old erotic three-shell game of the Middle Ages is, I think, indisputable. In order to pursue the good, one had to consort with evil, often both in kind and degree. As far as painting, design and statuary were concerned, this confidence game followed the developing technologies of artists: woodcuts, etchings, paintings, metal casting methods and so on.

As we view the progress of erotic art (or all art) of pictures from the medieval period through the Renaissance, it seems to me that the invention of central perspective in Italy between 1420 and 1430 was an event of extraordinary importance. A revolution occurred when artists burst their old limits to the new realm of realism provided by formulae for creating the illusion of depth on two dimensional surfaces. Nowhere is it more noticeable and moving than in what *I* call erotic art, though the artists of the day may have considered it many other things. Suddenly, nudes, satyrs, orgies and all manner of previously stylized cartoon sexuality took on, literally, a new dimension, possibly indicating that this new technique of and by itself created a new or revised interpretation of eroticism. Again, it is difficult to tell. Stylization, even to the extent of eliminating central perspective today, need not diminish artistic erotic content. In fact, to some people, it may enhance it. Since *all* painting in the West responded to the revolution of central perspective, it *must* have included *all* works designed all or in part for erotic arousal.

One monument to perspective and the world it opened up for the painter, the Sistine Chapel in the Vatican, is a familiar example of the way that Rennaisance artists dealt with the many faces of love and the ambiguity of passions. It is seen in both of Michaelangelo's masterpieces there: one redolent with youth and faith, and the other bitter and dispirited. Both are statements of enormous affective power (erotic and non-erotic) in large measure because of the illusory magic of central perspective.

So much has been written about various erotic aspects of the Elizabethan theatre that it is hopeless to undertake a non-controversial analysis of the period or of the Bard himself, as either a dramatist or a poet. What some of us frequently forget, however, is that all roles in Shakespeare's plays were performed entirely by men: that Ophelia, Juliet, Desdemona, Cleopatra and Goneril were young boys at the Globe. In what ways this convention has subsequently distorted critical views of his dramas and comedies, we cannot know, particularly in those where "men" dress as "women" and vice versa as part of the plots, and where the fun or mischief in the play is an erotic double-cross. One recent and fascinating distortion of our conventional, hundred-year-old (or more) erotic interpretation of *Macbeth* by Roman Polanski in his film version of the drama throws the entire play off center for the modern viewer—or, possibly, it throws it right back onto its *original* center after centuries of distortion. Lady Macbeth is played as a sensuous Playboy bunny, a sexpot who gets her kicks by manipulating, in *every* possible way, a young, handsome, horny but somewhat naive *Macbeth,* who is something less than the ballsy stud she would have for a husband.

Having seen so many modern, sexually sanitary *Macbeths,* I found the film both exciting and enjoyable, and wonder whether or not such a version may have simply exploited as erotic heterosexuality the obvious homosexuality implicit (or explicit) in its original performances at the Globe, no home of prudish decorum for audiences, actors or writers. Once again, the modern critic finds himself, in every respect, far, far removed in time and space from the first Enobarbus, Lear, Iago and Hamlet. What credit to Shakespeare's genius that his Hamlet serves as well for a case study in Freudian psychoanalysis as it does for a modern moral lesson on the uses and abuses of power when seen from the sidelines by Rosencranz and Guildenstern! Nor should we forget that *Romeo and Juliet,* far from being a sentimental poem to true love destroyed by an obdurate social order, may well constitute Shakespeare's stern warning by "the fearful passage of their death mark'd love" that the romantic idealism and sex drive of two immature, misguided youngsters are just "poor sacrifices to our enmity," in old man Capulet's words. I can read the play as a brittle sermon on the follies of the paths down which untutored eroticism leads the sorts of boys and girls who should keep away from one another lest they court disaster. Although I have never seen it staged this way, I would like to.

The Invention of the Pornograph

One of the qualifications for the status of genius is to be born at exactly the right time in the right place—not a day lost or given. Among the talents of William Shakespeare, this was not the least of them: to be the right man with the right talent in the right place at the right time. But possibly I am referring to a symbol bigger than Shakespeare the actor, part-time playwright and prosodist. Had he never lived, the Elizabethan Age would still have been one of the greatest in the annals of Western arts, especially if living itself can be considered an art. This was the period of Marlowe, Webster, Beaumont, Fletcher and the first original, sophisticated comic mind in English, Ben Johnson. It was also a period of geographical exploration, heroism and grand confrontation between nations and rulers. In truth, the Elizabethan era was not only English. It represented a larger move in European social reform, the secularization of the Renaissance, as the Reformation swept Europe's creative chemistry away from the Vatican and into new, great empires of commerce that were to burgeon during the seventeenth and eighteenth centuries. In England, it was an unsettled period marking the decline of one ruling house, the rise of another, and finally a revolution that was effectively to close the book on the Renaissance and its peculiar creative energy forever.

An age of confusion had begun. Shakespeare is the monument (one of many) to the death of those moments in European history when piety, rebellion, inchoate nationalism, classicism, secular power and superstition were all welded for a short period into a sort of creativity and vigor unknown before or since in the Christian era. In its own terms, it was also a period in which types of eroticism developed that can be better understood by our culture than any types that preceded it, even if we have to turn the eroticism on its head to induce it to tickle our loins. Shakespeare died in 1616. French literature and drama bloomed shortly thereafter in an erotic burst of fire ending with one of the greatest comic talents in our tradition, Jean Baptiste Molière, who, from my viewpoint at least, bested even Shakespeare.

To have nerve enough to chortle at the neo-classicism of the French secular Renaissance (now dying, if not dead), to blend wonderfully sharp satire of royalty, nobles and kings who would be gods on earth (right in front of their noses) into a theatrical tradition sprinkled here and there with flavors of Greek comedy and Roman vulgarity, all spiced with a retinue of *Commedia d'ell Arte* characters who had, quite literally, been strolling the Italian boards for centuries, and to command the respect especially of those who were fried in his own oven, was quite an accomplishment! If the record is correct, Shakespeare bent over backwards to appease Elizabeth and the Tudor nobles. If the record is correct, Molière enlisted not only the support but the theatrical cooperation of the same hypocrites, liars, fools and fakes he paraded before his audiences of French nobility.

The very words "the court of Louis XIV" have a vague erotic sound about them, and so do relics of it that we discover here and there in France today. To our eyes, somehow, rococo remains a style of giddy design and naughty eroticism. To Molière, it was the perfect medium for mecurial audacity and grist for the mill of his satire. "Devilish" is a good word for this secular comedian, devilishly funny, devilishly sharp and devilishly clever in the way that he courted the noble patrons that he stripped almost to the bone on his stage. Concerning the entire canard, he even had nerve enough to announce from the stage, "I think it a very grievous punishment . . . to display myself to fools, and to expose our compositions to the barbarous judgments of the stupid." [10]

For the English-speaking world, however, the Restoration's last burst of light and dying neo-classicism represents the change from remote history to, roughly speaking, "modernity." The date marking the beginning of the modern era of eroticism is elusive, naturally, because its evolution was erratic during the declining years of the Renaissance, and Europe was (because of problems of transportation and communication) a much larger place in the seventeenth century than it is today.

Note please, the direction in which technology was then taking Europe. The printing press was invented and developed between the years 1450 and 1500. By 1550, it had spread throughout the continent. Few people, however, could read. During the next hundred and fifty years or so, exploration, invention and commerce produced a new and ambitious middle class. The ancient grip of religion on reading or on "the book" was loosened. Selective and undemocratic in today's terms, the raw *number* of people who therefore learned to read—who *had* to learn to read—who could afford books and introduced themselves at will to various types of printed erotic stimulation (henceforth reserved, I would guess, for literate city dwellers and the wealthy) grew and grew. What I am getting at is that the energetic flair of Europe's classical revival, the Renaissance, burned out in part because its spirit was incompatible with too many books, with solitary reading, with the tastes of a large middle class, with utilitarian education and, last but not least, with the general conservative thrust of the Reformation, itself a stepchild of the printed page. Our circle is therefore complete. We are not quite back in the Middle Ages, but the social and cultural vigor that took Europe out of them left in its wake a world of considerably diminished color.

This is not to say that this social change came easily. It did not. Royal families, vested interests, old aristocracies of privilege, and even such vagabonds as actors and poets and painters and others depended upon and attempted to revive a remembered time when the church's monopoly on art and the burst let loose by the discovery of Greece and Rome glorified man in the image of God. But they fought a losing battle against change. Fight, they could. Win, they could not. The printing press was the most powerful technological instrument yet invented and, like *all* technology, its power was not discovered until men had been using it for a long time. By then, the universal church had been fractured into countless sects, regionalism was now turning into nationalism, commerce brought an infinite number of diverting corruptions to European soil, and whatever "erotic man" had been up until the end of the seventeenth century, give or take a little here and there, he would never be again! He died with the "universal man" of the Renaissance.

In England, the sheer pressure of events hurried things along. By the end of the seventeenth century, the British king (or His Majesty's Stationer) lost his privilege to censor books prior to publication, a right that even the rebel Cromwell—or *especially* Cromwell—had guarded assiduously throughout his dictatorship. The press was now "free"—at least free from prior impositions, and it has remained free in this way to date in England, although the colonies did not abide as closely by the new laws at the turn of the century as did the mother country. And apparently a new class of printed literature quite suddenly appeared, or at least came to the attention of the state. We discover that the term "obscene libel" (what we might call "pornography" today) first appeared quite unexpectedly in British law in 1727. Or so legal historians tell us.

Both the fact and the date are important agreed-upon historical symbols, but they are also both quite incorrect.[11] Note that I have already observed above that *every* instrument of communications technology has been placed to the services of eroticism (or pornography) shortly after its invention. This is, of course, true of printing. Much of it—in England and elsewhere—was at first illegally printed and circulated, that is, it lacked whatever imprimatur was considered necessary for proper literature during the sixteenth and seventeenth centuries. That such documents in circulation rarely called attention to themselves is also not surprising. Few were printed. They were expensive and apparently reserved mainly for private collections of higher churchmen and civil administrators who, in one way or another, decided which laws were to be enforced and which were not.

The date is also bogus, although the real one has been lost. We only know that in 1727, one Edmund Curll, the father of contemporary pornographic publishing, according to one authority, was convicted at long last for publishing a volume called *Venus in the Cloister; or the Nun in Her Smock,* a document to which we shall turn shortly. Now, Curll had been publishing erotic materials openly since 1708, about half a dozen years after the last precautionary license was stamped upon English books.[12] His output included, among other items, a translation of the *Satrycon,* and he was in and out of trouble for a long time. *Venus* proved his downfall, however. According to one authority:

. . . fair numbers of prosecutions had been brought before this particular case came before the courts; some were successful and others unsuccessful. But sooner or later, more especially after the disappearance of the Licensing Act from the statute book, the ordinary courts (the State Trials) were bound to take cognisance of an "obscene libel" (pornography) as the offence of publishing an indecent work came to be legally known.[13]

For the record, some of these "prosecutions" have indeed been preserved but certainly not all of them. They began in 1677, when some foreign books containing what would be called today "explicit sex" caused the official closure of a London bookshop for a few hours. Other printers and publishers were simply fined by lower courts, or the offending manuscripts were simply set aflame by constabulary action. One supposedly pornographic poem, *The Fifteen Plagues of a Maidenhead,* actually found its way to the Queen's Bench Court in 1708, but the presiding justice threw the case out of court because the poem, while admittedly "bawdy," was not a libel against anybody's person and, he lamented correctly, "There is no law to punish it." [14]

Granting that the poem (for which I have searched without success) was indeed erotic, lewd or *something,* the vital point here is that Mr. Justice Powell could not find it obscene because, apparently, he did not understand what obscenity was—a problem that has by no means been entirely solved to date. He mentions in the court record, and then dismisses as irrelevant, the behavior of one of history's lost heroes, Sir Charles Sedley, who, during the reign of Charles II (in the former century), was convicted of unruly behavior. It was to Sir Charles who jurists often turned for more than one hundred years to try to discover the precise nature of obscenity— whether its mischief lay in errant eroticism or outrageous behavior that might harm others physically, mentally or whatever, which is still a legal problem of some pith.

Sir Charles had apparently 1) stood naked upon a balcony (on a date not preserved for us), 2) flung some bottles down upon a crowd and, if I read the interpretations of the interpretations of his trial correctly, 3) pissed upon the crowd beneath him, or at least filled said bottles with urine! As noted, the *exact* reason for Sir Charles' conviction on the charge of disorderly conduct continued to bother jurists in Britain and England for a century and a half. Was he convicted because of his nudity and because the presumed nudity entailed eroticism? Was he convicted because of the harm he *might* have done people by throwing bottles? Was he convicted because unwilling victims were exposed to his "golden shower"? Was he convicted because he was obviously as drunk as a skunk in a period of history when men boasted of the "bottom" they were able to reach in heavy drinking without appearing intoxicated, and when such behavior on the part of a noblemen may have been considered more outrageous than similar simple mischief by a commoner? What damage *had* he done the public safety—and how had he done it?

Mr. Justice Powell in 1708 obviously believed that the conviction had mainly to do with Sir Charles' prankish physical endangerment of the people below him, in one way or another. (In America, incidentally, a Philadelphia court, in *1815,* reviewing this case in the United States' first obscenity action, took the position that Sir Charles was found guilty only of exposing his nude body to public view!) Because of Powell's broad construction of the common law, *Maidenhead* (or its publisher or bookseller) was found not guilty of "obscene libel." The volume hurt no one, and, as Powell said, he could find no law anywhere to indicate that obscenity actually libeled anybody. And so to hell with the government's charge!

Similar protections were responsible for the dismissal from actions of a number of dubious documents that neither the courts nor the public, in this age of gossip and scandal fanned by people like Addison, Steele, Defoe and Swift, knew quite how to deal with. The Earl of Rochester's horny play, *Sodom,* and various of his poems, written during the preceding century, found their way in and out of court, but none of them apparently ever sustained a significant or lasting conviction, despite the fact that they were neither more nor less erotic than Curll's publication, *Venus in the Cloister.* They were, however, noticed, and, as a result, the *notion* of obscenity found its way into British law—with nothing to support it in common law or statute except the idea that it *might* constitute some sort of libel against somebody, somehow. And so things stood for well over a century before *Venus'* eventual conviction in 1721.

I suppose that *Venus in the Cloister* is paradigmatic enough to serve English history as its first "obscene" book. In this symbolic sense, it is indeed significant, although copies of it (under its original name at least) have vanished over the years. Let me relate it to the invention of what I like to call the "pornograph," a fairly modern instrument of legal (and cultural) technology (or technique) that turns erotic writing, pictures, poems and/or radio programs into "pornography," and which in legal terms alone places these communications into a *special* class of speech, like privileged speech on the floor of Congress, at least as far as certain kinds of laws and customs are concerned.

My concept of the pornograph is meant neither as whimsey nor criticism. Before the conviction of Curll, much erotic literature had naturally been printed in England, as we have seen, almost from the day Caxton first set up his press in Westminster. Seventeenth-century England fairly drips with translations of documents like Aretino's erotic dialogues written in Italian during the immediate post-printing press period. (The author's life, 1492–1556, fits almost exactly into this period.) These documents found their way to England in the seventeenth century and were there called *The Whore's Rhetoriek.* They consisted of candid dialogues on sexual matters between nuns, wives and prostitutes, the latter part of the work achieving greatest notice and fame. Using today's standards, and translating the Restoration's overblown language into common English, you or I might well consider these documents hard-core pornography, but in their time they seemed no cause for social or judicial alarm.

Venus was probably little different from the rest of the erotic material extant in its day, except possibly for its anti-clerical thrust—although in the eighteenth century, anti-popism in Britain was not unpopular. Written by a French clergyman, the Abbé Barrin, whose pen name in English was the Abbé DuPrat (interpret as you please), *Venus* was advertised with the claim that "the amours herein displayed . . . (are) not to be paralleled for their agreeable entertainment in any romance or novel hitherto extant."

The book *was* popular—one strike against it! Other similar volumes were published in its wake—strike two! And the so-called "age of scandal," even for journals like *The Spectator* and *The Tatler,* was coming to an end—strike three! A sea change was also in process concerning the idea (or nature) of eroticism as understood by the public, possibly for the first time in history on so large a scale and certainly for the first time in England. Eroticism of certain types was therefore about to be turned into obscenity. The puzzle of who "obscene libel" could hurt had found its invisible victim: the *public,* who *might* be corrupted to vice and immorality by erotic emotions. This idea, which is easy for the modern reader to understand—if not sympathize with—was a distinctive result of the invention of the pornograph.

Sir Philip Yorke, the King's Attorney General, put the matter in succinct contemporary terms (1727) in an argument that would have been laughed out of court a century before:

> What I insist upon is that this is an offense at common law as it tends to corrupt the morals of the King's subjects and is against the peace of the King. Peace includes good order and government, and that peace may be broken in many instances without an actual force: 1) if it be an act against the constitution of the civil government, 2) if it be against religion and 3) if against morality. I do not insist that every immoral act is indictable, such as telling a lie or the like, but if it is destructive of morality in general, if it does or may affect all the King's subjects, then it is an offense of a public nature. And upon this distinction it is that acts of fornication are not punishable in the temporal courts and bawdy houses are.* [15]

In spite of a powerful dissent by one of the sitting justices to the effect that Curll had caused no breach of the peace the way Sir Charles Smedley had, the majority view was expressed by Chief Justice Lord Raymond in November, 1827. "If it (a published work) reflects upon religion, virtue or morality," he said, "it tends to disturb the civil order of society. I think it is a temporal offence."

Curll was pilloried for an hour, although he used a ruse to minimize the crowd's abuses by distributing pamphlets claiming that he was being

---

* This legal distinction remains in force *de facto* in British-American law to this day.

punished for political reasons. He was also fined and placed on probation. Curll steered clear of the law for the rest of his life, although in the years before he died in 1747, he continued to publish some questionable books, such as *The Pleasures of Coition,* an eighteenth-century version of *The Joy of Sex.*

Justice Raymond invented the early pornograph by transmuting "eroticism" into "obscenity" precisely at a time when progress in science, libertarian government, technology and education clearly signaled that a new era of liberal enlightenment in arts, letters, manners and morals might be just down the path.

It was not.

Pornography and Print

If you do them justice, you will esteem me perfectly consistent in the incense I burn to Virtue. If I have painted Vice in all its gayest colors, if I have deck'd it with flowers, it has been solely in order to make the worthier, the solmner sacrifice of it to Virtue.

—John Cleland

LIKE OTHER DANGEROUS new inventions, the pornograph was to lie almost unused for nearly one hundred years. As we shall see, it was an important century for the development of modern eroticism, especially erotic writing. It was a time when the notion of "obscenity," "obscene libel" or what we today call—using the classical word—"pornography" was well watered and grew most benignly. Few writers or publishers were unlucky or indiscreet enough to be brought before a court of justice in England or the colonies for writing or printing dirty books. One exception, however, was the noted parliamentarian, John Wilkes, who was unwise or mischievous enough to parody, in 1763, Alexander Pope's *Essay on Man* in a work entitled *An Essay on Woman*.

The unusual aspects of *An Essay on Woman* (and one other of Wilkes' masterpieces) gives us some insight to the gathering tangle of cultural sensibilities that would turn the eighteenth century into a paradise, both for writers of obscenity of many kinds and for those who would employ law, religion, popular opinion and other weapons to attempt to surpress or eliminate it. The *Essay* also tells us something about the role of the press in British—and American—culture.

A major issue surrounding *An Essay on Woman* was simply the fact that it was written by Wilkes, or so it was claimed, although it may have been penned by one Thomas Potter and merely printed at Wilkes' behest. Wilkes (1727–1797) was a British revolutionist in the tradition of similar impious heroes who brewed and won the American Revolution on colonial shores. In fact, Wilkes, almost from the beginning of his career as a political reformer, was anti-monarchal on both specific and general grounds and a firm supporter of the rebel cause in America. His expulsion from the House of Commons, his various trials and exile are beside the point here, except insofar as he spent his lifetime, a long one, playing the role of a political, social and cultural non-conformist and rebel, at times a public anathema and at times a popular hero. His entire colorful career was spent tilting against the aristocracy, the establishment and monarchist stuffed shirts.

Of less importance is the fact that, compared to much erotic literature of the period, *An Essay on Woman* was neither "obscene libel" nor even "obscene" in any present or later construction of the term. It was an irreverent parody of the Pope, ninety-four lines long, containing a rude paraphrase of a hymn, replete with notes supposedly written by a Bishop Warburton. It was satire; it was blasphemy. But it bore little similarity to *Venus* or her *Cloister*. In addition, only *twelve* copies of the document were printed. Two, however, found their way into the hands of Wilkes' enemies, one of them the Lord Sandwich, who read the entire poem to a shocked House of Lords. Once again, sources are not agreed upon dates, but, between 1863 and 1869, Wilkes was convicted of publishing "libels" and fined. His conviction had both strong religious and political colors in it, combined as it was with outrage at Wilkes' constant attacks against the King and his secretary of state.[1]

The Temper of the Times

I mention Wilkes because his was just about the only outstanding prosecution on either side of the Atlantic directed toward any sort of behavior that might be regarded today as "obscene" until 1815 in the United States (as previously mentioned). And even this early example occurs in an ambiguous context. American law did not really set itself to using the pornograph until 1821, exactly ninety-four years after Curll's light-hearted martyrdom at the hands of Justice Raymond in London!

It would therefore seem at first glance that the eighteenth century was a lackluster period for printed erotica. But nothing could be further from the truth. In many ways, this was a period of glorious irreverence and, in slightly exaggerated fashion, Wilkes was as much a man of his time as Thomas Paine, Ben Franklin or Thomas Jefferson. A tradition of eroticism in English, discussed in the previous chapter, had finally developed, and much of the general sense of freedom that had its origins in the philosophy of John Locke pervaded the secular world, even in matters of sexual decorum.

In Britain, the King was God's instrument of established religion. It is, accordingly, self-evident how and why religious freedom and secular self-determination—or anti-monarchism—were stamped on two faces of the same coin. Thus, deists, atheists, Quakers and others insisted, in the last analysis, on going to heaven or hell (if such there were) on their own steam and not at the behest of man, king or book.

During this critical century, pornographic literature as we know it today (including drawings, paintings and woodcuts) was *neither* legal nor illegal. As we have also seen in the last chapter, British law stood in no posture to take any position for or against it. In England, permissible boundaries of decency or decorum were kept fairly wide for both the man in the street and the aristocracy.

For the former, gin, cheap, powerful booze, had been invented as a side-product of oppressive industrialism. Hence William Bolitho's aphorism, that "gin is the shortest way out of Manchester," is a true one. In fact, hard spirits were—and remain—one of the shortest ways out of anywhere, not only for oppressed workingmen but for competitive scholars and aristocrats, especially in a time of great stress and social mobility. One by-product of alcohol was therefore much strange and libertine behavior that was (and is) conveniently blunted culturally by the semantics of the words "intoxication" or "drunkenness," a fact true also in the colonies, where rum was the particular drug of choice.

Erotica proliferated in such a climate (I like to believe) *because* of the revolutionary spirit and inclinations to freedom espoused noisily by men (and women) like Wilkes. These folk were not necessarily philosophers or politicians, and probably most of them were dimly aware, at best, of Locke's thinking that so powerfully influenced the West during this and the following century. The test of propriety regarding all freedoms—but particularly freedom of the press—did not at the time seem to lie in common law, in the courts or in arbitrary authority but in consensus within the social order itself. In other words, as long as individuals did not abuse too severely *any* freedoms of others (given privileges of class, age and education—as well as money), *private* behaviors—even possible "obscene libels" or the use of the pornograph—remained largely matters almost entirely related to whether one found his own way to heaven or hell as I have noted, not unlike the way one handled (or neglected to handle) his personal relationship with God or His various churches.

The population of the American colonies, in these regards, was a good deal more noticeably variegated than that of the mother country, largely because of the secular power of certain religions in certain territories, where the matter of one's personal freedom in regard to common morals was something of a public concern. Morals were only provided with slim and often temporary legal protection, because British law was, by and

large, followed in the colonies. Much has been made of the influence of the
Puritans of New England, a cultural thrust that extended down into the
colony of New York. (Some say *too* much, particularly as the idea has
been analyzed by European sociologists.[2]) Puritanism, of course, not only
took a harsh stand in regard to flagrant eroticism but also on drinking and
piety in general, although it was not unaffected by—and itself effected—
the political rebellion of 1776.

New England, the cradle of Puritanism, let us remember, was also the
cradle of the American Revolution, a fact that seems contradictory on face.
It is not, however, largely because the Puritan influence and way of life
built into it provided enormous scope for, and invitations to, both excesses
and hypocrisy, one the handmaiden of the other. The record, I think,
shows that, despite blue laws and fiery sermons, the Puritan blade was
blunted sooner and more easily than many, including the imaginative
Hawthorne, would have us believe, and much of what remains is myth,
including *The Scarlet Letter*. Witches were indeed burned and exorcised,
but certain freedoms—particularly the spread of erotic communication,
curiously in the interests of efficient cultural purification—seem to have
been encouraged by these practices, which is nothing new in history, as we
shall see.

The Quakers and similar sects were another matter, but again an
anomalous one. Ben Franklin is as good an example of a man of his time
as anyone else: an exile from New England's repression because he was a
Quaker, who found his way to the freedoms of Philadelphia, where he
practiced his religion and succeeded at more arts and skills than one man
today could begin to master. Among other things, of course, Ben produced
his own charming erotica in the 1740s for limited circulation: in my opinion, his excellent *Advice to a Young Man Choosing a Mistress* (choose an
older woman!), his risque *Polly Baker's Speech,* defending illegitimacy of
birth, and his delightful *Letter to the Royal Academy at Brussels,* on the
frequently pursued comic theme of the social consequences of farting.[3]
(How erotic the latter is remains open to debate as does all scatology, a
problem we shall have eventually to face.) As far as personal behavior is
concerned, Franklin is famous to this day for his own personal contribution to the population of illegitimate children in colonial Pennsylvania.
Nor did he apparently spurn the hospitality of the orgiastic "Hell Fire
Club" in London, or the sexual favors of a number of women, especially
when he served, in his advanced years, as America's emissary to the French
court.

Hypocrisy in this case? Cursory judgments of geniuses, especially
Quakers, are invariably unwise! Common wisdom encourages a distorted
view of the degrees of personal freedom in all matters—not only those
related to spirit and ceremony—that the Quaker faith both permits and encourages. As an epigramist, Franklin's advice to others was like the advice
to others offered by many of us, not necessarily based upon our prescrip-

tions for *self*-discipline but rather the discipline we would like to see exercised in others. In this respect, and many others, Franklin was both typical and exceptional by the main criteria used to judge men in his time. He was also possessed of enough self-insight and realism to judge himself for the man he was, not the man others might believe him to be, or so his autobiography indicates. He was fortunate to have lived when he did!

The main reason, legalisms aside, that obscenity seemed to flourish in the seventeenth century to the degree that we can call the era the "cradle of pornography" (a phrase that Franklin might have enjoyed) was simply that it was largely a private matter that was efficiently restricted regarding distribution and output. Factors involved were the way printed materials were produced, with hand-set type laboriously printed on instruments not too different from the original press used by Gutenberg centuries before. Paper was made mostly from linen. It was not mass produced. The art of reproducing pictures required great skill, and so did binding books, which were usually bound in animal skins. All books, be they obscene libels or Bibles, were in short supply and expensive. So were newspapers and the first magazines that appeared in London during this period. While anyone could *look* at a book, ownership was restricted to those who wanted them badly (such as scholars and clergy) and to those who could afford them to develop their own personal libraries, which were as fashionable a sign of status then as they are today.

The main factor, however, that inhibited the broad cultural influence of print in the eighteenth century was the same problem that restricted it in the sixteenth and probably delayed the invention of movable type in Europe until the fifteenth century, although it was feasible long before this. I am referring to severe limitations upon literacy in both England and America; rarely did the percentage of the population who were able to read in either country rise as high as ten percent. This was a seldom reached outer limit, despite the absence of both slavery and relative freedom for women in Britain (as opposed to the colonies) and the sophistication of much of the life in cities like London and Boston. Anyone could *look at* (and understand) woodcuts and etchings of people fucking—and of these there was not exactly a shortage—but such delights were often bound in books that were invariably expensive and not likely to be seen by any but the rich.

The true record of sex for play and pay in the colonies—and later in the new United States—is hindered by poor bookkeeping and even worse written history.[4] In England, lower-class whoring and higher-class randiness was, for many possible reasons, chronicled with considerable exactitude, thanks in part to writers of pornography. From the point of view of the whorehouse keeper, the eighteenth century was, in large part, a glorious period of bull markets, wide freedom and, almost inevitably, considerable prosperity.

This is not to say that the masses would not have been interested in obscene print if they had been able to read, but it would, most probably, only have gilded the lily of life for them. Permissiveness in the air reached the streets and naturally ran into the sewers as well.

The societal repressions that were later to bloom into the flower of Victorianism were gathering early steam at the time among exactly the same clerical, scholarly, aristocratic and, to some degree, mercantile minority, who bought and read the small amount of pornography in print. A precedent was being set that would require only two liberating factors during the nineteenth century to, in effect, open the modern era of print eroticism and the elaborate system of repression that arrived with it.

In the first place, literacy and education, at least on basal levels, had to be spread widely within and between social classes before any seeds of repression might bear fruit. This is precisely what *did* happen, most obviously in the new United States, where education, although not granted constitutionally as a civil right to anybody, was mysticized into a necessary byproduct of democratic choice. Until the post-Civil War period, following the wake of reformers like Horace Mann in the first half of the century, there was nothing similar to free universal education that was understood to be a *functional* desideratum of democracy, but this was indeed the direction in which the new nation was moving.

In Britain too, literacy was rapidly spreading, being no longer the province of the scholarly or leisure classes, but now a necessity for the conduct of business throughout an increasingly commercially oriented Empire. The Crown required an army of educated (or semi-educated, according to Noël Coward) administrators and functionaries, as well as clutches of bureaucrats at home to conduct the complex affairs of an industrial, economically and politically imperialistic nation.

Revulsion at (and reform of) the oppressive factory system and at the exploitation of lower-class children also had something to do on both shores with the humane desire to educate them. Such early crusades were based on the equivocal assumption that they were better off in school than in coal mines or at home—but *not* (yet) better off than as apprentices to an artisan or skilled laborer. The beginning of the present century with its labor union movement furthered that idea.

Second, technology came to the service of obscenity—at least to the bulk of it that had been written during the 1700s. The steam press was invented in Germany in the early nineteenth century. It was in general use for nearly all types of printing in most medium to large cities in both England and the United States by the 1840s. It was naturally and immediately put to use printing multiple copies of almost the entire trove of erotic literature that had been accumulated in English since the time of William Caxton—and probably before him. A new literate public was now ready to buy such books and pamphlets at prices that were relatively high compared to legitimate newspapers and magazines. It was not lack of enterprise that limited the production of obscenity of all kinds, but only the fact that printers' type was still set by hand and flat-bed printing remained a relatively slow process, even when powered by a steam engine. Not only print was produced in this manner, but drawings as well, an aspect of eroticism we shall treat in Chapter 4.

Culture in all its aspects, especially moral and legal, responded to these changes, as we shall see. For the moment, let us look more carefully at the birth of modern pornography in print during the eighteenth century.

Fanny Hill: A Model Woman

I think it is difficult to exaggerate the importance of John Cleland to the development of erotic literature in English either as art or as sheer erotica. The enormous range of pornographic (more or less) heterosexual fictions and quasi-fictions of print and screen that glut today's market are in countless ways rewritten versions of *Fanny Hill* and, I believe, so are many of their homosexual brothers (and sisters). On this list, I must, of course, include the literary output of Xaviera Hollander and all other happy hookers and pimps and their ghost-writers by the hundreds who have turned to the literary life during the past fifteen or so years, as well as the editors and writers of such slick and/or sloppy sex journals as *Hustler, Screw* and their imitators in other languages.[5]

How could *one* book have such an enormous influence on literature for so long with such intensity? Even so-called "serious" erotica like Lawrence's *Lady Chatterley's Lover* reflects fractured images of *Fanny,* not only in theme but in style and literary approach to the issue of fucking across class lines in merry England, among other things. Nearly every woman (or female surrogate) in modern pornography in English, including much contemporary filmic raunch, *is,* in one degree or another, *Fanny Hill* in one or another guise. I think I am correct to include here Molly Bloom as well as poor Constance Chatterley and, although they were not born in print, the heroines of the films *Deep Throat* and *Behind the Green Door,* both stories having been based on anecdotes of unknown vintage.

Fanny Hill is all the more remarkable because it contains not a single so-called "obscene" word or expletive, although the vocabulary available to Cleland contained a greater amount of such terms in the late 1740s than were available to Shakespeare in Elizabethan England. Nor was *Fanny Hill* the first book of its kind in circulation when it was written, or the first, or only (or some might say "best") at the time that steam presses and translations eventually blanketed the world with copies of it. Some works that pre-dated it by only a few years, such as the anonymous *A New Description of Merryland* (first published in 1740, nine years before *Fanny Hill*), are far more ingenious, and much of the erotica available in England at the time (extant today) is quite similar to *Fanny Hill.* So are "legitimate" contemporary novels that did *not* share *Fanny's* peculiar fate, such as Richardson's *Pamela,* Fielding's *Tom Jones,* Smollett's *Roderick Random* and Sterne's *Tristam Shandy.*[6]

I suppose some may consider it less than reverent to compare these latter literary monuments to *Fanny Hill,* although, to paraphrase Mark Twain, I would judge only about a third less. Cleland is sometimes accused by his detractors of monomania (a literary weakness that easily becomes a virtue at the hands of social reformers who turn their talents to writing), of exaggeration, of distortion, of being a poor historian and so forth and so forth. In short, Cleland suffers from the same major abuses to which all criticism puts most highly creative artists most of the time, because here is the easiest trick that the critic can pull out of his bag of chestnuts: indicting a writer (or painter or playwright or filmmaker) for not doing what he or she had not intended to do in the first place.

The last virtue for which one justifiably looks in *Fanny Hill* is realism, and we have every reason to believe that Cleland did not intend the book to be a model of verisimilitude. As fanciful an artist as Cleland writing erotica for the purpose of arousing or shocking his readers, however, could not help the later assumption of his role as a documentarian, as even the shoddiest pornographic filmmaker of fifty years ago—in spite of his original objectives—is seen by today's social historian. Certainly Cleland had intimate knowledge of the whorehouses of London, their keepers, like Mrs. Brown and Mrs. Cole, and the sorts of "honourable gentlemen" who patronized them. The stories that Cleland's assorted prostitutes tell about their seduction into the ways of sex, the amazingly fastidious orgies and various sexual combinations, while probably highly fanciful, provide the reader with insights, not only into the erotic imagination of the author but also into the stream of social and cultural reality from which they were drawn.

Fanny Hill's main attraction as both literature and art, is, of course, exactly what Cleland, who received twenty guineas for writing it (a fee probably equivalent to $2500 or so in purchasing power today), originally intended. The forty-year-old vagabond was first, up to mischief—an old euphemism for today's term "liberation"—and second, trying to induce erections in his readers of the day, presumably all male. That *Fanny Hill* remained actively in worldwide circulation for 230 years after the publication of its first part; that an artist of no less skill and reputation than William Hogarth turned his pen, within ten years of the publication of *Fanny,* to his illustrated "Harlot's Progress" (a picture story that ended, unlike *Fanny,* most unhappily); that *Fanny Hill* apparently retains for many modern readers its erotic thrust in our age of *Hustler* and Technicolor porno queens; that Cleland clearly anticipated experimental, empirical and theoretical evidence, supposedly generated by the Freudian cranium, that females enjoy sex as much, if not more than, men (despite the insistence of members both of the psychological and medical fraternities that *nobody* believed this until the genesis of contemporary sexology at the hands of A. Ellis, Kinsey, Masters or some other offspring of the present century's best thinking); that the entire dynamic of lesbianism as sheer fun was described magnificently by Cleland with a deadpan realism and that he postulated that the phenomenon of female homosexuality, while less physiologically dramatic than its male counterpart, was (and is) a far more widespread phenomenon than popular culture (and popular socio-psychology) indicates; that *all* of these qualities and more are true of *Fanny Hill* illustrates the extent to which it is indeed an exceptional liter-ary landmark on many counts—and may even excuse this incredibly long run-on sentence.

These, I think, were among the main things that Cleland attempted to accomplish—in addition to making money, the usual first attack by which critics have tried to dismiss *Fanny Hill,* but which is actually an irrelevant matter. I am certain that Homer did not sing of the Trojan War unless his palm was crossed with silver; the only writers who's sanities are suspect in the history of literature are those who did *not* write for money. (Dr. John-son's observation to this effect has been justified by history. May I amplify it with further speculation that anything written without a profit motive is probably worth no more than what it earns and that the bulk of the *bad* writing at any time in history—especially today—is that for which no remuneration is received.) Comparing Cleland with Restoration play-wrights, romantic novelists or even his own contemporaries may be an in-teresting intellectual exercise, but it is quite beside the point of his ac-complishments.

Erotica was Cleland's primary objective, and language, via print, was his medium. To this end he created the girl Fanny, real or otherwise, the paradigm of nearly all erotica in our tradition since the seventeenth cen-tury. Fanny is a whore who, partly because of fate's caprices and partly because of her lusty nature, is lured from innocence to prostitution via a lengthy affair with a young man she truly loves. Having been deserted by him and suffering the miscarriage of his baby, she returns to the world of commercial sex, where, one way or another, by means of her own experi-ences and of those of her fellow strumpets, she becomes involved in sexual adventures both conventional and highly imaginative—and enjoyable—in the doing and telling.

Fate finally treats her nobly by bestowing upon her the legacy of an el-derly infatuated customer who conveniently dies. Thus does Fanny rise in the course of the book, told as two first-person letters to an apparently high-born acquaintance (a frequent format for similar books to the present day), from rags to riches. Fanny is also finally restored to the arms of the man originally responsible for her defloration: her true love, thereby giv-ing, in her words, "legal parentage to those fine children you have seen by this happiest of matches." Fanny ends up as a loving mother and wife, a veritable literary precursor of so many other women, regarded by society as virtuous but with dark pasts or secret lives in Winesburg, Ohio; Peyton Place; that area of Pennsylvania known to its inhabitants as "John O'Hara country;" and other locales, these days usually suburban.

The plot of *Fanny Hill* is, of course, capricious, arbitrary, inconsistent, meandering and, at times, non-existent, but no more so than in many other so-called English "classics" of the period. Plots, in those early days of the relatively modern storytelling device of the novel were largely concerns of stage dramatists and not prose writers.

This tradition of novelistic near-plotless discourse has continued to this day in erotic literature for the best of reasons. Emphasis is placed upon description, character, action, anatomy, feeling, emotion and the believability of the numerous necessary personal encounters upon which erotic narrative centers. The plots are simply devices to bring together likely—or unlikely—participants in sexual behavior. They occur in ways startlingly similar to the stratagems that sexually predatory men and women contrive to arrange their encounters in contemporary Western culture: by arranging an unlikely (even bizarre) situation, possibly social, possibly commercial or possiblty both, where highly specific and much-desired sexual encounters can and will take place.

Two qualifications for these liaisons are obviously necessary: one, a social field or arena for the action (whatever it is), and two, the common psychological disposition of the participants to indulge in certain kinds of sexual activity, which are invariably circumscribed by convention. A so-called "swinging" married couple, therefore, that join an anonymous club of similar "swingers" is, in a real sense, *plotting* the occasion and content of its desired sexual encounters. An erotic novel or story about such encounters needs merely to create convincingly the characters' motivations and the circumstances of these interactions. Complexities of plot are likely to distract the reader from the author's objective. The events must not, naturally, be incredible (beyond certain limits), but the main burden of the story will (and must) center then upon the erotic behavior first and foremost.

All too few erotic writers, including the most subtle and artful since Cleland, have recognized this point. At any rate, if what we *call* "pornography" does not succeed in being pornographic, then its other qualities are quite beside the point. Much of my own experience with dull literary (and filmed) erotica stems from an author's *over*emphasis on plot, or on the convolutions of circumstances that get, say, a fifty-year-old bisexual male and a teenaged brother and sister into a remote hilltop cabin where the youngsters are totally at the mercy of the older man's imaginative carnal designs. Here we see nice *circumstances* for literary eroticism but a story that may easily fail due to overly clever plotting. Eroticism here will probably take the form of incest, male homosexuality, multiple anal male-female penetrations and so forth, with or without (probably with) more than a little sadomasochism. Into the story go various props, from chains and whips to enema bags (depending upon erotic objectives) and the possible introduction of other characters (people? animals? a sex-starved ancient hag of a female hermit?) with nearly unlimited possibilities. Character development is vital, but it cannot involve the convoluted cleverness of a writer of British espionage novels. This would blur the focus upon the erotic.

Note that out of the wild, spontaneous situation above, I have already begun to write an erotic novel that I shall never write, simply because I am not a novelist. (I have no personal scruples about erotic writing.) I have *not*—as erotic writers are often asked of by critics—begun with credible characters and/or the kind of plot elements that we today demand from credible fiction, not even of the sort that seem manufactured for sensational movies. Cleland was luckier than most pornographers today, because his literary environment required from him precisely those elements that yielded a novel (or whatever you want to call it) that *had* to be quite believable, entertaining and illuminating but, above all, had to remain fundamentally erotic. In simple terms, Cleland was culturally and psychologically free to make *stimulus to masturbation* his first objective in *Fanny Hill*. This he unquestionably accomplished, at least for his male readers—and probably for numerous females too. Merely that his art stands the test of time *within* our contemporary erotic vocabularly (as Ovid's poetry, for instance, outside of this same vocabulary, *cannot*) is of high critical interest because of what it reveals about the temporal, social and cultural origins of that vocabulary, to say nothing of the psychological.

For Fanny of the golden heart is the prototype of literary ladies of all kinds, including some of the documentarily damned females in Flaubert, Dickens and Dreiser, of even Mae West and the public *persona* of Linda Lovelace. The golden-hearted strumpet must also enjoy her sex and possess a nearly magical cunt of honey. Hers is the rare talent of being able to masculinize the often pathetic men around her, while, because of her super-libido, being allowed to dally with other females who also find her irrestible.

Whether or not such whores exist in reality—or have ever existed or may have existed—matters little. I am hardly experienced enough to guess. Certainly we do not find them in our documentary of realistic literature of contemporary prostitution.[7] Most of us who, for one reason or another, have had occasion to share the company of prostitutes may have, at times, met an occasional lady who seemed to fit the pattern for the short term. Our perceptions, however, tend to be selective. Nor do I for one moment hesitate to believe that (even and especially in the whoring trade) life often does imitate art: that is, that prostitutes will often play the role of the literary strumpet for their own edification and/or that of their patrons.

From a special perspective, therefore, does Truman Capote observe Holly Golightly. And Holly, modeled upon a real person, saw herself as—what? Even Capote does not venture too constricting a guess in his gentle psychological portrait. Further, because he is not involved with her sexually, Holly can play a credible role for him as the kind of unreal prostitute both he and she *want* her to be: a romantic one. Note that in the novel, *Breakfast at Tiffany's,* he avoids the sexual mechanics of Holly's life. Her fucking occurs in another world from the one Capote so delightfully describes, which is to say that she really doesn't fuck (as a character in the novel) at all.[8]

Fanny Hill fucks indeed, but this is not the source of her charm as the first person narrator of Cleland's classic. Whatever happens to Fanny is done *to her* for the most part, in the tradition of the heroines of English novels through most of the nineteenth century. And this is one outstanding ingenuous aspect of her character that remains constant. She becomes a professional purveyor of sex but never a hardened one. She is also miraculously observant, far more acute (through Cleland) in describing emotions and reactions of females than males. The males in Fanny Hill are, as a matter of fact, usually dull, although they are often seemingly colorful types of rakes and roués at first glance. Nearly all are a good deal less sensitive than the women—mostly whores—and more tiresomely characterized. This characterological aspect of heterosexual pornography has more or less continued to the present, largely, I suspect, in direct or indirect imitation of Cleland's success at high eroticism in Fanny Hill. (The great exception is, of course, the Victorian autobiography *My Secret Life,* but this document flies in the face of many traditions that have survived in other print pornography. See pp. 74–78.

I cannot resist the urge to quote in order to illustrate my points, although I feel irreverent about quoting from *Fanny Hill,* because the reader either has read the entire document or should have and because pieces and bits do not give justice to what Cleland accomplished in communicating eroticism, not only in discrete sections but throughout the whole of his two-part book. Compared with later, lesser, similar attempts—including the bulk of pornographic literature today—one finds in *Fanny Hill* no "dirty parts" or purple paragraphs that little boys of my generation might have read while masturbating in the men's room at school. (This activity, during the nineteen-thirties and forties, involved books that ranged from *Studs Lonigan* by James T. Farrell to Henry Miller's *Tropic* volumes [the latter illegally smuggled into the country, supposedly from Paris but perhaps not, for they were printed in Scandanavia or Holland in English] and even, as difficult as it may seem for my younger readers to believe, contraband editions of the third *Lady Chatterley's Lover,* which was also illegally obtained from abroad.)

No, *Fanny Hill* makes poor fodder for instant, separate masturbatory fantasies except in large chunks (rather than total "scenes") and not by reading the book alone but by fusing memory with imagination. For this reason, I suspect that *Fanny Hill* may have been one of the *first* books that many of my generation (and others before it) really *read* from start to finish. We did not skim or study it from an outline, as we did school assignments, because we *had* to read it. For example, I was introduced to *Fanny* at the time I was supposed to be reading *Silas Marner* and/or *A Tale of Two Cities,* I forget which. Masturbation being more important than scholarship, I imagine I shared the experience with millions of other American youngsters of having my first genuine *literary* experience via Cleland, an experience in which my English teachers at New York's Stuyvesant High School played no part, despite their good intentions and, by today's standards, near-genius teaching skills.

Added to this, my initiation, are all the pornographic photographs—homo-and heterosexual—so-called "dirty funnies," privately printed or copied erotic short stories that circulated throughout most large all-boys high schools, and all other great "turn-ons" of my adolescence. To what effect? I cannot say. Like service in the army, it all had to do with growing up, and subsequent choices by intent and by chance of sexual and intellectual directions during stormy adult years that were to follow in many other schools and on three continents, all of which included nervous breakdowns, reintegrations, quondam psychoanalysis, chronic alcoholism and myriad other autobiographical matters that will emerge with suitable candor if required, mostly in the last section of this volume.

Education occurs only partly in school, and, even for the dullest of us, I do not believe it ever stops while we live; it simple slows down or changes orientation. Causes and effects, excluding certain skills or techniques possibly, are difficult to locate in human growth and development, except as fashion dictates we *should* locate them. Thus, for instance, a Yale graduate *should* display certain characteristics of a Yale education, whatever that is. Most manage to do just this, although some do not, except to the degree that they merely and occasionally play the role of Yale graduates. All of them, however, seem to know what qualities are expected of a "Yale man," none of them primarily relating to academic matters.

Having protested too much then, let me extract a segment of *Fanny,* one of the most delightful in the book: her introduction to the delights of lesbianism. Fanny, a girl of fourteen, has found her way to London and a brothel operated by a Mrs. Brown. She is a virgin, nubile, hardly a mature woman, and is turned over to a considerably older professional, Phoebe, for her sex education. Phoebe, presumably nude, induces Fanny to strip for bed, lies down beside her and kisses her "with all the fervour that perfect innocence knew." Fanny herself continues the narrative.*

> Encouraged by this, her (Phoebe's) hands became extremely free and wandered over my whole body with touches, squeezes, pressures, that rather warmed and surprised me with their novelty, than they either shocked or alarmed me.
>
> The flattering praises that she intermingled with these invasions, con-

---

* Comments appear in Reference Notes at the end of the book to avoid breaking continuity.

tributed also not a little to bribe my passiveness; and, knowing no ill, I feared none, especially from one who had prevented all doubts of her womanhood by conducting my hands to a pair of breasts that hung loosely down, in a size and volume that sufficiently distinguished her sex, to me at least, who had never made any other comparison.

I lay there all tame and passive as she could wish, whilst her freedom raised no other emotions but those of a strange, and, till then, unfelt pleasure. Every part of me was open and exposed to the licentious course of her hands, which, like lambent fire, ran over my whole body, and thawed all coldness as they went.

My breasts, if it is not bold a figure to call so two hard, firm, rising hillocks, that just began to show themselves, or signify anything to the touch, employed and amused her hands awhile, till, slipping down lower, over a smooth track, she could just feel the soft silk down, that had, but a few months before, put forth and garnished the mount-pleasure of those parts and promised to spread a grateful shelter over the seat of the most exquisite sensation, which had been, till that instant, the seat of the most insensible innocence.[9] Her fingers play'd and strove to twine in the young tendrils of that moss, which nature has contrived at once for use and ornament.[10]

But, not content with these outer posts, she now attempts the main spot, and began to twitch, to insinuate, and at length to force an introduction of a finger into the quick itself, in such a manner, that, had she not proceeded by insensible gradations that inflamed me beyond the power of modesty to oppose its resistance to their progress, I should have jump'd of bed and cried for help against such strange assaults.

Instead of which, her lascivious touches had lighted up a new fire that wanton'd through all my veins, but fixed with violence in that center appointed them by nature, where the first strange hands were now busied in feeling, compressing the lips, then opening them again, with a finger between, till an "Oh!" expressed her hurting me, where the narrowness of the unbroken passage refused its entrance to any depth.[11]

In the meantime, the extension of my limbs, languid stretchings, sighs, short heavings, all conspired to assure that experienced wanton that I was more pleased than offended at her proceedings, which she seasoned with repeated kisses and exclamations such as, "Oh! what a charming creature thou art! . . . What a happy man will he be that first makes a woman of you! . . . Oh! that I were a man for your sake!" . . . with the like broken expressions, interrupted by kisses as fierce and fervent as ever I received from the other sex!

For my part, I was transported, confused, and out of myself; feelings so new were too much for me. My heated and alarmed senses were in a tumult that robbed me of all liberty of thought; tears of pleasure gush'd from my eyes, and somewhat assuaged the fire that raged over me.

Phoebe herself, the hackney'd, thoroughbred Phoebe, to whom all modes and devices of pleasure were known and familiar, found, it seems, in this exercise of her art to break young girls, the gratification of one of those arbitrary tastes for which there is no accounting. Not that she hated men, or did not prefer them to her own sex; but when she met such occasions as this was, a satiety of enjoyments in the common road, perhaps too, a secret bias, inclined to make the most of pleasure wherever she could find it, without distinction of sexes.[12]

In this view, now well assured that she had, by her touches, sufficiently inflamed me for her purpose, she rolled down the bed cloaths (sic) gently, and I saw myself stretched nak'd, my shift being turned up to my neck, whilst I had no power or sense to oppose it. Even my glowing blushes expressed more desire than modesty, whilst the candle, left (to be sure not undesignedly) burning, threw a full light on my whole body.

"No," says Phoebe, "you must not, my sweet girl, think to hide all these treasures from me. My sight must be feasted as well as my touch . . . I must devour with my eyes this springing BOSOM . . . Suffer me to kiss it . . . I have not seen it enough . . . Let me kiss it once more . . , What firm, smooth white flesh is here! . . . How delicately shaped! . . . Then this delicious down! . . . Oh! let me view the small, dear, tender cleft! . . . This is too much, I cannot bear it! . . . I must . . . I must . . ." Here she took my hand, and in a transport carried it to where you will easily guess. But what a difference in the state of the thing! . . . A spreading thicket of bushy curls marked the full-grown, complete woman. Then the cavity to which she guided my hand easily received it; and as soon as she felt it within her, she moved herself to and fro, with so rapid a friction, that I presently withdrew it, wet and clammy, when instantly Phoebe grew more composed, after two or three sighs, and heart-fetched Ohs! and giving me a kiss that seemed to exhale her soul through her lips, she replaced the bed cloaths (sic) over us.

Note, at this point, that the narrative continues with a critical sentence of obeisance to morality—a crude one, the seriousness of which is denied both by the style and content of Fanny's narrative before and after it. "What a pleasure she had found I will not say," Fanny continues, "but this I know, that the first sparks of kindling nature, the first ideas of pollution, were caught by me that night; and that the acquaintance and communication with the bad of our own sex is often as fatal to innocence as all the seductions of the other."[13] This said, Fanny continues on her merry way to defloration, romance, wantonness and finally a fast and contrived redemption, all told in the same simplistic moral tone as the extract above and, in both segments of the novel, as well crafted.

Fanny's Sons and Daughters

The Kronhausens, twenty years ago, identified most, if not all, classic pornography as "erotic realism." But they have more recently apparently modified both this term and the literary stylism it represents, although its use introduces for us an interesting question, particularly apt when discussing books like *Fanny Hill,* as the section above demonstrates.[14]

What arises is an undiminished question that bothers and tortures all erotic communications, particularly those in print but also drawings, photography, films, live sex shows and interpersonal eroticism: How *real* is *real*, and *when* is reality *real*?

This is not a frivolous or capricious question. Nor is it a philosopher's puzzle that ends with a cosmological or ontological answer that turns out to be, inevitably and always, a problem of language or symbolic thought. It is far more mundane and obvious and does not strain epistemological assumptions in the least, although all eroticism does present us, as we shall learn in the final sections of this book, with a world view of world views (and/or a psychology of a psychology) that might be called a metaphilosophy.

Come to think of it, our immediate *problem* is indeed confined to a metasexuality—that is, a lexicon of certain symbols, styles and cultural meanings that, in turn, define the meaning of those aspects of culture we have defined in the West as "arousing," "erotic" or "sexual."

Let me explain. *Fanny Hill* is as good a place to start as any, although I might have centered upon the most fantastic erotic underground art, or some near-documentary account of sexual behavior, such as Frank Harris' autobiography or Hubert Selby Jr.'s *Last Exit for Brooklyn*. The problem we face is by no means peculiar to eroticism alone, but it cannot be avoided in the analysis of eroticism the way it can be for other forms of literature and art.

To dwell (in Kronhausens' early terms) in any form of literature on the physical realities of human existence serves, quite correctly, to bring such poetry, novels or even sentences "closer to life." Thus, regardless of the envelope of fantasy within which it is sealed, literature in which characters pee, shit, fart—but most particularly fuck and, more important than fuck, live the life of the libido in their dreams, motivations and feelings—*must be* more "realistic" than similar literature (or *any* literature) in which this is *not* true. In its way, then, Rabelais' *Gargantua* is more realistic than Melville's *Billy Budd,* because it admits a wider recognition of the ongoing physical human condition and thus, especially but not entirely, to the analysis of Freudians like the Kronhausens.

A drama critic once objected to the sound of a flushing toilet on stage in the New York production of Tennessee Williams' *A Streetcar Named Desire* and observed that serious American drama had turned a vital and irrecoverable corner at that moment. He was entirely correct in his conclusion! Regardless of his sensibilities or the conventions of the contemporary theatre, the fact that people had to use toilets regularly had been almost an unmentionable on the legitimate stage up to that time. A shitting, peeing character in *Streetcar* was thus a more realistic one—as a human being— than Williams' previous non-defecating, non-urinating people in *The Glass Menagerie*. In one dimension—and one only—the theatre had indeed achieved a new realism.

Imagine, now, a literature in which people do not grow old or die— not so fantastic an idea, considering the pith of popular literature of the

American movies and television for the past half century or, with exceptions, the seventy-year-old literature of the comic strips. The introduction to art of aging and death, psychological schools aside, is therefore also a move toward realism. Note that the video and film play, *The Middle of the Night,* was considered in its time by critics as *realistic,* merely because it recognized aging as an inevitable process that did not necessarily diminish vital human appetites: An elderly man falls in love with a young girl and seeks the audience's compassion and sympathy. The comic strip, *Gasoline Alley,* remains spookily *realistic,* because the people in it are born, die, get old, and the history of the strip itself has now moved it beyond the lifetime of its creator, Frank King, who planned it all exactly this way.

The dimension of erotic realism may therefore be explained self-evidently. Fanny Hill is simply, from one point of view, a heroine who is more *real* than those in contemporary novels and in most literature before or after her. She has a functioning cunt, an asshole, and the BOSOMS that are, like most human females, quite operational and busy throughout life. She enjoys sex. She even enjoys whoring and is possessed of a full-blown sensual nature. Cleland writes (in the first person singular) as if she has spent thousands of hours on the analyst's couch, contacting the depths of her subconscious, her libido and/or id. *Fanny Hill* is therefore a *real* book in the same sense that *Gargantua* is, because erotic realism or eroticism, certainly *one* of the most insistent aspects of the humanness of us all (even if not nearly so insistently so as Drs. Freud, Reik and Kronhausen would have us assume), is a vital aspect of the story. In fact, it *is* the story.

A counter-argument, naturally, grants Cleland and writers like him their sharp sociological eyes and abilities to describe human emotion but emphasizes the continued, romantic aspects of plot, the shallowness of characters. It also brings up one point, agreed upon in nearly all of epistemologies, that there is more to life than the operation of our alimentary canals and sexual systems and that *this* other part is the most important segment of the laundry line upon which the integuments of existence are hung. Man is, by nature, the argument says, a divided animal. The sphinx told us this long, long ago by his (her) very existence! Those qualities that make man truly human are those that he does *not* share with the rest of the planet's mammalia: intellect, divinity, self-awareness and so on. These unshared dimensions of existence are the proper and rewarding constituents of literary or any other kind of reality.

This is true enough, were it not for the grand tyranny observed by Bernard Shaw, among others, that men are "dragged down from their fool's paradise by their bodies: hunger and cold and thirst, age and decay and disease, death above all, (that) make them slaves of *reality* . . . ." In this, of course, Shaw includes the tyranny of endocrine systems and both the frailty and mystery of our central nervous systems, all discouragingly real, and all, to his Don Juan, negators of romantic, godly and idealistic illusions in life. (Shaw's Devil here plays the role of the idealist!) [15]

I am convinced that the contradiction between these arguments can only be answered by a metaphysical reach, but we have not yet traveled far enough in this book to attempt such heroics. Suffice it to say here that, within our recent erotic tradition—the tradition of expanding numbers of readers in the West, proliferating printing presses and cheap books—*Fanny Hill* has become a landmark, more imitated, in one way or another, than any work of narrative fiction or drama ever written in English—or so I guess.

Pornography in print proliferated in England and subsequently in the United States, especially after attention was attracted to the first legislation against it in both countries during the early decades of the nineteenth century, and later, because of the articulation of the famous "Hicklin rule" in England in 1868, which stands as the first definition of obscenity as a legal entity. The rule was clearly articulated in such a manner that it might subsequently establish clear precedents for the identification of eroticism, which was an aspect necessary for its commercialization. With the coming of Victorianism, every move made against print pornography only seemed to stimulate its production—legally or illegally, though mostly the latter.

I realize that I invite nothing but trouble from apostles of the current social and psychological "liberations" through which we are living, but I do *not* believe that the great age of print pornography is either in the present moment or in the recent past. (Nor is the present moment, in our tradition, the great age of anything of moment, except transistorized mathematical machines, advertising on television and efficient explosives!) This is not easy to say with an entirely straight face, living as we are in a culture where thousands of paperback volumes and specialized magazines cater to every sexual whim with an overkill that is difficult to imagine, and where sex emporiums of the kinds that have lately opened in such cities as New York and San Francisco and similar tourist traps proliferate in Scandinavia, Holland and Germany.

Neither volume nor specialty, taken alone, says much about quality, however. I am the first to admit that specialized publications featuring photographs, drawings and copious prose about sex or countless photographs of teenaged boys masturbating and sucking one another's engorged genitals may indeed offer one an impression, at least, of the extraordinary power of modern mass communications techniques to spread information that was once confined to a few specialists to new millions of seekers of enlightenment!

One factor makes me pause, though, and that is the relatively high prices currently placed upon such delights as sadomasochistic photographs and prose, books about lesbians, women and large dogs, and so on. The main factor that has historically distinguished the spread of mass communications from class communications is low unit price. While, therefore, we may indeed live in a quasi-great age of banal, pathetic, rotten acting and infantile theatrical writing insofar as domestic drama (or soap opera of television and film) is concerned, I doubt that we can make similar claims concerning print pornography. Let me equivocate a bit where magazines like *Hustler, Playboy* and *Penthouse* are (or may be) concerned, for I question the purity of their eroticism—and even the eroticism of such successful (but by no means cheap) but sloppier journals like *Screw. None* of these publications (or their imitators) are given over entirely to eroticism.

As Al Goldstein, co-founder of *Screw* once divulged to me, "I try to keep socially redeeming material out of the damn thing, but that's impossible. How can you talk about fucking all the time? I'm up to my ass in politics, social crap, my own pet hates and enthusiasm, and I'm still making a buck. As a *sex* weekly, *Screw* is not what I intended it to be back in the late sixties when I started it. If we ever get into real trouble, I'll bet it will be over politics or something, not because of our fuck features." [16] In terms of total content, the actual count of the proportion of erotic to non-erotic materials in many other publications (including advertising) is quite surprising. Impressionistically, the erotic photographs and stories simply attract the peruser's attention and create a false impression.

For many reasons, then, our time and place must in the history of print pornography take second place in the modern world to the Victorian era—a period that by no means ended with the death of the Queen but continued into the periods of Edward and George. Historical emphasis is here usually placed upon Britain. But the effects of Victorianism were felt as strongly in the United States as in any other country of the world, with France a poor third and Germany not far behind. Had Victorianism not spread this far and wide, it would not have found its way, say, into French psychology and, via Constantin Stanislavsky and others, into Russian aesthetics, the cornerstone of today's Soviet realism in theatre, literature and graphic art. If it had not spread to Germany, Sigmund Freud could not have developed his schemata of repression, the subconscious and libido into the viable social heresy it was to become, particularly in the United States, where subsequent subcultures of prohibitionism, religiosity, artistic screwballism, subjective literature and movie aesthetics all required a suitable apostle and found him in Freud.

Skipping ahead a bit, I would say that the cultural revolution against the purity and refinement of Victorianism was a *genuine* revolution in that it came from *within* the social ethic itself and was led by potent figures who were themselves products of an older, defeated regime. It could not have succeeded otherwise. Arguments are also sometimes given that somehow—in mystery—Victorianism and Puritanism joined hands in the New World and, less credibly, in England, Germany and (somehow) Czarist Russia as well, to provide Victorianism with extraordinary conspiratorial power over ethical, moral and artistic life in many nations of the world. Max Weber notwithstanding, I have severe doubts that the Protestant ethic had much to do with Victorianism, even in the United

States, except to enforce or provide temporary rationales for the swing of a mighty pendulum that had begun in England.

In fact, Victorianism was born, spread and sanctioned less by the religious noises of Bishop Wilberforce in England or by Anthony Comstock in America than by a combination of other, mainly historical, forces.

First, popular democracy, loosely associated with the period of Jackson's presidency in the United States, saw a tremendous, broadly based, ever-more-powerful inclination—an inclination that lasted until the end of the century—to provide *basic education* for as many people as possible, that is, an education that was more or less confined to reading, writing and cyphering for the middle and some of the lower classes in England and America. It was for these groups, which included large immigrant populations in the United States, that reading alone had tremendous symbolic value. The desire to read was not necessarily a return to older Protestant values, because many more types of literature than Bibles were consumed by the masses. Nor was it a return by Jews to "the book;" the rabbis taught most of the religious only enough prayers (in Hebrew and by rote) to get them born, circumcised, bar mizvahed, married and finally buried.

No, reading was, by this time in our tradition, a *privilege* of class and status. The jump from lower to middle class, or middle to upper-middle, could not be made by means of literacy alone. But literacy *was* essential for mobility. Along with reading and writing came job opportunities, a place in the commercial community, money and all the things that money could buy, which was especially important in the New World. Popular democracy, let us remember, neither was nor is entirely a political or cultural concept. It is and always has been decidedly economic, even in capitalist cultures, as Black Americans and women of all colors and others keep reminding the rest of us—as if we did not already know.

Second, the various technologies used for the spread of printed persuasion were becoming more available, as were the methods of distributing printed material to the middle and upper-lower classes—in short, to those who could read, including both women and children. *The London Times* operated its own steam press in the early part of the nineteenth century. The first mass circulating newspaper opened its doors in New York City in 1832. By the 1840s, rotary presses were developed. Mergenthaler invented his Linotype two decades later and, with the invention of other, similar devices, the setting of print was turned from a craft into a speedy technology during the years that followed the American Civil War.

Third, the economies of the English-speaking countries had produced a system of print subsidy called advertising that helped to spread newspapers and magazines far and wide at reasonable costs. Even without advertising, books, prints and other documents were priced within the economic reach of great masses of the public and freely and easily obtained.

Now—neither the ability to read nor the technologies of mass communications dictate *what* is read, nor by whom. (McLuhanism being dead, we can, I think, accept this as axiomatic.) A treasure trove of erotica (including ancient documents that were perceived, in the erotic framework of the nineteenth century, as arousing, even though arousal might not have been their original function) were simply waiting to be set in type, printed and sold. Fortunes might have been made at this sort of enterprise. The bulk of this extant material was indeed fairly new and easy to read, a product of the licentious "age of scandal" we have already glimpsed in the eighteenth century. Indeed, I grant that it was also an "age of exploitation," poverty and cruel labor in factories or mines. But it was also a fabulous period of sensuality in print, and, for those who could afford it, plenty of whorehouse sexuality for sale, "liberated" females in the modern sense of the word (considerable freedom for lesbians and others) and of debauchery writ large—in somewhat greater measure I think, in England than in the United States.

Fanny Hill was an example. By the nineteenth century, great audiences were waiting for *Fanny, if* they could simply get their hands on copies of the book. To achieve this end stood hundreds, eventually thousands, of steam presses (most made by Hoe and Company in the United States) to print volumes of *Fanny,* illustrated, if necessary, by Currier and Ives and colored by hand, to slake this new literary thirst. Before this machinery of mass culture could be turned to pursuits of this kind or, more accurately, just at about the *same time* that the mass press began to assimilate the pornograph, Queen Victoria and the retinue of alarmed aristocracy for whom she spoke held up their hands and said "No!"

It was not the Queen herself but the aristocracy at home and abroad—both of wealth and letters—rich people, powerful people, scholars and politicians, who were the instigators of Victorian morality; they were gorgeous hypocrites, just about every one of them, for self-evident reasons. They—or their fathers—were precisely the same sort of people who had made up the membership of the "Hell Fire Clubs" of the previous century. Many of them owned privately printed copies of *Fanny Hill* and troves of other forbidden gems besides.

Their public alarms, therefore, at the spread of pornography in print among the masses was based upon what, to their own eyes, was the best evidence possible. As victims of the beast, and as veterans of countless hours of jerking-off while reading copious erotic fantasies in "translations from the French" (many written in London or New York) that *they alone* could afford to buy and that *they alone* could read, they well understood the evil inherent in this novel aspect of the communications revolution. Possibilities of epidemics of self-abuse ran rampant, of hazards of drowning in tidal waves of semen, of nations replete with deflorated fourteen-year-old girls, of populations fucking in the streets and of similar evils beyond imagining caused them to close ranks.

Victoria's army was therefore not only ready to serve, but it sent its armored Joan of Arc right into battle on the cultural front and, despite subversion from Darwinists and intellectuals who operated *within* the moral codes of the time, from scientists like Freud to writers like Dickens and Stephen Crane, Victorianism was a moral success—on the surface at any rate. It lived as it was born, in utter hypocrisy, of course. But few people (other than Queen Victoria) expected anything better of it. Pornography and erotic communications were therefore saved for the classes. Males among the masses were expected to get natural hard-ons, gratuitous hard-ons or self-generated hard-ons. Women were (more or less) supposed to eschew sex entirely, except for procreation, the pursuit of which, in the middle and lower classes, was so successful a moral imperative that happily only a high infant and child mortality rate saved both countries from a population glut that might have generated mass revolutions well in advance of the ones that (for other reasons) turned countries like Russia into the Soviet Republic.

Regarding Puritanism, I imagine that the last word has not been said, because the ghost of Cotton Mather is still being flayed in certain libertarian circles—entirely in the United States, naturally. Note, however, that American (and British) Catholics were not—and never had been—Puritans. More than this, the very words "Protestant ethic" remain anathema to them. Catholicism, however, found its peculiar haven in Victorian morality.

New England's Victorian proclivities, that continue to the present, are incorrectly associated by simplists with early Puritanism. This, of course, is nonsense. The observation may apply to a few aristocratic families in Boston that, like the fictional George Apley's, had run pretty much to intellectual seed by the start of this century. No, Victorianism found its best nineteenth century allies in Massachusetts among the immigrant Irish—the incipient Kennedy dynasties—that were on the rise and gaining power and wealth during the period roughly from the end of the Civil War to the present and mostly in the city of the Bean and Cod. Nowhere, incidentally, was Victorian morality regarding erotica more severely enforced in English-speaking cultures than in what is now the Irish Republic. Nor has this oppression entirely abated to the present day. It was rebellion against this unlikely Irish-Catholic–Victorian alliance that propelled such geniuses as Shaw, Joyce and O'Casey to England, where each in his own way took up his own cudgels against Victorianism.

Had Victorianism and Puritanism (or the Protestant ethic) mated as convivially in the entire United States, the morality of an *English* Queen would never—*could* never—have been courted as warmly by the American Catholic Church as it was until what appears to have been a partial or complete surrender was achieved as recently as the past decade. Nor was it a Protestant ethic that guided the destiny of such pressure groups as the National Organization for Decent Literature and the Legion of Decency in their attempt—long past their day in the sun—to keep the spirits of two enemies, Queen Victoria and Cotton Mather, alive.

It was something else, far more complicated—to which we shall return.

An Era of Refinement

Refinement is a force that moves in many directions. In an abstract way, rough strands of any substance—culture included—become finer and finer as they multiply in number, like molten glass being spun into fibers and finally into clumps of *erzatz* wool. The more refined, in any sense, is any one of man's endeavors, the more varied it becomes in style and manner, the more discreet, and the more it tends toward quantification, measuring, counting, qualification, definition, taxonomy and other instrumentation that separate that one strand from another. I think that the analog computer is one of the most refined instruments that man has yet created, and although it is still used for fairly crude and rough purposes, its functions have been refined already to a large but finite number. Its functions may turn out to be infinite.

Victorian refinement functioned on a cultural and subcultural level, and, thank heaven, we shall be dealing only with certain aspects of the latter here. To the former, however, one must genuflect, largely because of the tenacity, fecundity (and hence modernity) of Victorian rules, regulations, strictures and similar impositions upon the "presentation of self in everyday life," in the words of Erwin Goffman. In the Victorian period, harsh lines circumscribing this "presentation" were drawn in almost every direction in nearly every way possible across one's biological, social and cultural life: according to sex, age, education, locality of birth, school (or its absence), manner of speech, dress, gesture, and so on and so on. All the factors functioned as they do today, being indicators and determinants of roles in the theatre of life, but without the investiture of flexibility and exception that contemporary behavioral sciences and experience have taught us.[17]

One look at a manual for young ladies of the period on their behavior when entertaining gentlemen guests at home—or just on going "abroad" to do a bit of shopping—indicates, in part, how people can refine their life, when they set their minds to it. (I sometimes wonder, when reading perceptive, descriptive works like those of Goffman, whether our own time and place is much less fractionalized and refined in these matters, or whether our unwritten behavioral manuals are any less oppressive than they were in the Victorian period. The rituals that must accompany the so-called "joy" of sex—homo- or hetero—appropriate behavior for the divorced male, how to act and look like a millionaire, how to be an aging parent, how to face death according to prescribed thanatological procedures and other abstruse aspects of life have become, in recent years, subjects for books that turn into best-sellers. Yes, we laugh at the Victorians, but they may well be laughing at us from their feathered choirs right at this moment! [18])

Of Victorian culture, I cannot sing either praise or disdain! Societal mores, personal and social, do not move in a linear way: they swing the way a pendulum does from extreme to extreme. Any point along the path seems like a time of *change* or *progress* rather than the reactive vector it really is. John Stuart Mill was not the first to notice this phenomenon, and immersed as he was in the fabric of Victorian life, he could not help but note that the general societal tone of the freedoms that had marked the previous century was coming to an end, as law and custom seemed to be placing greater and greater restraints upon personal liberties of every kind. He therefore looked to logic and an age of reason (long past) to justify his observation that liberty was in danger, disappearing from the world around him at the same time that a myth of freedom was being promulgated by the popular press and by less perceptive philosophers. [19]

That Victorianism was an inevitable result of all factors—economic, educational, cultural, medical, political—that had distinguished the century that preceeded it is an observation blessed only by the gods of hindsight, for whom all things past are inevitable. At the risk of repetition, I think that the greatness of Victorianism lies in the heterodoxy of the men (and women) who rose directly to meet its challenges. I have mentioned some, but add the playwrights Schnitzler and Wilde, the statesman Disraeli, painters like Monet and Cezanne, the poet Whitman, the actor Booth, the magician Robert Houdin, scientists such as Clerk-Maxwell, inventors such as Edison and others, coming often from strange and unlikely corners of society, whose peculiar geniuses were able to flourish only in a world of refinements that they could somehow ingest, rise above or fight against.

In subcultural worlds, the Victorian refinement of a special interest in erotica baffles the mind. Hurried, as a shy pornographer must be, I would like, for example, to dwell upon the pages of *Screw*'s antecedent, *The Pearl*, but I have neither time nor skill.

One observation here, however, is in order. Victorian refinement in pornography and erotica has become, by no means, a lost art—if art it ever was or is. The subject-matter categories in my local porno book store at the present moment would gladden the heart and twitter the tastes of a Victorian specialist—or generalist—in vicarious erotica. Titles and subjects run into exquisite specialties: sadomasochism inflicted upon a Negro girl by blond pederastists, desert island settings where lesbians literally torture (and screw) to death a shipwrecked sailor, anal fucking of pregnant women, drinking milk from the breasts of lactating mothers, child abuse, rape, coprophagy, murder, necrophilia, urinary fun and games and similar delights beyond belief. (I refer here to *print* only—that is, products, one assumes, of imagination—although I must confess that I have also recently *seen* some of the above, real and simulated, both in motion pictures and in live exhibitions, as well as having read about them.)

One contemporary neo-Victorian is a long-time hero of mine, the indefatigable Gershon Legman, who has spent years categorizing, indexing and cross-indexing almost every off-color joke that has ever been told.[20] This American expatriate has for years championed the cause of pornography and literary erotica (folk, joke, in prose, in poems) and inveighed also against the literature of violence. Legman's monomaniacal, scholarly passion is comparable to that of Pisanus Fraxi or of Henry Spencer Ashbee, whose scholarship concerning Victorian erotica in its day was prodigious. Neither Kinsey's academic researchers, whose present collection of pornography is formidable, nor the famed Vatican collection reflect the dedicated *labor amoris* of either Ashbee or Legman.

To Legman we shall return, noting here merely that he is a man born in the wrong century. He does not deserve to suffer this era of sexual liberation in print into which he has survived, having been turned, for his many brave nonconformities, into a mere pendant, along with his bad-boy contemporary (more or less and also writing from abroad), Henry Miller. Legman and Miller did not deserve the punishment of living so long that they would finally hear their rebellions and obscene yowls described by critics—and even college students—as "tame stuff." How sad to contemplate yesterday's rebels when they outlive their revolutions! Only the cleverest of them contrive both to be born and die *exactly* at the right times.

Ashbee was born (1834) and died (1900) at *exactly* the right time! Between 1877 and 1885, the independently wealthy Ashbee, whose money came from legitimate businesses (so we are told), published three remarkable volumes, the first of which was the *Index Librorum Prohibitorum: Being Notes Bio-Biblio-Icono-graphical and Critical, on Curious and Uncommon Books,* a satire in title of the Vatican's *Index Liborum Prohibitorum,* or list of prohibited books. (Ashbee was, among other things, violently anti-Catholic.) Although such documents may also have appeared in other languages, "Pisanus Fraxi's" masterpiece stands as the first annotated and reasonably complete bibliography of erotica in English, although it dealt with books and materials in many languages written up to the year 1885.

The *Index* was published in 1877. It was followed by the *Centuria Librorum Absconditorum (The century of Lost Books)* in 1879 and finally by *Catena Librorum Tacendorum (The Restraint of Secret Books)* in 1885. Privately published, the total work remains one of the few documents of its kind concerning Victorian and pre-Victorian pornography of all types— fiction, non-fiction, prose, poetry, paintings, prints, etchings and even some still photographs—based, one assumes, on Ashbee's own collection of 15,299 rare books that he left, upon his death, to the British Museum. The museum seems to have taken the entire lot, because many extremely rare editions of non-pornographic books were also included in the gift, most notably *all* of the editions and translations of *Don Quixote* published up to that time.[21]

Steven Marcus, in his delightful book on Victorian depravity, comments upon Ashbee's inconsistencies, his scholarly contradictions and his pedantry, as well as the natural, typical Victorian hypocrisy of scholar-as-lecher and/or lecher-as-scholar. Ashbee certainly covered his beloved subject, *more* than covered it when he felt like it, particularly by quoting verbatim from pornographic works, describing drawings and, in effect, achieving his obvious erotic ends in the name of bibliophilia. He attempted to let the reader know that he, like most pornographers of his day, knew the difference between virtue and vice, good and bad. He recognized that the books he loved were not everyone's cup of tea and that they might indeed corrupt the vulnerable. But apparently and obviously he was enchanted, enthralled and thrilled by them, as many a supposedly objective scholar of erotica has been and is, the present writer not excluded.

His problem, shared by academics studying erotica from Freud to Kinsey to Marcus himself (and to me), is simply that academics are invariably more than just academics; they are frequently schizoid scholars. The Victorian era was a period of cultural schizophrenia writ large in life and refined to a high degree in literature. Nobody was more torn apart by it than Ashbee, although Wilde, Gilbert, Stevenson, Dodgson and other Victorian literary culture heroes shared, in one degree or another, his exact problem.

Marcus writes a fitting obituary for Ashbee's three volume index when he states: "(T)he fanatical quoting, the invariable literalness and precision, the infinitude of references, operate in the end not to master the subject but to reproduce on another level . . . the original chaos they were intended to bring under command."[22] Scholars of erotica owe much to Pisanus Fraxi, and I suppose historians do too. But his frequent and deadpan justifications for his obsession with refinement do not wash any better today than Plutarch's or Suetonius' claims to objectivity of history in their biographies of the great figures of the ancient world. One may learn a lot from a propagandist, but what we learn makes the propagandist nonetheless an advocate.

Marcus' evaluation is correct. But Marcus also gives due credit for the extraordinary motivation that impelled Ashbee toward the particular *kind* of refinement he chose in describing the literature that he obviously relished. Ashbee displayed an impulse typical (and not unexpected) of Victorian culture at large: that of *refinement for its own sake*—as a natural virtue. To find this tendency among the British upper classes located in the Victorian subculture of pornography is a little amusing, possibly surprising, but to Marcus also typically Victorian. This tradition continues, of course, as indicated in my previous devotions to G. Legman and other quixotic latter-day Ashbees. I offer this tribute both seriously and in wild amusement, a contradiction that would not bother Gilbert or Wilde or Stevenson or Lewis Carroll.

Notes from the Underground

Ashbee and his bibliography and possibly almost all print pornography dating from whenever to the present fade to near insignificance when compared to the eleven-volume work by "A Victorian Gentleman" that was published in full in two volumes in the United States in 1966, comprising some 2,400 pages and originally selling for thirty dollars. The books contained a knowing and scholarly introduction, naturally enough by Gershon Legman himself, much of it discussing the problem, not of who actually *wrote* the work, but of the possibility that it came from the pen of Pisanus Fraxi himself, a claim that seems to me unlikely on stylistic grounds alone.[23]

The name of the true author of *My Secret Life* is quite irrelevant to its value as pornographic prose. He was most likely in his time a literary nonentity and will probably remain so forever. What is important is the authenticity of the manuscripts that make up the opus (and therefore the heroism of the total endeavor) and the extraordinary literary abilities demonstrated in selective descriptions of aspects of the life apparently lived by the author—in other words and mostly, its quality and reliability as a memoir.

The autobiographer who calls himself (infrequently) "Walter," was born about 1820. In his sparsely self-described non-erotic business and social career, he went from rags to riches a number of times, alternated between sickness and health, traveled widely, and was married at least once. He began writing about his erotic experiences (that started in infancy) in the 1830s and finally decided years later to have his volumes printed, a project undertaken in Holland and completed in 1894. One cannot doubt that he received a good education for his time—although not necessarily at a university. He was widely read (his favorite book apparently being *Fanny Hill*), and he well deserved to be called "a gentleman" by all criteria of the day.

Are the events and encounters in *My Secret Life* true? Here is a question that cannot be answered, nor will it probably ever be. What we may be certain of is that they are *based* upon truth, largely because so much of their pith is of a piece with extant cultural history of the Victorian social so-called "underbelly" and because even the apparent inconsistencies in the volume make historical sense. Walter is forgetful exactly when he *should* be. His exaggerations and (possibly) fantasies are neither too frequent nor infrequent to be anything but real, and the pains he takes to cover his own identification and the identification of others are both scrupulous and properly inept.

Upon first reading *My Secret Life*, one is inclined to dismiss it as masturbatory fantasy not entirely unlike the recent cultism that has attempted to turn Sherlock Holmes into a genuine historical figure. (Or is it the cult of Dr. Watson?) But these doubts easily wear away. Walter has erotic and emotional ups and downs, too candidly and expertly described, in my opinion, to be just the fictional imaginings of masturbating megalomania. His writing style matures as he does. The physiology he describes, organs, odors, dialogues and sexual caprices all have the ring of truth, unlike most fictional erotica past and present.

I believe *My Secret Life* and accept it as authentic, mainly because I cannot conceive of any motives, other than those given by the author, for writing it: first, because writing amused him; second, because Walter apparently could not stop; and, finally, his desire to make in permanent form a "contribution to psychology" as he understood it. Certainly he did not endeavor to make money from the venture, the pornographer's usual incentive. The work is simply too long, too repetitious and was printed in such a small first edition (six copies recorded; Legman claims a few more) that the project probably cost Walter far more than it could possibly have realized.

Might the whole thing have been a mischief on the part, say, of Ashbee? Elaborate hoaxes contrived toward no end but deviltry do exist in history and still continue to grip the popular mind, constantly being fed by rascals fused by rascality! (Flying saucers are one long-running example.) *Fanny Hill*, at least as an autobiography, was, naturally, a hoax. Why not *My Secret Life*?

The claim, far from dead, does not wash for me. Although parts of *My Secret Life* indeed read like a *poor* Victorian novel, poor Victorian novels, like *East Lynne* for instance, may well have reflected the way people lived and thought in the past century more accurately than many of us think they do. No, were it literary hoax, *My Secret Life* would not need to proliferate into eleven volumes and then be subjected to an almost clandestine private publication. Nor did it need to be as scrupulously and carefully written as it was, nor as dripping with the arcana of Victorian subcultural refinement.

Walter's monomania, nevertheless, is little less than heroic—and astounding! *My Secret Life* deals *only* (or almost only) with Walter's endocrine system: his casually fucked women, his whores, his orgies, his occasional homosexual experiments (for which he hates himself after satiation, a Victorian masochistic thread that runs throughout the entire narrative), his patterns of masturbation (called "frigging"), his "gamahunching" (known colloquially in America today as "going down" male to female, or female to male, or any other combination you may contrive), his voyeurism and bouts of unconventional, somewhat imaginative acting out of fantasy—but mostly fucking, fucking and more fucking. Of considerable literary interest to the critic of *My Secret Life* is therefore why it is not duller than it turns out to be. I suspect the reason stems mainly from the author's variations of literary style and his changes of perspective upon *both* life and sex as he grows older.

Walter's monomania is naturally erotic. The book is really the autobiography of the author's penis for the most part, and a penis as the indefatigable hero of any volume is, of and by itself, a fascinating literary concept. (One recent pornographic film, discussed subsequently, used this device by creating and characterizing a "talking cunt," a charming diversion from most dross of this genre. The film is *Pussy Talk*.)

While the Ashbees and Legmans of the literary world have refined their inclinations to the degree that they are talking *about* erotica for the most part, Walter is forever generating erotica and obviously enjoying most of it, albeit compulsively. The only other author in the history of erotica with whom I am familiar who approaches this end is the Marquis de Sade, a monomaniac in a French, rather than English, tradition. De Sade, however, unlike Walter, soon tired of detailed observation—and even of imagination. In his copious final works, we find a man whose life has been enervated of the erotic, working out cold-blooded mathematical combinations of sex acts and bestialities between males, females, relatives, friends, royalty, servants, animals and such literally in outline form! Casanova, also writing and living outside of the English tradition, was too busy being a preacher, teacher, alchemist, gambler, musician, spy and satirist to *have lived* any sort of secret life!

No, eroticism reaches a singularity of purpose and theme in *My Secret Life* that has been arrived at neither before nor since its publication. Walter's devotion to purpose, his almost perfect sense of selectivity and his immaculate delimitation of autobiography to the life of his genitals—or to the non-connubial part of the life of them—is a singular and almost perfect inverse manifestation of Victorian propriety. Unlike de Sade, Walter was not mad, at least in the legal sense. Unlike Casonova or Don Juan, he was not a professional adventurer. Unlike Ashbee, he had little urge for scholarship or bent for pedantry. He was an average Victorian gentleman of extraordinary sexual appetites and an extraordinary, quite unrealistic, sense of their importance to the scheme of things.

The function for Walter himself of the writing of *My Secret Life* is discouragingly clear. It served him as a subfunction of his enormous sexual drive. Erotic behavior produces for most of us reservoirs of memories upon which we often draw in times of enforced celibacy or personal desperation in the service of comforting either sensuality or arousal. Many of us seem to find our way into this path for masturbatory, artistic or ego-enhancing purposes as life winds along. I suppose such erotic storage and its subsequent utility may be considered quite normal. Walter, on the other hand, made of memory an art of sorts, obviously reliving his exploits with relish and masturbatory fervor as he wrote: an end in itself.

Unlike *Fanny Hill*, *My Secret Life* is episodic, climactic and sequential; in fact, it is a document probably born in bursts of masturbation relating to the incidents depicted, in which the characters swirl to orgasms and reach tumescense, then satiation (and often self-disdain), in the way that wild sexuality often leads. We shall never know for certain if Walter's pleasures in recording his exploits reached or exceeded the actual pleasures he writes about or (possibly) invents, and we shall never know. I suspect that they did, given the sense of mischief and sin that Victorianism itself permitted him in the very act of keeping his memoir, hiding it and working on it in secret.

An analogy to Walter's behavior may be found in the vain hope among many young people that their frequency of masturbation will decrease once sexual intercourse begins. For males at least, a good deal of empirical evidence indicates that the converse is true; masturbation increases after American youths "get their first piece." I believe (without much available and decent data on the subject) that the same is true of young females—at least among those who have permitted me to bring up the subject with them for the past thirty years—and in the experience of psychotherapists I have questioned.

Eroticism therefore feeds—or may feed—upon itself, upon reality, upon art. I think this is particularly true in climates of repression, when and where the individual is forced by culture and social constraints to present for the most part a non-erotic persona to others in his "presentation of self" in most of the important aspects of his life. I cannot—like Marcus—conceive, however, of Victorian England and America as a neatly two-tiered cultural world, even though many Victorians themselves believed that they inhabited such a world.

Victorianism did not produce a front *versus* an underbelly, like a tortoise right-side up or upside down! Too much of one world was swept into the other, which is an important and significant aspect of the descriptive side of *My Secret Life* that is frequently overlooked. Licentiousness and so-called vice were indeed placed at one end of a continuum, and Stevenson's *Child's Garden of Verses* may well have been found at the other, but there was plenty of slack for play between the two. The latter's *Dr. Jekyll and Mr. Hyde* and Wilde's *Picture of Dorian Gray* may center upon metaphors that have come closer to the truth than much conventional Victorian cultural history.

Walter's secret life was, let us remember, just *one* secret life among (probably) millions during this marvelous period of refinement and manners. Walter's rebellion merely foreshadowed, or carried to refined extremes, what other "gentlemen," some his contemporaries and others who followed, attempted to accomplish in print in the years to come. In England, D. H. Lawrence comes immediately to mind as an enormously gifted novelist, emerging painfully from Victorian refinements, who could not, eventually, satisfy himself that he was writing about "real" life without an explicit re-creation of the "secret life" of Lady Chatterley's cunt, although he tried his best to hide her obtrusive organ in the two early versions of his novel, *Lady Chatterley's Lover*. By the 1920s, Lawrence was impelled by the ghost of Victorianism, now well behind him, to dip into the vocabulary of erotic print, just as Walter had more than a generation before, with, in the words of Walter himself, a slice of life "intended to be a true story and not a lie."

What then of "erotic realism"?

I think the term is another tautology.

Erotic Pictures

There is no such thing as the faithful copying of physical reality. As far as the human body is concerned, nature does not commit itself in its visual appearance to any particular pattern that can be correctly copied.

—Rudolph Arnheim

IF ONE STICKS TO the *aesthetics of visual art* taken *alone,* it is quite simple to argue down the fundamental cultural-social-erotic nexua for which I have up to this point spoken and upon which one main assumption of this volume rests, including our eventual entry into the thorny world of theory articulation in the final chapters.

To associate the erotic—or pornography—with visual imagery alone is like associating pure "art" with music only. Both are done, but they are also most unprofitable endeavors. We have all, for example, heard music called a "universal language" (or "international language"), and, I suppose, to some degree it is. Many Japanese today seem to have acclimatized their ears to Western music, classical and/or popular. Many of our most skilled western musicians today come from backgrounds where their grandfathers would have heard in Chopin or Mozart only cacophony and would have discovered melodies in tonal scales foreign entirely to their progeny's ears.

At the Chinese opera, however, a certain primitive musical universality does indeed obtain even for me, and I have a "tin ear." Cymbals clash as warriors fight over the hand of the princess. The lute seems indeed bucolic (or peaceful) as the lovers stroll on a bridge over a stream, and

79

even discordant noises of despair or death activate in me what I assume to
be the proper sorts of emotions—for a minute or two. So too do I recall
the song of the muezzin in Tunis and the impact of what seemed to be a
hundred radios all playing at the same time as I walked along the narrow
streets of Algiers' famous Casbah surrounded by Moslems' popular and
sacred music. Nearly thirty years have passed since I lived for a short time
in the world where these sounds that were strident to me were perceived as
perfect harmonies to others. A short time was all my nervous system
required to adjust to these noises, and, as I began to enjoy the taste of
lamb's eye and cous-cous, I also began to hear some of these divine
sounds.[1]

For anybody with ears, therefore, certain aspects of music may indeed
be "universal" and may point in the direction of something like a possible
pan-communication between cultures, though they might run a spectrum
of highly different colorations in other respects. This curiosity, of course, is
entirely the function of music's nearly total abstract quality when not serving either as sound effect or anamnesis, when not given a lyric to carry or
when a theme (like "pastorale," "nocture" or such) has not been imposed
upon it. The clearest examples of the wonderful abstraction of music are,
of course, the simplest: the ocarina, the penny-whistle or the sounds
mothers make when they coo babies to sleep. I think that all the rest of
whatever so-called "meaning" is found in music—and I cannot deny
meaning merely because I personally receive so little of it—is the result of
special types of vocabulary training that reflect, like all similar training, the
skills of the teacher, the nature of the vocabulary, its cultural structures
that connect it to various aspects of society and, most important, the apti-
tudes of the student.

These are all functions of time and place and, in absence of evidence
to the contrary, I think of heredity too. No wonder, therefore, the claim,
which has been so frequently made by critics as different from one another
as Walter Pater and Bernard Shaw, that, in effect, music remains the apoth-
eosis of art. Of course it is! And this is exactly its greatest weakness—and
greatest strength—as a mediator of meaning between people. All art, this
argument must then run, moves toward perfection as it moves toward abstraction. With such an assumption I cannot argue, as long as the discussion remains in the affective domain of art and art alone.

The same principle probably (some would say "inevitably") applies to
pictorial art as well, although I would have a dandy time trying to convince most music lovers (at any point on the cultural taste scale in the
West) that the most beautiful pictures and paintings and sculptures on
display (or, at any rate, the most *moving*) must of necessity be those that
are most abstract and therefore devoid of references to nature and nature's
symbols. Aestheticians have found a neat way out of this problem by
carefully creating different categories of aesthetics for different arts. But
the inconsistency will persist as long as musicians and music critics keep

talking about "pear-shaped tones" and "blue notes" and other matters that relate what we hear to what we see according to a semiotic rather than a simple effect in nature—like the thunder clap that follows the lightning flash or the squeak that comes from the mouse whose tail is pinched.

I think this subject, at least for our purposes, closes with this observation: To date, nobody in any culture of which I have heard has been able to devise a *pornography of music* or anything like it, although anamnesis or association may provide in certain kinds of music subjective erotic triggers in the listener. When I hear sentimental music like *As Time Goes By,* for instance, even my tin ear yields to an image of Dooley Wilson at the piano at Rick's Casino in Hollywood's version of Casablanca in a world of adolescent fantasy, just as the tunes that accompanied the old-time stripteasers in burlesque shows allow me to taste for a second the *ersatz* reprise of pubescent sin in the days before I knew what sin was.

Pictorial Eroticism and Meaning

As pictorial art moves from abstraction to representation, so does the possibility of finding cross-cultural, non-timebound eroticism increase. There is plenty of it around, and the reason is obvious—but not without interest.

Briefly, eroticism in every culture deals with more or less the same physical data. What we *see,* therefore, in pictures and statues of people must, in terms of meaning, be in large part invariable, concrete and far from abstract. It is precisely this natural concreteness that gives pictorial eroticism *some* of its universality. Curiously, this is quite the opposite of music's cross-cultural proclivities that derive, it seems, from its near total abstraction or whatever affective subjective powers sound alone communicates between cultures to human ears.

In the erotic domain, sexuality, for example, is visually a constant: all fucking (properly defined) involves male and female genitalia (and always has) in much the same way wherever it happens. Nudity may or may not be involved; it often is *not.* Deviations practiced in human sensual behavior have remained remarkably constant throughout varieties of cultures: anal intercourse, homosexual acts (male and female), sucking genitalia; even scatalogical acts like "golden showers" and shit fetishes, while not as universal as male and female masturbation, turn up again and again in mankind's sexual history. Since men and women are all biologically similar, the combinations available to the erotic artist are quite finite and predetermined by anatomy, although his artistic interpretations of what he sees (or sometimes imagines) are not. In this respect, I think of the famous ink drawing by Tomi Ungerer, showing a girl sucking, fucking, masturbating and fondling a wall of disembodied pricks and balls. (See Figure 2.) Here is a clever and imaginative conceit, physically absurd and freed to some degree from nature but nevertheless circumscribed by the limitations

Figure 2: Imagination Versus Anatomy

Figure 3: Giotto de Bondone's Erotic Christian *Doomsday*.

of female anatomy, the human form and the nature of the physical contact required in male-female sex. This drawing, I suspect, would be (and is) universally appreciated—but only because of the *concrete* nature of its representation, not its abstract qualities which to my culture-bound eye are neither absent nor negligible.

Erotic illustration, however, shares with eroticism in print its diminution of cross-cultural communicative power at exactly the same place: the semiotic and symbolic levels of meaning transactions. As behavior is turned by artists into symbols, and/or as an aesthetic becomes increasingly important to the meaning of erotic picturization, so does the possibility that the original erotic qualities of the picture or statue may be lost in time or distance increase. The early Venuses we have previously discussed *may be* examples: highly charged erotic figures when they were made but simply crude representations of fat-assed females today to me. Giotto diBondone's famous *Doomsday* fresco, painted early in the fourteenth century, may have been (probably was) about as erotic a painting as a Christian could conceive of at the time *in a semiotic* sense, but it looks simply macabre to contemporary sensibilities. (See Figure 3.) So were most of the well-known priapic woodcuts of about the same period.

There is nothing puzzling about this diminution, if we remember that *all* written and spoken language is symbolic, and that *all* grammars, syntaxes and meanings have been processed by semiotics before they are expressed in their entirety—or almost entirely. Pictures and statues, in the degree that they *can* represent nature as we see it, are not prone to any symbolic distortion. If symbols are used or if a semiotic filter is placed over what the artist sees, it is for one of two reasons. First, he may not be able to represent nature the ways he sees it because he does not possess the proper or suitable technique. *All* painters and illustrators, for instance, before the fifteenth century in Europe had to find ways of compensating for their lack of knowledge of central perspective. Some anthropologists claim that they made up for this lack of technique by *perceiving* nature in two dimensions, but this smells of sophistry, and I doubt it. These artists merely imitated nature as best—and as beautifully—as they could, compensating with beauty for what they could not achieve in realism in many, many instances.

The other possibility relates entirely to the particular semiotic in which the artist is communicating. We are all acquainted with Japanese erotica and its enormously exaggerated cunts and cocks set in scenes that seem to deny their genital crudity by means of elaborate and delightful chinoiseries (literally). (See Figures 4 and 5.) The artists who drew them—and continue to draw them—are calling attention to the pornographic nature of their work in a typically Japanese way: by a type of exaggeration that, to the Occidental eye, may look silly rather than erotic.[2] Today, for instance, we tend to look at the highly charged erotic paintings of Hieronymous Bosch largely as masterpieces of good (or bad) humor and may fail

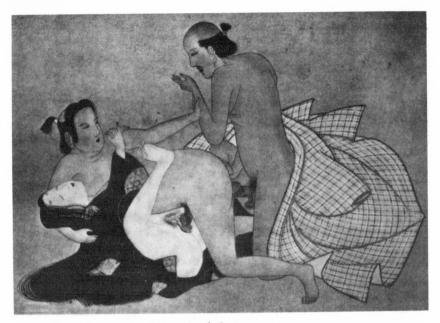

Figure 4: Japanese Scroll, Seventeenth Century

to react to them as eroticism, although other cultures have found them highly sensual during the five hundred or so years since they were painted. The same may be said about many of the caricatures of Goya or the drawings of Blake. In every instance, the intrusive factor is the semiotic of meaning and symbol structure that the artist chose (or had chosen for him) and within which he was communicating.[3]

Most of us learn a good deal about these distortive matters while we are quite young and dismiss them with a phrase about each having his own taste or "different strokes for different folks." But the principle we are dealing with is quite complex. Among other things, it applies almost entirely to the visual domain, or is, at least, most obvious and unsubtle when applied to what we *see,* rather than what we smell, feel, taste or possibly hear. So we discover—true or not—that Helen of Troy was a hag, that Cleopatra looked (if present extant reliefs of her face are accurate) like a wizened witch and that sexiness among certain African tribes is related to slashed lips with platters forced into them or necks distorted to giraffe-like lengths by the imposition of necklaces on them since birth. Time and place even work their mischief in tiny dimensions: The Floradora Girls bespoke a type of beauty that would not be understood by devotees of *Charlie's Angels,* and, thank heaven, *Playboy* bunnies defy the erotic imaginations of much of the world. Hindu statuary, famous for its erotic power, seems quaint to our eyes. Their elephants are about as stimulating to Western sensibilities as Indian couples entwined in complicated screwing positions.

Figure 5: Japanese Scroll, Twentieth Century

(See Figure 6.) Pictorial erotica on the walls of the houses of Pompey appear to be comic caricatures—possibly a bit naughty, but fit even for the eyes of your maiden aunt. (See Figures 7 and 8.)

Erotic relativism? I doubt that so facile a notion explains much. Despite strictures of cultural education, our erotic natures may merely be far more malleable than common wisdom tells us. Patterns of inter-marriage (or inter-fucking) between races and/or different people raised in different erotic traditions are, and have been historically, too insistent to ignore. Consider, for instance, the total demolition of the so-called "pure Negro" gene in America, probably *before* 1900, and the massive introduction of British "blood" into India during the relatively short period of the Empire's hegemony there. Hardly a Japanese lives today who does not display many Caucasian, probably Ainu, characteristics, such as body hair and (in men) baldness. The aboriginal Ainu, like our American Indians, crossbred with their conquerors, the Orientals.

For all our barriers of communication and transportation via national borders, warfare, differences in caste and, mostly, the myth of so-called "erotic relativism"—and hence sexual "selectivity"—we are fast becoming a world of mongrels, a state of affairs that frankly pleases me, because it offers mankind a political chance to survive as a species—*if* we mongrelize fast enough. Possibly Tibet or Afghanistan have been in some measure excluded from this trend, but I doubt it. Everywhere else one goes—with the exception of aboriginal preserves like those in Australia—one observes that the term "race" is becoming an increasingly relative matter, visible enough to fuss about but vanishing nevertheless at a remarkably rapid rate. Were eroticism or erotic phenomena culture-bound to the degree that

Figure 6: Relic of Indian Frieze, approximately 1000 A.D.

many would have it, such earth-shattering changes could not have indeed overtaken this planet, mostly during the past 250 years.[4]

Were we to speak of "aesthetic relativism," I think we might come closer to the operational mark, as long as we recognize that aesthetics are not anthropological or psychological matters but rather functions of philosophy or aspects of intellect that intrude eventually into our emotional lives. What *seem* to be erotic variation in what we see (and I am referring here only to the visual aspects of life) are, in fact, only reflections of our cultural training in aesthetics (a fragile training at best) and part of the philosophical anchor we have thrown out to the real world, so that its values may be related one with another, and so that we may control it to the degree that we fool ourselves into believing that it offers us security. In this sense, then, despite our training, we are all philosophers, like it or not.

Accept a hypothetical situation: A gang of teenage males are "hanging out" in front of an urban pool hall, simply "watching all the girls go by," as the song says. The boys are hardly aesthetes, certainly not philosophers and hardly aware of what they are up to as cogs in culture. Yet, as the girls indeed "go by," highly selective discriminatory judgments of them are made according to exquisitely complicated aesthetic judgments. This one will receive whistles and cat-calls. The next will achieve stony silence. The next will hear a reference to her walk, the sway of her buttocks or the angle at which her bosoms protrude from her blouse and so forth. Aesthetic judgments of a most complicated nature are made, and consensus is reached among the judges with remarkable clarity and speed, although the stimuli are highly specialized, culture-bound and temporally arbitrary—as most aesthetic judgments tend to be. More to the point is the fact that each one of the auditors knows that the ultimate physical erotic potential of *all* the passing females is, in theory, just about the same. The actual physiological state of their primary (and secondary) sex organs has little or nothing to do with the way they *look,* and, as eventual objects of erotic plea-

Figure 7: Pompeiian Wall Art, Tourists' Favorites

Figure 8: Famous Wall Fresco at Pompeii

sure, the sad fact remains that each of these human females is physiologically more like all the others than different from them! What we are dealing with are functional aesthetics almost entirely and a crude but dramatic example of the intellectual life of man (or males) at work, an *aperçu* that it might be difficult to convince many of today's liberated females of, even in theory.

What we come to then, in conclusion, is analytically somewhat distressing to me (and possibly contradictory to some other, later claims) that visual eroticism and erotic transactions by picture, when pictures represent nature, have a good deal to do with the cultural meaning of "beauty" at any time or place. Not only does this slide pictorial erotic communications squarely in the domain of philosophy (and the least precise or logical sort of philosophy), but it complicates the entire matter of meaning by referring erotic meaning to whatever aesthetic principles are agreed upon by a particular community of taste makers. What *should be* the simplest invariables in the world, the sight of nudes of either sex, representations of sex acts and so on (all of which begin their visual journeys into art entirely with what people *see with their own eyes*) are now hurled into the world of aesthetic "laws," with their degrees of abstraction and even technological factors such as color photographs versus black and white prints and the capacity of devices like the hologram apparently to simulate nature exactly. (Aesthetic perfection or aesthetic travesty? Ask the gurus of pop art! The issue *must become* a major artistic argument as the technology of holography advances.)

One anthropological possibility, of course, has to do with man's own self-image, a matter far more complicated than the sight he sees in a mirror or in the waters of a brook.[5] The theory that the ancient Egyptians, for instance, created self-images that replicate, more or less, the pictures that were drawn and scraped on the walls of their tombs and pottery is no more absurd, fundamentally, than the claim that Americans see themselves the way they are pictured in the comic strips. A study, incidentally, of the changes in the visual aspects of the latter art form during its short history is quite illuminating in this respect. It is hyperbolic analysis because comic art is hyperbole. But I have known real life Hans and Fritzes, Major Hooples and Charlie Browns, not only as characters but as visual incarnations of life imitating art. I therefore credit the thesis that self-image is a function of the *start* of the art of creating images with some validity and power for speculation, remembering particularly that we are living in an age mostly of two dimensional idealizations of life by means of photographs, snapshots, films and portraitures, and that our own self-images are as tyranized by stylization and artificiality as were those of the Egyptians. How else can we explain lipstick, nail polish, razors, moustaches, changing fashions in dress, "nose jobs," contact lenses, rings, cufflinks, fancy sunglasses and on and on?

In many ways, therefore, the very concept of natural representation by means of picture is at the outset suspect, even when the picture appears in a textbook for taxonomical purposes, and it is more than suspect if and when full human representations and human behaviors are concerned. Once again, the latter applies to textbook illustrations and the aesthetically disastrous motion picture photography of most sexual therapy films. It may also help to explain the apparent lack of erotic content in certain supposedly pornographic pictures for certain people under certain conditions, especially when the subject matter of the picture (or slice of life it portrays) is filled with potentials for erotic communication.

Because this is an artistic problem that must remain unsettled regardless of how much anthropologists and others want to solve it, we are certainly not going to square its circle here to the satisfaction either of scientists or of aestheticians. The phrase, "Erotic picturization is what it *is*," may sound like Gertrude Stein, but it turns out to be about the only general statement that we are able to make irrevocably about erotic pictures and the way we use them to communicate. We shall, therefore, avoid the problems of the music critics of this world—and, incidentally, an enigma that Morse Peckham found intolerable—by simply refusing to face, at this early point at least, whether the visual face of pornography *may* at times be art or, possibly more to the point, whether the aesthetic apogee of *all art is erotic communication by means of picture,* sketched, painted, photographed, or simply seen in mirrors suspended from the counterpane of one's own bed! The suggestion is simply unfair—not because of the usual semantic dodge that "it all depends what you mean by art," or "I don't know much about art but . . . ," but because it asks us to make psychocultural distinctions about which we must remain fundamentally ignorant until we learn more about how man ingests culture and how his various concepts of self relate to his entire perceptual process (or processes). Such a problem is not serious—or any more serious than my own tone-deafness (an ongoing despair for my wife, a music lover) or the fact that, behaviorally, I suppose, I am cast in the role of a *music hater.*[6] I am not disparaging the cultural value of visual art or its potential for civilizing and stabilizing many aspects of society, but due respect must be paid to the blind, the color-blind and those whose facilities for appreciating various types of relationships (say spacial objects, numbers or mathematics) are limited by accident or heredity. Not a bit of evidence exists that such individuals are diminished in their capacities for sexual stimulation or erotic communication one jot more than the most gifted visual artist (or mathematician) among us. Nature, in other words, answers back whatever tendencies we may display to over-generalize the function of vision in general in conveying meaning from human to human with a puzzle. To be precise, it is the extraordinary capacity of many people, blind since birth, to deal in as full a range—or a fuller one—of erotic transactions as the average sighted person or the individual with supersensory vision like fine artists.

With our *caveats* entered, however, let us note that pictorial art has been throughout much of history, and remains today, one of the most useful and used methods of non-interpersonal erotic communication, just as the sense of vision itself has been a normative concomitant of individual erotic feeling and expression as long as men have walked the planet. (Suitable analogies are also available in the animal kingdom, if indeed they are relevant to *any* discussion of meaning.) The most interesting aspect of visual eroticism is its pervasiveness throughout culture, its immunity from institutionalized education and its general acceptance by societies as an inevitable part of satisfactory acculturation. In fact, one criterion for that which any culture calls "sanity" is the acceptance, for most purposes, of that culture's visual aesthetic—*particularly* in erotic matters—as a conveyor of affective and cognitive meaning among the population. In this sense, then, I suppose we can say that pictorial art is not only a civilizing force, but it is an integument of the meaning of "civilization" itself—but *only* in regard to what we *learn* about society by means of what we see.

The Vocabulary of Pictures

The term "vocabulary" is simply a manner of speaking, of course, but it is a far better word than the abused "medium," which has been bleached almost entirely of meaning by McLuhanesque publicity and by other contemporary academic obscurists. In a linguistic sense, the true vocabulary of pictures can comprise only one thing: words, each one in various degrees and according to each particular language a mini-picture, part representational (of something), part symbolic and entirely a cultural convenience—in fact, an efficient recording mechanism.

There is nothing wrong, fattening or immoral, however, about looking to a culture's pictures for a vocabulary of sorts, composed usually of ideas or symbols that can be expressed in words but are more interestingly displayed pictorially. Groupings of pictures that are roughly analogous to taxonomies or types of vocabularies are possible to describe, accurately, and taken together, boil down to what we call "style." One strange aspect of the evolution of pictorial style is that it, like linguistic development, is entirely cumulative: that is, as new styles drive out, replace or live side-by-side with the old, the old ones are also replicated and copied by new artists, albeit sometimes with self-conscious effort. Imitating former styles (or vocabularies) of the past is, however, probably far easier for visual artists than for those who work with spoken or written languages, no matter how clever they are.

Such is the cumulative value of the visual arts, for instance, that today a skilled commercial artist can emulate the style of the woodcut without resorting to carving wood, or he can create "new" (although patently bogus) "Roman" frescoes with acrylic paints. Costume designers and set decorators for film and stage often show an uncanny mastery of the simulation of the arts of the past, and in its way the ability to create a convincing theatrical forum for a cinematic Caesar in more or less "true" Roman fashion is a profound exhibition of virtuosity of intellect. The research involved is considerable and far more a problem, I have noticed, than the actual creative artistic process that renders the artist's idea into, first, a design and, finally, into a three-dimensional setting. It is an artistic challenge to intelligence, and one that receives all too little respect.

Word vocabularies are also *somewhat* cumulative, but in a different way. They pose different problems, in that verbal or literary style is more abstract, in general, then visual art and requires a different—but no less formidable—type of intelligence to handle convincingly. I can offhand think of four writers, for instance, who have attempted to write in the style of Shakespeare: Percy MacKaye, Bernard Shaw, Barbara Garson and Tom Stoppard. All have failed miserably—to write in the style of Shakespeare! (That each in his or her own way also succeeded in making some sort of point, dramatic, literary or satirical, is beside my point.)

The purist may note, in the last analysis (and only the last), that there is something so subtly distinctive about literary style and vocabulary that it is nearly impossible to imitate convincingly even writers like Conan Doyle, Ian Fleming, Zane Grey and/or Robert Service, much less Shakespeare, although for the life of me I cannot fully understand why. On the other hand, the works of fine art forgers like Elmyr de Hory are legion, and I have heard many responsible estimates that a sizable fraction of the world's masterpieces of painting in the great collections of the West are fakes. For a galaxy of reasons, it matters little that most fine art experts are not too anxious to question the authenticity of many of these admittedly superb paintings. The important lesson they teach us lies in their example of the cumulative tendency in pictorial art, as opposed to vocabularies of other types.[7]

Because it tends toward accumulations of meaning, erotic art also tends to get more and more interesting as history passes in both the East and the West—interesting, that is, but not necessarily erotic, a quality that it is simply impossible to judge outside of original cultural frameworks. On the other hand, both talent and genius are easily recognized. The accompanying illustration from an ancient piece of a Grecian vase may not inspire poetry in us, but it is arresting and clever, though painted for Lord knows what purposes. (See Figure 9.) Posture, figure, pose, positions of nightcaps and slippers and shaved (or plucked) pubic hair are all simple but iconographically delightful, a quality as perfect, in its way, as the superb designs that Christian Thomsen created for Royal Copenhagen on porcelain within a similar circle during the first years of this century. (See Figure 10.) Comparing Thomsen's famous Madonna with Greek erotica may, indeed, seem to some sacrilegious, but it clearly demonstrates how ceramic art—and the challenge of filling a circular form with a satisfying picture—increases in complexity as artistic media develop over centuries, while the human fundament of artistic talent, vision or genius, seems to

Figure 9: Ancient Grecian Vase (Note border.)

Figure 10: First Royal Copenhagen Xmas Plate (Note border.)

remain fairly constant. The comparison is quite fair, I think, even considering the Greek artist's paucity of tools, materials and aesthetic knowledge and the sophisticated knowledge and overglaze method of porcelain manufacture employed by Thompsen, to say nothing of the rich religious heritage he exploits.

Interest indeed grows as methods of rendering erotic pictures become, loosely speaking, more and more literal or photographic and as the visual artist gains command of more and more methods of manipulating visual reality in clever ways to express in ever wider vocabularies the fundamental idea he had in mind. The flat, frontal viewpoint or plane of nearly all erotic etchings, prints, paintings and sketches up until the end of the nineteenth century was broken with the invention of photography and the subsequent influence of Impressionism in our era. Moving the artist's plane of vision at first through a multitude of angles made erotic ideas clearer and certainly widened the vocabulary of expression. It did not necessarily improve talents, artistic vision, cleverness or, possibly, prurience, as a look through any history of erotic art will demonstrate at a glance. Many eighteenth-century French engravings, for example, juxtapose delightfully the refinements of court dress, costume, furniture and the end of rococo with stunningly obsessive amusing scenes of, for instance, lesbian anal erotic play, exhibitionism and all manner of delights that helped to bestow upon France its reputation (undeserved) as the erotic Mecca of the West. (See Figures 11 and 12.) Sadly, English artists from Cruikshank to Rowlandson drew equally amusing sketches a century or so later; many of them were anonymous artists who directly imitated the French. But nothing about the English, even the distinctive sensuousness of Aubrey Beardsley, succeeded in making English art look quite as wicked (or as much fun) as French art—and, by Beardsley's time, the French were already publishing *La Vie Parisienne*. (So naughty were the pages of the latter publication that Hugh Hefner's artists reached directly to them for their lovely little pen-and-ink "playmates" that, once upon a time, gave *Playboy* much of its own playful, sensuous look of fun.)

Interest is not eroticism, however, and, as the myth of French pornographic hegemony indicates, the erotic content of pictures has, unfortunately, little to do with interest *per se* or with the breadth of vocabulary *per se*. In this respect, erotic art and erotic behavior are extremely similar, and in this respect are they both also different from erotic speech and writing. Fucking, sucking, feeling, prodding, poking and the rest of the agenda of erotic visual representation, like erotic behavior, have remained static matters since the first artist took up his pen in antiquity. I imagine that most human erotic behavior has also remained much the same, although every student of pornography and sexuality has to rediscover this for him or herself, it seems. Sexual variety at any moment in history is easily mistaken, by therapists, physicians and intellectuals (especially) for sexual novelty.

Figure 11: Eighteenth Century Rococo Raunch   *Figure 12:* The Medium Is the Message

A good deal of education is necessary before one realizes that the wildest sensual notion of which he or she can conceive is merely a familiar part of the wild notions conceived by humans, male and female, throughout history. To publicize it no more signifies any sort of liberation or revolution in the sexual mores of the moment than would be the declamation of the multitude of ways one may, in imagination, quench his or her physical thirst. (De Sade was not the first—nor will he be the last—delusive gull who believed that, because he had the talent to scandalize, he also had the talent to create a revolution by telling others what, in fact, most of them who had any brains already knew about the impossibility of the human situation and the ironies of nature. Revolutions require novel thinking and what we call "ideology.")

Let me concede, therefore, not only the possibility but the *fact* of pan-eroticism in the visual domain. Cocksucking in the medieval Orient is re-

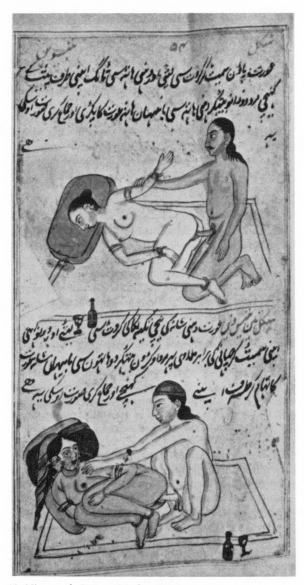

Figure 13: Nineteenth Century Moslem Erotica

markably similar to cocksucking in twentieth-century Italy, and there are both interesting and uninteresting ways to depict this act. Choice of medium and artistic vocabulary will have little to do with it other than to display the talents of the artist who chooses to illustrate it. Thus does its erotic value depend, in the end, upon two dimensions, neither of which are circumscribed by the tools an artist uses and both of which remain an essential criteria of visual artistic expression.

One is the cultural world view of the artist: what he is allowed to *see* by convention and experience and/or what the gods may or may not permit him to represent visually. The absence of abundant (or much) interesting Moslem erotic art, for example, is the direct result of the Mosaic proscription against visual representations of God's image—meaning men and women too—with the strange exception of the human hand, an organ with few erotic possibilities.

Islamic erotic drawings exist, however, and were circulated especially during the nineteenth century, when they served, for the most part apparently, instructional ends; they usually crudely represented heterosexual acts that were confined to male and female genitals—the male, incidentally, almost invariably dominating the female, regardless of her position. (See Figure 13.) Most Moslem aesthetic talent, however, was lavished upon abstract design, mosaics and the arts of decoration to such a degree that its influence is still felt in every culture touched by civilizations of the Near East, giving near certain evidence that erotic picturization is *not* a necessary or invariable concomitant of beauty. (The latter position has been opposed by many since antiquity and has recently moved from the Freudian couch to vacuous commentary about artifacts like "sexy automobiles" and similar absurdities.)

The other is an ephemeral continuum of human value that slides between what we call "talent" in its prosaic manifestations and "genius," when it is truly invested with a novelty of insight or is able, somehow, to transcend the sort of cultural determinism mentioned above. Here, of course, I lock horns with Professor Peckham (if I read him correctly) and what I gather to be a consensus of critical opinion that the quality of art may be independent of any *particular* and/or popular "talent to amuse," in Noël Coward's phrase, or *particular* play upon emotions.

In this connection, I must also deal with often quoted Wildian epigrams that deny quality to art in the realm of obscenity, pornography or content in general and place total emphasis upon "good" and "bad" art or other simple polar categories. This I do with pleasure, because even a cursory scrutiny of visual erotica over the centuries and into the present demonstrates beyond a doubt that certain artists (and photographers) enjoy a peculiar *talent* for the erotic, a *genius* for the erotic or simply a *bent* for the erotic and are merely mediocre at best when dealing with other sorts of subjects.[8] The visual domain permits, therefore, the assumption of such a concept as "a talent to arouse," again to paraphrase Coward, or, if it serves us better, a talent-genius for visual eroticism and eroticism alone. The Marquis Von Bayros is a good example. (See Figures 14 and 15.)

In theory, and only in theory, visual eroticism reached its apex with the invention of the photographic camera, which supposedly reproduces exactly what the eye sees on a two- or three-dimensional surface—a description of photography that completely misses the point of a photograph's fundamental psychological function. Photography, of course, nei-

14: The Marquis Von Bayros: A Talent to Arouse

Figure 15: Von Bayros: Elegant Monomania

ther was nor is the ultimate solution to the problem of describing the visual aspects of man's world, any more than tape recording was (or is) the ultimate solution to the problem of reproducing all the possible sounds in our environment or even the human use of spoken words. Indeed, both photography and tape recording *may,* under certain circumstances, simulate more or less exactly what sometimes appears in nature, but neither a photograph nor a tape *is* what it simulates, and whatever is simulated is just *one* set of highly selected possibilities out of millions of possible arrangements of the content or subject matter at hand.

I have written elsewhere—in agreement with Arnheim and his psychologically oriented analysis of art—that the invention of photography in the nineteenth century was, for the visual arts, largely a culturally liberating force, although it has been viewed by many quite differently.[9] In the West, from the invention of central perspective to the invention of the still camera (a period of about four and a half centuries), artists attempted much of the time to compete with nature as they tried to reproduce, as realistically as possible, a visage of an external world. Some tried harder than others, naturally, but their still-life and scenic paintings and portraits and even sketches, in various ways, were usually judged according to their fidelity to the natural world. In fact, much art is still evaluated in some measure in this way. Sheer imitation of the natural world, for instance, is the fundamental satirical point of contemporary "pop artists": Coke bottles, Marilyn Monroe, soup cans, comic strips, and plastic gee-gaws have, they say, replaced nature in modern life, and the artist's obligation has been classically to reproduce whatever is regarded as natural as authentically as possible. Hence, "pop" in all its manifestations, including statues that may easily be mistaken for living people.

(As far as I know, this notion was created—or given substance—by Ivan Karp, who was not an artist but an artistic entrepreneur, a fact that befits the entire mystique of "pop," itself a product of technology, industrialization, exploitation, conspicuous consumption and, mostly, the extraordinary prices that are commanded in affluent cultures by the most commonplace of common places—for example, most real estate in most of the world—profits from which are of a piece with the extraordinary prices the "junk" of pop art commands in the art market.)

Photography changed pictorial art. Of slight concern to us at the moment is the impetus that it gave new schools of expression like Impressionism, Expressionism, Structuralism, Cubism, Surrealism and so forth. After ingesting the talents of the camera, *all* artists in our culture—or most of them—were forced to re-appraise their social function. Realistic exposition of nature could be—or would now be—accomplished with ease by photography, they thought simplistically. What on earth might they use their unique talents to expose now?

Their answer was both simple and intelligent. They could paint and draw what they *saw,* not necessarily what an object or person *looked like.* If, therefore, a garden of flowers broke up into a myriad of colorful vectors in the summer sunshine, *this* was what a Cezanne might now paint, not a literal translation of what the garden looked like to *others.* Second, the inner-life of the artist might be externalized and removed as far as he or she wished from nature's visual tyranny, even into the world of feeling and thus almost entirely devoid of natural pictorial meaning.

The works of most non-realistic artists since World War I show this retreat into self, both in graphic art and in sculpture. Art became, quite properly I think, a manifestation of the new science of psychology, as it moved further and further away from the new technology of photography. So it continues, even into the world of popular illustration by such interesting talents as LeRoy Neiman, whose utter lack of subtlety and highly sophisticated stylism produces works of unusual vigor and clarity.

Photography, in its early years, basked in the patent illusion that it had captured the vocabulary of the visual arts entirely in its snare. For a long time, many critics and artists appeared to believe this as a truism. Edward Steichen was, I suppose, one of the first photographers to show that the idea was irrefutably untrue. But any number of nineteenth-century camera artists—even Brady and Muybridge in their special ways—had already clearly demonstrated that no camera, no matter how it was used, was able to determine the subject of a photograph or control the nature of its visual representation. This was entirely the province of the photographer. Any idiot could snap a Kodak, but the results (except by chance) were rough equivalents to what happens when an untrained person tries to draw a picture. A world of difference exists between the so-called "snapshot" and the "photograph," as great a difference as between primitive art and fine art, if not greater.

The vocabulary of the visual arts in the hands of photographers was, naturally, influenced by developing technology but little more than were other artistic technologies—etchings, lithography, zincography and such. In the end, any single photograph was distinguished by content and modified by style and reflected, just as surely as nineteenth-century British painting did, the visual vocabulary that the artist had selected to use.

Germane to our concerns is the fact that even the crudest snapshot may display some erotic power, and, to the credit of the sensibilities of those who view it, it may correctly be considered pornographic. Much the same might be said of primitive paintings or statuary, their degree of eroticism usually depending less upon the skill of the artist than upon the imagination of the viewer. I remember, for instance, the first pornographic photograph shown me eons ago: a quasi-snapshot, as I recall, of a frightened-looking female on her back with a man, who was lying on his side and, with grim determination, was inserting his erect penis into her vagina. Both were apparently lying on a plain wooden floor, God knows where!

For all its crudity, I recall that this photograph was not, in any sense, simply a representation of nature but rather an *attempt* at art, simply because the couple had been posed in such a way as to highlight the prick-cunt nexus, no matter what discomfort it entailed for them. People—most people, anyway—do not fuck in this manner, and, although I was twelve years old at the time, I was able to figure this out immediately. On the other hand, for precisely the same reasons, the photograph's aphrodisiac power upon me was enormous, and I held that particular photograph in my imagination for at least a year of masturbatory fantasies, mostly I suppose because it was not replaced by any others that were as artfully posed.

I doubt that a primitive painting or statue would have had the same effect on me at the time, but we are dealing here with the psychology of adolescent perception rather than the art of eroticism or even—strictly speaking—pornography. What the photograph did—as I assume it must for many children—was to affirm visually a fact that I already knew: that people fuck—and in much the same way that the crude "dirty" prose to which I had been exposed also told me they did.

I suppose an issue can be made concerning erotic photography of all kinds—as opposed to erotic drawing and painting—that, no matter how fanciful and imaginatively a pornographic photographer has chosen his background, lit his subject, and so on, the resulting statement always says primarily, *"These people* are fucking," or have fucked or are doing whatever they are doing. In this manner one is always impressed deeply and immediately by an irrefutable connection between photography and life, and absolutely nothing will eliminate it. On the other hand, competing qualities of the various visual arts, including photography, do not necessarily yield the same sorts of competition in aesthetic or emotional or cognitive reactions. In another context, for example, I cannot explain or qualify sensibly which, in general, I have found were more moving or horrible: drawings of concentration camp inmates made during or after World War II by former inmates, or the conventional news photographs to which we have all been exposed of children being led to gas ovens and bodies piled in pits like cords of wood. To answer that both are horrifying simply begs the question of equivalency.

This dilemma—clearer than the one that faces us concerning literary eroticism but essentially the same—dramatizes our perfectly natural psychological confusion when we try to juxtapose the persuasive power of fiction against non-fiction. A clear line between them simply *does not exist.* Much fiction, we have been told again and again, has crept into most so-called history, and it is impossible for a writer to create fiction without employing models in real life in one way or another. The difference between the two for both is a matter of degree, not a matter of kind. This is obvious.

The same ambiguity exists in the shadow area where photography merges with other types of visual art and vice versa, which is to say almost always—except possibly when faced with the entirely artless nonsense of the amateur's snapshot. Simply put, what are the aesthetic, emotional or intellectual consequences to *me* of the fact that Edward Weston's green peppers, sand dunes and nudes were once part of nature and as real as the pencil with which I write? None—or very little. From the other side of the continuum, what are the aesthetic, affective and cognitive consequences of the fact that David's *Marat Assassinated* is not Marat at all, and the canvas may, for all we know, look nothing like the real event did—and I pick David because of the meta-theatrical flavor of all his paintings? David's dead Marat belongs to exactly the same class of reality past as Weston's peppers, and the difference of the media through which they are brought to us over the years means little or nothing.

Logically and psychologically, however, erotic photography does—and must—also make a statement *about* reality. The usual puritan question, asked since the dark ages of erotic photography is, "Who on earth would pose for such photographs?" This naive question is the immediate consequence of relating photography quickly—too quickly—to real life, and may, for certain people (certainly twelve year old boys), succeed at exacerbating emotions for a time. On the other hand, one rarely hears the question, "Who would produce such a woodcut or paint such a water-color?" when an anonymous erotic drawing or painting hangs on a wall. (Exceptions, of course, are exhibitions of the works of living artists who create little or nothing *but* erotica. After attending a show of Betty Dodson's *oeuvres,* for instance, one is entitled to a few uncertainties about the woman who created them, although I am not entirely certain what the uncertainties are likely to be *about.*) Photography's relationship to reality is, I think, a temporary matter, not unlike painting's relationship to imagination, at least as far as still pictures are concerned. (In the next chapter, we shall be concerned about some of the complications that occur when pictures—both photographed and painted—appear to move via motion pictures and, necessarily, enhance the relationship of photography to life itself and thus to reality.)

One of the most interesting ways to test this aspect of erotic visual communication is to compare fairly old pornographic graphic art with old pornographic photographs. The latter are not easy to find, except in Al Goldstein's *Screw* and in his overpriced collections called *Smut from the Past.* The main problem with Goldstein's archival documents, however, is that they are poorly reproduced and abominably printed. One gets their general flavor, at any rate.

In an Edwardian living room setting, a man with an elegant patent leather head of hair is licking the clitoris of a buxom lady, who represents the epitome of beauty in a style long past; this scene presents us indeed with a photographic "slice of life" from yesterday's world. It is, however, *so* removed from cultural reality as we know it that the question of *who* these long-dead people *were* is irrelevant. The photograph is therefore psychologically mated with, say, a similar etching of the period in terms of emotional power. As we compare the two, the question of erotic communication now depends almost entirely upon the artistry of the photography and/or the artist who created the etching. The seam between fiction and non-fiction is smoothed out in much the same way that often occurs in other documents from the past: Suetonius' biographies of the twelve Caesars might as well *be* fiction from a contemporary viewpoint (some say they *are*—in large part!). Petronius Arbiter's *Satyricon* might as well be non-fiction for all the difference it makes to the contemporary student of life in ancient Rome.

A New Vocabulary?

Sheer common sense tells me that the cumulative vocabulary of un-moving visual erotic communication ends in photography. I find this also an unsettling truism, because the technological end product of still photography has by no means been reached—nor may it ever be—and future developments may present problems both in art and in the ways in which we define "reality" that are impossible to anticipate and ramify strangely into erotic communications.

Although I imagine one must exist somewhere, nobody has yet seen fit to invite me to view a pornographic (or even vaguely erotic) hologram. But what of this next inevitable step? Photography's first major trauma, equivalent to the discovery of central perspective in the world of the graphic arts, will, I think, occur with the perfection of the three-dimensional photograph, a step that has almost been reached. In such representations, certain constructions of reality will seem to be duplicated more faithfully than by present methods. Will such a powerful technology modify or break the apparent continuum of erotic art from primitivism to sophisticated replication by means of today's technologies? What will the effect be on other arts, particularly sculpture and ceramic work?

The answer, of course, is that such an invention cannot change many things in the *short* run, any more than the discovery of central perspective did. For a time, such three dimensional photographs will live, as central perspective did, on novelty alone and as *coups d'oeil*. They may survive this way for a hundred years. I imagine that the major effects of three-dimensional pornograph will be to diminish slightly the potency of live sex shows and to crimp the style of a small percentage of voyeurs, who are, after all, usually more interested in the *reality* of what they see than what they see. Voyeurs, however, are often strangely and curiously imaginative. Holograms will test the powers of creation of artists in an erotic vein in much the same way as contemporary photography does. Three-dimensional photographs will be both artful and artless, just as contemporary photography is. And who knows how long it will be before an Edward Land develops a technique for taking holographic snapshots that are developed immediately, returning us, possibly, to an age of copper-coated baby shoes and plaster casts of hands and faces of the dead that existed before photography offered us the illusion of freezing time.

What such a technology will not and cannot do is either expand greatly or contract the erotic vocabulary of visual art or accomplish any more than central perspective did during its first two centuries of life. Central perspective did not change the *artistic* perspective of the West until the Renaissance, when the Church placed new and nearly impossible demands on artists to reconstruct a sacred past and to glorify the Christ and his works. Such a fuse ignited an explosion of change. But it remained for quite a while in only one geographical part of Europe, as it awaited its philosophical and cultural mandates from elsewhere. A similar challenge does *not* await the second phase of erotic photography at the moment, at least as far as I can determine or dare predict, especially since a current era of pseudo, so-called "liberation" has permiteed the old *sub rosa* visual erotic vocabulary such increased currency in the Western World.

In the *long* run, who can say? The very forces that do not make holography much of a challenge to erotic visualization at the moment may be interpreted by future photographers as a barrier to be broken or a wall to be climbed. How they will accomplish these ends, I cannot say, but their first attempts are likely to be prosaic and uncomprehending—as prosaic and uncomprehending as the use of three-dimensional motion pictures has been to date, both for the erotic and conventional cinema, and as discouraging as the prospect of 3-D television is.

New technologies in the visual arts, of course, have almost nothing to say to visual artists of and by themselves. If Muybridge and Marey parsed the vocabulary of physical motion—especially human and animal motion—it was because, for one reason or another, each man wanted desperately to find out something about motion, not in order to use a new technology. Muybridge was an artist and Marey was a physiologist, and the instrument they used to take their professional interests further than others had was the still camera.[10] Countless other sorts of gadgets invented since might have accomplished the same end, but the camera of their period was the one they were naturally forced to use, because it held out the greatest promise of success.

Of one thing we can be, I think, more or less certain concerning still pictures but not, as we shall soon see, motion pictures. No matter what the still photograph becomes in the foreseeable future, it will remain a relatively poor way of capturing human reality but an excellent way of capturing human ideality. Given the proper technology, one may reasonably expect that its art may well reach new heights of selective reality in this latter respect, heights which Turner, Monet and a number of other artists achieved with oil paints before the era of photography fractured selective reality as a *desideratum* of fine art—and, incidentally, of erotic art as well. By no means will holography be able to give us reproductions of sexual acts with the same precision that it is able to show us what collectors' coins look like. (This is done so well that the hologram and the coin are literally impossible to tell apart). But even these exact and sterile reproductions are selective visions of the currency photographed and are quite unsatisfactory for the numismatic expert who needs to feel and see a coin at different angles and touch it before he can really say anything of numismatic interest about it.

Visual eroticism will remain, along with other visual arts, a difficult test of talent and selectivity, partly independent of whatever photographic art *per se* becomes in the future and partly dependent upon it, as has been true of the classical relationship of erotic graphics to other art since antiquity. As long as we rely upon the visual image we receive of frozen reality in responding to pictures, erotic content will remain a function of our erotic imaginations—both for the individual (aged twelve or sixty) who is looking at the picture and for the selective powers of the artist, photographer or technician who, by choice and a multitude of other factors, acts as surrogate for the viewer.

Like all art, visual eroticism will depend in the last analysis upon its capacity for stimulating imaginations *beyond* the cognitive point or meaning to which the work actually takes it. One principle of aesthetics that applies to nearly all representations of human beings—that is, to anything except sheer design or still life—is the sense of the flux of time one receives from the picture or statue. Most effective visual art since antiquity has informed its viewers of two fundamental propositions about its subjects: They have *come to* the moment they were captured on stone, canvas, paper or whatever, and they will *move beyond* this instant into a future behavior of some kind. (Even and especially comic strips display this quality, exacerbated when they are drawn by geniuses like George Herriman of *Krazy Kat* fame.) It may be trite to note that the more talented the artist, the clearer and more imaginative these past and future possibilities seem to sensitive observers; this is exactly the quality that makes da Vinci's *Mona Lisa* substantively and obviously different from all other Madonnaesque females painted by other artists during the fifteenth and sixteenth centuries, and some of them are magnificent.

Pictorial eroticism ideally demands no less of the illusions of time past and time future. Whether the achievement of such fluidity is equal to more than or less than similar tests we put to other types of drawings, paintings and photographs is an excellent question, but its answer must naturally be equivocal and of semantic (or possibly moral) interest only. In fact, we are asking the futile question of whether eroticism (or pornography) can indeed be called "art," a problem that I gladly, at this point, leave in the hands of critics like Professor Peckham. The main distinguishing feature of erotic art (when held against other types of art or other types of eroticism) is its indisputable potential for crossing great barriers of culture and enormous wastelands of time, possibly to a greater degree than any other type of art I can think of. Certainly eroticism is more cross-culturally durable than ideals and notions of human "beauty," which may change in our era in a generation; this is an aesthetic point of considerable significance when contemplating the long history and inevitable future of what are often called "dirty pictures." The reason, of course, has to do mostly with the invariable natures of human erotic acts and organs, not the skill of the artists or the sensitivities of the viewers. The facts remain that persistent emotional power and meaning has been a major and invariable element in erotic art over the ages and that it has withered least of any (or most) other artistic qualities at the hands of father time or with the change of customs.

:: 5

Cinematic Pornography

*Alienation is the most common state of the knowledgeable
movie audience, and though it has the peculiar rewards of
connoisseurship, a miser's delight in small favors, we long
to be surprised out of it—not a suspension of disbelief nor
to a Brechtian kind of alienation, but to pleasure, something a man can call good without self-disgust.*

—Pauline Kael

As of 1968 or so, give or take a few years, the locus of the word "fine," as
used in the United States (and France) for the idea of "refinement," made a
quantum jump toward the so-called "art of the film." Traditionalists and
museum-goers as well as gallery owners may deny this and point to newly
expanded markets in etchings and oil paintings. Nobel prize authors, playwrights and Pulitzer prize poets and prizewinning architects (is there any
other kind?) may rattle manuscripts and pictures of bridges and buildings.
No end of fuss will probably ensue until I (or whoever makes the arguments) back down a bit. And why not back down? Nobody with brains is
really prepared to argue seriously for the virtues of the living theatre versus
the movies, for instance. The argument is ridiculous anyway. There is no
living theatre; there are *productions*. There are no movies; there is only
this movie and *that* movie.

Backing down a little is not, however, concession. I doubt that anyone will object to a revised comment that the movies have become, in the
West at any rate, one of the new "darlings" of the arts.

The word is a good one, the title of a British film in the middle sixties
that was prophetic more than titular. It spoke with open candor about

105

sexual hypocrisy, the characters used bad language and it made a trenchant contemporary statement about the banal state of contemporary morality that many movies, before and since, seem to have made as well or better than most novels and live drama in English during the past twenty years. Indeed, *Darling* was a paradigmatic title. Possibly the name alone, along with its commercial success, contained a message for other filmmakers in America and England.

What I have just called "movies" had by now come to be called "films" and "cinema" even in high schools, and people began to earn graduate degrees in something called "cinema studies." Movie criticism, which had long been mostly a facet of journalism, took on the colors of a literary art and fractured into groups that might loosely be called "aesthetic." These groups replaced crude political orientations that, along with the "I know what I like!" type of criticism, made up in large part the literature of cinema since its invention. What were called film "theories" now proliferated and were not limited any longer to the obtuse writings of an Eisenstein or the perfunctory but thoughtful observations of a Panofsky or an Arnheim or the dense simplistics (when all was said and done) of a Kracauer or Robert Gessner.

While it did not happen overnight, cinema theory eventually joined hands tentatively with philosophy—particularly existential philosophy and the wide and baffling world of semiotics and/or symbology, symbolic logic and the philosophical component of psychoanalysis, among other modern movements. Some of this theory, like McLuhanism, seemed to be a good deal more religious than intellectual.[1]

Similar cultural change was *not* happening in other arts. Possibly it has never happened before to *any* medium of communication with such intensity and so quickly and will never happen again.

The apparent results in terms of film production, were catastrophic to the established order. In a number of her sharp critiques, Pauline Kael has noted that, at about this time, successful movies and good movies turned a corner from films that put the burden of intellect upon an audience by means of their implicit excellence of character construction (*Five Easy Pieces* is one example) to films that, in Kael's words, *"delivered"* that is, did the cerebral and emotional work of the audience for them. Among the latter, we find the hyper-violent movies like *Death Wish,* optical *tours de force* like *Star Wars* and even such ambitious ambiguities as *2001: A Space Odyssey* and *A Clockwork Orange*—films, in other words, that were devised for kicks.

Kael loads all the standard socio-economic-cultural causal factors in her basket: the end of the Vietnam war, recession, reactions to student violence in the late sixties and so forth. As far as she goes, she may well be right. One factor she seems to neglect, however, is that, with the liberation of movies from traditional restraints of censorship, which had begun to sail full speed by 1970, films were now *delivering* more than they ever had in the erotic domain, and with a new precision. That they delivered a lot of other things at the same time was probably inevitable and intentional.

One pornographic film, openly playing anywhere in America at a respectable theatre admitting all over the age of twenty-one who could afford admission, was a sufficient cultural-causal breakthrough into the new age of film! And I am not referring here to the timid, sneaky half-baked fake sensuality of *The Last Tango in Paris* or the *non sequiturs* of *I Am Curious Yellow* but the real thing. *Deep Throat* delivered! *The School Girl* delivered! *Teenage Fantasies* delivered! *Behind the Green Door* delivered! How could the theatrical film ever be the same again?

I have a poor memory for dialogue, but I believe one prophetic scene in the short but shocking *The Devil in Miss Jones* sums it all up for most of the successful films we have lately seen on the market. Pleading with the Devil's accomplice not to be sent to hell, the Faustian Miss Jones says, in effect, "I'll do *anything* to stay here (in limbo)," to which Lucifer's philosopher responds, "How can you do *anything* now that you have done *everything?*" What anti-monopoly legislation and television could not accomplish, the movies, as a mass art in the West, may have already done to themselves by delivering the same thing too many times to the same audiences. *Exorcists, Jaws, Airports* and *Omens* may all, in their various incarnations, simply have delivered too much too well to keep the old art of theatrically conceived films in financially viable shape. An audience that has seen one has seen them all, and eventually the shortage of what in Hollywood is called "product" (meaning movies people will pay to see) may become so acute, and the remaining types of films so unexciting, that the films will go the way of the circus and in pretty much the same manner.[2]

I respect Kael, but I do not think causes and effects—mine or hers— can, at this moment, be sorted out to explain what has happened to the movies or, for that matter, to predict very clearly what will happen to them when, for instance, cable television becomes universal, connected and interconnected, across the United States in five years or so. The present moment is a time of ambiguity, but nevertheless, certain facts seem irrefutable regarding cinema art, cause and effect notwithstanding, each of differing importance though in no predictable way. In short:

1. Movies have achieved a new status as fine art among those who fancy themselves the intelligensia. Theories abound.
2. Book titles about movies, movie stars, biographies and autobiographies, volumes about directors, studies of film genres, the production of specific films on the market are starting to rival the number of cookbooks. These volumes range from expensive coffeetable volumes in homage to people such as Monroe or Disney to pocket volumes of esoteric criticism and everything in between. I suppose this is paradox. Interest in the dominantly "visual art" of film (sheer nonsense!)

has created a boom in print book publishing! Everybody who has ever been to the movies seems to want to write a book about them. Many unfortunately do.

3. "The study of film"—which can mean anything—has become academically respectable from grade school to Ph.D. programs. Nearly anything, apparently, can be "studied," from how to make a movie to the psycho-sexual meaning of avian symbols in Hitchcock's *The Birds*. Courses are given in Chaplin, and erudite scholars argue about signification in the westerns of John Ford.

4. Interest is growing in old movies—among them "lost" or "forgotten" films—not only for exhibition on television but in academia and our museum culture. The number of obviously profitable non-theatrical 16 mm film rental organizations has grown, just as the catalogues of these companies (some of them pretty good texts of film history) have gotten a good deal thicker and more and more elaborate in the past few years. Rental prices have also risen considerably. It may cost as much as $300 to show a chic European film like a Bergman opus *once* in a school classroom; $150 to rent a Fred Astaire–Ginger Rogers oldie; $50–75 for a Grade B horror stinker of the thirties, depending probably on what studio made it and who is in it.

5. In most cities of the United States, and in many shopping centers and drive-ins, it is possible for adult Americans to pay anywhere from $2 to $6 to see a fairly well-made film in full color displaying openly— but not always attractively—nearly every type of sexual behavior, homo- and hetero-sexual, and not necessarily confined to humans with human partners. I cannot begin to list what is available on the market for the patient voyeur, except to note that the cinema has learned to write large and with profit the masturbatory fantasies of a fairly large, loyal and mostly male audience that, I think, is a good deal more variegated in a lot of ways than common wisdom would have us believe.[3] The agenda for the American porno film has been drawn neatly by the tenor and tone of the sexual fantasies of all of us, male and female, and in many ways.[4]

Stag Versus Social Value

Even if I had the time, leisure and support, I doubt that I could (or would want to) attempt a definitive or even cursory history of erotic cinema. At the moment, I, like most scholars in the field (if scholars we are), am satisfied with the more or less well told history of this aspect of cinema written in the sixties by Knight and Alpert for slick magazine consumption.[5] In addition, a number of inexpensively made but illuminating porno movies, called *A History of the Blue Movie, Hollywood Blue* and the like, have done, in my opinion, a workmanlike though far from thorough job in this respect, and in some ways better than that of most film historians of the printed page.

While I cannot deride conventional scholarship brought to any art, craft or aspect of culture, my general disposition enhances a long-held bias where and when film history is concerned: that most of it is best told on celluloid, and that the recent proliferation of books on cinema is simply a sign that a not-so-new communication medium is attempting to wrap itself in the respectable cloth of literary criticism and aesthetics resulting in phenomenon number 2, that is listed above. As circumstantially difficult as it may be to produce films about films, and as bothersome as it is to project and study them, they are worth the effort. Literary recapitulations, even cleverly written and copiously illustrated, tend to miss the point of what the movies—particularly erotic movies—are all about both in letter and spirit.[6] Nor is this a problem confined mainly to erotic films; it refers itself to practically all aspects of film history, except those that are mainly organizational or legal or that emphasize literary aspects of the cinema.

I shall be no more successful at writing a history, therefore, of sex in cinema than I have been with the various media discussed in the previous chapters—possibly less successful, because films are peculiarly ephemeral, many have been destroyed, nobody has seen all of them (of even one type) and clear techniques for analyzing them, while not impossible, are cumbersome. Most important, however, is the application of the principle that pornography and technology seek each other out like north and south poles of magnets. So it has been with films.

Who cares what the first erotic film was: Little Egypt doing her belly dance at the Columbian Exposition of 1893; a French strip-tease film, *LeBain,* now lost but said to have been made in 1896; or *Le Voyeur,* also lost, of 1907? Most of the earliest—and best—are described second-hand in film literature, and all we can be certain of is that, by the time the first so-called "legitimate" film parlors opened up in the United States (about 1905), a considerable clandestine erotic film industry apparently existed, and its traffic was international. The earliest stag film that I have seen is supposed to have been made in 1915 and is known, among other titles, as *A Free Ride.* It involves a man, an automobile and two girls, both of whom he eventually and vigorously screws in a wooded glade.

This often cited "landmark" film came along rather late in motion picture history, and its preservation is, I am sure, more or less accidental. Griffith had already made his short films for Biograph, and they clearly recognized the audience appeal of implicit—but innocent—eroticism. By 1915, Griffith's cameras were already finishing his full-length Civil War epic, *The Birth of a Nation.* French filmmakers before and since Melies had been playing games with "naughty-but-nice" themes for the general audience, as had filmmakers other than Griffith, to the degree that in 1915 state censorship of movies—probably quite innocent movies—drew from the Supreme Court its *Mutual Decision,* discussed in Part II of this volume. This decision legitimized legal control of motion picture exhibition on the basis of the principle that films were not a form of speech, hence they were not covered by our Constitution's First Amendment. This state of affairs would not be rectified until some forty or so years later when, by degrees and painfully, the *Mutual Decision* was slowly reversed by the Warren Court over a period of roughly eighteen years.

In their pure form, therefore, and forgetting for the moment such ambiguous entities as one or two scenes in Griffith's *Intolerance,* early De-Mille *opera,* vamps and shieks and a short period of surprising candor in the early thirties, most of the best—if "best" is the word we are looking for—eroticism in movies in America and abroad was to be found in clandestine, illegal films known as "stags," "pornographic films" or simply "dirty movies." At least, as a medium of communication, filmmakers were free in these films to attempt to achieve erotic communication as an end in itself, unencumbered by subterfuge or distraction.

That no *Fanny Hill* emerged from this genre should not surprise us. There are those who claim that no cinematic equivalent to *Fanny Hill* is yet to be found among the corpus of hard-core erotica that today swells our film vaults. I would disagree on principle and naturally without proof, pointing possibly to Gerard Damiano's *The Devil in Miss Jones,* the previously mentioned French *Pussy Talk* (1975) and/or Armand Weston's recent *Take Off.* My disagreement, however, might, even if correct, miss the main point of the comparison between media. *Fanny Hill* was more or less in existence at the birth of the novel (at any rate, in English) and was a precursor of a novelistic tradition that covered far more territory than the portrayal of pornography or eroticism. Films that might be measured by *Fanny Hill's* artistic yardstick did not appear until the cinema medium itself was about seventy-five years old and had developed the technical, artistic and stylized traditions and techniques that filmmakers like Damiano, Weston and others might draw on. What is irrefutably true is that the movies as a storytelling medium have produced no John Cleland—for obvious reasons.

Early erotic films available for viewing today happily lack the furtive and sleazy qualities that later examples—particularly those made in the thirties and after—display. Filmmakers seem agreed that this is because the early films were made by professional filmmakers, who were the only people who had access to production equipment, and that these individuals took some pride in their art. The performing is as difficult to judge by today's standards as most Hollywood movies of times long past and presents something of an enigma. Who the actors in them were, we do not know, although they were probably prostitutes, pimps and the same more or less deviant show business types who appear in porno films today, individuals totally inept at the art of acting. (There is no question as to the ineptitude of individuals appearing in stag films during the thirties and forties!) That these performances, as well as the productions, were so professional says little laudatory about the techniques of acting in silent films. Some of the porno clowns and comedians, for instance, are just as funny as the Hollywood stars they are obviously imitating, and many of the girls are every bit as enchanting as some of the well-known silent screen actresses!

Professional pride caused films like *The Casting Couch* (1924) to be so neatly made, acted and edited, as well as amusing, from start to final sight gag. But ubiquitous home movies put an end to most of these erotic romps by the late twenties. Except for the tricky business of developing film and making duplicates, motion pictures became anybody's game, and most of the pornographic films made until World War II and for a few years after look just that way. Plots were thin or non-existent, photography was poor and the entire enterprise often centered upon the bizarre—Mexican women and large dogs, gang rapes, scatology, two lesbians with Coke bottles, dildoes or simply one's own inclinations, unlikely orgies, and so on. The people were not particularly attractive—though perhaps more attractive than Candy Barr's male and female accomplices in the famous stag film *Smart Alek* (1951), which was reputed to have been shot in a motel in Houston, Texas. (A female accomplice, called on the telephone to help Candy satisfy her lover, steps into the motel room directly from the closet!)

An interesting psychosexual tradition of erotic cinema that seems to have developed during this time—exactly when, one cannot be sure—is the inclusion in most pornographic films of visual evidence of an orgasm on the part of the male actor. That stag films displayed the "real thing" as far as females were concerned was, and is, an equivocal matter. Anal heterosexual fucking was, for instance, always what it seemed to be, and photographers made sure that viewers could plainly see which orifice was penetrated, but whether the female was enjoying the encounter or suffering it was another matter. Simulation and dissembling have been, since time *in memoriam,* the only *real* talents required of the prostitute, and the same qualities were *sine qua non* for women photographed in these films. True, some of the females I have seen screwing dogs have not looked particularly happy about it, and some others seemingly objected to such mundane matters as anal penetration, cocksucking and/or being the recipients of urological fun and games, but even these displays of distaste and pain may have been simulated to arouse viewers and/or to convince them of the verisimilitude of the action.

(No such problems faced—or face—lesbian scenes included in motion picture pornography since its earliest days. My personal reaction to the many displays of lesbian encounters of various kinds that I have viewed in countless hours of pornographic films—and at live exhibitions in the United States and Europe—is that the female participants usually *appear* to enjoy them more than they do heterosexual encounters. I include here the obligatory lesbian scenes that one sees today in nearly every contemporary X-rated porno film. I have seen far fewer male homosexual films, but I have also been impressed by the apparent unusual spontaneity of the erotic performance in these movies, except for the nearly invariable tendency, noticeable over fifty years and in different cultures, for the male involved in the passive role in rectal fucking to turn his face away from the camera. This, no doubt, is meant to draw attention away from grim expressions that make it difficult to distinguish the rictus of pain from erotic pleasure. Similar grimaces on the faces of males achieving orgasm, however, have been permitted in erotic films since their beginnings.)

Male performers, however, may attest to their degree of stimulation in two notable ways that females cannot: the presence of an erection and visible evidence of an orgasm by means of "come shots," or "money shots" as they are known to contemporary pornographers. Come shots are seen in some of the earliest pornographic films, most frequently as the result of, or part of, scenes displaying women sucking male organs. During the twenties, efforts were made to make these come shots as naturalistic as possible. A girl might bring a man to orgasm and let the semen roll from her mouth. The next shot might show her licking her lips in close-up. Or she might withdraw the penis from her mouth and jerk it off to orgasm, often allowing the fluid to spurt in her face—a practice later to become a convention of both the stag film and recent theatre and peep-show pornos.

At what point this major convention for males, the withdrawal of the prick from the cunt to achieve the non-realistic, stylized come shot (often helped by a bit of masturbation), became nearly obligatory in these movies, it is difficult to tell. By the thirties, however, it had become an entrenched tradition, a sign of the *bona fides* of the male performer. Certain recent X-rated films have purposely eschewed come shots (*Sometime, Sweet Susan* [1973], a better than average attempt at telling a psychologically interesting story, is one of them) in the interest of filmic reality, but, by and large, it is a staple of Western pornography on film. Sometimes, as in the famous *Behind the Green Door* (1972), another recent movie, it has been carried to surrealism by repetition and optical work in the cinema laboratory.

Mechanically, it is simply the filmic use of *coitus interruptus,* possibly the oldest (but not most reliable) method of birth control known to most cultures. Cinematically, it demands that a close-up shot of the ejaculating prick and/or of the face of the male performer while coming be clearly photographed along with the discharge of semen that finds its own resting place on the back or abdomen of his partner, depending on her position. Frequent post-orgasmic action shows either the man placing his penis (if it remains erect) back into the vagina or the woman playing with the sperm fluid, possibly rubbing it upon herself or tasting it, while often smiling at the camera.

I know nothing about how such scenes were made before the modern period of erotic cinema, but today a certain amount of cinema trickery is possible in their execution, even to the degree of faking an orgasm by means of a rubber-tubed instrument and/or substituting concentrated milk or a solution of egg whites, milk and sugar for genuine ejaculate, both in shooting and editing the come shots. A convention, strangely enough, that denies the sequential integrity of most live human fucking—wherein the semen is only vaguely visible after the penis is withdrawn—may thus be artificially recreated and/or simulated so that the audience will see evidence, albeit bogus, that a sex act has *really* occurred. Other simulations of this sort, of course, are not uncommon in conventional films where they perform the same kind of purpose: to simulate the stylization of reality. All violent cinema deaths, for instance, are faked in this way, employing artificial blood instead of semen and usually taking advantage more fully of the magic of time-stop photography. So are scenes of Indian massacres and hand-to-hand combat. (The choreography in the final fight scene of the recent popular film *Rocky* is an excellent example of this stylized filmic legerdemain.)

Stag films by no means returned to their earlier general technical stature after World War II but, by and large, the worst of them were frequently kept out of the *sub rosa* market. One must remember, however, what they were: black and white silent films for the most part, made and distributed illegally for highly inflated prices. That some of them seem to be as professionally made as they are is not easy to explain. On the marketplace itself, little distinction was made between old and new, well-made or jerry-built. One famous and somewhat superior example, *The Nun's Story* (1950), records expertly on well-lit black and white film the simple heterosexual violation of an attractive, somewhat Latinesque sister of the cloth by a harmless-looking young man. This movie was also circulated under the title *College Coed* in a version in which the three or four minutes at the start that established the girl as a nun are entirely cut. Nothing in the latter version smacks of the notion of "violation."

This was also a time when older style, quasi-legal "exploitation movies" were beginning to respond to changing post-war morality in both Europe and the United States. It coincided with a series of continual assaults upon city and state censorship that would eventually, and probably for the indeterminate future, bring theatrical movies under the protective arm of the First Amendment of the United States Constitution.

So-called "exploitation movies" were by no means offsprings of the fifties, nor is anyone today *exactly* certain what an "exploitation" feature was (or is), except that they were (and are) not distributed through normal channels and were usually exhibited in sleazy movie houses, the managers of which promised more than they delivered in terms of nudity, sin and/or sex (sometimes all three, but sometimes none of them). How erotic one considered these movies in their day of glory depends, I suppose, on the eyes of the beholders (at the time) and on their expectations and imaginations. The most daring of them today receives, possibly, an R rating (if it is rated), unless it deals in an extraordinary amount of explicit violence and sadism. The only element they had in common usually were low budgets and filmic ineptitude of every possible type and a potential for "exploitation"—hence the name.

"Exploitation" subjects, until the middle sixties, ran a strange gamut of the "forbidden." Some might be concerned with medical subjects such as venereal disease and/or birth control. Sex education, in a broad sense, was a popular topic: One of the all-time money makers among exploitation movies included clinical footage of the birth of a baby. Some were photographs of burlesque or strip-tease dancers doing relatively tame versions of their live acts. Others centered on the use of narcotics, drugs and alcohol in pseudo-documentary or fictional style. The fifties saw an upsurge of exploitation nudist films: some serious, some comic, some involving burlesque strippers, who added "name value" to the movies. An occasional nudie would be shot on location in a country like Bali, where a certain amount of female nudity is the *status quo*. Occasionally, some of them would actually be propelled by a plot. I remember one nameless British film of this period that told the story of a prim young London socialite who inherited a nudist camp from her eccentric grandfather. By the final reel, the heroine is converted to the healthy cultism she discovers when she journeys to the country to examine her bizarre property—as well as to a handsome male nudist who leads her to the alter.

Because of local censorship, even this sort of nudity was more visually implicit than real, although I repeat that judging the erotic content of this genre is nearly impossible from the vantage point of the moment. Neither complete frontal nudity nor pubic hair appeared in most of them until the sixties, and only then in glimpses and (forgive me!) snatches. By and large, these films are tributes to the craft of cinema editing—cuts and cross-cuts that give the impression of more naked flesh than one actually sees.

According to Turon and Zito, in their popular book on porno films, the director, Russ Meyer, later known for his suggestive and lush pseudo-pornographic and highly imaginative fantasies like *Vixen* (1968), introduced to the exploitation market the "nudie-cutie" film with a fairly clever quickie, photographed in color, entitled *The Immoral Mr. Teas* (1959). Its action developed from an amusing premise. A comic actor, intoxicated by the after-effects of an anesthetic, somehow or another thinks he sees all the men and women he meets in the nude. *Mr. Teas* was both highly exploitable and extremely successful. In effect, it began a decade's evolution in motion pictures that eventually led to the hard-cord porno films which were ubiquitous by the end of the sixties.

Whatever the fine points of the vanished genre of "nudie cuties" were, they did not include much originality or sophistication of a high order. By and large, nudity was their outstanding feature—usually female nudity as seen by a voyeuristic central character—and whatever sexual meaning the voyeurism contained was achieved either by implication in the script or suggestion in selection of shots and editing. Most of them were inexpensive, independent productions, the work of professional filmmakers operating under the pressures of low budgets and short, rapid-fire shooting schedules.

From the mid- to the later sixties, with a new porno film market just around the corner, "exploitation films" grew bolder and less suggestive. Producers, directors and actors gave advertisers and exhibitors plenty to exploit as they vied with one another to outdo themselves, dealing, usually, though still by implication, with all manner of violence, sado-masochism and voodoo in their movies. They were still nude, but year by year they became less and less cute, as the producers began to explore topics such as rape, cannibalism, vampirism, mass murder, incest and all manners of sexual deviation.

Once again, the actual erotic content of these films is today difficult to judge. Much was left to the imagination of the viewer and the acting, photography and directing were frequently so poor and hurried that more was asked of even a gullible audience of frustrates than their imaginations were able to bring to the films. Producers and directors like Meyer and David Friedman were sometimes able to transcend the general quality of these movies—in films such as Meyer's early work, *Lorna* (1964)—but, because it was often as easy to exploit a bad film as a good one, neither writers, directors nor performers felt much impetus to aim for better than mediocre work that did not cost much to produce.

Illegal stag and legal exploitation movies did not join forces at one single moment of metamorphosis, but the two types of erotica were, in nature, form and objective moving closer and closer. John Stuart Mill has written that the tendency to censor will always increase in society unless some force is brought to bear against it. The reverse, however, is also likely to be true: Liberality and candor in communications, and erotic candor in particular, will tend to increase in the absence of restraints. By the end of the sixties, most *legal* restraints that *might* have kept stag films under the counter and exploitation films reasonably circumspect had been exhausted.

For all practical purposes, the films were now *certainly* forms of speech, protected fully by the Constitution. Like speech in general, their freedom was not *absolute* under any and all circumstances, but most state and city censoring bodies had been legally eliminated. As the result of a number of Supreme Court decisions (discussed in Chapter 6), the standing definition of the term "obscenity" (a class of speech definitely *not* protected then or now by the First Ammendment) had been widened to include various types of communication (films among them) hitherto closed to it. In addition, the Court insisted that speech of any sort could not be obscene unless it was "utterly without redeeming social value," a mischief phrase that places an enormous burden upon the word "utterly."

The question has never been settled, but it was asked often enough, as the courts tackled the growing permissiveness of exploitation features and the appearance of stag films in movie theatres across the nation in one or another manifestation. Is *The Casting Couch* "utterly" without redeeming social value? (Not, one presumes, if it tells you how certain Hollywood actresses at one time got their parts in films. The film's moral precedes the end title: "The only way to become a star is to get under a good director and work your way up.") Certainly films that displayed how men and women might heighten sexual enjoyment could not be "utterly" devoid of social value, especially if such movies as *Man and Wife* and *He and She* left little, if any, of this education to the audience's imagination by the late sixties and early seventies. The same was true of a host of other equally enlightening documentary-style color films. A number of European movies that today we would label "soft-core" pornography followed more or less credible story lines during this period, probably the most notable being the Swedish import *Without a Stitch* (1969), which chronicled the amusing adventures of a frigid heroine who follows—to the letter—the libertine advice of her sex therapist.

At the heart of the question of whether or not this or that film was "utterly without redeeming social value" were many vexing questions, usually evaded by courts but found in the underlying rationale that opened up a new era of eroticism for American movies. Fundamentally, is a nude human body "utterly" without redeeming social value? Is an erect male penis? A vagina? A couple fucking? (To some, sexual intercourse stands for the ultimate of social value! What sort of societies would our species have *without* it?) Examples of deviant sexual behavior? (You mean to say that, taken as a whole or in part, Baron Richard von Krafft-Ebing's *Psychopathia Sexualis* is "utterly" devoid of social value?) And so forth, and so forth and so forth.[7]

Into these legal muddy waters jumped a number of American erotic filmmakers, most notably John Lamb and Alex de Renzy. In 1969, an erotic trade show was held in Copenhagen, attracting not only merchandizers of erotica but a large tourist crowd as well, coming as it did upon the heels of the legalization of all pornography in Denmark. This experiment in universal license has since been modified considerably for reasons to be discussed subsequently in this book. There could be no doubt about the social interest, value or relevance of this specific event, which had been planned to become a yearly festival, a tradition that lasted for all of two years! American (as well as European) filmmakers were there in full force ogling the occasion from every possible angle. The result was a number of feature films of a pseudo-documentary nature, the "redeeming social value" of which could hardly be questioned in court. On the other hand, neither could their obvious "prurience," the word our courts have, in recent years, chosen to associate with slim definitions of "obscenity."

Entitled *Sexual Freedom in Denmark, Censorship in Denmark: A New Approach* and similar straight-faced, straight-laced names, the films purported to tell the *truth* about the modern sociological phenomenon of Danish permissiveness in general and this exposition in particular. This they certainly did, thus justifying their status as documents, and they were so contrived that they fairly dripped of the "redeeming social value" required under the law at the time, even without the use of the weasel word "utterly."

What lawyers and others did not seem aware of then (1970), in the rapid shock syndromes that both pro- and anti-civil libertarians experienced upon the release of these pictures, was that the films threw a metaphorical but bright spotlight on the weakness of the Supreme Court's notion that pornography (or obscenity) might *ever* be classified as "utterly without redeeming social value."

First, it is and has been since the seventeenth century generally understood in British-American tradition and law that *truth* is, under most conditions, socially utilitarian, and all of these films, alas, told the truth. Neither the law nor the general public, however, were quite ready to accept the more stark general principle that *truth and truth alone does not always have social value for everybody at all times under all circumstances.* Were a motion picture camera, for instance, to follow any one of us around for twenty-four hours, the result would show *truly* how we live. But the social utility (except, possibly for medical or psychiatric diagnosis) of scenes of our urinating, shitting, farting and blowing our noses, to say nothing of our drooling, scratching and nail biting, is moot and of dubious documentary value. For the most part, for instance, characters in the most realistic stories, plays, novels and historical documents do not (often) piss and (rarely) shit, a remarkable phenomenon if you think of it, but a literary convention relating to human privacy that is almost universally accepted.

Second, the particular truth that these films displayed created a fascinating problem of meta-cinema or meta-theatre, a play within a play, wherein the *second* play must always be a *true* play—that is, it is in *truth* a drama.[8] The strolling players in every production of *Hamlet,* accordingly, are putting on a *true* play, in that they are pretending to be actors putting on a drama devised by Hamlet to unsettle his uncle. The rest of the actors in *Hamlet*—Hamlet himself, Gertrude, Polonius, Laertes—are not showing us natural truth: they are pretending to be a group of people involved in a retelling by Shakespeare of a story of court intrigue that is supposedly a part of Danish history. So are the players when they listen to Hamlet's directions to them. But the moment they begin playing actors, they are doing, in truth, exactly what they are doing in the natural world: acting. Into this neat trap of logic fell *Censorship in Denmark* and its brethren, except the trap turned out to offer them a special kind of protective custody.

Thus was *truth* vindicated for these films on *two* levels. On one hand, they were accurate but possibly legally vulnerable; for example, a filmed tour through an Algerian whorehouse might indeed be true but still open to the question of whether or not it is "utterly without redeeming social value." (My memory of such Algerian establishments is slightly hazy, but I personally would not desire the obligation of making such a judgment. In all seriousness, I imagine my decision would depend, in large measure, simply on how the tour was conducted!) On the other hand, not only were these films simple truths, but they contained meta-dramas: true performances put on for real audiences of real people—performances *not* simulated for the *films* but for other purposes.

Censorship in Denmark was the best, and best remembered, of these movies. Two examples of long sequences from it will suffice to give the reader its flavor. In one case—possibly the most honest and clearest—we join an audience of voyeurs at what I presume to be a nightclub watching an act called "Olga and Her Sex Circus." The audience is visible in the foreground, as a team of three beautiful nude girls, two white, one Negro, indulge at length in every manner of lesbian relationship possible for their three lithe, limber and attractive young human skeletal and muscular systems. This includes one remarkable sequence showing one girl bending over with her head between another's legs chewing at her genitals, while Olga herself fingers and licks the anus of the second girl, stopping every now and then to indicate to the (nightclub) audience how much she is enjoying the romp. From the girl in the middle we get little reaction: merely fervid continuation of her sucking and eager submission to the rectal manipulation. All we see of the audience—mercifully—is the back of individual heads!

Another sequence is a bit more obtuse in its meta-theatricality, but its point is equally clear, and its end, the framing of hard-core pornography within a meta-dramatic boundary of truth (and possibly a social value of a documentary nature), may even be clearer. The trick is simple: De Renzy's camera crew simply visits the site of *another* camera crew that is making a pornographic film and some still erotic photographs at the same time. Thus, we see a man, who we are told is actually a Danish sailor, wearing his uniform at the start but later happily cavorting nude with an attractive prostitute, using both his own resources and those of a mechanical vibrator to stimulate the young lady, as both sets of cameras grind away. The uninhibited duo even stop for refreshment in the middle of the filming, and, when the sailor begins losing his erection, the woman, alarmed, does what she can to get his mind away from food to where, in the businesslike business of creating pornography, it belongs. She succeeds.

More than any other films of the sixties, *Censorship in Denmark* and others like it (possibly not as well made) clearly indicated that cinematic erotica, now freed by statute from censorship, would and could move in no other direction than the replication of the old, illegal "stag films," albeit with a quantum of social significance (if necessary) thrown in to satisfy obscenity laws. Now the movies were more expensively made, longer, in color and openly available to all except children, who were excluded anyway by State statutes as infants from First Amendment guarantees and immune from consideration in most legislation censoring artistic expression. The same Supreme Court that had hoped, by defining "obscenity" in terms of social utility, to widen the limits of erotic expression in films enough to permit movies that the Court had judged modestly indiscreet to be freely shown, had, in fact, ended up legitimizing almost *any* type of cinema that the mind could devise! It was not until 1973 that a more conservative Court than the one which had brought the films into the contemporary age of erotica attempted to remediate the situation created by its predecessor. For many reasons, it failed.

The social and juridical background demonstrating why this later Supreme Court *had* to fail will be discussed in Chapters 6 and 7. At the moment, while we are concentrating on movies, let us consider just one general and universal legal principle that inevitably (and incorrectly) is reduced to the phrase, "You cannot legislate morals!" Morals—personal rights and wrongs—of course, have been, are and will continue to be determined, particularly in modern technological countries where interdependency of people is a necessity of social function, by law and law alone that may, at certain times, fly directly into the face of custom, upbringing, religion and even biological imperatives. That certain people will break such laws is, I think, inevitable. But, if they are apprehended and tried for their transgressions, society will usually find a way to punish them. What *all* law requires, however, over a long period of time, is either the assertive and authoritative force of a possibly modest but effective public opinion— not necessarily a majority or plurality—or a functional curtain or smoke screen of obscurantism behind which the law may hide in order to *prevent* public opinion from undermining it. (America's attempt at alcoholic prohibition lost its general public support, even among most small but powerful groups, in the heat and light of the twenties. The moral issue it treated—alcoholic consumption—was, like pornography, quite a clear cut one; there is nothing ambiguous about drinking or not drinking. Problems facing marijuana laws today are obviously more complex in every respect, including the personal moral issues and demands for choice they present to many young people.)

No, the problem of porno films in our culture does not relate in pith to home truths or myths about regulating morals, but rather to the fact that law cannot turn back the moving fingers of culture and custom and fashion, all of which may only be vaguely related to moral issues or consensual ideas of right and wrong. We cannot, for instance, undo the impression that *any* technology has made upon society, as Jacques Ellul has so aptly observed, and as (mis-named) ecologists would have us today attempt to do by idealizing a benign world of nature that, in fact, has never existed. Neither laws nor public policy can return to us an ideal of education that included, as signs of a cultured person, a knowledge of Latin and Greek. Nor is legislation capable of restoring sanctity to marriage vows, once an integral part of value systems in former cultures, any more than it can restore the apprentice system or the barter system to society's work-a-day world.

What I am saying, in effect, is that the law has no power to *unmake* *Censorship in Denmark* or *Deep Throat* or any film that has substantively influenced culture, custom and/or fashion, and it cannot risk trying to do so without revealing its own ineffectuality. I suppose this principle relates as trenchantly to *Potemkin* and *Citizen Kane* and to several Fellini films as it does in countless subtle ways to the contemporary pornographic epic. In the legitimate theatre, for instance, those of us who saw the first performance of *Oklahoma* when it tried-out in New Haven were perfectly well aware at the time—in fact, we discussed it for days—of what was self evident: that the Broadway musical would never be, could never be, the same again. A cultural landmark—for better or worse—had somehow passed, and a long cycle would have to swing the pendulum of art and theatre to return it, if ever, to what it had been.

The Erotic Apotheosis?

I would be bending judgment in favor of closure if I maintained at the end of this part of this book that, in its peculiar way, erotic expression has produced during the past few centuries, first, absorbing and integrating traditions of narration and verbal fancy and, second, a pictorial tradition that, when blended by the skilled filmmaker, achieved, *voici,* an ultimately perfect (to the moment anyway) medium of surrogate erotic communication: the pornographic movie. On the other hand, I find merit in this notion, if I may be allowed in searching it out to use selected examples of certain unique pornographic films made in recent years.

One has to travel far and look widely and long through the history of erotica to find anything as irreverent (and irrelevant even to eroticism in places) as Peter Locke's ironically titled film, *It Happened in Hollywood* (1973). The movie, in fact, goes to extraordinary pains to signal to the audience its distinctive New York origins and mad Brooklynesque impressions of the movie industry. Scatological, more than slightly anti-Semitic and wildly inventive (including a pornographic acrobatic act featuring an indescribable "erotic bicycle"), this spoof of the making of Biblical movies was a stepchild of the Al Goldstein–James Buckley (at that time) publication *Screw,* and nothing quite like it has been made before or since. More to the point is that its crazy sex, horrible puns (Samson, in a scene from *Samson and Delilah,* carries Samsonite luggage) and whacky raunch are not the sort of things that are, can or should be imitated. Might it best be described as a kind of *Helzapoppin* on film or neo-Marx Brothers romp written and produced by psychopaths? It is certainly one of the most uninhibited comic films I have ever seen that is, in large part, genuinely funny as well as voyeuristically appealing.

(Goldstein himself appears in the film, is sucked to an orgasm by a young girl dressed—I think—as a Roman slave and then ejaculates into a silver salver subsequently set aflame, a la *Crepes Flambé*—all for no reason that I can detect, except that Goldstein thought that it would be fun to appear in the picture. He admits today that it was. But he was crushed, he says, when the actress who had blown him in front of the cameras during the morning shyly refused to join him at luncheon. Of such strange professionalism is pornography compounded, especially in films, forcing me to wonder if Aristotle's concern about erotica in the Poetics might not maintain its relevance today: The Greek aesthetician, as we shall see, did not worry about the effects of pornography upon *audiences*. This he understood to be healthy. His fundamental concern was for the morals of the *actors* and *actresses* in the satyr plays of his day. Goldstein, for many reasons—none of them Aristotle's—has happily not appeared in a porno film since *It Happened in Hollywood*.)

Looking at some others more quickly, a valid although overtold moral lesson in *The Devil in Miss Jones* was taught in a uniquely sensual although uneven manner. The film's success resulted largely from the convincing performance of an accomplished actress, the pseudonymous Georgina Spelvin, who manages convincingly to transform the central character in stages, from a desperate virgin who slits her wrists into a fascinating nymphomaniac and finally into a masturbating frustrate (in hell), despite the thinness of both concept and script. (Spelvin, incidentally, is the only erotic actor or actress currently working in porno films who is a seasoned performer with considerable professional experience on the Broadway stage. Most of the rest are neophytes and/or amateurs, some with slight talent, some more or less more attractive than others, and all, of course, with the exhibitionist's proclivity to perform sex acts believably in the public arena of the usually brightly lit film stage, wherever it may be.)

Behind the Green Door (1972) exploits, in a peculiar, meta-theatrical way, both the degradation and sexual virtuosity of a kidnapped girl (the beautiful model, blonde Marilyn Chambers), who is sexually exploited in a lush Edwardian setting for an audience of a group of grotesque voyeurs (thin, fat, short, tall and so on), all of whom are stimulated by the performance to their own final frenetic and bizarre orgy. Here the Mitchell brothers of California produced—over-produced, I think—a carnival of contrasts, not the least interesting sequence of which is Ms. Chambers' beautifully photographed simultaneous seduction by a group of dark-haired lesbians and her subsequent scenes with a pantheresque Negro, Johnny Keyes. Provocative, fantastic contrast as a vehicle for eroticism, like the *Beauty and the Beast* fable, is one powerful stimulus often missing from these cheaply made films. *Behind the Green Door* stands as a notable exception, or at least as one where the theme is believable as a vehicle for such filmic and dramatic contrasts.

I have already mentioned the remarkable French movie *Pussy Talk,* a delightful conceit that evolves from the uncomfortable discovery by a lovely Parisian housewife that her cunt has taken on a life of its own! It (the cunt) begins to talk and argue with her, displaying particular dissatisfaction with her husband and choice of men. News of the talking vagina spreads throughout the country—somehow involving a female psychiatrist. The movie eventually introduces an enterprising reporter who interviews the cunt while its owner is drugged—and so forth into wild plot configurations that baffle the imagination. Lusty flashback scenes of the cunt's (that is, the heroine's) early life are fancifully told: her defloration by the nose of a puppet (yes!), a wild seduction scene involving another young girl and a teacher and her insane but convincing seduction of a young priest in a confessional booth—both seen rocking in copulatory rhythm at scene's end. In addition, the cunt is frequently lip-sync animated as it speaks, and some scenes are photographed from what I suppose must be an infra-vaginal perspective: as the organ looks out and observes the world around it. *Pussy Talk* is a unique erotic adventure that, for reasons I have not been able to determine, seems to have disappeared entirely from American exhibition after its initial run. It succeeded, nevertheless, in balancing erotic interest with inventive storytelling and excellent film production, a rare accomplishment for this genre.

Armond Weston's *Take Off* (1978) is the only other recent satirical film in a class with *Pussy Talk,* at least in my admittedly limited experience. In this movie, however, Weston's crafty direction, the professionalism of the film and, mostly, the cleverness of the plot distracted me from its considerable erotic content, a danger that baffles and discourages many filmmakers less talented than Weston. Employing a familiar cast of American porno actors (including Spelvin), Weston coached amusing and credible performances from nearly all of them, especially Wade Nichols. Where the acting is weak, the loveliness of performers such as Leslie Boveé more than compensates for moments of amateurism. A version of Oscar Wilde's *The Picture of Dorian Gray,* Weston's mysterious aging portrait here becomes a reel of porno film, made in the twenties, that ages while the real Gray (re-named Green) remains young through the thirties, forties, fifties, and sixties.

Once this premise is established, the following sequences are all cinematic spoofs: Cagney gangster films, Bogart movies, Brando films and generation gap stories of the sixties. It is so witty and well told for the most part that the pornography—even eroticism—slides into the background of what is, in fact, a cinematic topical review of the kind that used to grace the Broadway stage. Thanks to television's mania for old movies, the satirized films are familiar—over familiar—to the audience, and therefore to see them kidded in the context of pornography is less sexually arousing than simply joyful. A healthy male is able to laugh with an erection but, to some degree (and for different people, I imagine), *Take Off*'s sharp devilish humor and skillful production seems to me to exploit sexuality in the service of comedy, instead of the other, more familiar way around. *Take Off* also seems to be one recent hard-core porno film that definitely interests American women, or so exhibitors report, whether it be erotically, humorously, or both, it is impossible to determine. (For what the news is worth, much of the shooting script was written by a professional writer, a clever woman. And my own wife, who tells me that she is quite sensitive to the erotic stimulus in many films, even tea as weak as *Last Tango in Paris* or *The Night Porter,* enjoyed *Take Off*—and she remembers it largely as a comedy rather than an erotic statement.)

Using these films as examples, I have, I am afraid, overstated my case, having fallen into the trap of a Ciceronian argument. Although successful erotic communications of *any* and *all* types may well be exceptions rather than rules, I must make it clear that the films cited above are extreme exceptions—not only to the measure of present pornographic films, but to the part that erotic behavior has, in general, played in cinematic history since its silent-picture beginnings.[9]

I am certain that I detect a trend, ever growing in the United States, and signaled by the organization of erotic film producers into a bona fide association, commercially and self-protectively motivated to be sure, that is of serious concern for the future of this film genre. Known as the Adult Film Association of America, this group's present activities are devoted mainly to mutual aid in legal stands against censorship of various kinds. But many of its members are undoubtedly interested also in the erotic film as a medium of communication and in the unexplored potential these movies may have for telling stories and dealing with fiction, fantasy and even documentary in unique and ingenious ways.[10] Among other endeavors, the society presents yearly awards (similar in intent to those given by the Motion Picture Academy of Arts and Science) for acting, directing, screenwriting, costumes (yes!), music, editing and cinematography, that are fairly judged by meaningful criteria for the most part and certainly well earned by the recipients, considering the special nature of their talents, I would say.[11]

Trends come and trends go, however. The future of the AFAA is in the hands of fashion, law, commerce and a hundred variables that I cannot predict. When one stumbles upon a sophisticated, well-produced and thoroughly professional film such as *Sex World* (1978), based in concept upon the successful *Westworld,* some of the artistic potential of the erotic film and the power of the medium to communicate erotic ideas may seem momentarily a good deal clearer in fancy than they are in fact. (This expertly made but somewhat uninspired film was, incidentally, recommended to me by a number of my most intelligent female students in New York who are seriously interested in cinema art and discovered it while searching for an X-rated film they were compelled to see for a college course on the problems of censorship.)

Sex World deals with the erotic fantasies of a number of people who attend a resort where, by means of science-fiction voodoo, their masturbatory dreams are gratified with scientific precision, an interesting "before and after" plot concept that might have been handled more cleverly than it was.

What I gather that my students found so attractive in the film, however, was the *possibility* of exploring with candor certain nonconscious and/or repressed appetites within characters (and maybe within themselves) in imaginative ways that are particularly powerful when transferred to the cinema medium. *Sex World,* both in premise and production, is a good deal more erotic than *Take Off,* mainly because the theme itself (like that of *The Devil in Miss Jones*) is based upon an erotic premise, while *Take Off* really is not. Pornographic content in both films is about equal and quite similar, with particular emphasis upon lesbian sequences involving extraordinarily beautiful girls. *Take Off* is, all things considered, the superior, although many contrasts between the two are worthy of close scrutiny by film buffs.

When viewing movies of this sort, however, including even the work of homosexually oriented directors such as Wakefield Poole—*The Boys in the Sand* (sic) (1971) and *Bijou* (1972)—I find it too simple and unsatisfying merely to postulate that films, as surrogate erotic communications, hold out possibilities for transfers of emotion and meaning that are merely suggested, but rarely reached, by older media like words and still pictures of various types. Two powerful factors, one social and one psychological, militate against what I suppose I must call the "effectiveness" of erotic cinema, particularly contemporary pornography as we are familiar with it. And either or both may bury them as prospective art forms and/or as erotic media, particularly the latter.

First, erotic films have, since their earliest illegal days, shared with other specialized forms of mass (or, in a sense, "class") communications the promise and sometimes the fulfillment of enormous profits for slight investments: profits on investments that have run as large as a thousand percent or more. These profits, unfortunately, are not necessarily rewards for excellence in filmmaking in any (including an erotic) construction, but rather from the films' appeal of novelty and their ability to reach that part of an X-rated film audience at a given moment whose appetite gnaws mostly for the new, the unusual and the bizarre. One film imported from Europe—entirely a miserable production—featuring a girl copulating with various animals (including a pig) recently brought to its distributor enormous grosses. So has one far better movie that featured a pair of identical female twins, identically lovely incidentally, who indulged in various homosexual acts, one with the other—not uncommon behavior, incidentally, between twins, both male and female (which would seem to have more in common physiologically with masturbation than with interpersonal sex, an irony that I happily turn over to psychiatric research). A presently popular movie features the adventures of a rapist enema freak, who assaults females (including two actresses playing sisters) by forcing them to have intercourse with him; he subsequently urinates on them and then, "to cleanse their sins," gives them enemas. (See Note 2, this chapter, at the end of the book.)

An erotic film producer recently snorted to me that "films like these give pornography a bad name!" and it is hard to disagree with him. But we (and he) must realize that eroticism, by its nature, does not incline to obey conventions or strictures of either intellect or art. I have viewed many films such as those described above, and I find that this problem is neither evaded nor solved by comparing, in a rational manner, the so-called "cinematic values" of porno films with similar values in collateral films of other sorts.

Sexual deviance may, for instance, share many common characteristics with human violence—and I am willing to exclude homosexual behavior *per se* as a type of deviance from my comparison. While violence as an *idea* is often intellectually repellent to supposedly civilized peoples, its attractions in life and art (and particularly in drama and graphic art) are irrefutable and profound. In fact, *both* sexual deviance and violence may be traced back to the great dramas of antiquity, and their thread may be followed with ease in drama, poetry and painting to the present moment. Violence and deviances, for all we know, may be prices we pay for so-called "civilized" culture as well as the necessary sublimations and cooperations that such cultures force upon us, a theme treated again and in more detail later in this volume. In the end, there is (and seems to have been for a long time in both the West and the East) money to be made from bestiality, child pornography, oddball sexuality and scatology of the least subtle type—money in large multiples from small, high-risk investments.

At some point on the road to excess, the abuses which this motive may cause—such as the so-called "snuff" films, the cinema recording of a supposedly bona fide murder of a (usually) female performer—may amplify the many present demands for censorship of *all* erotic celluloid or movies that pass a certain point of candor. Such demands are usually shotgun blasts rather than carefully aimed single bullets, an example being the present absurd tendency of academic do-gooders to lump into one heap all so-called televised "violence." As a result of this childish generalization of violence out of context, I assume that they would purge American television of the *one* classical dramatic element that has been apparently indispensable for the composition of nearly all types of stories both for children and adults since antiquity in every culture! This sort of mindless opposition to dramatic and fictional violence is exactly what José Ortega y Gasset refers to when he speaks of cultural "barbarians" attacking the arts.

Second, a more curious factor, not unrelated to the first, is the psychological one that may fairly be called, I think, "erotic discount." It has to do with the apparent tendency for erotic communications to lose their power of arousal when they are not accompanied by erotic behavior. Had somebody suggested to me, for instance, when and where I gained (physical) maturity that a time would come in my life when pornographic films and/or live sex shows would, by virtue of repetition alone, turn into nothing more or less than sheer boredom two-thirds of the time, I would have doubted his or her sanity.

Now, I admit that both age and circumstances have, to some degree, jaded me, but I share this reactive phenomenon with countless young people I know (most of them, incidentally, males) who seem normally lusty in their personal lives but sadly sated in their vicarious ones. Films, of course, are not the only medium that leads one to this fatigue, but, possibly, they lead to it more noticeably than either words or pictures—and more drastically. One must *attend* a film, seek it out, view it under specific conditions at a certain time and on certain occasions. Still pictures and prose are more strategically malleable and may be perused according to one's mood and/or at leisure. A movie, at present, simply cannot be opened and closed like a book.

Let me admit that I find something disconsoling in the fact that so many young people find yesterday's shocking cinema commonplace, and that values of the commonplace have changed so quickly in the contemporary world. In one decade or so, the once-shocking aspects of *I Am Curious, Yellow* turned into howls of derision from student audiences, as did the precious soft-core obscurities of *Last Tango in Paris*, a heinously made film, saved in its day (somewhat like *A Clockwork Orange*) by invading private personal domains of its characters with a fake candor slightly ahead of its time. Similar to a carnival freak show, *Last Tango* attracted the curious to "such events that only come to town once a year" as a cover for execrable writing, directing, editing and (sadly) acting.

If the cultural and artistic directions in which we are moving eventually blur distinctions between pornographic movies and movies in general, we shall be traveling in a salubrious direction. But I doubt that this eventuality is even remotely possible at present. Despite sagacious arguments to the contrary, like those of Lawrence Becker,[12] we shall, I am afraid, force ourselves to continue making distinctions concerning the value of films according to bogus moral criteria rather than those drawn from aesthetics, simply because the former are easy distinctions to handle—to lecture about, write about, argue about. One of the most aesthetically perfect films of the thirties, for example, is *Triumph of the Will,* a moral disaster because of the deification of Adolf Hitler by its toady but talented director. By way of contrast, the single most insistently moral film I have seen in years is a Hollywood flop called *Harry in Your Pocket.* It was a failure, I think, although it was brilliantly written, because the film was too slickly directed and poorly cast—except for Walter Pidgeon as an old, idealistic pickpocket. In other words, it was a discordant, aesthetic mess but a moral triumph.[13]

As long as cinematic erotic communications are burdened with the moral impedimenta they carry right now, it will be quite simple to criticize these films—or deny them criticism, as many newspapers like *The New York Times* do today according to a vague moral "policy"—but neither the causes of art nor morality will thereby be fairly served. In the long run, similar to other media we have discussed in the past chapters, the maturation of cinema as art and communication will only be delayed by such false distinctions.

When movies, in particular, fall victim to the critic and to audiences as judges of public morals, we discover in their fairly lengthy history periods of foolishness, banality and ineptitude raised by the gods of success into bogus golden eras of art. One simply has to look back at the meretricious films (and plays and books) that thrilled us into superlatives before and during World War II because they rooted for the right team. They illustrate, I think, one clear dimension of the difficult axiom that morality, art and communications live in separate intellectual domains and bespeak different heuristic processes—possibly even epistemologies—no matter how, why, when and where circumstances cause them to overlap.

It Happened in Hollywood: Rare photo of Al Goldstein (beard on face) in costume for zany porno romp. Milky Way Productions.

Penelope Lamour, the girl with the vocal vagin the French import, *Pussy Talk*. Mature Films 1975 by Catalyst Productions, Inc.

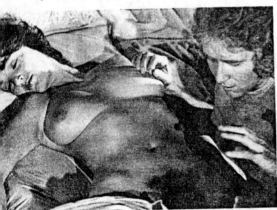

Pussy Talk: The premise: Penelope Lamour's talking organ babbles on even while she is unconscious. Mature Films.

Pussy Talk: Penelope's organ remembers her sc days and a male teacher, a common porno the (Actress is another girl, probably in mid-teens.) ture Films.

Pussy Talk: The adult Penelope at the movie, un the spell of the talking pussy, leading her astr Mature Films.

Take Off: Wade Nichols and Georgina Spelvin. The "Dorian Gray" hero is bewitched in the nineteen-twenties. Mature Films © 1978. A Maturpix Release.

Nichols and Spelvin. The bewitchment is cinematic. This frolic is captured (by a Von Stroheim chauffeur) on an unseen camera. The film image ages; Nichols does not. Mature Films.

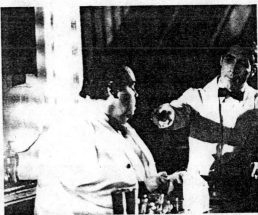

"Dorian" Nichols in the 'thirties *a la* Cagney. Unexpected switch is the bagel in the face. Mature films.

In the forties, Nichols imitates Bogart, selling passports for intimate favors—from females, not bartender. Mature Films.

he ageless Nichols as Brando *cum* motorcycle in
he 'fifties. Satire in sequence is clever, sharp. Ma-
ure Films.

The 'sixties scene with weirdos, drugs and gener
tion gap does not succeed. Nichols is "hip," b
cinema parody is unclear. Mature Films.

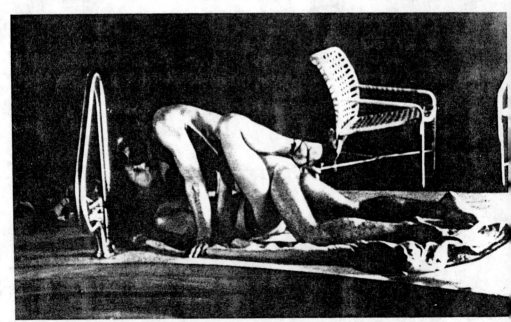

A final fling in the present with lovely Leslie Bovee
before "Dorian" Nichols' geriatric finale. Mature
Films.

PART TWO

:: THE PRESENT

The Vanishing Censor

I would give the broad sweep of the First Amendment full support. I have the same confidence in the ability of our people to reject noxious literature as I have in their capacity to sort out the true from the false in theology, economics, politics or any other field. (Emphasis added.)

—William O. Douglas,
Roth vs. United States, 345 U.S. 476 (1957) *

LAWS GOVERNING EROTIC COMMUNICATIONS reside in a disaster area of history that is almost as old as law itself. In general, the wider the scope that is aimed for in discourse and behavior by a legislative system, the more trouble erotic freedom itself—in speech and in action—tends to create. Dictatorships and effective monarchies usually display little concern about the relationships of *law* to *sexual feeling,* however it may be communicated. The Mosaic code tells us simply not to covet our neighbor's wife at the cost of God's displeasure. And that, more or less, is that! The fact that I get an erection when my neighbor's wife in a bikini hangs up her wet wash on the lawn becomes pretty much a matter between God and me. Here is merely one other tyranny of nature (or of God's practical jokes), and I suppose that in a society governed by the law of Moses, what I choose to do about the matter as well as what my neighbor's wife chooses to do about *me* turn into non-negotiable legal matters. If I am caught breaking the Lord's commandment, I suppose I shall be expelled

---

* I have used the literary "vs." for all court citations, as opposed to the correct legal "v.," lest any reader mistakenly assume that I am either a lawyer or jurist.

from the tribe or community. This is the risk I run in a theistic dictatorship. Nothing—but nothing—can be done, either about my mischievous hard-on or about the way the woman next door looks when she puts her laundry out to dry, except personal exercises in self-control and decorum of dress and behavior. Here are matters peculiarly immune, most of the time, to legal niceties, because, explaining them crudely, they seem inherent to what laymen call "human nature" and are difficult—sometimes impossible—to control.

Difficulties arise and are compounded when increasingly subtle measures of freedom are added to social and cultural restraints, according to what the law says, what it does *not* say and how it is applied. These difficulties have historically (and continue to) turn into tornadoes of confusion in complicated cultures that regard themselves as "libertarian" and/or when restraints of law are bent back upon themselves to preserve some measure of anarchy, anti-restraint or, as we often call it, "freedom" to disagree with the law. Such laws are intended specifically to *restrain legal restraint*. I can offer no sane argument to deny that such counter-restraints are often necessary when a complex culture conducts its affairs in brambles and thickets of rules and regulations that govern (or impinge upon) almost every aspect of human behavior from birth to death.

Into this tangle must be introduced some legal prohibitions against restraint, if any small clearing is to exist and be maintained (even symbolically) for the exercise of free expression or behavior—in effect, a little patch of anarchy in a bureaucraticized universe. (A major irony here is that, as contemporary cultures move in the direction of this libertine construction of the word "freedom," the number and spread of legal restraints placed upon individual choice and behavior seem to correspondingly increase to an extraordinary degree.)

This problem is not particularly or entirely a curse of modernity, although there are few modern libertarian cultures that have managed to avoid it, those being perhaps one or two dictatorships and other kinds of oligarchies seen popping up at a rapid rate in the so-called "third world," where one does not look in law books for rules on free discourse or behavior but is able to "buy" the right by living "above the law"—either by special statute or by owning a submachine gun.

In seventeenth-century England, this paradox disturbed John Milton just as much as it has disturbed recent philosophers of freedom such as Sidney Hook and Zechariah Chafee; nor were James Madison and Thomas Jefferson unaware of it in an age that was infused with enormous faith—greater than ours today—in the rational side of man's nature as a social control.

One major historical and topical confusion that has certainly resulted from this self-evident irony when applied to the erotic domain is happily of equal discouraging concern (or blind-spot non-concern) to ardent libertarians *and* to conservative bluenoses alike. It is also, fortunately, a major

matter concerning both eroticism as a culture trait and erotic communications as they have been formalized by all the media we have discussed in Part I of this volume. It stems from the tendency—perhaps inevitable, perhaps not—so notable in Justice Douglas' words that introduce
the chapter (excerpted from a Supreme Court decision concerning the legal
protection of erotic literature)—for the law to regard sexuality *in action* almost entirely as if it were a socio-political vector of some kind.

This assumption is so general and widely accepted that it may often
be, as we shall see, both explicitly affirmed and implicitly denied in the
same paragraph by our wisest judges and solons, and nobody appears to
notice or care. From a pragmatic viewpoint, however, and leaving the
semantics of the matter aside, neither eroticism nor erotic communications
have, when the water boils out of the pot, *anything whatever to do with
freedom of speech, press or religion or any of the great libertarian instruments that we hold so closely to the heart of our tradition!* Nine-tenths
of the now multitudinous problems surrounding contemporary censorship
derive inevitably from an endemic misunderstanding of this state of affairs
and a grand yearning that things were somehow different, that is to say
pure voluntaristic thinking. The degree to which the reader at this point
thinks that the writer has suddenly gone mad is exactly the degree to
which voluntarism governs his philosophical notions of Western law.

The courts, again as we shall see, have, in the past generation, firmly
faced this problem of malconstruction and wild assumption by refusing to
admit it exists! "Obscenity," they repeat *ad nauseam,* "is not covered by
the *First Amendment,*" and it is therefore immune from any but backhanded legal protection. The question of whether obscenity can even be
defined will be discussed below. I, for one, think it most definitely *can.* But
let us grant temporarily that we know what it is. Let us call it for the time
being an "erotic itch," so that *you* and *I,* at least, know what we are talking about, even if certain lawyers do not, cannot or will not.

So—granting that the communication of an erotic itch by means of
words, print, picture, films, or whatever is not considered legally a class of
speech, the question remains concerning what indeed the nature of such a
message *is.* On one hand, libertarians and permissive liberals of various
sociological and psychological schools insist that it *is* indeed a form of
what we otherwise call "speech." Justice Douglas, I suppose, leads this
pack. If eroticism is indeed speech, it must then be considered a socio-political instrument, mainly because speech (and the communication of
speech) has been encodified as a special form of activity in our legal tradition because of its intimate relationship with vital social and political
processes, particularly in a state that considers itself a republic. Arguing
for the political significance of sexuality (in any of its forms) is and has
long been possible as a sort of psycho-historical conceit. But it is a pragmatically inert practice, leaving us with grand propositions such as argu-

ments about the relative sex appeal of John Kennedy and Richard M. Nixon or the Marquis de Sade's ravings in life and fiction concerning eroticism as an instrument of political power. (The latter's ideas have indeed influenced the work of fabricators of historical fiction and Hollywood epics.)

Far more puzzling is the fate of eroticism in all of its manifestations if we do *not* regard it as "speech." If my collection of porno photographs is not protected by the same law that guarantee my rights of self-expression, if *Hustler* and *Screw* are not true "magazines" and "*news*papers," if their editors are not "gentlemen of the *press*" and if Linda Lovelace and Jennifer Welles are not exponents of socio-political ideation, what manner of human communication *are* we dealing with?

An easy answer is "feeling," pure and simple. But there is an enormous difference between the communication of such "feelings" as pain or pity *per se* and the complexities of erotic communication. Also, the simple fact is that we are *not* dealing entirely (or necessarily mostly) with feeling alone. If we were, no claim that eroticism is indeed speech would be remotely possible. Pain and pity are each unique and certainly may be *involved* in the communication of authentic speech, which is duly protected by law. To accept some feelings as modifiers and to reject others is naturally absurd, so eroticism must therefore receive the same sort of legal recognition as other feelings, as well as the same rights to the same type of protection. To maintain, therefore, as all the high courts in our history have (with occasional dissents from men like Douglas), that obscenity is not speech helps jurists to handle individual legal contests at given moments, but the concept inevitably flunks even a freshman philosophy test. Excluding eroticism from one category (thought or feeling) means that it must be in another category, and here the juridical brain has failed us. Eroticism is thrown into a trash bin of mysticism, where most enterprises like art and poetry and emotion reside, because their relevance to social and political domains is rejected by jurists who neither understand nor appreciate them.

Worse still is the, by now, obvious truth that the whole problem is not a problem at all but a canard that simply does not exist except in juridical minds! If you want to pass a law in your community prohibiting the sale of "fruits" and then legislate that strawberries are not fruits, I suppose you can, if the courts will uphold your sophistry. What I mean is that free speech deals with a class of behavior that may well bump into eroticism every now and then but, in the main, has almost nothing to do first, with its nature and, far more important, second, with its function. No court in the world would, I believe, maintain that the expletives used by the participants in the Watergate scandals (and recorded on tape) were *not* of political significance and therefore not speech, but, at the same time, only a maniac philologist would claim that the word "shit" *taken alone* has

socio-political significance enough to be protected by the Bill of Rights—
for example, if it were, without explanation, written in five foot letters on
a billboard over Lafayette Park.

We end up with an intolerable situation—from a legal point of view.
Insofar as erotic behavior and communication are *entirely* erotic (that is,
concerned with feeling and sexual activity at the psychic and personal
level), they are not political vectors. They are not activities of the individual in his role as a *citizen,* although they may or may not impinge on any
and all sorts of social institutions and even be responsible for the genesis of
some of them. But eroticism is not part of the pivotal *function* of any of
these activities in terms of their socio-political significance. Kitchen stoves,
for example, are not results of man's appetites; they result from his perceived need, which is socially determined, to cook food, and are, when all
is said and done, cultural conventions. Men eat. But their kitchen stoves
are not a function of their eating. Eating is a function of cooking, and, let
us remember, one can also cook without a stove.

Like man's physical appetite and the satisfaction of it, erotic communications may occur in many (or most) dimensions irrelevant to legal
sanctions protecting free speech, just as other appetites may come and go
without the slightest relationship to a kitchen stove. In our civilization,
however, when one thinks of a balanced diet or a good meal, a kitchen
stove (or some sort of stove) is usually involved in the thought—so much
so that the ideas of "appetite," "eating" and "diet" may all involve stoves.
Reduced to bare essentials of living, we would probably include a stove
among the other necessities of life, like automobiles and flush toilets. Of
course, this idea of "necessity" is pure nonsense, but it is exactly the same
sort of nonsense that relates erotic communications as a legal entity to
libertarian ideas such as freedom of speech.

The Definitional Dodge

Because we do not create—and have not created—clear categories in
which to place eroticism, the conventional legal black or white solution to
the problem appears to most people reasonable, no matter how untenable
it is in fact. If eroticism (or obscenity, extracted from the larger universe)
is not speech, how can you tell where speech begins or ends, particularly
when so much that is obscene is identical with that which *is* protected as
speech, except that it uses different words and/or centers on different concerns or subjects. If obscenity *is* speech, by what rationale does the law
protect it, except that it *should* be protected because, essentially, some
(mystical) authorities say that freedom is good, or that people cannot fulfill their true destinies without freedom to act as they please—or similar
cant. What is lacking is a *reason,* a viable social and political reason, for
all laws that protect human freedom (create our clearings in the un-
derbrush) and that relate directly to the collective welfare of the majority

of citizens in a certain culture, not God's (or nature's) implicit or explicit commandments.

One does not need to be a juridical philosopher to comprehend that most legal confusion results from blatant statutory absurdity, from laws that contradict one another or from common behaviors that contradict laws. If our Supreme Court, at the present writing, is going to insist that race legally cannot be a factor in the selection of professional school students by university administrators, and, at the same time, uphold the constitutionality of so-called "affirmative action" (or academic admission preference) on the basis of race, we are obviously heading for trouble, the least dangerous part of which will be confusion. This does not mean that it is impossible to live with certain contradictions in law. Indeed we already do. But what is necessary is a willingness on the part of the public, the courts, the police and other keepers of the cultural flame to accept an *Alice in Wonderland* world and scrupulously avoid noticing that their beloved social institutions, however right or wrong, simply do not make sense at the outset. If a people are somehow induced to worry long and hard enough about the morality of a single, relatively trivial socio-political issue (from the budget of the CIA to the abuse of power by a Nixon), there seems to be little need to examine the basic rationality of the institutions that produced the issue in the first place. (in the instances mentioned, being first, the necessity for a counter-revolutionary intelligence agency like the CIA and, second, an ever-increasingly powerful executive arm of federal government.)

So it stands also with the problem of eroticism, which is neatly divided into two camps at the outset by the great majority of jurists: the many who would solve the "problem" of obscenity—as they see it—by claiming that it is not speech and therefore not protected by the Bill of Rights; and the very few (Legman and Douglas and who else? Henry Miller?) who claim eroticism damn well *is* speech, period. The latter group take recourse to folk wisdom and common sense. If it looks like a rabbit, hops like a rabbit, smells like a rabbit and eats like a rabbit, it is probably a rabbit—although, dear reader, it may be a wallaby. So great is the majority of our best thinkers who would exclude eroticism (as long as it is called "obscenity") from the First Amendment, however, that hardly a major free speech decision has come from our Supreme Court in the past thirty years that has not affirmed—in these or similar words—that "obscenity is not within the area of constitutionally protected speech or press." [1] Again, period.

One ploy by which it is possible to deal with most nonsense is to explain it or refine it in an absurd way, a fact that then makes either the explanation or the nonsense seem sensible. *If* one accepts the relevance of eroticism *per se* to speech *per se,* it then behooves those who take either side of the argument above—and if one argues at all, he must choose heads or tails in this matter at one time or another—to throw the entire matter into the sewer by claiming simply that it is *impossible* to define "obscenity" in any case. So what is the argument all about? Rules cannot be created if their objects cannot be identified and described.

Here we meet the cheapest shot in our legalistic discussion so far, mainly on grounds of 1) patent inaccuracy, 2) irrelevance, 3) lack of intrinsic sense and 4) non-utility. Yet, it is and has been heard many times, most notably I suppose in Justice Potter Stewart's famous 1964 short opinion in the *Jacobellis* case. Considering the matter of how the Supreme Court had been up to that time defining obscenity when related to specific books, he wrote:

> It is possible to read the Court's opinion in *Roth vs. United States* and *Alberts vs. California* . . . in a variety of ways. In saying this, I imply no criticism of the Court, which in these cases was faced with the task of trying to define what may be indefinable. I have reached the conclusion, which I think is confirmed at least by negative implication in the court's decisions since *Roth and Alberts,* that under the First and Fourteenth Amendments criminal laws in this area are limited to hard-core pornography. I shall not attempt further to define the kinds of material I understand to be embraced within that shorthand description, and perhaps I could never succeed in intelligibly doing so. *But I know it when I see it,* and the motion picture involved in this case is not that.[2]

How avidly have jurists and others clung since 1964 to the tiny fibre of Justice Stewart's uncertainty—or to his certainty that he would know pornography if he saw it! So would we all know it if we saw it, but the result of such a test is obfuscation, and jurists—like the public at large—know little about the languages of communication or communication by language. Yes, it is just possible that we *may* or *may not* be able to define "hard-core obscenity," "obscenity," "the erotic," "pornography" or any of the terms we have used so freely in this book for all people for all time, or even for some people at certain times, but the severe question arises as to how relevant the definition of anything is to its inclusion in or exclusion from an idea in law.

Part of the answer to the curious claim that obscenity and its relatives cannot be defined—and therefore may be neither excluded from nor protected by law, one assumes—is that much law is and has always dealt with poorly defined matters. But this is just one part of the answer, and the most obvious one.

What, in the name of Korzybski, are "rights" anyway, as the word is used in the Bill of *Rights?* At one time they included my freedom, almost on the top of the list, to own a gun in working condition without asking anyone's permission! I have no such unilateral right today—or rather the idea of "rights" has changed. I would like to hear the definition of "insanity" as "knowledge of right from wrong" defined with any precision. Cerebral knowledge? Emotional knowledge? My right? Your wrong? How much knowledge? How consistent? How deep? (Say, three minutes at four feet?) "Consent," I think, has something to do with rape. I should also like to see it clearly defined. Can a woman who may have enjoyed sexual congress in rape "consent" to her fucking after the fact? You bet she can, and I wonder how many women *do!* We shall never know. Show me a man or woman of "sound mind and body," and I will show you a deranged person (according to some "experts' " opinions) who is on his or her speedy way to the graveyard (and I may not need an expert—just common sense). Anyone who has ever served on a jury has wrestled with semantic cuties such as "premeditated" murder, especially when a time span between meditation and deed is not specified, but the notion of "spontaneity" is. But this could be a period lasting from a second to a generation, depending upon many factors.

Law built around notions of eroticism in any of its forms simply cannot replicate corporate law or contract law. It is social law and must deal with many of the gray areas that society itself must also ingest and deal with. In another but similar domain, I think I might join Potter Stewart in claiming that *I* know a "clear and present danger" to our republic when I see it. But my degree of certainty in no manner clarifies the haziness of this bewildering concept as applied to any *one* case; and so it has been since it was first articulated by Justice Holmes more than sixty years ago. What is important legally, I suppose, is that "clear and present dangers" to nations indeed *do exist,* like it or not, and they will continue to exist whether or not courts in the protection of a state against such dangers can define where to draw the line without creating the greater and simultaneous danger of legislated paranoia.

No reasonable claimant would declare, I think, that obscenity, pornography, and such *cannot* be *in some manner* defined. Anything, I suppose, admits of a definition even if, as the gawker said at Barnum's museum about the elephant he was viewing, "There ain't no such animal!" What is missing is a *good* definition or—to be more precise—so good a definition that neither experts nor judges nor juries nor any other human agency will be necessary to determine whether or not the item at hands fits the description. A litmus test! An atomic clock test! An absolute test! A *scientific* test!

Were we to demand such tests of the language used in nine-tenths of our laws, we would, I fear, have no laws. To request this much, therefore, of terms like "obscenity," "hard-core pornography," "scatology," is to ask for what, on one side, may be impossible. But, on the other, we require merely that such terms make as much sense as—or more than—other concepts in laws of socio-political relevance—terms such as "life, liberty and the pursuit of happiness," for instance, or "equality," to start a long list.

To observe, accordingly, that lawyers and jurists have done a particularly poor job in creating any sort of litmus test for the obscene simply reprises one of the major curiosities of law that so amused many clear-sighted Victorian and Edwardian Englishmen: that a large fraction of legal problems that face any state, particularly modern ones, are mainly linguistic and/or functions of language and meaning at a level so fundamental that one hesitates to call them "semantic." Psychology, as William James noted long ago, found a similar weakness in forensic medicine and eventually called it "psychosomatics" or "the mind-body continuum," in that "sickness" and "health" in these domains turned out to be mainly manners of speaking—for instance, when one deals with the enormous ephemera of "mental health" or with medicine's so-called "fight" against the perfectly normal and inevitable phenomenon of death.[3] Both medicine and law, of course, must court both obfuscation and professionalism by elliptical speech. But their confusions reach even deeper objectives, because these so-called "professions" must also deal with the ironies, confusions and caprices of the real world while maintaining, in public at any rate, an image of detachment—scientific or just snobbish.

One example in the present context: When Al Goldstein of *Screw* talks about obscene movies or the kind of cinema that left Justice Stewart wordless, he calls them "fuck films." Goldstein is neither a lawyer nor judge, but even a jurist would have no trouble comprehending the kind of cinema to which he is referring. I cannot, however, imagine a Supreme Court Justice, let alone a circuit judge, calling a fuck film a "fuck film." Legal reluctance to call something by a name that both describes and defines it is the same sort of chicanery that literally forced a noted dermatologist recently to call a nervous itch I brought him for diagnosis "neurodermatitis"—and to mail me a bill for twenty-five dollars for his services!

One therefore admires *any* jurist anywhere who even attempts to define terms like "obscenity," and, keeping one's eye on the doughnut rather than on the hole, must grudgingly respect the efforts the law has spent in this respect when compared to most other serious matters it attempts to parse in common English. Sir Alexander Cockburn, a linguistic victim of his times, showed more than a modicum of bravery in his attempt to articulate what became known as the "Hicklin rule" in British and American statute. Cockburn's definition of obscenity was misnamed (as most similar definitions are), because Benjamin Hicklin, the recorder of London and intermediate-appeals judge, found in 1867 a pamphlet called *The Confessional Unmasked, Showing the Depravity of the Romish Priesthood; the Iniquity of the Confessional, and the Questions Put to Females in Confession* outside the domain of British obscenity law at the time. In Part I, we examined the crudities of such law in the nineteenth century. But some question seemed to exist at the time as to whether the offending pamphlet was in specific violation of *Lord Campbell's Act,* a piece of 1857 legislation directed against the inundation of London with mass-produced obscene literature. The Act had been created by a Parliament that wanted to have its cake and eat it, not by outlawing obscene literature for the educated or privileged classes but by preventing its spread via the steam press to the impressionable masses.

Three aspects of the Act were notable, all of them for their libertarian thrust rather than for their puritanism. First, the legislation was directed only against printed materials sold in public shops that were available to the common man. *Underground* copies of *Fanny Hill* and her sisters (by this time, in fancy editions) were therefore safe. Second, obscenity was only considered present if the document at hand might corrupt the morals of the young, thereby exempting prolix, complicated or sophisticated works by and for educated men of letters. Third, some sort of judgment had legally to be made of the intensity and nature of the degree of shock that an offending document might engender in a healthy mind—once again, backhanded protection of pornography as upper-class amusement at the expense of the supposedly weaker, average man in the street.[4]

Recorder Hicklin could not see how the "Confessional" pamphlet came within the definition of obscenity implied in *Lord Campbell's Act,* nor why its distributor, one Henry Scott, should be punished. Like Potter Stewart, Hicklin indeed *intuited* that much of the pamphlet was obscene, but it was also an anti-Catholic tract written and distributed for the apparently honest but knavish and quite legal reason of undermining British popery. Neither was it printed to corrupt the morals of the young as, say, a similar pamphlet attacking the Church of England might. Nor did Hicklin think that it would disturb notably the equilibrium of the balanced mind. Only the fact that it was on *public sale* brought the document to the Recorder's Court.

Hicklin's judgment was far from naive, nor was it particularly "liberal" or "permissive" in today's sense of the words. The document contained exact quotes from anti-Catholic theologians of repute, some of it was written in Church Latin and at least half of it was, at most, mischievous propaganda. The rest was for its day pretty raunchy. So-called "dirty words" were used, and the supposed depravities of the Catholic Clergy in the privacy of their confessional booths was lasciviously described. On the basis of the fact that about half of the document was deemed highly erotic, the police (at the urging of a community organization) had arrested Scott and impounded 250 copies of the document.

On the basis of the fact that half of the document was *not* erotic, Hicklin ordered Scott's release and the pamphlets returned to him. Of considerable significance to the Recorder was the issue of *intent,* raised by Hicklin. Scott's *intention,* he felt, stemmed from a reasonable motive: to protest religious practices with which he disagreed in a forthright and honest manner. If, in his ardor to accomplish this end, he had to flirt with obscenity, the means were justified by his ends and Britain's tradition of free speech. (Hicklin, incidentally, had no English Bill of Rights in which to seek shelter; he had merely an accumulation of English law and tradition—mostly the latter.)

An appeal was brought to the Court of Queen's Bench, with Lord Chief Justice Cockburn presiding. Hicklin's decision was reversed. In framing his own decision, Cockburn was now forced to articulate the first *legal* definition of obscenity in British or American law of which I know, and to which every *legal* definition from that day to this has been, in one way or another, intimately related. Cockburn's reasoning, preserved in the record of his decision, constituted a nicely tempered analysis of cause and effect, centering mainly upon the fact that effect of any type might have nothing to do with its intended cause, but that the law, nevertheless, owed it to the public to protect it from effects irrelevant to presumed or apparent or intended causes; it is the same argument that today lies at the core of the anti-pollution and ecology movements in America. By way of illustration, a concurring colleague of Cockburn cited such precedents as "the case in which a person carried a child which was suffering from a dangerous disease along a public road to the danger of the health of all those who happened to be on that road." It was held to be a misdemeanor, without its being alleged that the defendant intended that anybody should catch the disease.[5]

The fact, then, that the central objective of the "Confessional" was anti-Catholic was not the problem to which Cockburn addressed himself. As to the importance of this primary objective, Cockburn noted:

> . . . (u)pon the grounds of motive the recorder (Hicklin) thought an indictment could not have been sustained, inasmuch as to the maintenance of the indictment it would have been necessary that the intention should have been alleged and proved, namely, that of corrupting the public mind by the obscene matter in question. In that respect, I differ from the recorder. I think that if there be an infraction of the law the intention of the law *must be* inferred, and the criminal character of the publication is not affected or qualified by there being some ulterior project in view (which is the immediate and primary object of the parties) of a different and honest character.
>
> It is quite clear that publishing an obscene book is an offense against the law of the land. It is perfectly true . . . that there are a great many publications of high repute in the literary productions of this country the tendency of which is immodest, and, if you please, immoral, and possibly there might have been subject matter for indictment in many of the works which have been referred to (in the previous argument).

Here the influence of Victorianism begins clearly to salt the flavor of Justice Cockburn's traditionally British reactionary broad-minded attitude until it becomes, somewhat reluctantly I imagine, inundated by the generally protective thrust of much other liberal legislation in this period and in the years to come, as well as by more than a dash of contemporary prudery. Cockburn forges ahead:

> But it is not to be said, because there are in many standard and established works objectionable passages, that therefore the law is not as alleged on the part of this (anti-Hicklin) prosecution, namely, that obscene works are the subject matter of the indictment; *and I think the test*

of obscenity is this, whether the tendency of the matter charged as obscene is to deprave and corrupt those whose minds are open to such immoral influences, and into whose hands a publication of this sort may fall.[6]

Nothing in Cockburn's decision should come as a surprise to us, except possibly that 1868 is late in the game for British law to react in such specific terms to the spread of erotic literature to the middle (and even lower) classes. Such material had been printed on steam presses for over a generation! Had Cockburn's court not attempted subsequently to define "the obscene," another court would surely have had to do so in short order. Victorianism's devils, be they men, women or ideas, had by this time to be concretized and symbolized most precisely, simply because it is impossible to wage a war against a faceless evil—particularly a war involving morals, fashions and freedom of behavior.

America's problems were somewhat different from those of the British, not because the intensity of Victorianism was felt less in the United States than in England, but because one severe legal obstacle had to be surmounted before censorship of any sort might have the force of law—and sheer definitional difficulties were puny when held next to it. I refer to the Bill of Rights and the plain, explicit wording of the First Amendment, especially the words "no law," "freedom of speech" and "the press." Under the influence of social danger—or perceived social danger—the Bill of Rights was not, nor has it ever been, an insurmountable obstacle to abrogations of the behaviors it supposedly protects. Where and when there is sufficient will there is a way to circumvent the most fundamental legal freedoms in every society man has known, including (and possibly especially) our own, yesterday, today and, it is safe to predict, tomorrow.

Definitions be damned! Not to hang our courts up upon the snares and barbs of trivia, we eventually borrowed Cockburn's definition from England. Instead of an urbane jurist, we in the United States produced, as an instrument of definition-by-doing, the monomaniacal Anthony Comstock. He was born in 1844 in Connecticut, a Congregationalist by religion and a veteran of the Civil War, and died in New York City in 1915.

Comstock was neither a jurist nor a politician nor an elected official nor a writer of much erudition or skill. He was simply a man with a mission.[7] He also possessed enough gall, as I think Dorothy Parker once said, to be divided into three parts. Whatever he accomplished in life was powered by his enormous faith in himself and sheer nerve. Few men find their way into the dictionary, but the word "Comstockery" did—into some dictionaries, at least—and this alone is no mean feat of excellence and/or uniqueness.

Unique Comstock was, even in Victorian America, but he was also very much a product of his time. As a young man, employed merely as a clerk, he formed, in 1872, a coalition of Protestant leaders in New York City (among them J.P. Morgan) and the YMCA in order to organize, first, a Committee for the Suppression of Vice, which was later to be known as a "Society." Comstock himself became its secretary, a post he maintained for the rest of his life. Not a sophisticated British jurist, Comstock could not be and never was much concerned with niceties of definitions of terms like "obscenity," "art," "eroticism" and so forth. What he *was* concerned with was "vice," pure and simple, and vice, like the devil, has powers to assume many pleasing shapes.

Not only did Comstock know vice when he saw it, he knew it when no one else saw it, and he set himself to extirpate it in his fine Puritan fashion. How interesting to note that, although Anglican influences were essential for the Victorian climate in which Comstock thrived, his style was much like that of an early Puritan fanatic, a nineteenth-century Cotton Mather or The Protestant Ethic incarnate but gone wild! Neither Catholics nor Jews, by and large, avidly supported him or the Society. Comstock's success and national influence was largely related to the true-blue WASPish American Establishment of his day. In other words, he spoke the same language as the power elite.

Comstock yearned for results, and these he achieved. In his way, I suppose he managed to define the term "obscenity" for all practical purposes in the United States until about World War I. In 1868, New York State had forbidden traffic in "obscene literature" (no definition, of course). In five years, using his home state's nebulous legal action as a wedge, Comstock had lobbied so vigorously for his cause in Washington that his great legacy, the "Comstock Postal Laws," were passed by Congress and subsequently became laws of the land. Although they related only to materials carried through the United States mails, their influence upon our culture at large was enormous and amorphous, and it continues to the present moment.

The so-called "Comstock Laws" deal specifically with "mailing obscene or crime-inciting matter," although they reflect an amazing lack of interest in just what either "obscenity" or "crime incitement" are. Nineteenth-century legislators, like legislators today, apparently contented themselves with the knowledge that judges and juries would have somehow to dissect and parse these matters. The legislation itself was filled with endless—and near meaningless—definition by synonym, as I choose to call it. Thus we find endless sentences describing literature that is "obscene, lewd, lascivious, filthy, indecent, immoral" and so on "and (literature) that may incite arson, murder, assassination or produce abortion" and such. Such materials were, of course, banned from the United States mails, and suitable heavy fines and prison sentences were meted out to those who were found guilty of mailing them.[8] Although modified over the years in countless ways, our postal regulations still echo the hysterical voice of Anthony Comstock, because these laws remain the skeleton upon which postal regulations regarding appropriate carriage for the country's mails still hang.

Comstock himself was lucky enough not to outlive America's need for him. He spent most his life in pursuit of "vice." His Society lived after him, almost up to the present era, when its fires were finally spent and its mission over. He crusaded at every forum available to him against the sin he saw in art, in society, in education, in classical literature—in fact, everywhere that obscenity might raise its head, which was everywhere! Comstock's career was lucrative and his fame (or notoriety) was enormous. He was energetic and indefatigable. But Comstock finally went to his grave quite literally never having known what he had been talking about all his life—as a new generation of jurists was about to discover.

How could so powerful a force as that exercised by an Anthony Comstock gain such power and last so long clinging so ardently only to a nebulous notion of "vice"? Once again, I must note that in life (and law) one does not require precise definitions in order to make crucial decisions, as anyone who has ever married (or divorced) anyone with whom they fell in (or out of) love knows. A typical legal approach to a problem of corruption at the time—and in some places today—may be extracted from an obscure obscenity decision written by a judge in the New York State Court of Appeals *as late as 1884,* many years after Britain's Hicklin rule. It is typical of the temper of the times, and it resonates Comstockery:

> It does not require an expert in art or literature to determine whether a picture is obscene or whether printed words are offensive to decency and good morals. *These are matters which fall within the range of normal intelligence,* and a jury does not require to be informed by an expert before pronouncing on them. . . . The question of whether a picture of writing is obscene is one of the plainest that can be presented to a jury, and under the guidance of a discreet judge, there is little danger of their reaching a wrong decision.[9]

All of the above, mind you, was written in the absence of any operational definition or set of criteria by which to judge obscenity, decency or offensiveness! In terms of results, before and since, such legal sophistry not only works, it works *often,* and, quite possibly, the law cannot function without it.[10]

Death by Definition

I think my case has been made (for the most part) in support of the fact that one of the great legal mistakes in this century was (and continues to be) taking too seriously in court Potter Stewart's (and others') feelings of confusion when faced with eroticism in certain manifestations and then forcing the courts to deal with what they see and feel in a purely definitional context. As much as I abhor both psycho-history and (worse!) psycho-legalistics, I am inclined to suggest that Stewart and others in the same fix feel deep confusions regarding obscenity that are linguistic, semantic or legal only *in part,* and that the rest is, or may be, panic, guilt, pain in pleasure or pleasure in pain, "politeness or spleen" (in I. A. Richards' phrase) or something else irrelevant to their roles as mediators of justice.

Nor has the law tried all possibilities, if the search for a definition does continue to the present day, (and I am not so sure that it does, except halfheartedly). Many things may be defined by what they are *not.* How else does one efficiently describe a catatonic mental patient, a (supposed) extra-terrestrial object or the state that matrimony reaches much of the time before husband and wife seek a divorce? Although I have some juridical blood in my veins, I shall not be tempted to square any circles at the moment, but the erotic photograph of two men and one woman I am holding in front of me while I write this is as notable for what it is *not* as for what it *is.* (I would not ask my publishers to reproduce this gem, but it is a graphic color photograph of an attractive redheaded female being screwed anally and vaginally at the same time by two young men, an unsolicited advertisement, incidentally, sent to me through the mails for a silent, Super 8mm reel of motion picture film.)

I grant that the picture is manifestly prurient, as far as *I* am concerned. Like Potter Stewart, I know what it is when I see it, and, presumably also like him, I know this largely because of specific genital commotion men (and women) often feel when they see photographs of this type. (We shall take up the problem of exactly *what* women feel in Chapters 9 and 10.) But this sort of test, as we know, gets us nowhere. The picture itself has, however, certain negative qualities which *may* be helpful in defining its nature and status as pornography. (Despite the interest—and obvious pleasure—I take in it, I must classify it as both "pornographic" and "obscene"!)

1. It is aesthetic junk—a snapshot.
2. Because it is posed, it lacks spontaneity and, most important, it looks it.
3. The individuals involved are blatantly ignoring their own rights to privacy regarding critical functions of their bodies.
4. The sex act depicted is outside the limits of normative behavior.
5. Its major function is neither cognitive nor emotional response but apparently commercial reply.
6. It does not address *me* in my role as a citizen—or in any other role, for that matter, except as a physically mature male human being.
7. It manifests no assumptions of dignity insofar as essential factors of masculinity or femininity are concerned. Both are exploited as fully as possible.
8. Sexuality is, insofar as one sees in the photograph, related neither to love, reproduction or pleasure. (The men are grim; the girl looks pained—and probably is!)

9. The photograph accomplishes nothing cerebral or emotional for me *except* genital commotion (a hard-on). It was apparently intended to accomplish nothing more, not only for me but for anyone else viewing it.
10. The photograph displays little continuity with real life, current or past, fiction or social reality. The people are anonymous and severed from the society and culture in which they were born, will live and will die.

Now, I grant that some fairly innocuous and innocent photographs may accurately be described as I have described the one above—in part. I also grant that Potter Stewart may have seen films, read books or seen photographs that do not apply to my statements above, again in part. On the other hand, the photograph is so lacking in value (not just social value but aesthetic, cognitive, mischievous and, except for prurience, emotional value) that, upon second thought, I would not insult my readers' intelligence and sensitivities by even *implying* to my publisher that anything about it is relevant to this chapter, any more than I would ask him to include a blank page in a book so that you can see what nothing looks like!

Now, I grant also that these negatively oriented characteristics cannot precisely *define* obscenity (or any of its relatives) in ways that jurists like to have things defined. But, as we have seen, society does not create categories to please jurists or civil libertarians, philosophers or scholars. What I am driving at is that, given certain parameters of meaning, it is perfectly possible to create criteria for literature, art, photography and any and all means of communication that relate to some—or all—of the issues I have listed, and to articulate more that may be relevant to some other picture, prose or poetry under *other* circumstances in *another* time. Then it is possible to note what *that* particular communication fails to communicate—or what a judge, jury, critic (or group of them) *thinks* is *not*, but should be communicated by it. Let me admit that we are here dealing with definition by consensus, in much the same way as we define such qualities as "greatness," "respectability" and even "social utility." But many definitions in law rest ultimately on reasonable consensus and serve quite satisfactorily, if and when the *criteria* for those consensuses are clear enough.

When the criteria are not clear, we are in trouble, and positively oriented criteria present us with the most trouble. For example, Justice Cockburn's assumption that obscenity must "deprave and corrupt." This is an equivocal notion on face, largely because all of us must indulge in behaviors that would be obscene if they were fully communicated to others in the rounds of daily life, as I have noted. What Cockburn's criterion had, however, was the virtue of simplicity, and that is all.

By the twentieth century, naturally, other ideas had crept into the original definition of obscenity, and *all* of them, as we shall see, were more or less useless, finally rendering the definition so narrow as to apply to nothing—not even my porno photograph—and leading to the eventual canard that obscenity is impossible to define. Obviously, obscenity is neither impossible to identify *nor* to define, if we know reasonably well what we are talking about ("I know it when I see it!") and if we approach it by looking at what it does *not* accomplish as a human communication rather than what it *does*.

One such complex notion—and one of the most absurd—is the concept, derived from French law of *l'homme moyen senseul,* which, for reasons that would be out of place here, relate better to French culture (and language) than to ours. The concept boils down in plain English to the idea of referring judgment to "the average man," whoever and wherever he may be. After 1933, the accepted definition of obscenity in the United States was bounced against "the average man"—in law, almost invariably. Almost invariably the results were disastrous.

In 1869, Justice Cockburn *could not* have used the average man as his authoritative auditor of possible obscenity. Too many privileged but more or less "average" Victorians would be caught in the trap, and so Cockburn concentrated on the effects of obscenity upon, presumably, those who might be "depraved and corrupted" by it, whether or not they were average. One of the most interesting aspects of the personality of our Victorian gentlemen (Chapter 4) known as "Walter" is precisely how average he seems to think he is, and, his sex life aside, how average he was.[11] By the middle thirties, with a different climate obtained, tests for obscenity began to be measured, in court and elsewhere, against broader social backgrounds than just depravity and corruption.

The first major American use of the "average man" idea (in the context of obscenity) is found in Justice John Woolsey's famous *Ulysses* decision.[12] This in itself is odd. Little in the novel, James Joyce's *Ulysses,* was aimed at the "average" reader of novels. It was—and is—caviar for the General, but Judge Woolsey, in attempting to determine whether or not the book (which puzzled him) was obscene, asked two friends to read it in order to confirm his opinion that it was not. They agreed with him. "It is only with the (n.b.) normal person that the law is concerned. Such a test as I have described, therefore, is the only proper test in the case of a book like *Ulysses,*" he wrote. (Note that Woolsey's initial legal construction of "normal" turned into "average" in short order. In any culture, there are, of course, far fewer "normal" than "average" people.)

Upon appeal, *Ulysses* and Woolsey's decision went to the Second Circuit Court of Appeals, where Justices Augustus Hand and Learned Hand agreed with Woolsey, Justice Manton dissenting.[13] Augustus Hand, in his well-known affirmation of Woolsey, emphasized a point that may or may not have been implicit originally in the Hicklin rule: that the work should be judged as a *totality.* Thus, he concludes that the dominant nature of the volume probably will not promote lust in the reader—of course, the "average" reader. Even in Manton's dissent, the point seemed implicit. To disregard the effect of the book upon its likely readers would, in his words, "show an utter disregard for the standards of decency of the community as a whole and an utter disregard for the effect of the book upon the *average,* less sophisticated member of society." [14] Farewell to normalcy!

As of 1934, then and therefore, any definition of obscenity would have to apply to the *effects* of the item in question upon the *average* man, both a process impossible to demonstrate and a witness impossible to locate! How remarkable, however, that both conservatives like Manton and liberals like the cousins Hand could agree that this particular criterion was not only relevant, but it was germane to locating eroticism in law. How great a blow this definitional desecration of the Hicklin rule would be to judicial Comstockery might well have surprised all four jurists involved in the liberation of Joyce's Molly Bloom. In building up a definition of obscenity, what was naturally happening was that positive criteria for judgment (that were legally logical and semantically sufficient unto their own day) were beginning to be piled one upon the other like layers of baklava crust. That these criteria were impossible to test against hard (or soft) evidence in the real world seemed to be noticed only by a few. Fewer still observed that, despite their judicial vocabulary and authority, they were also nonsensical.

In a way, the entire legal structure surrounding obscenity of all sorts was at this time being set up for Justice Stewart's exasperation thirty years later! But it did not stop there. Death by definition is an evolutionary process.

The idea of "averageness" had now to be *socialized,* another step in judging the positive characteristics of obscenity that had been impossible for Justice Cockburn to conceive of—just as impossible as it is for me to make much sense of 110 years after *Hicklin.* The law however forged ahead. Eroticism, obviously, was a function not only of individual temperament but also of cultural consensus, a proposition covered in the early chapters of this book. To speak, therefore, of obscenity in a nudist colony is quite different from talking about it at High Mass at Saint Peter's in Rome—just as eroticism is different today in almost every part of the Western world from what it was two generations ago. If we want to understand our own erotic natures, we must consider this fact, and it is certainly a legitimate cornerstone to the comprehension of erotic communication.

On the other hand, this relativism is not a firm hook upon which one can hang a definition of obscenity, mainly because, among many reasons, an infinite number of cultural and subcultural groupings create infinite variations of possible obscenities. Eroticism, therefore, must lie on some sort of continuum, which is different even for the individuals who make up a single group—say a family—as different as the morning of youth from the darkness of old age. We are back again trying to create averages where none can be measured, even if they exist.

James Kirkpatrick, a clever student of censorship and law, singles out 1935 as the year when, in Chicago and New York, a number of obscenity actions were thrown out of court because jurists could not comprehend how the accused documents violated what were becoming known as "community standards." [15] But it was not until as late as 1954 that "contemporary community standards" began forcefully to intrude into legal constructions of obscenity as standards according to which a court of law was supposed to act. This is not to say that this idea had not been unstated but understood in a number of obscenity decisions before then. It had indeed. But it was specifically cited by a California District Judge in denying the claim of a postmaster that some "girlie" films transported by mail violated the Comstock Laws. Unlike many judges involved in such actions, Ernest A. Tolin actually looked at the films and wrote a common sense essay about how standards change in different times and places and concluded that these movies were certainly worthy of "community acceptance." He warned, however, that if films such as these promoted the "general corruption of morals" they would not be mailable, because postal regulations were subject to all of society's notions of morality at any given time. [16]

Finally, the Supreme Court set for itself two nearly impossible positive hurdles in a brave attempt to articulate once and for all a clear definition of obscenity. One was literary-artistic and the other was psychological. If man's laws, in their long and majestic history, have at any time clashed more fiercely with any two epistemologies similar to those involving artistic—particularly literary—criticism and the study of human thought, feeling and behavior that we call "psychology," I cannot think of when or where. Nor—with a few exceptions—am I able to think of any organized body of college graduates potentially *less* competent to make cogent judgments in these domains than the hundred or more jurists who have graced the high bench since 1789 to the present! Also—and I hate generalizing about any professional group—I cannot imagine many kinds of education *less* likely to sensitize a man or woman's artistic-literary and psychological perceptions than one in the law as taught by nine-tenths of the law schools in the United States during the past half century.

Yet, in my experience, neither ignorance nor lack of perception has ever diminished the reformist energies of lawyers, politicians, teachers and writers! Where Justice Cockburn had been most circumspect in his use of the words, "whether the tendency of the matter charged as obscene" is corruptive, American jurists wanted either to nail this tendency to the wall or to discover its shortcomings for certain and to *prove* the results of obscenity upon those exposed to it—whatever they might be. Thus did our courts begin looking for "dominant themes" in works of literature and art, and courts and juries were requested (harking back to *Ulysses*) to look at *gestalts* rather than at this part or that part of various works taken out of context.

These, of course, are reasonable literary and artistic requests. They are not so reasonable as *legal* requests, simply because precise measures of themes of books, plays, paintings and films do not exist and, in many instances, are matters of opinion. What on earth is the dominant theme of *Alice in Wonderland?* Of *The Devil in Miss Jones?* Of *The Picture of Dorian Grey?* Of *Paradise Lost?* Of van Gogh's self-portrait? Of *Man and Superman?* If I must judge everything as a whole, every part of it is equal, then, to every other part of it—unless I can prove otherwise! In this matter, I can only offer opinion but not proof. Instructions to juvenile delinquents on how to steal automobiles or grow Deadly Nightshade plants at home may then be neutralized in a magazine that also includes recipes for fudge and instructions for leading elderly ladies across the street! Taking such controversial books as *Mademoiselle DeMaupin,* Marie Stopes' *Married Love, Ulysses, Strange Fruit* or the writings of William Faulkner, James T. Farrell, Calder Willingham, D. H. Lawrence and Henry Miller as a "whole" became an automatic legal reflex by the end of the fifties that did not even eventually require the services of a literary critic. To the untutored, the impossible in matters such as these not only becomes possible, it becomes simple, and as such it was achieved pretty much by formula.

But the creature "wholeness" strangles itself when, for instance, one examines a well-made pack of pornographic playing cards, each showing a porno still in perfect color. One may still play Patience with the deck, do card tricks and/or anything and everything that can be done with any other deck of cards. Forgetting for the moment any moral judgment we may make of such a deck of cards, the words "taken as a whole" (with or without "dominant theme" considerations) catch in the throat—if indeed we are building a definition of obscenity! No, in point of fact we are *unbuilding* a definition. The *dominant* theme of *any* pack of playing cards is their function as playing cards, quite obviously—an artist might be able to argue otherwise but certainly a lawyer could not. Taken as a *whole* (and with a nod to Gertrude Stein) a pack of cards is a pack of cards. Anyone who denies this is fit for what our courts used to call an "alienist." To define, therefore, a "proper" deck of cards is, of course, impossible. In the history of playing cards, too many kinds of designs have at various times been "proper" for us to accept any one as superior to another.[17]

A deck of cards is not a novel, a film, a drawing or a photograph; as an example of an art or craft or the work of an artisan, it is a relatively uncomplicated cultural cluster of symbols when compared with most novels, films, drawings and even many photographs, especially, I think, in regard to whatever its "wholeness" or its "dominant theme" may be. The rainstorm of ambiguities let loose, therefore, by literary-artistic criteria of this sort in the courtroom pointed eventually in the direction of chaos and finally to absurdity. Almost anything, taken as some kind of "whole" or another, is a significant culture trait of the society that produced it! Sigmund Freud found no end of symbolic and cultural importance in the meanest of dirty ethnic jokes (especially the "sick" variety), and, taken as a "whole," the scatology of small children is not unrelated to the cultural tone of adult society, a point that writers such as Richard Hughes and William Golding have made so well in the past few decades that it is now a truism.

In law, the concepts of "dominant theme" and "wholeness" found their first and fullest acceptances by a major national judicial body in the Supreme Court's *Roth–Alberts* decisions of 1957, which are discussed below.[18] It was not until 1966, however, that both ideas joined in chaos and curdled into absurdity.

In a famous decision, officially known as *Memoirs vs. Massachusetts,* we meet our old friend *Fanny Hill* again, apparently none the worse after well over two hundred years of circulation.[19] The burning issue of 1966 was whether Cleland's classic was obscene or not, which by this time meant simply whether the book was eligible for protection by the First Amendment. While similar broadside issues came up in other cases before the high tribunal, they had yet to be clarified as neatly as they were in this case. The Attorney General of the State of Massachusetts had brought *Fanny* to law before a Superior Court judge who found her exploits indeed obscene. Now, in the light of the accepted "dominant theme" and "wholeness" doctrines of the *Roth–Alberts* case, the high court had to decide one matter and one matter only: the "obscenity" of *Fanny Hill.* If, among other criteria noted above and below, the dominant theme of the book was *not* obscene, *Fanny* could pitch her tent—or make her bed—protected by the umbra of the Bill of Rights.

The six judges who voted to absolve *Fanny Hill* of prurience recognized clearly the importance of their judgments. There existed no shortage of so-called "literary" evidence that had been offered in the lower trial and had been sniffed at in court. The book was by now a classic, sometimes even studied at universities. It was *probably* a work of art, although we had not in the sixties (and have not now) a clear legal definition of "art," but the idea of "erotic art" was as much in the air at the time as it is today. The Court fancied itself liberal, but certain problems nevertheless arose when they applied the "wholeness" and "dominant theme" tests directly to Cleland's masterpiece. *Fanny Hill* still, they recognized, *might* be obscene, *particularly* in regard to its dominant theme and the author's unrelieved pursuit of prurience. In order to eliminate any doubt, therefore, they thought to close the door finally upon the matter by an explicit statement of what these two ideas mean *for legal purposes.* What they did not—and could not—realize was that they were building a time bomb that would consign their precious notion of *obscenity as non-speech* to virtual oblivion! Only Justice Douglas in his concurrence and Justices Clark, Harlan and White in their dissents seemed to sniff hints of the trouble ahead.

Justices Brennan, Warren and Fortas, joined silently by Black and Stewart and grumpily by Douglas, forged ahead.

The mountain labored and what come forth may have looked like a mouse, but it was a mean and dangerous little critter. The decision set the scene for the one major *legal* question about obscenity that still remained to be answered: "Why bother with censorship at all, when nothing on earth or under the sky could conceivably be judged 'obscene' by the criteria—lawyers criteria—set up in *Memoirs?*" What might this grand pronouncement conceivably be? Simply the, by now, chilling and familiar wheeze that in order for something to be "obscene" it must also be, in Brennan's words, "utterly without redeeming social value!"

The mischief word in both law and logic lay, as I have noted, in the word "utterly." With this phrase, a legal structure that for better or worse had taken ninety-eight years to develop from *Hicklin* to *Memoirs* came tumbling down, or so it seemed at the time. Is that photograph I was looking at a few pages ago "utterly without redeeming social value?" Of course not! *Any* photograph, because it is a photograph (a record of reality) must have *some* social value, and so must a book, mainly because *somebody* wrote it. (Some lawyers cited the correct pagination of books as a socially significant quality!) All movies, even Uncle Albert's out-of-focus mementos of your family picnic, have *some* kind of social value. If I say "fuck you" to a policeman, the social value of my statement is immediately obvious. Once again, in a world of chaos, all specific examples of anything are absurd—and endless. Certainly freedom of discourse in the United States had been widened immeasurably by this idea. Whether this principle has ever helped any student of erotic communications to clarify any of the mysteries he or she faces is, as lawyers say, "moot."

Finally, the Supreme Court turned to psychology in asking, as a critical criterion of obscenity, that films and literature—or any other communication—appeal to *prurient* interest. We already know that prurience is an itch, and the word "itch" as used here constitutes a reasonable metaphor. So, in my opinion at any rate, the court fared slightly better in the world of psychology than it did with art and literature—but not much better. The idea of "prurience" (or its metaphor) had, quite clearly I think, been present in the "depravity" and "corruption" criteria of Cockburn's *Hicklin* decision but only—and wisely—in terms of results that were not regarded by lawyers, teachers or parents to be quite as equivocal in 1868 as they are today. In fact, it is hard to find an obscenity decision in either England or the United States during the past century that does not, in one way or another, question whether the overall effect of the item under consideration might raise an erection or start the "itch" in most people (Again, normal people? Average people?) exposed to its stimulus.

Here we are faced with a perfectly valid psychological question that cannot have a valid psychological answer, unless hedged by such statistical terms as "empirical" or "normative"—both of which create more problems than they solve. Even as late as 1966, the year of *Memoirs,* publisher Ralph Ginzburg was convicted of pandering to the public itch by soliciting subscriptions for his various publications (*Eros* magazine, *The Housewife's Handbook on Selective Promiscuity* and a newsletter *Liaison,* all weak tea by today's standards) by means of lascivious mail-order promotion; this meant, in effect, that the promise of the advertising implied that the documents on sale were obscene and therefore appealed *to* prurience.[20] (The nature of the publications themselves were not the issue, and their status as obscenity—a doubtful one—was beside the legal point.) A close Court decision (5–4) upheld Ginzburg's conviction as a purveyor of *promised* prurience. He was fined and sent to jail.

But these late cases mattered little in the long run, mainly because the definition originally articulated in the *Roth–Alberts* case in 1957 had already managed to undefine "obscenity." It had set the profession of the censor on the same path that the trade of the blacksmith had taken years before. In fact, considering the speed at which the Supreme Court was murdering clear, legal criteria for obscenity, it is possible to argue that even the *Roth–Alberts* definition was less important than it seems, considering all the patching and filling and fancy footwork the Warren Court was forced to do in its wake during the next ten to fifteen years.

The term "obscenity" was heading for the same (or worse) legal hell as the word "insanity." The latter was legally meaningless in Britain until 1843, when a British court defined "legal insanity" as a "knowledge of right and wrong." It is on this perilous, thin and foolish thread of intellect that hang to this day determinations in the English-speaking world of whether or not a killer—or anyone else—may be held responsible for his or her acts. The "M'Naghten rule," named after the first murderer sent for a cure rather than a hanging, was widened somewhat in 1954 by the United States Court of Appeals to include "mental disease or defects" in its ambit, but the original definition in effect still stands. Its weakness is generally accepted by legal experts, who definitely do *not* know "madness" when they see it! Unlike "insanity," "obscenity" was murdered by scrupulousness and over-definition, and the killing was more brutal but possibly also quite "insane" in a legal sense.

On one hand, the scrupulous—and to Justice Douglas, unwise—exclusion of any speech, erotic, pornographic or exploitative, from the First Amendment set the stage for a slaughter. While I find the logic of Douglas' absolutism difficult to follow, he made an important point in an ironic way. To exclude *anything* from the protection of free speech in a permissive cultural climate, where almost any kind of speech somehow manages to get itself into public discourse, renders the exclusion eventually meaningless. A similar problem faced our law-enforcing—and eventually law-making—institutions in regard to the Eighteenth Amendment, which prohibited the manufacture and sale of liquor in the United States—as we have seen. The greatest harm done by prohibition was not to guzzlers who went blind drinking bathtub gin but to both the Constitution and collective popular respect for our police and law courts.

Much the same phenomenon occurred, Douglas says again and again, to obscene speech (or much of it) when it was defined as irrelevent and therefore outside the realm of protection by the First Amendment, that is, non-speech. Other kinds of speech that general consensus has long agreed should not be so protected—mislabeling, libel and even, under certain circumstances, private or confidential speech—ran into no such problem. In these matters courts could operate by reasonable, although sometimes tricky, definitions in order to obtain rough justice without damaging respect for and belief in the integrity of the Bill of Rights.

Over-definition produces different kinds of problems, and, because they are logical ones, it is difficult to understand how and why even the liberal Warren Court backed so neatly into them. Any type of fairly abstract mental phenomenon, the identification of which must meet an infinite number of indefinite criteria, will eventually cease to exist! Purists, for example, who argue that dramatic tragedy died with the Greeks of Athens are quite correct, *if* their criteria for dramatic tragedy are certain unique qualities displayed by three particular playwrights, all of whom lived within a few years of one another. Catholicism's claim to being the "true" church rests upon a similar definition, as does the Greek Orthodox Church's; similar are the Hebrew's argument that Judaism represents pure monotheism and the Moslem's conviction that Islam purified (by over-definition, I think) Judaism.

One is ready to forgive the religious their (possibly necessary) non-logic, because religion operates in the domain of faith, not social utility. It is more difficult to rationalize the progress (or regress) of the *Hicklin Rule* to the *Roth–Alberts* rule, which states in a roundabout manner, via Justice Brennan, that the test of obscenity is: "whether to the average person, applying contemporary community standards, the dominant theme of the material taken as a whole appeals to prurient interest." [21] Add to that the inevitable qualification that the speech, print or film in question must be, *a la Memoirs,* "utterly without redeeming social value," and "obscenity" disappears about as neatly as Harry Houdini used to get out of a padlocked trunk. Now you see it, now you don't.

The results of *Roth*—or, more properly, the cumulative results of the Warren Court—on erotic communications are difficult to determine, so few years having passed since the Court's intentions were clarified and began sending shock waves into American life. As we shall see, these vibrations became part of a cultural admixture during a period of moral revisionism. They coincided with changes in attitudes toward the old game of masculinized feminism, the politicization of homosexuality, scientific progress in birth control and abortion, as well as with apparently revised attitudes (particularly among the middle class) toward educational reform, artistic adventure in literature and cinema and with new manifestations of interest in certain erotic matters on the part of academics. The latter was felt especially among sociologists and psychologists, as well as in the medical field, mostly because of increasing fractionalization of numerous schools of psychotherapy, one of the sharpest schisms of which centered on the domain of sexuality. In all these matters, cause and results are twisted and mingled beyond present comprehension, and each also relates to national affluence, to our so-called "drug culture" and to most of the other social fireworks by which recent history has been read.

A critical power shortage in Norway during World War II that turned off all electric lights and radio broadcasting at dusk is said to have increased the number of births considerably, just as poverty in India may also easily be blamed for that nation's population glut. Changes in erotic behavior have throughout history often occurred as side products of this or that more or less irrelevant social change. Main currents of erotic communications respond to—and are responsive to—ever more subtle sorts of cultural stimuli as time passes. Man's quest for justice via law is but one of them.

Morals, Attitudes and Laws

If the agencies of amusement and art could recover a sense of the dignity of their social function, that of restoring vagrant feeling to a free acceptance of the good, the instinct of regulation—like an awkward gesture for recovering lost balance—would be put to rest.

—William Ernest Hocking

To SIT IN A CORNER with a plum pie and repeat the old chestnut that you cannot legislate morals does justice neither to art, poetry, or society. One hears one or another version of this negative truism in classrooms, from pulpits and in bull sessions with increasing frequency these days, but, as an aphorism, it goes back to fairyland, a retelling in modern dress of the story of Jack Horner, who affirmed his own goodness with a plum. As Michael, of today's fairyland in Mart Crowley's play, *The Boys in the Band,* says "one thing you can say for masturbation . . . you certainly don't have to look your best." In heuristic terms, one thing you can say for solipsism . . . you certainly don't have to worry about whether or not you make sense! Things have been the same in most fairylands for a long time.

I know of no period or place in the history of the West since the end of the Middle Ages where the law as an institution was actually able to keep squarely abreast of social change, or, for that matter, needed to. One of the more attractive aspects of the contemporary Kristol-Buckley "hip" conservatism is a recognition of this state of affairs, as opposed to the belt-line liberal's faith in law as a method of curing social evils that run all the way from venereal disease to poor housing to premeditated homicide.

Not only does our law run in kitty-and-tail circles regarding the drug-taking habits of our teenaged children (if pot and booze can be called

157

"drugs"), but I myself have to finesse an obsolete, complex legislative mouse maze in order to obtain sufficient quantities of the various medications that a physician has chosen for me to keep my blood pressure and metabolism in balance, all the while paying said leech a gigantic fee every time I need a prescription filled. What is most infuriating about this legislation is both its recentness and obsoleteness in its naive attempt to cure social evils by exacerbating them—which is also a solipsism if ever there was one. In 1909, my late father could buy morphine at almost any drug counter in the country, and, while addiction rates to hard drugs were higher in his youth than they are today, addiction was not regarded as a *social* problem amenable to the manipulation of law and therefore "legally" curable. In fact, hard-drug addiction was not one bit more curable in 1910 than it is today, but, by and large at present, different sorts of people get "hooked" on different sorts of drugs in different ways.[1]

Most negative wisdoms leave as residue merely broken rice cookies, little pieces of paper and nothing else. Money cannot buy happiness, naturally, but so what? On the positive side, comedian Joe. E. Lewis used to say that he would rather be miserably rich than poor, and I think he was nibbling at a profound truth. Regarding the law, we are living in an age of deep and telling experience in which we are discovering, issue by issue, all the things that laws *cannot* do in the personal, social, economic, artistic and philosophic domains of life. Every time we discover that some aspect of our faith in legal instruments is misplaced, we are nonplused for the moment but undaunted nevertheless in our faith, which I imagine is all for the best in the long run.

At the moment, for instance, we are discovering that the economic aspects of industrial culture are less amenable to legislation and manipulation than many economists working between the two world wars had thought. Milton Friedman, among others, seems to be slowly teaching us that we cannot "head off at the pass" recessions, inflations, booms and busts by means of Keynesian devices. The mechanisms we are trying to control appear to be steered by energies of extraordinary drive and a sense of direction akin to forces in the natural world—an eighteenth-century idea that was lost in the shuffle of the cards of history and recently rediscovered with glee by some and ruefully by others.[2]

I believe that it was A. N. Whitehead who first made the claim that changes in symbols are not only inevitable results of revolutions of all sorts but also relatively benign substitutes for revolution itself, where and when issues have not yet peaked to the point of rifles and grenades.[3] Laws and statues and regulations of most types are anti-anarchic instruments of a similar nature, though they are not as subtle or effective as symbolic ersatz revolutions. But, because we have faith in them and because many (maybe most) are enforceable to some degree, they function as conservative instruments for maintaining the general conformations of the *status quo* by preventing its violent upheaval.

Thus did the multitudinous agencies and executive actions of Roosevelt's so-called "New Deal" insulate America against the socialist-communist revolution into which she was apparently plunging in the thirties. To call Roosevelt, who was the archenemy of reaction and conservatism in his day, a reactionary or *instrument* of conservation seems hyperbolic. But one exaggerates little by noting that he and he alone made America safe for Wall Street, its cigar-smoking chairmen in executive boardrooms and the fat cats after World War II by heading off an impending revolution by means of laws, federal programs and legislation that were damned roundly as inchoate communism in their day.

The infamous Watergate affair shows us the flip side of the coin. Neither Nixon nor his co-conspirators were involved in acts of treason or up to dark mischief much more devious than I have seen eaten whole and swallowed by supposedly ethical administrators at numerous schools, colleges and universities. Nor was "Tricky Dick" notably trickier than the clutch of reporters and writers who, in ways still unchartered, broke into and exploited the Watergate nightmare. What *had* happened, however, was largely symbolic, and it portended in the consciences of both the public and the politicians of the right and left what *might* have happen if the spirit of the Watergate cover-up had succeeded and progressed from the oval office into other divisions of executive government, a point that Nixon himself, I imagine, simply cannot in good faith comprehend to this day. At the highest levels of government relatively simple laws of conduct were flouted in the face of an ad-libbed and ever-changing concept of "executive privilege," which did not exist!

The sense that was communicated to the public, the press, the Congress and even many of Nixon's supporters (myself included) *on the face of things* was that mischief in the oval office signified that the binding power of law was coming undone at a level of state where, in its symbolic way, it should *appear* at least to be inviolate and deserving of absolute respect. Oddly enough, the worst of the initial scandal (barring eighteen-and-a-half minutes of tape recording we know nothing about) was not too serious and was certainly not incommensurate with the way various other Presidents had used and abused executive powers; it did not involve any genuine "stonewalls" or "smoking guns" but only metaphorical-symbolic ones. Seen in this light, Nixon's resignation and pardon was indeed a shrewd deal, the alternative being, possibly, not only an impeachment but a hanging and a possible revolution with both genuine stone walls and smoking guns at the end of the trail.

I do not believe that I have chosen a particularly long-winded way to illustrate the exquisitely delicate relationship between law and morals as they interact in society today and perforce have always interacted where and when the personal conduct of people—from presidents, dictators and kings to bricklayers, mendicants and entertainers—has been judged by criteria of law for purposes, broadly speaking, of rewards and punishments.

Of course, morals cannot be legislated, if, as it seems, parameters of police (and/or presidential) power cannot be effectively assured. But positive aspects of the morals-law relationship make better and, I think, more sensible reading.

What the law *can* do is prevent such massive misunderstanding of right and wrong and good and bad in a particular culture so that all morals turn inward and function without the appearance—not necessarily the statistical truth—of consensus. In their simple way, laws are the ideals by which any or all of us should be able to measure the success or failure of our personal morality. For this reason, the pseudo-Hemingway notion that morality depends on what "feels good" may be a dangerous notion —to the degree that consensus as to what does or does not "feel good" to differing but important portions of the population *cannot* be judged and/or evaluated according to consensus *and* shared values. Note please that consensus alone means little or nothing, especially when that consensus is based on average (not normal) behavior as gleaned by survey and manipulated by statistics. In this sense, therefore, Kinsey's evidence about the ubiquity of certain sexual practices did not, as he claimed in his second (and final) study, generate a mandate for moral change. It simply indicated that changing times were around the corner. So they were.

Episodes of homosexual behavior *may* indeed characterize the average behavior of males and females in the United States at one or another phase of life, but in no sense does this mean that homosexuality is (or should be) regarded as either normal or moral. Were the vision requirements for drivers' licenses reduced to the average (not normal) eyesight of American men and women, our highways would see much more carnage than they do now! Were the attitudes of the average American as he prepares his federal income tax form translated into a moral norm of fiscal rectitude, I would fear strongly for the future of capitalistic private enterprise.

I cannot here pass judgment on the personal moral problems posed to individuals either by their homosexual yearnings and activities or by the inconsistencies of custom and law that they may face in pursuing what seems to them God-given appetites and destinies.[4] I am able, however, to sympathize with the sense of danger that is felt by the community at large when homosexual behavior, either male or female, is given ever wider and wider *legal* sanction and therefore symbolic cultural approval. Many well-meaning people caught up in movements such as Gay Liberation frequently do not fully understand that the last thing they require is so-called "liberation" from outworn *moral* codes. This they have and have had for a long time in much of the West.

What they are looking for is *legal* sanction of their private and public behavior. This is another matter entirely, and it is not solved by posing as an oppressed minority group—as if homosexuality, an abnormal, deviant but near-ubiquitous (at some time of life) and apparently benign way of achieving erotic pleasure is somehow politically equatable to racial, religious or doctrinal inheritance and/or choice. Not so! Jews, Blacks and women are born Jews, Blacks and women, and the matter is hardly open to controversy. Religiosity may even be pathological, but one usually converts to a different church because of faith and or conviction, not because of some as yet unexplainable psychosexual roulette game that obscures the etiology both of fagdom and lesbianism.

In other words, the moral nature of homosexuality, among other things, falls largely into the private, not public, domain of right and wrong. Just as you cannot legislate morals, you cannot un-legislate legal parameters of immorality, if both consensus and common values do not accept the assumptions upon which such legislation is based. In a smaller social domain, for instance, the recent removal of homosexuality as a mental illness (whatever that is!) from the roster of a medical association's behavioral disorders neither helps nor hinders nor changes the moral problems that face either *one* homosexual physician (the impetus for the reclassification) or countless others, whose behavioral and emotional disturbances bring them to psychiatrists. Not one bit! Some years ago, one of the finest diagnosticians in New York City had an equal reputation as a well-known homosexual, but it proved a matter irrelevant to his medical reputation and subsequently enormous practice. Even to single out the late Dag Hammarskjold as a great *homosexual* international figure seems absurd—as absurd as similar epithets hurled (mostly as insult by innuendo) at the late John Edgar Hoover; such "slurs" neither help nor hinder his reputation or place in history.

As far as I am able to determine, few, if any, civilized societies have been fully satisfied with the so-called moral "codes" that church, state and tradition have handed to them and by which individuals are supposed to live. Therefore, there is nothing particularly modern—or even twentieth century—about the multitude of "new moralities" through which I have lived in the United States, among them, war morality, the above-mentioned "tough guy" or Hemingway-Hammett morality, beat and/or hippie moralities (with their Eastern infusions of arbitrary mysticism), the moralities of boom and bust, the Nixon morality, the "new permissiveness" and so on. Nor is there anything unique about our time and place in the margin of difference that makes us feel—the young among us particularly—that our morals or the morals we bespeak are somehow at odds with, first, those morals by which we actually live and, second, moral imperatives provided by law.

This is precisely what made both the "hawks" of World War II and the "doves" of the Vietnam era such laughable figures in the long haul, having predicated both their desire for blood and guts in one case and peace and love in the other upon appeals to law in the name of crimes against humanity. Both "peace in our time" in one case and "senseless slaughter in a corrupt war" in the other were slogans—pure cant and greasy hypocrisy. While peace is and has always been supposedly the highest moral virtue about which we talk (and for which we legislate) in the West, we remain almost continually at war. In the same vein, while war is forever justified by making the world safe for something (or someone) or protecting innocent women, children and/or minorities, it remains the ultimate human outrage that invariably produces chaos and destruction as bad or worse than that which it is preventing or avenging! Problems of war and peace are simply the most obvious members of a large family of moral inconsistencies—"psychopathologies" they have been called by Erich Fromm and others—to which men have had to adjust their lives and behaviors during most of recorded history.

Morals and Basic Rights

As I ruminate about the corruptive nature of erotic communications and about the distances between professed idealism in life and law, I cannot but pause for a moment to evaluate some of my own sins and moral hypocrisies, which are necessary passports, I tell myself, for survival in a psychopathological world. My problem is (just as it is the problem of others who have attempted to qualify their own eroticism in terms of morals) the comparatively benign and harmless nature of that behavior and a sense of the irrelevance to morals of even the most arbitrary capricious and (possibly) damaging parts of it. Illegal abortions, broken hearts and ribs, mild venereal diseases, broken hearts and promises (possibly the worst items on the agenda) and intolerance of the sensuality of others all seem strangely innocuous at my age and as nothing compared to the short training I received in my youth to function as a brutal killer of other human beings. For this tiny period, dreamlike now in memory, I managed to sever psychological connections between what I believed, what I said I believed and what I knew were laws regarding human life. Yet I played the game with curious avidity. Thank God, I was never put in the position of having to kill anybody! I would probably have done it. Possibly I would even have enjoyed it without a twinge of moral discomfort, having fallen under the spell of facile slogans, political propaganda and institutionalized lies.

Certainly, like most of us, I have been subject to wide doctrinal moral swings over the years. But my own behavior reflects the simple influential roles that law and art and education play in the process of acculturation. While law and morality keep their distance one from the other, I think that they keep a stable distance in stable societies, and when they change they all change together. If, in a given culture, the three vectors—law, morals and behavior—all run along at about the same extent of alienation, one from the other, as generation moves into generation, such a culture has, I think, a good chance of surviving. Since the industrial revolution, however, and with opportunities for social mobility newly opened to large groups of people in America and Europe (and now in the so-called "third world"), such stable relationships have become exceptions rather than rules, posing the question, correctly I think, of whether present types of industrial cultures can endure very long. Like Jacques Ellul, and for many the same reasons that he gives, I cannot believe that the modern industrial state has much capacity for longevity, if the legal, moral and behavioral supports upon which it rests shift their relationships with every exigency of economics, science, fashion, invention and sheer mischief.[5]

In the last chapter, we observed the dramatic ways in which American democratic idealism has attempted to keep pace by means of law with moral and behavioral change, in the end apparently overshooting its mark to the degree that the law itself has opened the door to a number of things: further moral change for one, and a severe boomerang reaction for another, which is discussed later, primarily in Chapter 11. A far clearer illustration, but I fear a less dramatic one, may be found in the history of motion pictures in the United States and in their discreet relationship to the First Amendment of our Constitution.

While this is a story that has been told many times, it is archetypical of how the three cultural vectors of law, behavior and morality must (and do) both adjust and repel one another in the contemporary state. Causal factors are numerous, even in this limited domain, but the outlines of change themselves are clear, demonstrating the responsive nature of both law and morals to behavior as well as the reciprocity between them.

Motion pictures were a technological miracle, a curiosity, a business and a form of entertainment during the first decade of their life. Neither their inventors, exploiters, entrepreneurs nor performers had a clear notion of what they might become. Shortly after the turn of the century, a movie was enough of a curiosity to compete with performing seals as an act in a vaudeville show. Strollers along the boardwalks of Atlantic City or Brighton might stop to see peep shows, the contents of which, naughty, nice or historical, were always short and mercifully silent. These films (and some, at first, were made to synchronize loosely with primitive cylinder recordings) usually fell into one of a few categories: a popular performer doing an exerpt from his act, a photographed vaudeville turn, a sexy performer, such as a belly dancer or a bathing beauty, or an event of historical importance, such as the swearing in of a President or the signing of a treaty.

By 1905, the first motion picture parlors or theatres began catering to customers who might sit for an hour or longer and watch various short subjects (rarely longer than ten or twelve minutes) that flickered before them on bedsheet screens. During the next ten years, these modest parlors turned into the famous "nickelodeons," and after 1912 it was possible to view longer movies in legitimate theatres, seats to which were sold by reserved ticket. We know, of course, that underground erotic and pornographic films flourished during this period, but they were of little public concern. Films that were popular—and therefore made money—tended to center upon romantic melodramas, western adventures, farce comedies (by 1915 Charles Chaplin was an international star), the dramatization of sensational news stories, scandals and a sprinkling of historical dramas and classics with well-known stage actors.

That such cinema fare should, from its earliest days, attract the attention of civic groups of censors, local Comstocks and even state legislatures on moral grounds may seem strange when one views them today, particularly considering the generally liberal and free-spoken atmosphere in which the legitimate theatre, vaudeville and print media of the time lived.[6] The reason is similar to the reason that eighteenth-century British pornography did not become a legal problem until the middle of the nineteenth century. Neither vaudeville, theatre nor print offered direct access of their corruptive powers, whatever they were, to the young, the uneducated, or, in sum, to those whose defenses against corruption were not, it was understood, fully developed. Because of their silence, the immigrant part of the population, often illiterate and uncomfortable in English, found the movies an especially satisfying and economical form of entertainment in the cities where many of them settled. Children enjoyed them for much the same reasons.

As early as 1907, New York, a city rapidly filling with a lower-class population from Europe, instituted a haphazard system of film censorship. By 1909, censorship was affirmed by Chicago law, being directed specifically at two western movies, *The James Boys* and *Night Riders*. While eroticism was not the issue, the court wrote that these films represented "nothing but malicious mischief, arson and murder. They are both immoral, and their exhibition would necessarily be attended with evil effects upon youthful spectators."[7] The court noted as well that current standards of obscenity and morality were quite adequate as guides to the "average person" in judging such movies. Censorship was upheld.

State censorship laws directed at early movies such as these go back to 1911 in Pennsylvania; following was similar watchdog legislation in Kansas and Ohio in 1913 and in Maryland in 1916. New York State, incidentally, was not among the first states to set up boards of censorship for undesirable films. The reason that such a licensing law was delayed in New York for five years appears to have been the faith of certain civic leaders in an organization called the National Board of Censorship (later the Board of Review), which was designed to avoid legal pre-censorship by exerting pressure on the film industry to produce only "clean" films. The Board worked—and had a long life as a rating agency—but it came to be funded shortly by movie people themselves and, after World War I, no longer satisfied those who looked for a sieve finer than the one that a suspect industry itself applied via its own agency to standards of decorum in films. New York State began licensing films in 1921. It has the distinction of being one of the *last* states to stop licensing them, at a time when the legislative underpinnings of state control over the exhibition of films fell apart fifty or so years later.

By 1915, the problem of film censorship had reached national dimensions. Although D. W. Griffith had not yet released his epochal *The Birth of A Nation* and Cecil B. DeMille was still a neophyte director at work on a silent version of *Carmen,* movies were attracting wide and serious nationwide attention. Like most media innovation and inventions, they were viewed by many with suspicion—less for what they actually portrayed than what they might portray. They were popular with children and thus blamed by some for juvenile crime. For many, they obviously were substitutes for older forms of entertainment and amusement such as theatre-going and reading. In their attempts at comedy, they inevitably flirted with the risque and sometimes with scatological humor, real or implied. Love themes involving beautiful girls and handsome men constituted the spine of much movie fare from the start, just as they do today. Physical beauty and attractiveness became one desideratum of film stardom (not the only one!), and sexual attraction, it was clear, was the most powerful plot motivation that writers and directors could exploit in many ways.

With a mass audience apparently demanding to be stimulated emotionally in many ways by these early films, the appearance on the floor of the House of Representatives of the Hughes Bill of 1915 merely confirmed what was obvious. The bill, defeated in the light of simultaneous Supreme Court action regarding burgeoning state censorship, was a remarkable proposal; its intention was to set up a Federal Motion Picture Commission (similar to the later Federal Radio Commission and Federal Communications Commission) to regulate *all* motion pictures at the national level before they entered interstate commerce. The unborn FMPC was to be an arm of the Department of the Interior and would issue licenses to those films that were fit for Americans to see![8]

Granting a perceived necessity at the time to censor films, no such harsh mechanism as a federal commission was required. The states, it seemed, were perfectly willing, even anxious, to do the job themselves—providing, of course, they had a constitutional aegis to act as prior censors and licensors in regard to movies, despite the fact that they had no such right regarding printed literature or anything correctly called "speech." The theatre—except for pure "exhibitions" like freak shows, circuses and rodeos—was, and had been since the passage of the First Ammendment, in a quasi-legal category all its own, one that was not fully tested until recently, and even today has possibly not been tested thoroughly or enough. As we shall see, a live stage show is not only a form of *speech,* it is also a form of *behavior*—the behavior of living human beings in a certain community at a certain time. (A genuine assault or murder, therefore, that is part of a wild or screwball theatrical performance, cannot be immune from the law because it is part of a theatrical performance. We shall eventually examine this problem, which is shared in part by professional and amateur athletics such as boxing, wrestling and baseball.)

The main question facing censors, would-be censors and filmmakers alike was, in 1915, a relatively simple one: whether or not the movies fell within the province of the First Amendment—that is, whether they were speech—and, if they did, whether they were protected as is speech by the Constitution.

The answer, given by the Supreme Court in the famous *Mutual Case* was unanimous and unequivocal.[9] Granting the *nature* of the movies to which the justices addressed themselves in 1915, one can find little fault in their reasoning, which was clearly expressed in Justice McKenna's rejection of the Mutual Film Company's claim to First Amendment protection in the face of Ohio's attempt to pre-censor its products, as well as of a claim that the free-speech guarantees in the Ohio State Constitution itself were traduced by said censorship. The Court's landmark decision, which was to effect the development of films in America in many ways for many years, was relatively brief. Here are its salient points:

> (Motion pictures') power of amusement and, it may be education, the audiences they assemble, not only of women alone or of men alone, but together, not of adults only, but of children, make them the more insidious in corruption by a pretense of worthy purpose or if they should degenerate from worthy purpose. Indeed, we may go beyond that possibility. They take their attraction from the general interest, eager and wholesome it may be, in their subjects, but a prurient interest may be excited and appealed to. Besides, there are some things which should not have pictorial representation in public places and to all audiences. And not only the State of Ohio but other states have considered it to be in the interest of public *morals* and *welfare* to supervise motion picture exhibitions. We would have to shut our eyes to the facts of the world to regard the precaution unreasonable or the legislation to effect it a mere wanton interference with personal liberty.
>
> Are moving pictures within the principle (of the First Amendment) as it is contended they are? They, indeed, may be mediums of thought, but so are many things. So is the theatre, the circus, and all other shows and spectacles, and their performance may be thus brought by the like reasoning under the same immunity from repression or supervision as the public press—made the same agencies of civil liberties.
>
> As pointed out by the District Court, the police power is familiarly exercised in granting or withholding licenses as a means of their regulations. (State decisions cited.) The exercise of the power upon moving pictures has been sustained. (State decisions cited.) It seems not to have occurred to anybody in the cited cases that freedom of opinion was repressed. . . . The right of *property* was only considered as involved. It cannot be put out of view that the exhibition of motion pictures is a business pure and simple, originated and conducted for profit, like other spectacles, not to be regarded by the Ohio Constitution, we think, as part of

the press of the country or as organs of public opinion. They are representations of events, of ideas and sentiments *published and known,* vivid,
useful and entertaining no doubt, but . . . capable of evil, having power
for it, the greater because of their attractiveness and manner of exhibition. It was this capacity and power, and it may be in the experiencing of
them . . . that induced the State of Ohio to require censorship before
exhibition. . . . We cannot regard this as beyond the power of government.

It does not militate against the strength of these considerations that
motion pictures may be used to amuse and instruct in other places than
theatres—in churches, for instance, and in Sunday schools and in public
schools. Nor are we called upon to say on this record whether such exceptions would be within the provisions of the (censorship) statute, nor to
anticipate that it will be so declared by the state courts or so enforced by
the state officers.[10]

There are obviously many ways that McKenna's words may be interpreted. First, he was dealing with movies at their crudest and in their infancy: short films for the most part designed like circuses to amuse and
shock. Second, McKenna was operating in a near total vacuum of a
knowledge of cause and effect. Contemporary McLuhans at the time were
busy heralding movies as the eighth wonder of the world, a new language,
an educational instrument and a revolutionary hypnotic! If they were
right, films certainly had corruptive powers undreamed of by the authors
of the Bill of Rights. Third, they seemed to appeal to *all* the population
and especially to the most impressionable part of it—the young, the uneducated and women. Fourth, by analogy with live amusements, they
seemed also to stimulate audiences by means of corruptive example via *behavior* rather than by means of *ideas.* Fifth, the apparently suspicious face
of the motion pictures *business* was seen first and foremost by the Supreme
Court. Although McKenna has been over the years roundly and deeply attacked by scholars and jurists for this *apercu,* motion pictures *were* indeed
involved in more shady business manipulations—from manufacture of
equipment to patent rights, exhibition rights and cut-throat competition—
than the far older publishing industry during the preceding decades.

The clearest assumption running through McKenna's arguments—and
here I have no doubt that he was speaking for the entire Court—remains a
moral one, pure and simple. Nineteen hundred and fifteen may seem a late
date for the United States Supreme Court to formalize its position as a
guardian of public morality, but we must remember that the *Mutual* decision pre-dated the Prohibition Amendment by only two years. Women
were soon to be enfranchised to vote. In many ways (enough to fill a hefty
cultural history), legal instruments were being adjusted to the widening
distance between law and moral change that had already occurred in much
American culture during the slow fade-out of a great deal of Victorian idealism. In this respect, in the *Mutual* decision the Supreme Court felt it had

some obligation to the forces of reaction as it moved against what it saw as further and pernicious moral change that just *might* result from allowing motion pictures the same sort of freedom that the press was granted by the Bill of Rights. Whatever his failings, McKenna (and the Court) knew clearly the difference between right and wrong in the face of the law. The unanimous nature of the decision proves that little disputation—and not a single dissent, even from Holmes—would be stirred up in responsible circles by a common sense affirmation of what seemed then to be a basic constitutional delimitation.

Was the Court wrong? We know that a later Supreme Court reversed the *Mutual* decision, not once but a number of times, with increasing insistence. Most subsequent analysis of *Mutual vs. Ohio* tries to excuse McKenna for his fearful misreading of the nature of motion pictures, a misreading due to their crudeness and silence during what has been called, oddly, their "age of innocence." The possibility exists however that, entirely from a moral perspective, McKenna was (and is) quite correct about the moral dangers inherent in what David Manning White later called "the celluloid weapon," although McKenna could not possibly have comprehended the fact that there was nothing the judicial arm of government could do to prevent moral change in the long run, and certainly not by using the blunt instrument (in this instance) of the First Amendment against the powers of state censorship, as we shall later see.

Censored or uncensored, during the next forty-five years movies were, in fact, to have a profound effect on the morals of the United States, if we are to believe the sociologists and psychologists who claim that Hollywood films had wide-ranging effects upon both people and institutions in our culture.[11] Like all claims to causality regarding moral change, arguments and disagreements arise concerning whether this influence was good or bad. One thing is certain: Censorship as practiced by the various states could not stop it, nor could self-censorship by the Motion Picture Association of America in Hollywood (an organization of powerful producers, distributors and exhibitors) nor, especially and most notably, could the Supreme Court of the United States, who tried by means of its simple (and possibly naive) decision that films were neither speech nor an organ of the press and therefore not protected by the Constitution.

To my eye (a usually sympathetic one where hindsight is involved), McKenna was more correct than incorrect. What he could not comprehend, however, was that the Supreme Court, America's most potent instrument of control by check and balance, was simply fighting an inevitable rear-guard action in trying to maintain a prior but changing distance between morality, law and behavior as it was being expressed by means of motion picture technology. It took more than four decades for the distance between these three forces to become great enough for the law to be revised to meet moral codes that had changed and for the Court to attempt to address itself to reality. The only question that remains is whether by doing so a majority of the justices of the Supreme Court did or did not overcompensate for what they clearly considered a previous misjudgment.

Changing Morals and Changing Rights

One of the most amusing—and amazing—stories in recent constitutional history is the sticky, arbitrary and downright spooky way that, first, films crept under the legal umbrella of the First Amendment; second, how old structures that had treated them in old ways began to crumble; and third, how, with almost dreamlike hesitancy and in slow motion, this new freedom slid past the initial moral boundaries that were assumptively drawn for it and into glorious confusion. [12]

Here we discover a Court reversal, a change in legislative powers and a moral revision in law that are all fascinating mainly because they apparently lack the impact and power, say, of the Supreme Court's reversal of its previous stand that education might be "separate and equal" in the *Brown vs. the State of Georgia* decision of 1954. The latter almost immediately caused high drama to be written on the stage of history and began a stream of social and legislative civil rights actions that continue to this day, (attended by violence, much rhetoric and even assassination and murder). While its effects eventually may turn out to be as deep, lasting and permanent as those wrought by *Brown* (for right and wrong, good and evil, says the moralist), the result of the reversal of the *Mutual* decision was nearly the antithesis of the explosive civil rights mini-revolution set off by *Brown*—although in its way, it may also have legitimized a subsequent mini-revolution that would have happened anyway.

I cannot parse this history in the detail that it deserves; I can only indicate its main outlines and the moral climates through which it occurred. I need not dwell upon the technological and aesthetic developments of movies between 1915 and 1952, except to note that during the first twenty years after the *Mutual* decision, films developed into sophisticated devices for communicating dramatic and documentary events—if one considers faithful color reproduction as the last *major* development in the technology of modern cinema at mid-century. By 1935 (others would claim by 1930), most Hollywood films were comparable to plays, newspapers, books and other means of communication in their *potential* power to deal with the kind of ideation that the First Amendment was designed by its authors to protect, because the political power and influence of movies, again *potentially*, was by now beyond dispute.

A fair question at this point is why still another twenty or so years had to pass before the Supreme Court took notice of this fact, and thus allowed the *Mutual* decision to stand for so long.

The answer is complex, relating in part to a far from perfect judicial system that is an adequate instrument for dealing with *responses* to social and legal change but far more slipshod when it comes to *initiating* such changes, whether they be necessary or not. Powerful financial and commercial forces held strong interests in maintaining what eventually proved to be illegal monopolies (in Hollywood and New York) in the production, distribution and exhibition of American films. In effect, these powers were used in various ways, by means of trade associations, lobbies and other (mostly) political pressures, to maintain the status quo in the film industry and to keep the Justice Department (and, of course, the Supreme Court) at arm's length from the corporate boardrooms of filmland. Once the issue of commercial monopoly was brought into the federal courts, the adjacent issue of First Amendment rights would almost certainly be raised as well.

Filmmakers, wisely from their own point of view, knew that the reverse might also be true: Once legal inquisition into the constitutional rights of filmmakers, distributors and exhibitors found their way into the courts, further inquiry could easily elicit embarrassing questions about the legal and commercial obligations to law of these same wealthy entrepreneurs. This trade-off in silence lasted for about a decade before it even began to disintegrate. It took another ten—possibly twenty—years for the dust to settle to the degree that it caused the exact commercial upheaval that the filmmakers feared.

The major reason for the delay, from the judicial point of view, however, centers once again on the matter of public morality. In its long history, the American judicial arm of government has been more often than not a conservative force when it set itself to protecting the spirit—if not in the letter—of the First Amendment of the Bill of Rights. Considering the extraordinary and powerful influences of various social, political and even therapeutic movements that have changed and modified our ideas of government, economic and social justice and human rights (both to property and to happiness) that began, roughly speaking, at the time of the French Revolution and continued through Hegel, Marx, Darwin, Freud and up to the blander ideologists influential today in these domains, the Court has done a superb job. Resistance to new and conflicting "truths" that came and went and swayed, not only public opinion but the best academic thought in Europe and America, was, of course, necessary to maintain our eighteenth-century faith in rational republican (more-or-less) democratic government in order to prevent it from being plowed under by enormous and attractive new doctrines, which had shattered many older epistemologies during the preceding two centuries—most of them, in one way or another, by-products of science, and most of them, therefore and inevitably, somehow at odds with one another.[13]

In the face of so much revolutionary or near-revolutionary ideology, it has been a tendency of the judiciary (except in time of war or when the court has been "packed" with ideologists of one sort or another) to disturb the *status quo* as little as possible except where to do so might cause long-term harm to the Constitution as an instrument of law that binds our people, states and federal government (executive and legislative) into reason-

ably compatible companions. Of the many, many aspects of national life
to come into its ambit, I think it is safe to say that the ones that have
always presented the most difficult challenges to our Supreme Court are
those that have had to do with personal morals: those rights and wrongs
that have always been a mixed bag in so plural a nation as the United
States from its earliest days. In fact, I harbor a strong suspicion that many
of our finest constitutional jurists have tended to equate such moral domains of personality, belief and behavior primarily with the issue of religion. This being the case, any sort of legal determinations in regard to
morals fall—and have always fallen—*somewhere* inside the territory of the
First Amendment to the degree, at least, that they are related to "conscience," as the word is used in its theological sense.

Where and when morals broke the bonds of the First Amendment and
began to impinge upon the professed rights and wrongs of others or led to
illegalities, the amendment's implicit protection could not apply to them,
any more than it could to such "religions" as the Black Mass, which incor-
porated federal and state criminal acts into its practice. By and large, however, when moral matters have come up before the high bench, they have
been greeted with strong stony silence, the one great exception in American history being the reluctance of the Court to find the Prohibition
Amendment unconstitutional, which might have been possible but certainly would have been difficult in its time.

All of this is grade school talk for political scientists, but it provides a
background for understanding why the Court held back for so long a
change that seemed both reasonable and inevitable: that motion pictures
receive the direct protection of the Bill of Rights like any other form of literature. No congressional agency (like the FCC) acted for government in
licensing filmmakers, writers, directors or actors, which would have complicated the issue. The path was clear for the Court to act. But it did not,
as I have noted, because of strong influences within the cinema world, and
also because the sudden admission that the *Mutual* decision had been in
error might open for the Court a flood of moral problems it felt unable to
deal with effectively, or so it believed. That is, until 1952!

Not unexpectedly, it was indeed a religious issue that opened the Bill
of Rights door its first few inches for the cinema. Again in hindsight, I
think that the impetus *had* to come from the domain of religious freedom
as specified in the First Amendment, mainly because no other distinct *type*
of speech or print *is* specified in it except *religious* speech and print. That
is, the amendment singles out religion as immune from congressional legislation or, by implication in the Fourteenth Amendment, similar interference by any of the individual states. (Certainly, *true* speech, *witty* speech,
erotic speech or *boring* speech are not specifically mentioned in the Bill of
Rights, nor is the *political* press, the *fiction* press, the *scholarly* press or the
magazine press specified. The only *kind* of communication mentioned—
and that by implication—is *religious* communication. Of course, speech

and print are merely implied in the words "respecting an establishment of religion," but I know of few "religions" that can be "established" without utilizing both in one way or another.)

The issue before the Court in 1952 was the right of New York State's then perfectly legal board of censors to prohibit the showing of one sequence in an Italian film trilogy called *The Ways of Love. The Miracle,* one of the short films, was a simple and touching little story, beautifully played by Egyptian-born Anna Magnani, of a feeble minded peasant woman in Italy. She is raped, and, in the hysteria of the birth of the baby that results from her violation, the woman becomes convinced that she is the Virgin Mother and that her illegitimate child is the infant Jesus. Although the movie was made in 1950 and had played in Rome without offending the Vatican's film reviewer, its opening caused a storm among many New York Catholics. The New York censors (its State Board of Regents) withdrew the license it had previously given *The Ways of Love* on the grounds that the one sequence was "sacrilegious." "Sacrilege" was specifically spelled out in New York law as proper cause for film censorship.

That the Supreme Court *had to* find the New York censors—and therefore part of New York State's code of censorship—unconstitutional is of course significant, because this was the first hard chip chiseled away from the constitutionality of state and city pre-censorship of films. But this is more or less beside the point (and importance) of the decision as it relates to the domain of morals.

Justice Tom Clark, writing (once again) for a unanimous Court, cited a host of reasons for striking the word "sacrilege" from the censorship codes of the state and then, quite out of the blue and with amazing and uncharacteristic certitude, swung into the following observation:

> The present case is the first to present squarely to us the question whether motion pictures are within the ambit of protection which the First Amendment, through the Fourteenth, secures to any form of "speech" or "the press."
>
> It cannot be doubted that motion pictures are a significant medium for the communication of ideas. They may affect public attitudes and behavior in a variety of ways, ranging from a direct espousal of a political or social doctrine to the subtle shaping of thought which characterizes all artistic expression. The importance of the motion pictures as an organ of public opinion is not lessened by the fact that they are designed to entertain as well as inform. As was said in Winters vs. New York, 333 U.S. 507:
>
>> The line between the informing and the entertaining is too elusive for the protection of that basic right (a free press). Everyone is familiar with instances of propaganda through fiction. What is one man's amusement, teaches another's doctrine.
>
> It is urged that motion pictures do not fall within the First Amendment's aegis because their production, distribution, exhibition is a large

scale business conducted for private profit. We cannot agree. That books, newspapers, and magazines are published and sold for profit does not prevent them from being a form of expression whose liberty is safeguarded by the First Amendment. We fail to see why the operation for profit should have any different effect in the case of movies.

It is further urged that motion pictures possess a greater capacity for evil, particularly among the youth of a community, than other modes of expression. Even if one were to accept this hypothesis, it does not follow that motion pictures should be disqualified from First Amendment protection. If there be a capacity for evil it may be relevant in determining the permissible scope of community control, but it does not authorize substantially unbridled censorship such as we have here.

For the foregoing reasons, we conclude that expression by means of motion pictures is included within the free speech and free press guarantee of the First and Fourteenth Amendments. To the extent that language in the opinion in *Mutual Film Corp. vs. Industrial Commission,* 236 U.S. 230, is out of harmony with the views here set forth, we no longer adhere to it.[14]

Although I have no doubt that Justice Clark and his colleagues, to a man, knew exactly what the implications of this bold statement were, state censorship did not suddenly vanish. The *Miracle Decision,* as it came to be known, centered only upon sacrilege. Although the case was called a "landmark decision" almost from the first, considerable question remained as to how deeply the Supreme Court meant Clark's words to cut into the wider pumpkin of morality—if deeper than that which was merely circumscribed by religious doctrine. Taken alone, his words seemed to apply to a full spectrum of all morality—a spectrum of freedom *not even open at the time to the print media.* But was it even possible to take these paragraphs out of the context of the *Miracle Decision* as a whole? The only tangible results that the words quoted above produced for almost seven years was that state and city censors no longer denied licenses to films that somebody—anybody—might call "sacrilegious," if this was their only objectionable quality.

During these seven years, it was obvious that Clark's uncontested statement would have somehow to be tested in the crucible of experience and under extreme conditions. As long as the Court wavered concerning the applications of the First Amendment relative to sexual mores as they pertained to print itself, there was no way of determining, even at its widest points of implied permissiveness, exactly how Clark's observations applied to films.

The main point here is nonjudicial and therefore illustrative of the nexus between morals and law. The fifties was a period that saw progressive changes of many sorts in displayed public attitudes concerning sexuality—and therefore eroticism—in all the arts, in public discourse and to most observers in public morals as well. Moral change had become after World War I the *status quo* itself, and law that preserves the *status quo* does not automatically keep up with such change. If one event in American history is to be blamed (or praised) for the particular changes we observe in the fifties, I suppose it probably is the release of the first Kinsey report and the book's attendant publicity. One must also not forget that this was a period of extensive economic changes in popular arts such as the cinema. Films began a search for new audiences in the face of competition from free television and in doing so spoke with increasing candor, bringing the same excitement which both good and poor playwrights (or good playwrights like Tennessee Williams writing poor plays) brought to the theatre and subsequently to films, especially in erotic matters. Best-selling novelists—John O'Hara and Irwin Shaw are examples—who had once treated explicit sexuality with fuzzy pens now began to sharpen their purple prose. The word "fuck" became printable even by prestige publishers—if Ernest Hemingway used it. Causes or effects? Effects of what? Cultural historians guessed—and continue to guess—as many moral climates seesawed through the sixties. But one is never sure exactly what in Parrington's words the "main currents of American thought" are in the first place or what effect they are having upon the moral tonus of the nation's people. There were and are simply too many main currents and too many people!

Whatever tests the Supreme Court had now to face in regard to morality and movies, they did not occur in a vacuum or even at the high altitudes of judicial interpretation by the United States Constitution. Our date for the *Roth* decision is 1957. Along with the previously discussed criterion, "utterly without redeeming social value," a precise standard *had indeed* now been created by the Warren Court, or so they thought, for the limits of erotic permissiveness in print—and, by extenuation, to painting, sculpture and, by further extenuation, to photographs as well. It looked, in what turned out to be an illusion, as though *permanent* standards reflecting the moral tonus of an entire nation had been set forth by the Court with considerable clarity regarding First Amendment protection of the press and presumably of that ephemeral quality called "speech" as well. The question now was merely whether or not the same principles applied to motion pictures, as Clark had so boldly stated.

Like it or not, the Court was thereby forced to take a consistent position regarding films. Wisely, the test case for this principle was a film version of a novel that had once been banned by all American censoring agencies both formal and informal, from the Customs Department to the Watch and Ward Society of Boston; that film was of D. H. Lawrence's infamous *Lady Chatterley's Lover,* or, at least, Lawrence's third and highly explicit (although most unconvincingly written) version of the story. True, the film, a French import, did not contain the same colorful scenes of joyous fucking and genital worship—including flowers entwined in Constance Chatterley's pubic hairs—that the book did, but the adultery theme was quite clear and the nature of Lady Chatterley's extraordinary preoccupations with Mellors' sexual prowess was unmistakable. The film was fairly faithful to the book and well acted, although the direction and editing were somewhat sterile and bloodless. But it served the petitioners' (and their advocates') purposes nicely.

The *Lady Chatterley Decision,* as it came to be known, once again challenged the New York censors' right to withhold a license from a film and thereby prevent its exhibition in that state *now* on the grounds, not of sacrilege, but of whether the movie, according to New York statute, was all or in part "obscene, indecent, immoral, inhuman, sacrilegious (still quite unconstitutionally sitting in New York's law) or is of such a character that its exhibition would tend to corrupt morals or incite to crime." (The penultimate issue had been satisfactorily defined in a recent state statute as "a motion picture or part thereof, the dominant purpose or effect of which is erotic and pornographic, or which expressly or impliedly (sic) presents such acts as desirable, acceptable and proper patterns of behavior." [15])

Granting that films and print were now coeval, the *Lady Chatterly* case seemed to be moving into a direct collision with the previous *Roth* decision and the doctrine of "utterly without redeeming social value" in the *Memoirs* case. In order to avoid such a confrontation of issues, therefore, the Court turned to the central problem that set the stage for a test of the constitutionality of *all* the criteria contained in New York's film censorship laws. It headed directly toward the laws themselves *in principle* and to the question of whether or not state censorship of films was compatible with First Amendment protection of the press.

It *could* not be, of course! With a fine legal hand and firm moral conviction—but with much shakier psychological and aesthetic ground on which to stand, as we have seen—Justice Potter Stewart writes for the court (as if washing its hands of the whole business), "What New York has done, therefore, is to prevent the exhibition of a motion picture because that picture advocates an idea—that adultery, under certain circumstances, may be proper behavior."

Note please that Stewart chooses to deal with the moral–sexual problems raised by *Lady Chatterley's Lover* as problems of ideation or doctrine, not of eroticism or emotion or sexual feeling in any manner or construction! One intrinsic looseness of much law is that insanity, genius, beauty—as well as all forms of sexual arousal—*may* if necessary be twisted by the legal mind into "issues," just as Stewart does here. The subtleties and ebbs and flows of psychosis in an ever-changing social field *may* be transformed into the moral, legal issue of "a knowledge of right and wrong," for example. Stewart's dubious legerdemain is clear, regardless of the tenuousness of his assumption in the light of his famous comment, previously discussed, about knowing pornography when he sees it. (How?)

He continues:

Yet the First Amendment's basic guarantee is of freedom to advocate *ideas*. The State, quite simply, has thus struck at the very heart of constitutionally protected liberty.

It is contended that the State's action was justified because the motion picture attractively portrays a relationship which is contrary to the moral standards, the religious precepts, and the legal code of its citizenry. This argument misconceives what it is that the Constitution protects. Its guarantee is not confined to the expression of ideas that are conventional or shared by a majority. It protects advocacy of the opinion that adultery may sometimes be proper (n.b.) *no less than advocacy of socialism or the single tax* . . .

The inflexible command (of the) State Legislature thus cuts so close to the core of constitutional freedom as to make it quite needless in this case to examine the periphery. Specifically, there is no occasion to consider . . . that the State is entirely without power to require films to be licensed prior to their exhibition. Nor need we here determine whether, despite problems peculiar to motion pictures, the controls which a state may impose upon this medium of expression are precisely coextensive with those allowable for newspapers, books, or individual speech. It is well enough for the present case to reaffirm that motion pictures are within the First and Fourteenth Amendments' basic protection. (See *Joseph Burstyn Inc. vs. Wilson*.)

Nothing could be clearer. Justice Black, in concurrence, notes with good humor that the problem of censorship in the hands of the United States Supreme Court is being treated by "about the most inappropriate Supreme Board of Censors that could be found," as he squarely places films under the protection of the Bill of Rights. Justice Felix Frankfurter, about seventy-six years old at the time, seems to have missed Stewart's main point altogether and addresses himself instead to the issue of adultery, noting that Lawrence himself decried pornography or "dirt for dirt's sake" (or to be more accurate, "dirt for money's sake"). He finally and sagely notes:

Unless I misread the opinion of the court, it strikes down the New York legislation in order to escape the task of deciding whether a particular picture is entitled to the protection of expression under the Fourteenth Amendment. Such an exercise of judicial function, however onerous or ungrateful, inheres in the nature of the judicial enforcement of the Due Process Clause (of the amendment). We cannot escape such instance-by-instance, case-by-case applications of that clause in all varieties of situations that come before the court.

Up to a point, and unable to forecast the barrage of X-rated movies that was yet to come in the late sixties, he was more or less correct.

Justice Clark notes with considerable optimism and what turns out to be unwarranted faith that he does not believe that New York State is left powerless to ban what he calls "pornographic films" or those that portray *acts* of "immorality, perversion or lewdness." Of course, he therefore supports striking down New York's censorship laws.

Also, Justice Douglas repeats his familiar broadside contention that censorship of anything is unconstitutional.

One might think that the *Lady Chatterly* decision would finally have settled the matter regarding state and city film censorship or the state's legal guardianship of this aspect of public morality. It did not!

The riot act had indeed been read to New York's Board of Regents. But film pre-censorship—not geared as much now to Stewart's notion of "ideas" as to the "prurient interest" concept of the *Roth* decision and to the still vaguer notion of protections of the young against corruption and incitement to crime (which the court had not touched in *Lady Chatterley*)—continued to be practiced in a declining number of states and in a few cities. In other words, and in fascinating disregard both of federal judicial intent and decision, national laws (together with cultural moral change) were moving faster than state and local laws and statutes in practice. The difference is striking when one looks, for instance, at the Supreme Court's less convoluted reasoning and repeated tests in the matters, say, of school integration or disintegration of cinema monopolies, both being institutions that toppled pretty fast and dramatically as soon as local law enforcement agencies and the Department of Justice understood clearly the Court's new constitutional interpretations.

Few juridical issues are devoid entirely of morals, but the *entire* fabric of film censorship in the fifties was woven out of moral thread. This was probably the main reason that Justices such as Black, a wise liberal if ever there was one, and Frankfurter, a well-tempered one in his late years, always seemed so uncomfortable with them.

For a moment in 1961 in a 5–4 decision, it even seemed that the Court was about ready to give power *back* to censors where once it had taken it away. But the *Times Film Corp. vs. Chicago* case produced an equivocal decision in an equivocal case, and its best logic (and rhetoric) was saved for the persuasive dissent of Justice Warren (joined by the Court's "left wing—" Black, Douglas and Brennan).[16]

Times Films was one of those good legal battles that makes poor law. It seemed to force the Court out of the purely moral domain in a clever way in the interests of the petitioner, the City of Chicago, whose police department was attempting to retain its power to pre-censor movies.

The reason that *Times Films* looked like the beginning of the end of a trend was simple. The case was so contrived that the Court's decision was bleached white of any moral implications—except those in wild imagination. The film that had been exhibited without the necessary imprimatur from the Chicago police could hardly have been more innocent, being a version of Mozart's opera, *Don Giovanni*. The issue, by clever legal maneuvering, was deflected by the Chicago attorneys away from First Amendment concerns with so-called "issues" to the common sense question of whether or not Chicago's police department had a right (or obligation) to protect the citizens of the Windy City from harm if and when a movie (or presumably anything else) was brought into their domain that they were free to examine *before* circulation to establish its true nature, be it benign or malignant.

The point at issue, therefore, centered not on *what* the *Don Juan* movie was or was not but what it *might have been!* The Court up to this point had stopped short—as it has done up to the present moment—of asserting either that obscenity is protected by law or that *some* speech or print cannot *under certain circumstances* do damage to the citizens of a city, state or nation. *Don Juan,* therefore, *might have been* the most corruptive, evil and disgusting movie ever made (worse than our present "loops"), and the only legal way for the Chicago gendarmes to establish the fact was quite obviously for them to examine it before it did its presumed damage!

In its way, *Times Film* remains one of the most interesting of all the free-speech cases dealt with by the Warren Court, because it deals with the problem of censorship from a fresh perspective. Warren's dissent naturally tried to shift the issue back into its old framework, with his patient reviewing of the thrust of film censorship and moral change through which the Court had gone up to 1961. It was neither a great nor brilliant dissenting statement, but because *Times Film* like many interesting cases upheld such a poor law and was directed at so subtle an application of common wisdom, Warren's words were heeded. Now that nearly a full decade had passed since *Burstyn vs. Wilson* and since Justice Clark's unmistakable edict that motion pictures are included in the Bill of Rights, the entire case seemed to spur the Court to renewed incentive to give the *coup de grace* to legal prior censorship on First Amendment grounds come hell or high water.

We have previously seen that enormous changes were occurring in the American motion pictures industry at this time, changes that were reflective and directive of moral changes in society itself. New foreign films from England, France and Italy were making trenchant dramatic statements about the human condition (invariably including numerous erotic puzzles involved in that condition) with unmistakable seriousness, wisdom and art; the films were far better, in my opinion, than the legitimate stage, popular fiction or American movies at that time. One has to remember that this was the heyday of directors such as Frederico Fellini, Michaelangelo Antonioni, Akira Kurosawa, the young Roman Polanski (working in Poland), Alain Resnais, other "new wave" filmmakers in France and their imitators in England, as well as John Schlesinger and other outspoken directors and writers, some working in the United States. Exploitation films were also increasingly exploiting erotica, and the grand fireworks display of political and moral outrage that seared the rest of the decade was beginning to splutter with the Bay of Pigs fiasco and the Cuban Missile Crisis.

Looking backward, were liberals on the home front during the sixties engaged in anything more intensively then they were in legitimatizing moral change? Certainly not party politics; one of their own kind, Lyndon Johnson, was mercilessly sacrificed to their "cause." Certainly not ideology or intellectualism; "greening America" and Marcuse's meanderings may well have pushed much American intellectual life back one or two decades, until our scholarly perspective of the period cleared up a bit. Certainly not mysticism or religion, although the hippie and drug cultures were based loosely on profound misunderstandings of Eastern philosophy and revealed truths that, boiled down to their essences, turned out frequently to be as suicidal as they were transient.

Morality, however, was much at the center the stage of national attention. Main ancillary preoccupations, I suppose, were the morality of war, the morality of *this* war, the morality of urban living, the morality of the use of natural resources, the morality of cigarette smoking (tobacco and pot), the morality of the military draft, the morality of drug use, the morality of wearing animal hides and furs, the morality of eating meat and so forth. At dead center of all of these issues, however, one found erotic morality, the supposedly "new" sexual mores that found their symbolic expression in the puerile slogan, "Make love, not war!" (How would a more socially responsible notion, devoid of such products as over-population, nervous breakdowns and domestic tragedy, like "Make money, not war!" have appealed to the strident young activists of the sixties? It had been the operational but unspoken imperative for many during the fifties. Unfortunately, its *moral* tone was definitely not in harmony with the aims of the Woodstock generation. It was, however, entirely operational for their many wily exploiters who indeed made love and peace pay handsome profits!)

In the midst of all this civil activity and mass media noise, the Supreme Court was in the process of closing the books on movie censorship (and most other kinds of censorship), at least where and when the force of law rather than mutual agreement served as the instrument of enforcement.

Possibly the most trenchant comparison we can make between *Mutual vs. Ohio* and the two cases to be discussed in the opening pages of Chapter 8 is *not* the matter of how far films had come as vehicles for speech between 1915 and 1965 but the degree to which the moral tone of a nation and the general attitudes derived from those morals *appear* to have changed in just fifty years. We must remember, however, that in matters of morality fifty years is not a long time. In England, less than half a century was required for Victorian Codes to change the surface appearance of manners and mores in polite—and even impolite—society. Moral changes in recent history appear to occur with ever excessive rapidity and in spurts. Or so it seems to many elders today who lived as adults between the two world wars. But their reaction is, I think, in large part based on illusion born of many tiny stresses and strains that demand that they change their values as times change. Through the law-breaking twenties, the depressed thirties, the fearful forties and into the recent past, rights and wrongs in the erotic domains of life from birth (almost) to death (almost) may well turn out, when all the evidence is finally gathered and analyzed, to have been modified over the years by cultural change (or vice versa) with distressingly banal consistency.

The Sin Market

The basis of morality, as Shelley insisted, is laid not by preachers but by poets. Bad taste and crude responses are not mere flaws in an otherwise admirable person. They are actually a root evil from which other defects follow. No life can be excellent in which the elementary responses are disorganized and confused.

—I. A. Richards

THE READER, having followed the discussion in the past few chapters, should now experience a certain sense of inevitability, not necessarily about the liberation of motion pictures to become *bona fide* forms of human speech similar to the press, but from the eventual fallout and the more or less unforeseen by-products of what did indeed happen when two fairly recent events occurred. First, the *Mutual* decision was reversed in *fact* rather than merely in law, and second, the *Roth* decision, directed mainly to printed matter in words, in *fact* became an instrument for evaluating not only books but photographs, drawings and recordings and by extenuation live performances of various sorts and finally even loosely labeled "private clubs," "photographic studios" and "massage parlors."

My scrupulous avoidance of ascriptions of cause and effect to this or that during this period of moral and, I suppose, institutional change which peaked during the late sixties and first five years of the seventies is indicative both of cowardice and discomfort at interpreting too facilely and incorrectly currents of change that are still so close to the eyes of the wisest observer that they cannot be evaluated with requisite clarity.[1] I have been told that those who are in the eye of a hurricane are among the least reliable observers of the storm, and I tend to believe it.

What I *can* assert with some degree of certainty will seem painfully obvious to some, cause for considerable concern of a reactionary nature to others, and encourage a teapot tempest in yet others, who will deny that many of the changes they observe on the cultural horizon are more illusory than real. No question exists, to me at least, that the past generation has indeed seen a notable shift in the relationships between *law, morality* and *behavior* on a nationwide scale in the United States and probably in other English-speaking cultures as well, and this is as good a point to start from as any.

Obviously, the easiest element of these three vectors to quantify, qualify or explain is change in law, and this, more or less, is what we have been up to for the most of Part II of this volume. Changes in morality, we also know, tend to be ephemeral; one *feels* that they occur, but the evidence by which one demonstrates them is often discursive, impressionistic and vague. Usually one takes recourse eventually to proof in law that change has actually happened. And law, of and by itself, proves little. Behavior changes yield to the techniques of sociology—large and small group samples, statistical devices, and so on—all of which remain largely academic matters. I do not mean that they are necessarily incorrect or that they are frauds (as some, like Jacques Barzun, claim) but rather than they are highly *qualified* insights into truth that for the most part require almost as much special training to comprehend correctly as to gather and prepare. Thus, they remain most useful in the academy and do not mesh productively with most other sorts of data by which scientists and scholars observe culture.[2]

This is also a suitable place to observe that those who tend to blame or praise *one* single aspect of a vector for social changes regarding eroticism in general are, I believe, not only mistaken but grossly misled by their ideas of how and why attitudes and values change in cultures. I am attacking the popular position, bespeaking the "common wisdom," of many political and social conservatives and liberals, who are usually more political than social. The Warren Court, for instance, was *not* solely responsible for many of the factors that have been involved in the liberalization of so much legislation regarding erotic discourse during the past decades. The proof, as we shall eventually see in Part III, is that a *conservative* Supreme Court with a *conservative* Chief Justice and a *conservative* majority at his command was and is unable to produce constitutional interpretations that defy common sense, contemporary moral values or what the Court understands to be public opinion.

What the Warren Court has done, the Burger Court *cannot possibly undo.* In fact, its efforts, which are highly consonant with what the justices apparently believe to be the moral position of most Americans, have merely stimulated and encouraged the ever-widening ambit of permissiveness in erotic communications begun in the Warren years, in fact if not in intention! The hard truth is that, as of this writing, a single brutal attack upon the publisher of an erotic publication, *Hustler,* which left the man apparently paralyzed from the waist down, has since the incident probably had as much effect upon freedoms granted such publications as almost any legislative action has had in history, which is an irony for exponents of social amelioration through law to consider carefully.

De Facto Film Freedom and the Roth Decision.

One of the cases of interest that helped in its way to deliver the final blow to state prior censorship and all that is signified was by a twist of fate a challenge to the licensing powers of the State of Ohio, the original site of the *Mutual* action. As law I find *Jacobellis vs. Ohio* something of a disaster.[3] It is a 1964 decision reversing by a 6–3 decision Ohio's denial of an exhibition license to a film called *Les Amants.* It includes only one written dissent, by Justice Harlan, who expressed concern about the Supreme Court's tendency to take from the various states the task of judging whether or not individual films are obscene on a case-by-case basis. In light of the nature of the majority decision and concurrences, one sees his point.

Brennan's opinion (joined by Justice Goldberg) and White's, Steward's, Warren's and Clark's concurrences (some written) strike out at what seems, in light of the possible mischief caused by the *Times Film* decision, to be ten directions at the same time. All the above agree that movies indeed fall under the principle of the *Roth* decision and its subsequent modifications and that this test, and only this test, should be applied to the cinema. Who applies the test and when seems to cause no end of trouble, because implicit in the application of the test is a decision by a legal body whose right it may or may not be to pre-censor films (under *Times*), regardless of their constitutional status! In order, therefore, to avoid the incontestable common sense contradiction regarding the protection of a community that was raised in *Times Films,* a number of remedies are suggested, but none of them apparently expressed a firm conviction of the majority of the Court.

All six justices agree that state pre-censorship is *not* the answer. But all are troubled as to what is! Certainly community standards, perhaps even national standards, could be articulated and applied to such films that were genuinely "pornographic," because it was understood that *Roth* did not protect *truly* obscene films. The justices at this point seemed quite oblivious to how deeply the *Roth* definition and the phrase "utterly without redeeming social value" had cut into their collective and vaguely held notions of the nature of pornography and obscenity both in print and on film. In this regard, their assumptions indicate not how involved in moral change the Court had become in the middle sixties but simply how unrealistic and naive in these matters the liberal justices were at the time. Such a sentence as Justice Brennan's is a clear indication of this. "We thus reaffirm," he writes, "the position taken in *Roth* to the effect that the constitutional status of an allegedly obscene work must be determined on the basis of a national standard." For good measure, he adds, "It is, after all, a national Constitution we are expounding." [4]

In 1965, the *Times Film* issue was replayed, this time to a different tune in *Friedman vs. Maryland.* [5] The motion picture at hand, *Revenge at Daybreak,* had, like *Don Juan,* not been submitted to Maryland's censors, which was one of the few bodies left at this time that was still pre-censoring films at the state level. Unlike the decision in *Times Films,* however, the Court decided against the Maryland censors on the grounds that it is up to a censoring body to determine whether or not a film breaks the law—that is, whether it is obscene under the *Roth* principles. The burden of this proof lies with the state, which may not, via compulsory licensing, act on the assumption that all films *may* be guilty of such a crime. Furthermore, "to this end, the exhibitor must be assured, by statute or authoritative judicial construction, that the censor will, within a specified brief period of time, either issue a licence or go to court to restrain showing of the film." [6]

In effect, what the Court accomplished in *Friedman* (if it was their intention) was devilishly clever: to create conditions whereby the operation of a state censorship office would simply be physically impossible—or very difficult. In the first place, the censors would have to be mind readers in order to anticipate whether a film they had not seen was illegal or not, and, second, they would have to operate quickly, a demand that, given the resources and procedures needed for film pre-screening—particularly by New York State, which acted as censor for most other states for a fee—was procedurally nearly impossible.

Strangely, what the Court gave with one hand in *Friedman,* it *seemed* also to take away. *In principle* the idea of state censorship of movies was unquestionably upheld. *In practice* it was made more or less impossible, except after the fact of its exhibition. Therefore a film's initial exhibition *need not* require a license. State censors, caught in this elipse, soon dropped by the wayside, particularly in light of the Court's encouragement to make haste in their decisions, meaning that a film distributor not granted a license could at the very least initiate legal action against almost any censor to the effect that not *enough* haste had been made, no matter how quickly the censorship board had operated. The distributors were given a potent weapon.

The next important step, not only dooming to oblivion state censorship of films for reasons of obscenity, but also opening the possibility of redefining "obscenity" and "pornography" where films were concerned, did not occur at the level of the Supreme Court but in the actual application of the *Roth* principle to *individual* movies. This could now occur in nearly any courtroom in the nation—and did, to the degree that it became quite logically impossible to find *any* movie (including *Censorship in Denmark* or *The Casting Couch*) obscene or pornographic, although the latter word, shortened to "porn," described a whole new genre of publicly exhibited films. The *Roth* definition was simply too all-inclusive in the first place, and in the second, each and every film had also to be *entirely* devoid of social value.

I suppose the Swedish import, *I Am Curious Yellow,* helped considerably to establish this principle in law. A United States Circuit Court upheld the importation of the film and denied the Customs Department the right to prohibit its entry into the United States, almost entirely in the court's opinion (with one dissent which objected to the exploitative nature of the sex in the film), by virtue of its failure to meet the standards of obscenity or non-speech now set by the Supreme Court.[7]

I Am Curious Yellow was and is a curious film. Part—possibly as much as one-quarter—contained heterosexual scenes of simulated fucking, implied cock-sucking and cunt-licking—none of it explicit and all of it photographed poorly. The rest of the film was made up of bits and pieces of social comment that may or may not have been attempting to make some kind of socio-political statement about mores in Sweden *circa* 1967. A young plump blonde girl is its protagonist, and the sexuality in the film is both discreet and quite irrelevant to the rest of it and to its social observations; these observations are in themselves loose, disjoined and in spots almost surrealistic.

Because of the publicity it received, Grove Press, the distributor of *I Am Curious Yellow,* did a booming business in the United States. Grove published the script accompanied by numerous photographs from the film, especially nude pictures of its leading lady, Lena Nyman. For *Curious Yellow's* day in court, such noted literary and film figures as Hollis Alpert, Norman Mailer, Stanley Kauffman and John Simon testified on its behalf. (They may well have had cause, in the decade since then, to rethink their claims made for the artistry of a seriously flawed movie directed by a confused Vilgot Sjoman, who introduced his own presence, Brecht-style, into the movie occasionally, supposedly to explain what was going on.[8]) *Curious Yellow* played (with an X rating) to bewildered audiences in many neighborhood theatres throughout much of the United States. Sjoman's sequel, *I Am Curious Blue,* released a year or so after *Yellow,* contained more of the same sort of disordered filmmaking and was a total failure in America, hardly surviving its initial week in first-run theatres. The natural limits of audience gullibility had apparently been reached!

By 1968, however, law and logic had coalesced. The cinema in general was henceforth to be treated in court—until 1973—in much the same way that print was at the time. Nearly all forms of legal censorship had been or were about to be abandoned, except those which, in one way or another, traduced local ordinances or blatantly exposed statutory children to supposedly "corruptive" materials. But even in these instances, one might take recourse to the courts where, despite the *Friedman* principle of haste, a film could remain in litigation long enough so that a distributor would agree to edit it or cut it to bits just to get it into circulation.[9]

In addition, another Supreme Court decision (1969) protected the right of an individual to possess materials *in one's home,* which might *be* judged obscene in court, largely on the grounds that one's home is one's castle and that this private domain regarding films, pictures and literature should not be invaded by the state's arbiters of values.[10] A complicated matter, Justice Marshall's opinion of the Court constitutes a long-winded legal metaphor, spelling out the difference between private and public morals and legal barriers to privacy while denying the necessity for legislative control of invasion of it—under certain circumstances. This distinction was naturally necessitated by the reaffirmation of the Court (a ritual obeisance by now) that all speech could not be protected by the First and Fourteenth Amendments and that "obscenity," if you could find it, might still be extirpated by and under law—but not if owned and/or shown privately within the confines of your house or mine.

This adjudication is indeed a vague statement that may or may not wear well in the future. It has neither been tested severely nor often enough. A first-rate constitutional attorney once offered to defend me *gratis* on this principle alone if trouble was caused in a community where I was showing a film to an undergraduate class in media. The film, *The Devil in Miss Jones,* had in a court of law been found to be obscene in the particular county where my classroom was located. He was droolingly anxious to test the notion that a "home" or "household" might extend to a university undergraduate class, where the teacher is held to certain obligations and given certain rights *in loco parentis.* Unfortunately, my classroom was not raided, and I was scrupulous about keeping inquisitive visitors (including some of the college faculty and one dean who suddenly evidenced a hitherto undisclosed interest in the cinema) out of the place, partly by force.

I have also previewed numerous porn films in my rented apartment, permitting my wife and teenaged children, as well as one or two of their friends (with parental permission), to view 16mm prints of so-called XXX porn films that, for one reason or another, I found necessary to project at home, either to view repeatedly and closely or to transcribe dialogue—which is legitimate research for teaching and scholarly purposes, or so I claimed. The films, I fear, were visible from the apartments across the street, because the tropical plants I was growing at the time prevented me from closing my living room curtains. Would the principle in *Stanley vs. Georgia* have applied to me had my neighbors across the street noticed the films and called the police in those two or three instances when the movies in the versions I was showing had been previously judged obscene in the community in which I lived? Or even on the contention that the films up to now had been confined to specific theatres and not exhibited *gratis* on a street in Queens, New York, via my first-floor living room picture window? (Nobody called the police or anybody else!)

In some ways, the single most straightforward piece of judicial constitutional interpretation we have met so far in Part II of this book may be, in the long run, the most difficult to circumscribe and/or apply effectively (this being a later observation of Justice Burger in 1973, to which we shall turn eventually, when our present inquiry is concluded).

Eroticism, Morality and Sin

After the decline and fall of the Warren Court and the abrupt change in the Court caused by President Nixon's four appointments, President Ford's one, and the death or departure of the Court's most stalwart liberals: Warren himself, Hugo Black, William O. Douglas, Goldberg and Fortas (the latter two having served three and four years respectively), judicial interpretations of the United States Constitution anent moral problems raised by motion pictures began to shift gears. This change provides for us a notable case study in contemporary history centering on the incessant problem of maintaining what philosophers might call a "proper" relationship between public and private morality and the power of law. Because one cannot define "propriety" in this respect, the task may be nearly impossible, because every justice (or even every crackerbarrel constitutional lawyer) falls back in the end, as have most of our Supreme Court Justices—both liberal and conservative—on his own private interpretations of good and evil or, more precisely, his own sense of sin and his interpretation of it—the sense, not the sin.

To accuse the Warren Court—or the American Civil Liberties Union and/or any group of special interests—of having *caused* these moral changes is, of course, ridiculous. I have already attempted to make clear the point that the ultimate auditor of all laws in all cultures, those who check the checkers in effect, is the public itself, which expresses itself *whenever* and *however* that amorphous, amoeboid glob of silly-putty we call "public opinion" reveals itself to a society. More than one high court justice has sagely reflected on the inadequacy of nine aging, male, legal scholars to serve as weather vanes for shifts in the temperature of public opinion. Indeed, to the degree that the elite of society remain insulated from main currents of thought and behavior in that society, they are the poorest auditors of public values. Possibly the remarkable aspect of the Warren Court's relatively consistent behavior relating to erotic books and films is that, from today's perspective at least, the main thrusts of its decisions seem so highly consonant with what we now know (or think we know) about public opinion regarding these matters from 1950 to 1970. Whether, in the long run, such reflective wisdom is mainly an extension of judicial attitudes toward certain encroachments of government into aspects of private economic enterprise during this century, one can only guess. By and large, however, I think that we expect of jurists greater sophistication in economic (and political, educational and even philosophical) matters than in those that deal largely with matters like eroticism and art.

Some observers have called this twenty-year period one of "revolution" in American sexual mores in general. I have already indicated that I disagree with this hyperbole for the most part, novel methods of contraception, legalized abortion and newly "activated" homosexuality notwithstanding. *Something* revolutionary during this period at the level of interpersonal and mass communications has unquestionably occurred, although the question of whether such changes were not greater during the period of, say, 1910 to 1930 than in the Warren Court years is another matter that I am incompetent to judge fairly. Unfairly, I estimate the change to be just about as deep and as permanent.

That these last decades have been a time of considerable attitudinal change in regard to sexual morality among much of the American public, particularly the increasing number who now live in urban communities, is a good guess, but it is only a guess. Instruments for judging such public attitudes, however slickly they are presented and by whatever devices they are gleaned, remain suspect, whether they are attempted in the academic community or by pollsters like Roper, Gallup and company.[11] More ethical members of this community are careful to delineate exactly why and how the study of public attitudes—certainly at the depth of moral attitudes—is a dangerous, difficult and, at times, an impossible game.

The trend, forever rediscovered by sociologists, that young people tend to be more liberal in regard to sexual matters than their elders is a fatuous statement, an exercise in nugacity. This chestnut was given to me as axiomatic when I survived my first sociology course many, many years ago. I believe Socrates had something to say on the subject. Young people, naturally, grow eventually into middle-aged and old people, and this tension is continually in flux for what are probably inevitable reasons born of culture, custom and physiology, at least in the West. The crude street aphorism (from, unfortunately, the male perspective) that "a stiff prick has no conscience" was, for me—and I suspect for most men—more of a *functional* problem in youth than in late maturity, not because I have firmed my grip upon conscience and upon the moral rationalization it requires, but simply because I am not as disturbed (if that is the word) by the intensity and frequency of erections as I was when I was young! Translating rationalizations of behavior into moral imperatives, a tendency most of us show, swings us therefore in the direction of conservatism, caused less by ratiocination or wisdom than by the simple lack of testosterone in our blood streams.

For social change—and moral change—at the level of public discourse, we must, I am afraid, look more deeply into society than the superficial methods of opinion sampling favored by marketing and advertising people and sociologists do. Advertisers and the public relations fraternity find their instruments particularly useful *because,* as Aldous Huxley once observed, they center mostly upon the trivia of life: preferences in deodorants, cake mixes and television commercials and/or other matters regarded by the public—but not by manufacturers of deodorants, cake mixes and television commercials—as issues of precious little pith or consequence when compared to other aspects of living. These latter concerns rarely respond neatly to the sociologists' categorizations of race, religion, age, education, social status, economic worth, sex, place of residence and/or birth and so on, but, in one degree or another, crisscross all of them with different emphasis at different times in different parts of society, even as behavioral scientists enjoy stratifying it. My claim boils down, I suppose, to the belief that moral change is in public terms difficult or impossible to ascertain by means of the application of selected scientific procedures. When and if our social scientists "shut up" long enough for our poets and artists to tell them what is going on, we are likely to see behind what Ronald Knox called a "smoke screen of facts" something like the outlines of both reality and truth.

I suppose I want (but cannot have) my argument both ways: that, on one hand, there has occurred (and for all I know it is still occurring) an exploitative, cross-cultural change (hardly of revolutionary proportions) in the way communications, particularly in mass communications and so-called "modern" communication instruments, are being used today to disseminate erotic ideas and emotional stimuli. This means only two things, the first being an increase in "candor" and the second being a decrease in "privacy," in the sense that we call our primary—and used to call our secondary—sexual organs "private parts," access to which was limited to ourselves, physicians, intimates and morticians. Such notions of privacy were generally maintained, except in certain places under certain conditions such as burlesque shows, gang-bangs and in cases of the illicit circulation among male peers of private pornographic collections of print, pictures or films. Beyond its religious parameters in our culture, say, from 1900 to 1950 or later, part of the enjoyment of the circulation of such special group eroticism was not only its inherent voyeurism but also what I would call a secular sense of sin that tends to make all forbidden behavior enjoyable simply because it is forbidden—right up to the point of psychopathology.[12]

I am reminded of the story my students seem to enjoy of Dr. Johnson's friend, who loved pork so much he wished he were a Jew so that he might have the *double* pleasure of eating pork and committing a sin at the same time! Sam Johnson's friend was not much concerned with religion but with law, and the fact, often overlooked by criminologists, is that breaking the law may not only be profitable, it can also be fun—for perfectly normal people at certain times. When the fun spills beyond certain limits—as in the case of kleptomania, for instance, in societies where private property exists—we are indeed dealing with psychotic behavior, but the seeds of almost all psychopathology are usually found in normative behavior.

Getting back to my double-edged argument, I want to possess at the same time as I acknowledge the change an anchor of a different sort on the behavioral side of the argument, especially as it concerns life to death patterns of human erotic activity—including mental behavior (thus adding another dimension to much but not all taxonomical research into human sexuality),—and how these activities effect people in a given culture from birth to death over relatively long periods of time. I doubt, for example, that what is probably the most frequent and ubiquitous form of sexual behavior in which humans (and some apes) indulge, namely masturbation, has been much affected either by moral change or by notions of sin in the past hundred years, much less by mass communications and their content. To claim that my son in his teen years was stimulated to more vigorous masturbatory behavior by his collection of *Hustlers, Penthouses* and company (bought and paid for, alas, with money he had earned himself) than I was by Petty girls and/or photographs of Rita Hayworth in *Click* or *Look* or by the prose of James T. Farrell would be untestable, but testing would also be absurd. Patterns of female masturbation, because of their undramatic nature and opportunities for secrecy, as previously noted, are even more difficult to detect, but once again, in the absence of information to the contrary, I imagine their general nature—in adolesence at least—in the lives of my grandmother and my daughters was much the same.

Actual hetero- or homosexual behavior is a different matter, but, once again, persuasion via print and picture (as well as birth control devices) that seem to hurl the young into premarital screwing may be greater today than in my late mother's and father's day. But mom and pop in a less populated, less hurried period had more opportunities for privacy and experiment and Lord knows what else than is provided for today's kids. The latter seek out the comparative seclusion of places like drive-in theatres for what turns inevitably (just as it did in my generation) into sexual acrobatics in automobiles, front and rear—as well as in the rumble seats of my youth, a difficult task for neophytes to master.

I cannot prove but indeed sense a considerable degree of constancy in this class of behavior, especially because we usually measure the changes we *think* we see on social, economic, class or racial lines. Some changes may indeed occur, but they may merely signify variations of behavior among different groups both away from and toward certain types of socio-sexual permissiveness. Middle-class academics like me, for instance, tend to look at youth through a lens much distorted by our own shifting class position. One result is the pseudo-fact gleaned from our perceptions of much of the sexual behavior of young people during the so-called "hippie" years; mainly because the noticeable participants appeared to have come from middle-class environments, we expected, on the surface at least, far more decorous behavior than we found in their talk, publications, popular songs and antics. That hippiedom hardly effected the greater number of lower-class youngsters, including minority group members (except, possibly, to stimulate trade in certain illegal drugs), remained of little interest to bourgoise sociologists, psychologists and cultural historians and even less to our middle-class media of communications at the time—that is to say, all radio and television broadcasting, nearly all movies and all newspapers and mass-circulated magazines, except one or two.

A legitimate question then arises as to the nature and influence of erotic persuasion—or propaganda—which, in effect, has not only increased in amount enormously during the past generation, but also has been sanctioned by law as we have seen, has been spread by mass-marketing methods, has obviously had some sort of effect upon the collective moral tone of our nation and *must* have, in one way or another, forced both a new and an old generation to redefine *some* deeply held notions of sin itself.

Erotic Persuasion

The idea of "persuasion" as we understand it today is Greek and has come down to us in a relatively pristine state from the *Rhetoric* of Aristotle, a textbook on persuasive speech that has a peculiarly modern ring to it.[13] No known medium of communication has proven resistant to Aristotle's notion of the *enthymeme,* a triad of persuasive elements: first, the character of the persuader; second, the necessity to sway on one's behalf the emotions of the listener or listeners; and, third, the proof—or apparent proof—of the proposition at hand.[14]

In persuasive matters, Aristotle tells us, do not try to look for formulas, fundamental methods or rigid sets of principles. He likens the *enthymeme* to the dialectic mode of argument and thought: a *process* rather than a position or set of rules. Posterity has, however, turned its back on Aristotle and handed us a multitude of simplistic pseudo-rules centering on "glittering generalities," "bandwagons," "source-credibilities," "boomerangs," analogies to maps, territories and cows with exponents hanging from them. These games are simply the twentieth century's intellectual equivalent to the sort of junk meals served at fast-food franchises. When Paul Joseph Goebbels, grandmaster of Nazi deceit and treachery, reminded us some years ago that *propaganda itself has no essential method, only an objective,* he was doing what any other German Doctor of Philosophy would have done forty years ago. He was not, as many maintain, reaching back to the Italian arts of Machiavelli but simply quoting his Aristotle.

Another reason that the concept of persuasion has remained largely a rhetorical one is also, in part, Aristotelian. This is the close relationship in Western history, both in secular and religious matters, of persuasion to law, particularly in *courts* of law and in methods of adjudicating disputes.

The adversary system of obtaining rough justice pre-dates the Peri-

clean age, and over centuries, as we have seen, combined a moral dimension—like it or not—with the practice of competing persuasive arguments.
"Right" and "wrong" (or "justice" and "injustice") are, as we know,
largely understood today to be ultimate functions of persuasion, being
used according to whatever ground rules society sets forth at a given time
to effect the satisfaction that one feels when an argument—even an arithmetic or statistical one—persuades because it apparently makes sense. (I
say "apparently," because "sense" is always a function of the specific epistemology convivial to a given culture at a given time.)

Aristotle's great mistake was to construe persuasion ultimately as a
function of *language*, or, at least, to indicate that *speech* somehow has a
special affinity for persuasive discourse and vice versa. As a matter of fact,
he himself departs from the rhetorical confines of his discourse when he
discusses human character and the way it influences the persuasive nature
of an argument and the emotional vulnerabilities of an audience. The man
who wrote *The Poetics* could not have been so naive as to believe that
man's verbal communication environment had much influence over his
feelings and disposition insofar as the subjectively functional important
matters in life are concerned. Nor was he so naive. But the great technology of Grecian culture was the transition of the written word from poetry
to prose, and Aristotle may have seized this opportunity to show off a bit.

The important aspects of persuasion, future studies were to demonstrate, concerned mostly the *dynamics* of rhetoric. The assorted media
through which Aristotle's "proofs" and Dr. Goebbels "ends" are reached
are not irrelevant—they are merely comparatively unimportant. Over the
years, I have said and written many times that the most persuasive jot of
propaganda in the world today may well be a loaf of bread (or its equivalent), if we are not being lied to about the number of our fellow men who
live on a less-than-minimum daily caloric intake. I have personally met
many men and women who would have followed me into the fires of
hell—or done anything—for a loaf of bread or a square meal, much less a
shot of whiskey or a fix of heroin—so many, in fact, that if I ever believed
that human motivations and behavior began and ended with words—or
"media," as we call symbolic languages today—they were long ago put to
rest.

Nor do I believe that these starving individuals were and are too different from you and me. We are *all* hungry for something that mere mediated words, symbols and ideas cannot give us. The main tests, often, of
what we are worth in life, have to do mostly with *direct experience,* either
as we cross the hairs of a rifle's peepsite on another human being, fall
upon our knees in ecstasy in religious experience or sink a razor blade into
the arteries of our wrists, because, in all probability, words failed us just as
surely as they did Prince Hamlet.

I am not suddenly maintaining that language *cannot* be persuasive
and that trickery *cannot* work in selling snake oil at a carnival show. It
has and it does; the technological media of mass communication today

bring the carnival midway into the American home and has been so contrived as to get *us* to pay the pitchman to offer us his phony nostrums! What I *am* saying is that the fancy bottle his cure-all is packaged in is of relatively little consequence and that whatever he says may be said in countless ways. What *is* significant is the fact that my stomach hurts and that a man's bottle of elixir or little pink pills will, I hope, stop the pain. True enough, a great restaurateur once claimed that he "sold the sizzle, not the steak," but before sizzles worked the steak had to be pretty good and certainly chewable. That my stomach pains may yield to psychosomatic relief is also obvious, as well as the fact that something tastes better if it looks and *sounds* good. But these are relatively trivial sociopsychological matters when placed beside the curiosities involved in manipulating human beliefs, attitudes and opinions.

Given the flexibility of the triadic nature of persuasion, therefore, no *one* manner of framing a persuasive message is *intrinsically* superior to any other!

Some days I think that we all have fallen victim to Maxim Gorky's illconceived and archaic warning that the motion picture is somehow inherently hypnotic and therefore a device for diabolical persuasion to a degree that would surprise even Gorky, if he knew as much about hypnotism seventy years ago as Theodore X. Barber does today.[15] No, I am afraid motion pictures are not fundamentally more persuasive than open-air billboards. There is no good reason why they should be. Motion picture "stars" may well be persuasive in many contexts, but such individuals may be more effective for a given task smiling at you or me in effigy from a billboard than from a movie screen.

These few observations about persuasion in general may seem uncharacteristic and peculiarly cold-blooded, given the topic of this section. However, when one immerses oneself for a few years in a historical and functional study of how mankind has and does communicate erotic feeling and meaning from individual to individual and from individual to group, too much prior qualification is never enough!

The professionally skilled persuader in the school of Machiavelli (or any other school) shares with the expert in erotic communication one construction that is the hallmark of professionalism in all deceptive arts: a cold-blooded objectivity toward his or her skills and talents and an exceedingly businesslike attitude toward his or her audience. While my evidence is mainly empirical, I suggest that neither the propagandist nor the whore who enjoys his or her profession *too* much—or who allows emotion to get in the way of cold, calculating reason—is likely to be very successful or last long in his or her chosen career. The chances of finding a propagandist with a heart of gold are about as good as finding a prostitute with a heart of gold. Both of these stereotypes, I submit, are for the most part fictions, particularly in the latter case.

Erotic persuaders are in this respect no different from other persuaders or from other of the various types of magicians of the erotic that we have already met in this volume. Let me make clear that I exclude from the discussion people who may be amateur or professional gynecologists and obstetricians. Few of them seem to be really interested essentially in the dynamics of erotic pleasure, only in its mechanics and consequences. Nor do I include most psychiatrists—with quite a few exceptions, however, including Freudians, who, largely by means of literary tricks, manage to trivialize our old idea of "prurience" and somehow or other turn human sexuality into an exercise in verbal and ideological gamesmanship. For most of them, at best, sex is a literary exercise and erotic communications are viewed fundamentally as anti-intellectual.

On the other hand, I cannot claim that erotic persuasion is *exactly* the same as other types of social, political and cultural persuasion, except in one fundamental way. Sexual persuasion admits of a triadic, Aristotelian *enthymeme:* an erotic persuader, the command of human *feeling* rather than of *thought* and, finally, a proof. In the case of eroticism, the proof is usually the weakest part of the triad, because it so often turns out to be a rationalization (or a manifestation of selective perception or retention) that can be summed up in such pathetic sentences as "I had a good time at the time," or "I did it for love" or "How else do you get into show business these days?" [16]

Once we have cleared the basic hurdles of the triadic form that unites all propaganda and persuasion, the actual nature of the lion's share of erotic persuasion begins to show its peculiar and distinctive form. Distinctive? Well, not entirely, because in its overt manifestation, the appeal of sex is invariably modified by custom and culture and in many ways is similar to the appeal of religion, which is also invariably modified by custom and culture.

Holding *The Hite Report* up beside William James' *Varieties of Religious Experience* and noting where the data in both converge is, oddly, far from a thankless task. It is, in fact, illuminating. Both sexuality and religion are energized by similar tyrannies of the human situation and find their origins in the biological nature of our species, which, generally speaking, occurs on what, I think, constitutes an unexplainable continuum. For reasons none of us comprehend, we are all by definition born, most of us mate and continue our species, and then (quite unfairly it seems to me and regardless of how well we have served nature or biology), for all our best efforts, we are rewarded by an inevitable visit from the dark angel of death.

The point I am making is simply that our religious and sexual impulses share a wealth of mythical impetuses in common and produce a highly similar metaphysic that different people in different societies dip into in different ways. We are thus sustained by mysticisms that are often difficult, even in their personal physiological demands, to sever intellectually one from the other. But more of this later.

Priests and medicine men in white or black coats are forever hovering over our erotic lives with their ceremonies of "coming of age" and marriage and incest taboos, rites of circumcision, confessional boxes and so on. Grand masters of sexuality in many cultures (our own included) save our souls by means of therapeutic rituals and sex education. They also dispense all manners of voodoo along with a sacred technology of pills, ointments, gadgets, machines and medicines in an attempt to raise sexual experience, as we remember it at least, to the level of a so-called "spiritual experience," an improbable parallel alone by weight of the number of spiritual experiences most of us are able to withstand in one lifetime!

Let me therefore definitely modify my observation above that erotic persuasion is peculiar and distinctive. Peculiar, it may well be. But it is not as distinctive as it appears at first blush, because its peculiarity is shared by much religious persuasion, which is a matter for further inquiry in pages to come. In fact, there have been times in history—and the present moment may be one of them—possibly in the United States, possibly in Japan and possibly in Islam—when and where sexual and religious mysticism have been almost impossible to sever one from the other either attitudinally or behaviorally or both. Apparently such an era of double-duty metaphysics occurred at times both in ancient Greece and Rome and has been blamed—unjustly I think—for the destruction of both cultures, or at least for the decline of everything decent that these cultures produced—except children.

In this section, however, I shall not dwell upon religious persuasion, because it is too broad a topic to relate easily to the type of secular sin I mention above, and because, if we want them to, *all* paths of investigation into the modification of beliefs, attitudes, opinions and actions eventually bring us to spiritual concerns. Despite its insistent nature and eternally tyrannical hold on so many of our thoughts and actions, erotic persuasion employs a somewhat more parsimonious or economical set of phenomena than religion, possibly because mankind usually esteems it less important than the specific concerns of life and death upon which all religion pivots. (It is not!)

In simple terms, most of us live in the belief that we ourselves control our sexual appetites in one way or another and pursue our earthly objectives more or less *in spite of them;* on the contrary, we have been and are almost *entirely* at the mercy of whatever unseen forces deal out to us the Tarot cards of life and death.

Whatever else we may have learned about eroticism, many of us are shocked at exactly how illusory the degree of control we maintain upon what many call "sexual appeal" (in its broadest sense) turns out to be. I am not referring here to any enormously magnetic Shavian "life force" or neat little Freudian libido—both lovely conceits—but rather to the ubiquitous and deceptive nature of that aspect of the human condition which blinds most of us so completely and so much of the time to the influence of sexual persuasion on our cognitive processes and dispositions.

I no longer find it strange that much of the deepest wisdom one finds concerning these matters seems to come from those tortured most by it: religious celibates, including various saints, psychopaths and prisoners (sometimes one and the same) like Jean Genet and the Marquis de Sade, both before and during and after their incarceration. The major punishment of any and all forms of isolation—physical or psychological—is, I believe, erotic. And it is manifest in more dramatic and insistent ways than nutritional starvation or even thirst, because few automatic body mechanisms apparently modify the workings of our endocrine systems to any great degree, unless such deprivation is extended for long periods.

As I say, it is not the raw power of sexuality that amazes me, nor am I amazed by the extraordinary behaviors into which it induces otherwise apparently stable human beings. What does amaze me is our developing general attitudes toward *all* eroticism: that it is controllable, understandable, treatable, malleable, amenable to scientific investigation and quantification and that it is properly responsive to law, education, civilization and intellectual exploration—all those qualities our Supreme Court justices would ask of it. In short, from the persuasive point of view, pure prurience joins the supernatural and mysticisms such as fortune-telling and extrasensory perception (and I suppose even much religion) as a class of knowledge that we need but to wait a bit longer to turn into another modern technology. At the moment, many claim to have mastered its techniques; technology, for them, is just around the corner. Pedants dissect it with scientific scalpels and our "best minds" are these days worrying about it. Eroticism is just one more item on the agenda of the future that will, as Huxley predicted, respond to total human control in the Brave New World.

I shall avoid here any discussion of Aldous Huxley's batting average as a seer or haruspex but instead point to the dangers in regarding or thinking about *any* aspect of human mystery—including human eroticism—as a class of experience similar to disease of dysfunction for which there is an appropriate *cure* or *policy* (like, say, an "energy policy") that may be wrapped into a neat package for delivery at Christmas. Of course, this is precisely the sort of stupidity that persuaders (hidden and overt) and propagandists enjoy best. No one is more easily swayed in his opinions and attitudes than the person who, in John Stuart Mill's terms, holds them as a dogma or is absolutely certain of a specific truth, which can therefore be pulled from beneath his feet like a carpet, leaving him on the "ass" end of his convictions. (I call this Socratic stupidity, in honor of the man who, after speaking to all the wise men of Athens, concluded that he himself was the only wise man in town. While everybody else knew all the answers, he, Socrates, recognized that he knew almost none—and few of the relevant questions either.)

The temple of Socratic stupidity in our culture is the American university, where nearly everybody knows the answers to nearly everything. How appropriate, therefore, that a good number of porno film producers during the past decade have honored this fact by setting their mythic romps in academic environments: notably *The School Girl* and *Teenage Cheerleaders*. Their central theme is invariably the same and quite wise, I think, in its way: Those who are most easily diverted by erotic persuasion are those whose erotic natures have supposedly best been tamed by intellect, knowledge, civility and self-control. In these movies, even in films as innocent as *Animal House* (1978), this is the grand hypocrisy of American education from high school onward.

We play a round-game, however, when we create even crude minidramas like pornographic movies that, for most of us most of the time unfortunately, tell us little more than we already know. (It is precisely this finitude of novelty that, in the end, make a steady diet of pornography such a tortuous experience—with a few exceptions.) Most persuasion, most propaganda, most advertising and much education, I submit, functions, within wide erotic dimensions, not in Freudian terms but in metaphysical and mythical terms. Erotic persuasion, remember, began in myth in the Garden of Eden, where sexuality made its first connection with the fruit of knowledge, and this junction has really not changed much since Adam took his first bite of the apple. This may be why so much persuasion, so much propaganda, so much advertising and so much education seems so downright dull and repetitive to a public so super-saturated with so much of it for so much of their lives.

The Biblical parable, however, is more than a moral story. It is a perfectly adequate description of a deep human enigma—the same one discussed above. Adam's quest for knowledge yielded only Socratic stupidity. What other forms of life on our planet could not even begin to intellectualize—questions of existence and reproduction and death—mankind, once perfect in God's image, was now doomed forever fruitlessly to parse in his various languages. So great has man's wisdom grown that now he holds in his hands a capacity to eliminate his own species entirely if he wants to! However, the erotic mystery remains gorgeously intact, immune to the wisdom of both saints and murderers.

The wisdom of the Egyptians never ceases to amaze me! How beautifully their sphinx sums up the human paradox of erotic persuasion: a creature with the body of a wild animal and the head of a man—or of a god. Could any statement in mere words be clearer?

The Real World

Mass persuasion is but one marketing device used in those societies where minimum bodily needs have been met and a measure of "choice" is given to the buyer at the marketplace for the disposition of his cash or goods for barter. I cannot speak for any time or place other than my own with absolute certainty, mainly because such poor records have been kept in the past of the market for erotic activities (including prostitution) and the statistics upon which one must depend today are not much better.[17] The main commodity in the sex industry—if it indeed meets the criteria of "industrial" dimensions—is the aforesaid "mystique" of contemporary eroticism or simply the sense of "sin," à la Dr. Johnson's pork-loving friend.

Few of the many industries that meet the consuming public directly are without their unique investitures of mysticism, and I include at the top of the list the automobile industry, all of the communication industries, much of the American packaged drug and cosmetic trade and the clothing industry. All are haunted by strange social symbols of their own invention and, in some ways, are more responsive to what we today call "manipulation of images" than manipulation of substance. But between the idea and the reality (or, crudely, the promise and the performance), the gap we find in them is usually much, much smaller than in the sin market in any and all of its manifestations—including prostitution.

Here is one of the most frustrating aspects of erotic communications for those few people involved in it who are not motivated entirely by cash rewards. Here, too, if my recent experiences mean anything, is where I must take as exception even certain prostitutes, both male and female, who may not have hearts of gold but whose motives are also not *fundamentally* pecuniary—from Messalina in ancient Rome to Buñel's not-all-that-fictional cinematic *Belle de Jour,* wherein a housewife is impelled to whoring by frustration, boredom and guilt.

The sin market cannot fairly be characterized, however, by its exceptions—except to note that exceptions not only exist, but that one's attention is called to them because of their novelty, in much the way that one notices a rock protruding from a swiftly flowing stream. By and large, however, the contemporary erotic market of goods and services, ranging from massage parlors to peep shows to cinema to books, from magazines and live sex circuses to go-go bars and on and on, is a cheap, carnival world, which is three-fifths visible and open within legal limits (that vary considerably geographically—to about the same proportion, I would guess, as those of most American commodity markets). The distance between promise and delivery is enormous—so enormous that I have begun to wonder what sort of perpetual motion keeps certain parts of it moving so swiftly and lucratively. Alas, I must include prostitution in this general observation, despite its professional antiquity and eternal ubiquity and its many strata of specialization, most of the latter also related more closely to promises and images than to the nature of the services performed.[18]

The present market is supposed to involve at least two billion dollars (Forbes magazine claims *four* billion) in retail trade yearly, probably a conservative estimate; the former figure is confined to the United States alone and excludes substantial foreign connections involved in print, pictures and film. Experts on the President's Commission on Obscenity and Pornography denied forcefully that such enormous trade occurred in mediated "pornography and obscenity" alone—on the particular part of the market they could find and analyze—but the figure is, I think, nevertheless quite conservative by standards today. The reason is that for the most part every aspect of the sin market presents a face to the businessman of either the perfect investment or the near-perfect speculation. Capital costs tend to be low and easily controllable; expenses are also minimal. Risk, both financial and legal, have decreased about to the level of a time deposit in a Savings and Loan Association, and "investment" not "speculation" is the proper word for most of the market's use of capital funds. Mark-ups are unbelievably high: 600 to 1,000 percent are not unusual for books, novelties, films and magazines, and substantial profits are realized in relatively short periods of time. In certain instances, long-term net profits from a film such as *Deep Throat* are so large that they are absolutely incalculable!

As in many businesses, precious little of this profit finds its way to the creative talent(?) involved, the largest shares being reserved for investors, distributors and sales personnel of one sort or another. Crudely speaking, let us remember that the earnings of most busy whores are turned over to a pimp who, acting as agent and entrepreneur, lifts from her shoulders many problems not directly related to her profession. But let us remember that the effective pimp is also the prototypical investor, sometimes speculator, manager and manipulator in a competitive marketplace. This metaphor has been brilliantly brought to the stage both by Jean Giradoux and Jean Genet, as well as by Eugene O'Neill and others, in the guise of a figure who obtrudes into marketplace manipulations everywhere that competitive trade exists and sometimes even where no competition exists at all.

Common sense propels one to ask how a market so large can thrive so well when on a national basis conduits for sales and distribution seem hardly noticeable to most people—except in certain districts of large cities. The answer is that the market is not all that *large* but merely *profitable,* and it is pretty well exploited, both by those who approve and by those who disapprove of it. (Neither Gumps nor Neiman Marcus nor Saks Fifth Avenue are *large* stores when compared, say, to a Sears, Roebuck, but their prices—and mark-ups—are extraordinary, their publicity well placed and their sales volume formidable.)

Who makes how much and when, where and how remain a mystery, the answers to which the Internal Revenue Service would like to know as much as I would. One well-known publisher of a sex publication claims to "clear" between eighty and a hundred thousand dollars a year, yet complains of his enormous personal expenses, which are difficult to write off as tax deductions, and the financial strain of having to live in the high style of other publishers far richer than he is. In fact, he is a seething mass of bourgeois complaints centering on rent, marriage, raising children, the cost of restaurant meals, electricity, and so on, most of which I imagine are justified.

About eight hundred of America's fifteen thousand or so indoor and drive-in theatres show *nothing but* porno films. An equal number (or more) offer occasional X-rated movies and soft-core features. The former group, however, seems to have gathered to themselves a loyal audience that attends nearly everything they exhibit, good, bad or indifferent. Their admission prices on the average run higher than those of conventional motion picture houses. A few flea bags charge as little as $1.50 per admission, but a good number of posh houses in medium- and large-size cities sell tickets at $5 to $6 each. Rental prices for "knocked-down" 16mm prints of these films are about as expensive as any other kind on the market, even if they are used for educational purposes limited to classroom exhibition. Non-commercial rentals run from $150 to $300 a movie, and videocassettes (for home or club exhibition) sell and rent for somewhat less.

Despite the number of porn shops one observes in cities such as New York and San Francisco, the major part of the home erotic market is apparently carried on by mail. The important point here, however, is that *everything* is incredibly overpriced—that is, it sells for about double what a comparable item would cost were it not devoted to erotica. Two hundred feet of 8mm (or Super 8mm) color film, usually of the kind used in peepshow loops, will cost from $25 to $50, whether bought in a store or ordered from a mail-order house. Occasionally, one finds pornographic books discounted, but even the least ambitious of them (possibly comic reprints) cost about $5 or $6 per 64-page issue. Such novelties as playing cards with abominable pornographic photographs on them retail at from $5 to $10, and the list price for pornographic novels and other kinds of books runs from $2 for cheaply bound, poorly printed paperbacks to $20 for volumes slightly more respectably written and/or illustrated.*

While these prices are high, it is notable that these items are considerably cheaper than comparable goods were ten or twelve years ago, before the Supreme Court's interpretation of the First Amendment during the fifties and sixties changed so many regulations regarding pornography. Until it was "legalized," pornography of every sort literally bore no price; it consumed whatever the market would bear. The market often bore unbelievable retail price tags, because one was dealing with "hot" merchandise and wealthy customers for the most part.

Costs for personal services are difficult to generalize about, because they vary so in different parts of the United States and according to the way in which erotic environments are manipulated: on a one-to-one basis, in a massage parlor, in a fancy apartment or residence and so on. They are also functions of factors such as social milieu, race, education and class status. Roughly, the price per single male orgasm in the United States

---

* Because of these high mark-ups, inflation does *not* seem to have effected the prices of pornography much. They have been remarkably stable over the past several years and are apparently falling rather than rising for many items as of the autumn of 1979. Fees for the services of prostitutes seem, however, to be rising at roughly the rate of the cost of living index as one would expect.

begins today at $10 and may end almost anywhere. For the former sum, one may receive a more or less legitimate (and possibly legal) "hand job" at a massage parlor or bar—that may cost a little more, or possibly a little less, depending on many things. (I am excluding the near ubiquitous practice of tipping, which intrudes into nearly every aspect of the personal, live sex market, except in certain more or less theatrical exhibitions and sex shows.)

Despite advertising and handbills to the contrary, a visit to a "respectable" massage parlor in a fair-size city will usually cost a normal male from $75 to $100. Credit cards are often accepted. In sheer incremental terms, the customer may well have received his money's worth compared to a sleazy massage parlor "hand job": some erotic play and voyeurism with one or two girls, a "blow job" from one of them or conventional intercourse, a few drinks, a bath—and possibly even a *massage!* Transmission of disease, even athelete's foot, occurs infrequently at such institutions—an old tradition of well-run bordellos—simply because sanitation is a major precondition that protects the manager's investment and maintains whatever quantum of good will he or she needs to survive.

The world of free-lance whoredom, either the hetereosexual one or the homosexual (mostly male) one, is impossible for me to characterize clearly with any justice. Again, prices seem to start at about $10. Call girls in most prosperous areas receive about $50 per customer (the average coupling lasting about half an hour, including disrobing), but their expenses—clothes, rent, "protection," pimps, a "cover" profession (often acting or modeling)—are high. At the upper end of the scale, some doxies ask for (and receive) $100 for precisely the same service, or as much as $500 to entertain a traveling salesman or bank executive by joining him for dinner at a good restaurant, attending a night club, the theatre, opera or a concert with him—and so to bed until morning. Weekend companions of this sort are also available for as much (or as little) as $1,000, but these ladies are usually extraordinary girls, either taciturn or well spoken, fairly well educated, nicely groomed and dressed, and the last sort of women, naturally, that you or I would identify as a prostitute—certainly at first glance and even after considerable inspection.

Male prostitution has produced a looser, more sinister (to me) world, in which the marketable commodities—and price structures—seem quite different. By and large, the most popular male prostitutes are the youngest and, if I judge correctly, the most implicitly feminine—in looks, usually, rather than in style of dress or "swish" behavior. Race, clothes and social factors are critical here, and prices at the high end of the scale seem more reasonable than those for heterosexuals. Male prostitutes drift into the role of full-time "companion" (or "son") to older customers more frequently than their female counterparts and therefore sometimes retire from promiscuity, or at least from the sale of their erotic services, during their most potentially lucrative years.

Live shows and erotic performances in the United States are also quite various. America does not, at the moment, boast of any wide-open, wild erotic circuses on the scale of those currently running in Amsterdam, for instance, or in certain lush Parisian night clubs. But sex shows of sorts abound openly, even at country carnivals. The rock-bottom price charged to view a couple simulating screwing or to watch two girls or two men fondle one another is about $5, although it is possible to observe, from a window in a small booth, a nude woman dancing on a large mirrored table at certain peep-show parlors as cheaply as a quarter for roughly thirty seconds. (An automatic panel falls on the window obstructing your view until you feed a hungry slot machine another quarter!)

More elaborate burlesque shows—mere travesties of the delightfully vulgar (in the Latin sense) Minsky-type revues of a generation ago—cost about $5 to $10 per admission and are stripped down to bare essentials in almost every respect. On hand are two or three musicians (a drummer, a pianist with a small electric organ and possibly a bass player or clarinetist) and a half-dozen strip teasers (who strip more than tease), who may engage a member or two of the audience, if willing, in some light-hearted but genuine sex play, as well as a broken-down male comic from burlesque's past and (lately) even a male stripper. Cheaper shows dispense with live music and employ horrid rock tapes that blare cacophonies from electronic sound systems. Male homosexual counterparts are not substantially different.

Nightclub and bar shows are usually less elaborate, more erotically effective and more costly, but these charges derive mostly from inflated liquor and food prices, minimum and cover charges and the endless drinks that male customers often end up buying for the performers—who cleverly spit them out, frequently into frosted "chaser" glasses. Private shows for private "parties" may run from the mundane to the bizarre. In this world, one may meet girls who perform at stag parties and end up having sexual congress of some sort with every man in the house and in so doing are paid a lump sum of about $500. One also discovers a world of specialists and free-lance artists that boggles the imagination: a contortionist who can suck his own penis; a girl who performs multiple sex acts with two large dogs, one an Alsatian and the other a mixed-breed collie, both male, as well as offering her services, before and after her performance, to any men and women interested in having them for a fee of $25 per joust, credit cards *not* accepted; and so on. The latter young lady, quiet and well spoken off the job (I was about to write "in real life"), is fairly attractive and well groomed and claims to be an ex-school teacher (seventh grade) from West Virginia. I am not inclined to doubt anything she told me, so bored seemed she at my interview, which she granted as a favor to a mutual friend.

All of these girls—and men—seem to slip quite easily in and out of the porno film world, where their values in the flesh are frequently enhanced by their cinema reputations.

So-called "child porn," using children who either fuck or suck one another or other adults is another matter entirely, and one I have had no more luck in chasing down than has either the Congress of the United States or many enterprising newspaper reporters.[19] From what I can gather, "kiddie porn" seems usually to be a family enterprise or a cottage industry: siblings at play or mothers and/or fathers using their own well-trained children sexually in front of silent cameras which are often operated by another family member. For certain people the taboo break involved in this practice is enormous! I tend to be skeptical of much of the publicity recently given this aspect of the erotic market, because it fits the "sex and sin" mystique a bit *too* well by creating incestuous ironies that exacerbate the sin factor in erotica almost beyond reason—for instance, in the case of a silent color film of a nude lactating mother who puts her hungry infant aside in favor of a pair of male lovers who slabber at her breasts.

Whatever else one may say about it, so-called "child pornography" certainly *does* exist, and I have no doubt that somewhere live kiddie sex shows do too. But most of it remains illegal in the United States, and prices come extremely high for anything involving the multitude of risks involved in physically "corrupting a minor," a crime that only tangentially relates to the Bill of Rights, if at all.

It remains, however, the cumulative cultural experience of the human race that children of various ages and sexes have and will continue to serve as erotic stimulants for many adults, to say nothing of those dim exchanges of erotic pleasure that occurs within the world of childhood itself. Suffice it to say that at present the sin market is extremely sensitive to the exploitation of minors either as stimulants or customers, mainly because the corruption of children is a matter that the courts do not deal with as issues concerning speech, except where a pornographic novel or comic strip may center, as many do, on the violation of fictional children by adults or vice versa. Present commercial pornographic films often contain scenes of child rape, involving usually a "step father" forcing a young girl to suck and/or fuck him in an impressionistic "memory" sequence. But in every instance I have seen—with one exception (a French movie)—the child was played by a mature actress or by a girl over the age of consent where the film was made, who was made up and dressed to look young, sometimes even with her pubic hairs shaved or thinned a bit.

The general market about which I have been concerned is not, in any sense, the entire American market for the *erotic,* the lion's share of which, I would judge, is mediated to its customers in books openly published by established publishers (hardcover and paperback), manufacturers of large magazines, the advertising industry and the people who film and tape our television programs and movies (however they are rated), to say nothing of clothing manufacturers, so-called "fine" artists, sign painters and packaging specialists. No, what I am talking about is the "sin" market, its borders defined roughly as the places where middle-class candor or notions of privacy are freely and apparently gleefully celebrated in a spirit that I may easily call "twentieth-century Dionysian."

This world is part and parcel of the much-publicized phenomenon of "wife swapping" and "swinging," nude psychotherapy, excessive alcohol and excessive (but more or less legal) mild drug use and sexual liberation in general. Various investitures of novelty are added here and there to keep the mystique of sin always fresh and green, either as tokens of nonconformity or of nominal rebellion (which are usually temporary) against one's family, job, home, religion or past experiences. These provide psychic excitement and illusory risk by means of an interregnum from the quiet desperation of middle-class convention. This subculture appears to be a good deal bigger than it really is, because it almost invariably is at the center of much media attention, is noticed by passers-by and attracts the concern of law enforcement agencies. (A porno film theatre in a residential district protrudes into the environment like an unwanted erection; conventional movie houses are all but invisible!) It is also the cite of exchanges of tremendous amounts of money. On the other hand, certain aspects of it also appear to be less intrusive into culture at large than they really are, because they may be confined to delimited localities in cities and towns, sometimes operating under more or less innocent looking facades, and, like the "kootch" shows that travel with carnivals and fairs, are often pretty much taken for granted.

Except for the use of modern media of communication such as films, videotape and mass-printing mechanisms, the sin market is, of course, an old, old place, operating at this moment in the United States as freely and as openly and with almost as much protection by the law as it has been during the past century in the West. Considering the Victorian tradition from which we have so recently emerged, this is—or should be—quite sociologically and historically surprising. While it is certainly *different* from other sin markets—in the Orient, the Near East and in Europe (to varying degrees), despite their greater antiquity—it shares more factors in common with them than it is different from them. For this reason alone, a closer look is not out of order before we turn to our ultimate concerns.

The Dynamics of Prurience

Mass culture must desensitize us to the situations that folk culture, in its organic need to preserve both itself and the values it gave to life, surround with a sense of moral responsibility. Pop psychology, distributed through the media machine, too facilely identifies moral sensitivity with a sense of guilt. If the body is an appended gadget to the will; if it is something that can be narcotized, destroyed, made hostile to new life, frozen and stored for future use, sexually altered, then it is an instrument, a thing.

—John M. Phelan, in *Mediaworld*

NEITHER MORALS NOR ETHICS nor law need make either their primary or ultimate appeals to utility. In fact, the usefulness or destructiveness of any one of man's conventions may, anytime or anywhere, show little or no relevance to how well it lubricates or gums up ther wheels of society's progress or stability, either in the short or long run.

Since the onset of the Age of Reason, and with it the birth of the social sciences, this historical truism has presented intellectuals in the West with some of their greatest difficulties, even tragedies and often ironies. In fact, all ontologies (with the exception of those that are fundamentally nihilistic) seem to be biased somehow toward utility in one construction or another—if even an extremely vague one. If I am told to let my children starve and to suffer the plagues of the Egyptians through life in order that I may live on milk and honey in an afterlife, my suffering indeed serves a utilitarian purpose for *me,* quite aside from the Marxist interpretation of it as an instrument for preserving the economic *status quo*. Nor are such kinds of self-abnegatory demands for psychological utility just Christian monasticism or Protestant ethics carried to the nth degree: Issac Leib Peretz's famous story *Bunches Schweig* unearths this ontology in the ghetto streets of pre-World War I Warsaw and carries it to heaven with surprising beauty in an unlikely time and place. (The point of the story!)

Long before philosophers and psychologists of pragmatism, instrumentalism and behaviorism—or what you wish—had set the cornerstones of their thinking upon foundations of society's necessities, demands and functions, Hegel had reinterpreted all of history as a kind of technology that the *useful* sciences (there were no other kind) had given the Western world during the seventeenth and eighteenth centuries. This was the world of Bentham and Spencer, and in it grew the roots of contemporary sociology and modern social explanation. However man lived, his codes and creeds and beliefs and fantasies might ultimately, at the very least, be explained in some sort of utilitarian terms, possibly altruistic from a larger cultural viewpoint but usually self-centered and selfish when boiled down to individual motives—even to the personal motives of the saints.

We must expect, therefore, that when, where and if eroticism is indicted as an evil—even as a sin—the reason is usually a "Reason" (with a capital "R") that has something or other to do with personal dysfunction and/or destruction and, by implication, with the destruction of society. Where, when and if eroticism is defended as virtuous, the opposite is true: sexual excitation in one or another mode is seen as useful and therefore virtuous. Heaven knows, I myself have often used *both* arguments in this volume and, as a creature of my time, I suppose I shall continue to do so!

Taken alone, mere utilitarianism or the lack of it does not and cannot explain how and why men's social conventions are constructed in such a way as to justify primarily their ontologies rather than, say, the "greatest good for the greatest number," or "the least number," or "the next generation" or "the ease and comfort of the present moment."

Examples are too numerous and too uncomfortable to dwell upon for long: When a city is destroyed by an earthquake or a volcano's eruption, the inhabitants do not usually move to a new site. They build another city in the same place that eventually, as they surely know, must meet the same fate. Hindu wives of husbands prematurely dead used to throw themselves upon the funeral pyres of their spouses, or so they did until recent laws banned the practice of *suttee*. But it continues anyway. A famous and brilliant biologist falsified his data in order to justify a political construction of history rather than report accurately his findings concerning the growth of certain varieties of food crops. Men persist—and have persisted for centuries—in rushing off to fight wars that cannot be won, wars that will enervate them in the end and that obviously and inevitably will turn winners into losers and losers into winners in a multitude of ways. Need I continue?

All that Bernard Shaw's Devil and Don Juan had to do in order for the dream sequence of *Man and Superman* to be hailed by the best minds of our own century as "brilliant" was to list for one another the chronicle of such commonplaces. Shaw could indeed be brilliant when he had to be, but neither his Devil nor his Don Juan were portrayed as outstandingly intelligent. They merely told simple truths. This is the essence of most brilliant and scathing social commentary and satire: simple truths, or truths as seen by uncomplicated minds, minds that are not diverted by fashionable constructions of intellect that are apt to confuse cleverness with complexity.

In law books and according to countless definitions, morals and law are natural bed partners of utility. In action, as I think we have seen, they are closer to public consensus or public opinion than to reasonable public welfare in any sense. Cigarettes are outlawed because they kill us, but public consumption increases! Automobiles kill us too, but next to nothing is done to limit their use to sane proportions. Psychotically—and amazingly uneconomically—we gleefully smash into one another on streets and highways, while do-gooders blow copious hot air at the capitalists of Detroit—in much the same way that dynamite manufacturers were once (and sometimes *are*) blamed for wars. So our already confused lives and plundered pocketbooks are assaulted by passive restraints: we refuse to use seat belts and/or gadgets that prevent automotive death in favor of a life as a cripple or as a vegetable—if we are lucky! In the end, morals and law answer to public opinion, and public opinion answers to nothing but, as Walter Lippmann once told us, the cockeyed view of the world we live in that we like to call "reality" but that is in the end "public opinion." The circle is complete.

The odd version of this sad construction of "reality" refers perfectly in our own time and place to the matter of public communications, possibly to a greater degree to those that are politically and commercially oriented than to those whose functions are erotic. The first paradox here is that it behooves utility to be non- (or anti-) utilitarian! The established business and political order are best served if we, first, allow freedom of enterprise to dictate the destiny of our major channels of communication, and, second, continually affirm that their proclivity to ram propaganda designed for their welfare (not ours) down our throats (and here I refer largely to television) does not really have much effect on anybody either for better or for worse. That is, we must be made to believe that this persuasion is a neutral social vector, neither useful *nor* disfunctional in the upward march of culture.

In the first instance, this so-called "freedom" is an ideal rather than an accomplished or empirical fact, making up in emotional appeal what it lacks as a specific social technique. In the second, the *status quo* is uneasily maintained for the captains of the communications industries and their advertising brothers, because they, while contriving little that is patently evil or notably virtuous, seem to lubricate the wheels of our highly competitive, capitalist society. In this regard, therefore, established common wisdom turns the losers (the public) into winners and the winners (politicians and business interests) into—well, not exactly losers, but stolid pillars of the community and bearers of the burden of *noblesse oblige.*

In regard to most ideals of freedom, I am afraid that we are forced to accept this strange concordance of idealism and utility as one of the heritages that justifies what we believe to be a democratic form of government, the main problem of which, as G. K. Chesterton has said, is that it has never been tried. We know that Jefferson was aware of this futility in the democratic ideal, even in his modest vision of an aristocracy of natural talents. But he was clear in his conviction, even in old age, that failure in its pursuit was better than the success of any other type of socio-political order with which he was familiar. That his thinking has survived social theorists of the nineteenth century as well as the modern inroads of Skinnerian utopians (among others) should be apparent in the constructions by the United States Supreme Court of our Constitution regarding freedom of speech in the context of the preceding chapters of Part II of this book. Personally, I lack any more comfortable idealism by which to live in this context. So I am content to let the gods of paradox have their sway, joining, I suppose, most honest liberal legalists in our tradition, because like Jefferson I cannot find a better faith by which to live.

The second paradox is sneakier but no less a reconstruction of the faiths that give much to the vitality of American capitalism, accompanying its growth and, until the sixties at least, its generally accepted grandeur. Nearly two decades have passed since Joseph Klapper published his famous volume on the effects of mass communications, which demonstrated that the weight of evidence (at the time) indicated that "masscom" has little effect on anything in the realms of behavior and values, but it apparently does enhance or validate those values that are already accepted by culture or by various portions of it.[1] That Klapper himself eventually settled down as the resident social-science guru for CBS may or may not be beside the point in support of his claim that mass media—particularly television—are in a social sense non-utilitarian (or marginally utilitarian) and provide broadcasters and others with the clearest paths imaginable for (in serving commercial interests) maximizing the profits (and accordingly stimulating consumption) by any means imaginable and by thus paying minimal attention to the decorum of their output. The result was *highly* utilitarian from their point of view!

Klapper was guilty of nothing greater than putting down on the printed page what was already obvious to the parents of the kids who watched CBS' Saturday morning cartoon marathons. Finding evidence of outright corruption in the glut of "masscom" that is poured into a modern, capitalistic, industrial state is just about as hard as finding evidence of uplift—possibly harder! It does not matter much what kind of evidence you seek. One expert's opinion neutralizes another's. The findings of one empirical study deny the findings of the next. One laboratory experiment contradicts another laboratory experiment. The wisdom, therefore, of various social scientists—some writing while Klapper was still in knickers—who first told us that mass communications seem to do something to somebody some times, but that finding out exactly *what* they did (if the "what" exists) might be impossible has been justified over and over again. It continues to be in both less and more imposing environments than that of CBS' Bureau of Social Research. Much steam has also been pumped into this second paradox: As long as most "masscom" does not effect anybody, it is simply sound business practice to keep re-discovering that fact and spreading the news! Uselessness is extremely useful, and so the news has been sung in a pitch and key so strident and high that even dogs cannot hear it!

What is true of radio and television (and presumably most movies and even the press) is exactly to the point in any consideration of eroticism; it is even a hazier locus in which to locate the effects of human communication than Dr. McLuhan's ephemeral "global village." Problems intrude when the modern pornographer, possibly a college graduate in the humanities with an advanced degree in accounting, maintains seriously that *nobody* has ever really produced any reasonable evidence that obscenity (even granting that we know what it is) has ever hurt *anybody*— even small children (or especially small children). This exact conclusion was sustained by the report of the President's Commission on Obscenity and Pornography, which was commissioned by Lyndon Johnson toward the end of his term in office and delivered to President Nixon in 1970.[2] For reasons largely political, Nixon refused to accept the generally liberal majority conclusions of the report, which was the highly fashionable consensus of opinion that pornography did not seem to hurt anybody much (excluding children), and instead sided with the three minority dissents. But the findings of the commission and the pith of its recommendations—the elimination of obscenity laws—remain part of the record. Klapper, incidentally, was a member of the "expert" majority.

I emphasize fashion here because, by 1970, the United States had also lived through a number of investigations into the effects of violence, in movies and on television in particular, all sponsored by the federal government and all including some of the same social scientists that were members of the Commission on Pornography and Obscenity.[3] The studies are *all* remarkably similar and deal with almost identical types of highly equivocal evidence. Yet the violence reports claim that mayhem on the media *is* indeed corruptive and should be controlled by legislation, quite the opposite of the conclusions of the report dealing with pornography and obscenity! So Garry Wills notes correctly, looking over the political credentials of *all* the social scientists and others involved in *all* the studies, that "the Liberal View (sic) seems to be based on sound premises—that sex is good and violence is bad."[4] Political and social premises usually come before the evidence or the absence of it whenever the issues at hand are commerce, self-interest or fashion. But I shall return to this curious matter in Chapter 12.

The study to date of the effects of both erotica and violent communications of all kinds has been extensive, deep and voluminous. Again to the point of fashion, I would not even attempt to guess how many millions (billions?) of dollars have been spent attempting to understand causal relationships in these domains. I am certain beyond a shadow of doubt that the money could have been better spent by helping those unfortunates who cause trouble, or are in trouble of some sort, because of their sexual behaviors and/or by helping innocent victims of senseless violence wherever it occurs! But, no, such altruism violates an essential dictum of the ameliorative social sciences: that every social problem actually gets worse in proportion to the amount of money spent solving it. Accordingly, I defer to the academic-scientific viewpoint that research into the causes and effects of pornography and violence are worth every nickel spent on them, even if the outcomes of such research are entirely predictable before they are started. Better this in the academic world and print, I suppose, than social tinkering that further damages some cultural disaster area. And I include here the little-publicized warning from the Surgeon General's Office of the United States that violent television may be dangerous to our health. Like other, similar warnings, it did not seem to disturb anybody too much.

What ultimate conclusion might all of this research produce except what, for lack of a better term, I shall call the "Klapper principle?" Although members of various commissions and study groups may evaluate the weight of "evidence" this way or that (vide: the federal obscenity and pornography study vs. the federal violence studies), the results are differentially ambiguous, depending upon how you look at them. Into this void, therefore, rushes the Klapper principle: Since nobody can decide what affects whom and how, *nothing* probably affects *everybody* very much. And the results that we *think* we see from rampant pornography and movies and video that drip blood and gore are, in themselves, *functions* of other social factors that will one day be discovered. Media, says the principle, are both *directive* and *reflective* forces, and they only direct (or influence) that which they reflect (or absorb) from society at large and are powerless to initiate anything new. They are therefore innocent, because of a lack of evidence, of all invidious charges hurled at them, sensible or absurd.

For some reason that I fail absolutely to understand, most fashionable analysts of these matters agree on one thing: More and better education will help solve this reflective-directive dilemma or possibly even solve it entirely. This idea is peachy until somebody asks, "What do you mean by education?" Note that even a full-length and clinical treatise on the relationship of pornography and sexual deviance, concluding that there may and may not be a connection between the two (probably not), sermonizes about the value of *education* in untwisting what the authors have shown may be one of the most complicated and contorted problems in human psychology.[5] But "education" remains undefined.

So-called "education" is the great American panacea for nearly all problems. When a social or economic problem reaches cricial dimensions in the United States, we never revolt and rarely march in the streets, as they do in Europe and in South America—so say many sages. We offer college courses in the offending subjects! Our palliative for crime is the study of criminology; for drunkenness, courses of study in alcoholism; for aging, seminars in geriatrics; and for the ultimate personal and social problem, death, we have created a bright new academic specialty called "thanatology." The incidence of these problems remains constant, naturally, and sometimes increases while we are studying them, if we spend enough in solving them.

If this strange proclivity proves nothing else, the weight of experience—even with college and university studies of "education" themselves—demonstrates with awesome clarity that much schooling (at any level) tends to create more societal problems than it solves. This, I think, is exactly what the search for knowledge, wisdom, skill and civility *should* accomplish when it really works, from the Lyceum and Academy of Greece to the university of today. The philosophers of instrumental progressivism who "sold" education as a socio-political anodyne were well-meaning, misled soul-savers, and so they remain to the present moment.

Sex education is one example, but it is relevant to our concerns here. What enigmas in the sex lives of our children are *any* of our schools *competent* to untangle that cannot better be accomplished in a Nevada whorehouse, at a drive-in movie or in a motel room? My question is not capricious but based, as most sensible questions are, upon experience as a parent, a teacher and a student, and is directed to the obvious failure of many of our schools to teach even the most rudimentary aspects of contraception and prophylaxis.[6]

Effects of the Erotic

I shall follow Wills here in what I think is a perfectly satisfactory summary of how we know whatever we know, and how we know what we do *not* know, about the effects of erotica and pornography upon people—male and female, young and old.[7] In fact, it behooves any investigator in this field to follow *anybody* he or she can in this respect, so many are the questions that common sense, not to mention scientific sense, poses to assumptions, hypotheses, methodologies and conclusions relating, necessarily I submit, to an aspect of human behavior impossible to generalize about beyond certain commonplaces: for instance, the "shattering" news, as we shall see, that, under certain circumstances, certain types of erotica seem to be able to stimulate certain types of females in certain ways that are apparently not unlike the ways they also stimulate certain types of males.

For the most part, sociology and experimental psychology, past and present, seem oriented in large part to devastating old wives' tales by means of procedures that are called "sex research," a type of data gathering that leaves much to be desired. Much of what we think we know about the effects of all types of erotica—including that which is offered us by life—results from *surveys* of one sort or another. In sexual matters, the two published Kinsey documents, one on the American male and one on the female, are seminal works, but countless surveys of numerous kinds have followed in their wake, so many that they may be impossible to count.

Initial criticisms of the Kinsey studies remain relevant even to the more sophisticated sex studies done today—with various modifications. Surveys usually depend upon verbal answers to questions which are circumscribed by 1) language's ability to explain things, 2) the social setting in which questions are asked and answers are given, 3) the vocabulary of the respondent, and 4) the tendency of people to rationalize much of their behavior. While it is sometimes possible to get beyond verbal responses in measuring sexual arousal (see below), we are still not exactly sure of what we are measuring nor of the role that semantics at large play in posing questions or creating settings for responses. The longer, cleverer the survey used, theoretically, the more likely the answers are to be correct, again theoretically. But patience wears thin and contradictions within a plethora of answers to cleverly planned questions may be as indicative of misunderstanding, poor comprehension or boredom as they are of lying or dissembling. Ask me at what age I began masturbating, and my answer may well cover a four-year span, depending on how I interpret the word "masturbation" and depending on the state of my hazy memory at the time with regard to my own growth patterns. I will certainly provide you with an answer! The answer will be reliable "verbal behavior," the best I can do. This is better than nothing, I suppose! But how much better?

Other early criticisms are still fresh and may still apply to the glut of surveys one finds on the market these days. Population selection is a critical matter and, even among college students, individuals who are willing to answer either verbally or in writing, anonymously or identified, questions having to do with their sexual behavior or sexual feelings may not, I think, be divided into "people who *will* talk about matters like this" and "people who *will not*," which was the charge of distortive bias that was hurled at Kinsey decades ago. The matter is even far more subtle, as we shall see below, when eliciting erotic information from "people who *will* talk about matters like this." One person is unduly sensitive to homosexual matters, another simply "turns off" to any sentence containing a sensitive word—"fuck," "cunt," "prick," "asshole" and so forth.

Even relatively liberal college students may resent invasions into what they consider psychological privacy. Many, I have discovered, believe that the best way to protect such privacy is simply to lie, recognizing that in doing so they wield a devastating weapon of personal automony. I have gone through such phases myself, especially when political pollsters accost me. But I am not immune to the argument that the number of liars at any given moment is probably distributed equally among people of various political persuasions, although I *might* be persuaded to believe that registered Democrats lie more frequently than registered Republicans. In any case, nobody can prove I am wrong. (I am a registered member, at the moment, of neither party.)

Many people feel, and correctly I think, that the survey, no matter when or how it is used, remains the single most naive instrument available for ascertaining the nature of past, present or future *behaviors*. Naiveté, however, may or may not be a drawback to the usefulness of this instrument for certain purposes. If you want to find out what television program people watched last night, I suppose that *one* of the ways of finding out is to ask them, recognizing that certain distortions are inevitable and that one is always saddled with probabilities of error in sample selection, a matter that cannot completely be neutralized by statistical techniques, no matter how clever.

There is also a qualitative difference, at the moment anyway, between the question "Who are you going to vote for in next Tuesday's election?" and "How many times per week do you have sexual intercourse?"—a problem that neither statistics nor common wisdom can scare away. The essential naiveté of much social scientific empiricism is actually an asset to the validity of the answer one receives to the first question (and to its reliability too), but it is devastating to the latter, depending upon the setting in which the question is asked, the nature of the inquiry (live or written) and, most important, the psycho-sexual mind-life of the respondent.

Responses to surveys about sexual behavior fill volumes these days, not one of which is worth citing here. And, yes, I suppose most of these constitute reasonably accurate accounts of the verbal meanderings of women (largely) to open-ended questions about their sex lives. Heuristically, some of them remind me of the man who said about trees (not unwisely), "If you've seen one, you've seen 'em all."

Yes, interview ten prostitutes, and you may well conclude that all whores are frigid, or that all are lesbians, or that all of them resented their fathers. The annoying aspect of these assertions is that they are not *exactly* *in*correct! They simply do not reach far enough into the convoluted verbal responses one usually encounters when talking to assorted doxies, even if they are chosen from a cross section of the population in regard to race, religion, social and economic origin and so forth. To predict, therefore, that the next whore you interview will indulge in similar verbal behavior may well be correct, but it is also painfully superficial and next to useless—except for publication purposes.

All prostitutes are most decidedly *not* frigid, *not* lesbians and *not* victims of antagonistic fathers, despite what most of them may *say*. That most prostitutes have similar self-images *may be* true, but this also means little—as little as the fact that most teachers may also have similar pictures of themselves in their own heads or hearts or both. Nearly all dentists will give you certain similar answers in regard to certain aspects of their professional lives, but the answers will merely reflect that they have all been trained in the same way to answer certain sorts of questions and will have little to do with truth or candor or both. The worst part of the problem is that most dentists you talk to do not *know* how to verbalize their real attitudes, opinions or even their behaviors.

These surveys seem to prove only one thing and even that equivocally, if indeed they can be believed. Certain women (and men) talk or write interminably about sex if you give them the chance, and what they say in a given culture at a given time is predictable and repetitious to the point of nausea and beyond. But these are special people by virtue alone of their logorrhea, and throwing their responses together into a so-called "study" or "survey" constitutes an exercise in futility.

Wills' second category of causal studies are what he calls "quasi-experiments." This, I think, is as good a name for these sorts of games as any other. The book, cited above, on the effects of pornography on sexual deviants was compounded largely of this kind of experimental trickery.

Group studies may be set up so that identical questions are apparently asked different groups (i.e., heterosexual single males and homosexual single males; men and women; urban dwellers and rural dwellers). When one discovers different responses in any answers of the two groups, they may be manipulated into so-called "variables" that supposedly differentiate the groups. Therefore, I find myself in Group A if I have been *caught* at what is considered in my state as a "sex offense." If I have not been *caught* at the identical mischief and am not in jail, I am in Group B. Any differences in responses between the members of Group A and Group B will therefore be ascribed to the differences between "sex offenders" (Group A) and "normal males" (Group B). That the holes in such manipulative truth-seeking are large enough to admit trailer trucks seems to discourage neither sociologists nor psychologists. (In the situation above, the only *reliable* variable between the two groups is the fact that one is made up of people *caught* doing something illegal and the other of those who were *not*. I imagine their answers to a lot of questions of many kinds will be different one from the other, but what the difference illustrates, I cannot sensibly guess!)

At best, isolating single, selective variables that *might* affect sexual attitudes and behavior is a risky business. I am not even happy when eight-year-old girls in a single private school are compared to ten-year-old girls at the same school. The only *invariables* that serve research purposes that *may* have influences upon *all* aspects of these girls' lives are literally infinite, ranging from intelligence and constitutional differences to the multitude of domestic settings in which they live as well as the caprice of pure chance (such as the fact that a good number of the ten-year-olds have accepted lollypops from elderly gentlemen of quirky sexual proclivities who hangs around the local candy store but who eschew girls of eight because they are too young!).

The problem with these "quasi-experiments" is not their naiveté, because these sorts of manipulators make their naive—and usually honest—survey-taking brethren look like Solomons. It is rather that *anything* can literally be compared to *anything* if a common measure is used to quantify two (or more) observable, testable phenomena. It is therefore possible to compare the number of sex crimes committed in various cities with the number of porno theatres, adult book stores, ambulatory whores or, if you wish, sex education courses given in high schools or incidences of ownership of Japanese automobiles and hit pay dirt somewhere along the line, if you know something about computers and have sufficient gall. Chances are that the phenomena you are relating have little or nothing to do with one another. They may be the results of a common cause or causes; or B may cause A instead of vice versa. You are literally pursuing chaos and sometimes find yourself the victim of a situational practical joke.

The lowered incidence of sex crimes in Denmark after the legalization of pornography is an example of the latter, and a treacherous one at that.[8] Sex crimes *did* indeed diminish considerably with the coming of a free and open porno market—and almost immediately, mainly because the *main* sex crime in Denmark, possession and sale of pornography, was no longer a crime! As time passed, however, certain other sex crimes *did* apparently increase while others decreased according to factors that may or may not have had anything at all to do with the new porno laws. Rape incidence rose. But possibly a new Danish candor encouraged women to report a stable or decreasing number of rapes to the police more frequently. The number of indecent exposure arrests declined, but I am certain that in a city like Copenhagen definitions of what constitutes decent dress—already quite liberal before the relaxation of legislation concerning erotica—changed as other social factors changed. "Statistics are no longer significant," writes a knowledgeable observer of the Danish scene. "We can then only conclude that we cannot conclude anything, or that the situation with respect to crime has not changed much since the legalization of pornography, or that it has become worse.[9]

The observer lacks imagination. With a little statistical juggling, the situation he reports given his statistics could also "become better," depending, first, on how you define the word "better," and then on how you interpret an ambiguous social field and apply various quanta to it, comparing this to that until you hit a chance jackpot.

Wills also cites what he charitably calls "controlled experiments." These are obviously more fun to perform than any other kind of sex research (except perhaps participant-observation), but they are extremely dangerous instruments by which either to test hypotheses or derive workable generalizations. *In theory,* of course, a *single* controlled experiment might well answer once and for all time the question of what effect erotica (or violence or anything else) has upon people, if the experiment could be designed to operate with a large enough sample, proper controls and over a sufficient period of time. It would also be impossible to conduct, because *complete control* over *one* aspect of the subjects' lives (exposure to erotica) over a long period of time would be necessary. By this I mean that two groups of more or less fairly matched children (preferably) in reasonable number would have to be paired one with the other. The first would be shown erotica at certain intervals during their growth. The second would have to be kept in a cultural climate where it was impossible for them to get their hands on pornography of any kind. We would then educate the latter say, in a way entirely acceptable to the Girl Scouts of America or the established order of educationalists in the Office of Education of the Department of Health, Education and Welfare in Washington, D.C.

I do not mean that their education alone would have to be carefully controlled. So would all exposure of both groups to everything outside of the school room, where much of learning—possibly most of it—actually happens. Final results of this ideal experiment would then be determined only in the long run by means of a comparison of the life profiles of both groups. Were their sexual lives largely the same or different? Incidence of sexual deviance? Marriage patterns? Proclivities to crime? Religious impulses? General intelligence? Masturbatory behavior? And so forth almost endlessly, because I cannot think of the limits of what I might want to know about the differences or similarities between the two groups. No matter how limited our sample is according to the usual psychosociological variables that are desirable for similar experiments, the results, even if they showed only an *absence* of differences, would be most enlightening.

As I say, the experiment is quite impossible to perform—and I hope that it will remain impossible in the foreseeable future.

Falling short, therefore, of this idealism, experimenters have had to make do with less than perfect circumstances and conditions, which is to say that they have been forced to improvise. The effects of any psychological stimulus must, again in theory and often in practice, produce *some* sort of somatic change in people, and if change occurs, it may be measured. Thus, any number of indices may be used to show, at least, *immediate* sexual arousal: blood pressure, heart beat and such. In a number of recent instances even genital commotion itself has been measured with precise electronic calibration.[10] With males, in these experiments, the penis has been encircled with a device called a "penile strain gauge" that indicates both the nature and strength of their erections! (I am reminded of Al Goldstein's "Peter Meter" by which he rates pornographic films: one prick, two pricks, three pricks and so forth, as well as percentile rankings according to specific and general criteria. Goldstein, of course, performs this miracle—as do his male guest reviewers—without electronic help or wiring: *mirabile dictu*.)

Female participants in these experiments have been fitted with a gadget called a "photoplethysmograph" which is inserted into the vaginal canal. It measures pressure (cunt contractions, I presume) as well as blood volume change, both factors understood to be indices of sexual arousal when charted on a graph. (To the best of my knowledge, Goldstein has never wired up a female film reviewer in this manner.)

Individuals are then divided into various groups and exposed to all sorts of stimuli, including different types of erotica. Results, by and large, to such measurement tend not to be spectacular. Even so, they are open to many questions. First the population involved in such experiments must indeed be somewhat unusual folk, a largely self-selected group who permit their sex organs to be electrically wired, anticipating possibly that they are about to be exposed to red-hot sexual stimuli. (Many—or most—are bound to be disappointed.)

At any rate, I think I speak for most normal men of my age in saying here and now that *nobody alive* is going to wire up my dick for the advancement of knowledge or for any type of psychological experiment! If I require so much as a cystoscopic examination, I demand a general anesthetic! (Thirty years ago a satanic physician inserted a cystoscope into my water works under a local anesthetic, an experience I shall never forget. This sadistic leech mercifully died an untimely death at an early age, murdered, I assume, by one of his patients!) Nor do I imagine that many of my female students, past or present—some of whom have participated in my own fumbling surveys and helped me prepare materials for this book— would be particularly reliable subjects for these experiments, operating in the knowledge that an acrylic device with an electric eye is monitoring the behavior of their twats. Nor do I blame them. The attitude of most if not all of them who I actually questioned in regard to this matter was to simply look at me as if I had gone crazy! But I must admit that I do not possess the experimental psychologist's persuasive insouciance.

The gizmology provides, of course, only one method of eliciting small-group responses to direct erotic stimuli. You may always ask experimental participants what they felt. If you are foolish, you will trust their answers, which may have been motivated by any number of things from a desire to humor an eager experimenter to immediate and irrevocable hostility toward him or her. In any event, the human being becomes analogous to a laboratory mouse, and herein lies the greatest problem presented by these experiments, even granting that they must deal with select populations—who are usually willing college students. Despite the deep faiths of psychologists like Dr. Skinner, people are not mice—nor are they cats or dogs or pigeons, or even the people they were yesterday and/or will be tomorrow.

(Wills raises the possibility that most human guinea pigs actually devise methods of testing their own testers, a notion that John J. Sullivan, an experimental psychologist himself and former colleague, suggested to me many years ago. At the time, we were watching students in one of his classes at New York University perform identical experiments with a number of white rats and Skinner boxes. Recording the different learning rates of the various rats had created a fiercely competitive environment among the students, whose behavior the rats apparently were controlling magnificently. "Suppose," said Sullivan, "these rats know exactly what they are doing, take mental notes and compare them in a seminar discussion after I put them back in their cages!")

I said that the results of these experiments, by and large, are hardly spectacular and probably will not be of lasting consequence. First, they all show that people seem to be stimulated sexually by erotica of many types, which is hardly a well-kept secret. Second, they confirm what many people throughout recorded history have known and have stated clearly, among them our friend John Cleland (and also practically every writer of pornography before and since): that women as well as men are stimulated by erotic communications. The female response, in general, seems slightly different from that of males, due, I suppose, to the fact that a female "hard-on" is a metaphorical semantic convenience, even when considering an engorged clitoris as equivalent to an erection. The difference seems to center upon variant responses to slightly different sorts of stimuli, a matter taken up below and possibly better explained by an astute novelist or autobiographer than by an experimental psychologist. Many women respond more or less identically, I submit, to many men to precisely the same sorts of stimuli, a nearly mathematical reliability that may even be extrapolated from many current findings in the laboratory, granting them a validity they do not deserve.

Much is made of the old truism that in every culture man has known different sorts of responses to identical stimuli have been expected from people playing male and female roles—including homosexuals. The point is a good one. It obviously influences verbal and written responses to pornography as well as contaminates, to some degree, somatic reactions of females (and males) to erotica, depending especially upon the circumstances of exposure and whether or not their inhibitions have been freed by chemical or environmental means: liquor, pot, sedatives or stimulants, as well as the company they keep. A famous and now-classical study of female sex arousal concluded that the main sexual stimuli for college females were *men*.[11] There also remains a widely held belief, and some experimental evidence exists to support it, that women favor masochism in their pornography, which possibly explains the success of such strange documents as *The Story of O, Fear of Flying* and *Bedtime Story*—or possibly not.

No reliable test has yet appeared in print that indicates what kind of erotic biases, if any, attract or repel the majority of women of any age, social or educational group in our society. One hidden piece of datum, another open secret for centuries which has been lately confirmed by electronic gadgetry instead of the human hand, is that women apparently respond physically to pornography without being consciously aware of it, while men are almost invariably aware of physical sexual arousal. In a way, the still-hidden but great secret that explains the difference—if any—between male and female erotica may be extrapolated from this tiny crumb of insight, which is a side-product of contemporary experimentation that has not yet been considered seriously enough by psychologists and others.

In a highly sensitive and quite reasonable article on pornography for women, Lois Gould chews at most contemporary literature concerning pornography and females and then, being a novelist and a writer of uncommon sense, simply interviews fifty reasonably sensitive but disparately chosen female acquaintances at some length concerning the issue.[12] The pith of Gould's article seems to me to boil down to the conclusion that men prefer their erotica to be fairly specific and unambiguous, while women prefer more or less the same sort of thing but more discursively and subjectively handled. She writes: "Nearly all of the women I talked to agreed that depersonalized 'genitalized' sex, as represented in all classic male-oriented pornography, does not, and probably will not, appeal to them. Most of us did not know a single woman who had been 'reached' by the so-called 'new porn for women' for the simple reason that, as one woman put it, 'it's nothing but porn for men in drag.' "[13]

This observation agrees, incidentally, with most of the best empirical observation of female reactions to erotica. Nor does it argue with experimental findings apparently to the contrary, if one remembers that the *reactions* females feel may not necessarily reflect their true state of physical arousal and/or preparation for the sex act, masturbation or whatever else they do when they have been aroused. I hesitate to use the word "unconscious" here, because it will be misinterpreted. There is little doubt, however, that cultural conditioning as well as other learned differences between people create various and differing degrees of awareness of *responses* to erotica—so-called "response patterns," if we want to simplify or caricature a complex sensory process—that may all be quite similar, although they are perceived and reported differently.

During the past week, for instance, I had the opportunity, while waiting for a patient in a dental surgeon's recovery room, to note differential reactions of various individuals of different sexes and ages to stimuli that were all pretty much the same and which *could* not have differed as much as the patients' individual reactions, conscious or unconscious, to them. The dentist was apparently experiencing a bull market in extractions, and the anesthetics used on all patients were similar. But, as one noticed different reactions to the nasty experiences, those of sex were the clearest, to the degree that the dental assistants spoke to and handled the men and the women quite differently one from the other.

The situation was especially fortunate in that each patient was accompanied by a friend or relative who waited for him or her after surgery—the role I myself was playing. For each individual, the experience was therefore a "social" one, in that it was audited by at least one other person. By and large the males, even the adolescents, attempted to be nonchalant and stoical, some even to the degree that their blood clotted poorly because they would not follow instructions. The women tended to act wounded and vulnerable. They obviously found it socially permissible to cry (not one male did!) and to display considerable helplessness and even pointless rage and anger.

The circumstances of this event were quite specialized, contaminated in part by cosmetic dysfunctions, both real and feared, of tooth extraction. I am willing to accept the old notion that, if men had babies, there would be only one per family. On the other hand, I credit acculturation with enough power to understand entirely Noël Coward's offhand comment, after visiting the front lines during World War II and comparing British and American fighting men, about "sniveling little Brooklyn boys." Coward's words got him into trouble with former American admirers, but generalizations of this sort are invariably risky no matter how true they are. In Brooklyn's defense, let me note Shaw's observation that an Englishman thinks he is being moral when he is only being uncomfortable. British super-stoicism, no matter how unrealistic, has served its historical purposes, however, and contains a large measure of truth.

(Please do not misinterpret. In a dentist's office, I myself am as much a perfect coward as Ed Wynn was "the perfect fool." But I also go to absurd and often futile pains not to let it show. Implacably male, I'd say. Do not accuse me of punning, but Coward himself showed inordinate British stoicism at the end of his life when, crippled and moribund, he visited friends in New York and attended—at enormous discomfort to himself—revues that were made up of his songs and skits and performed by superb casts, knowing all the while that his days were numbered.[14])

So much for stoicism. Despite the supposed thrust of women's liberation, unisex and changing values in our society, sexual reaction, while organically a phenomenon of biological nature, invariably makes necessary a considerable amount of cultural role-playing. Because the bio-cultural mix is so variable, we probably would not understand it even if we were familiar with all of its constituents; nor have sociologists, psychologists and social psychologists made many productive inroads toward its mysteries. I see no reason, therefore, why a sensitive novelist like Gould may not be far better prepared to discuss female pornography (or *any* pornography) than dense clinicians and experimental types like the inventors of the photoplethysmograph.

The answer to the larger question of whether surrogate eroticism does *anybody*—even children and psychopaths—any harm, or any good as some claim, remains moot, all the more so after examining evidence that purports finally to answer the question in one way or another. Referring to the President's rejected obscenity investigators, Wills writes, "The Commission's real disservice to social science was the effort to disguise inadequacies of method, to pretend that they could be minimized where not obviated." [15] The "mysticism" of sex in culture simply negates much of the power of our best modern (and even ancient) methods of observing causes and effects in human beings. Eroticism is and has been nearly everywhere a holy aspect of the human condition, subject to non-rational taboos, rites, ceremonies, semantic games and mysteries, even to the godless. Searching for rational patterns of causality in an irrational universe reflects neither upon the adequacy of science to solve problems nor on the social utility of its peculiar ontology for that universe. This matter is discussed in greater detail in Chapter 12.

I am sure that my readers, however, are interested in the fact that much the same sort of observations may be made of most experiments and studies that attempt to find the causes of social *violence* either in television or in this or that other mass medium; this holds true for any other single culture trait or simple combination of them. If the history of human warfare tells us anything, it also displays clearly the mystical (*truly* "metaphysical" in the philological sense of the word) role that violence has played and continues to play in the really important affairs of men.

All the studies of all the king's children, *whether they produce results that show causal reactions between televised violence and children's behavior for the next hour, or whether they validate a thousand null hypotheses in this regard, are entirely meaningless!* [16] I am sorry to say that they are also entirely beside the point of the multitude of taboos and holy aspects of violence in culture; they produce irrelevant social scientific data almost by the ton, whether it comes from Klapper and/or cold-blooded psychological researchers like Stanley Milgram or from well-meant benevolent men of peace like Professor George Gerbner.

How fitting it is to consider here the absurdity of searching after knowledge that does not exist toward ends that cannot be reached, the absurdity being compounded by do-gooders among PTA and church groups, marching mothers in Boston, politicians like Senator Pastore and others who find virtue (if only on Sundays) in bemoaning the bad example that television sets for our children because of its heavy doses of violent action. When a noted psychiatrist like Irving D. Harris, therefore, raises an eyebrow in public at the "common knowledge" that teenage violence is a spin-off from televised violence, he is only adding an authoritative, experienced viewpoint to what common sense and clear thinking confirm again and again and again.[17]

Understand that I am *not* saying that either eroticism or violence may *not* foul up the lives of human beings and do untold damage to them *under certain circumstances*. But much the same claim might also accurately be made for reading, driving automobiles or bathing daily. Nor, in a still larger context, do I wish to absolve television in America nor the culture in which it thrives of its responsibility in underlining, exacerbating and glamorizing the least civilized and worst aspects of our Western tradition and laughing at the best! This is the kind of absolution offered by the Klappers of this world from stratospheric offices at CBS in New York. But the appalling condition, brought on by the pursuit of easy money and by delivering audiences to advertisers who have little choice but to pay or get out of business, *causes so many things, good and bad, in our culture* (mostly at the level of human attitudes and relationships, I suspect) that to single out violence (or sex) as prime and discreet factors of corruption is absurd and equal to blaming disease upon ambient evil spirits that jump into our bodies when we yawn.

Nor does the buck stop in executive suites on New York's Avenue of the Americas! Men and women of extraordinary irresponsibility and greed run, in effect, the *entire* "masscom" empire: television, radio, most magazines, most newspapers and two-thirds of the movies in our theatres for starters, each so-called "medium" so much the part of a total oligopoly of human attention and worship that it is impossible to peel one medium from the other. Nor may one say anything about any single component of so enormous a complex that it cannot be refuted by pointing to another part of the elephant, by denying that the elephant exists in the first place or by challenging the adequacy of the tape used to measure him or the accuracy of the eyesight of the measurer—or some other similar artful dodge.

Media and Effects of Effects

My business at hand is not to ask redundant questions like, "Why do publics that have been indirectly responsible for the major brutalities committed by man in his long history on this planet happen to enjoy certain kinds of films and television, especially in 'civilized' nations like Germany, Japan and the United States? Why are movies and television shows with a high degree of violent action in them so popular? Why, particularly, do children in these cultures find such action attractive?"

To avoid answering such questions, I have chosen eroticism not violence as the subject of this volume, although the two often walk hand in hand. Far more important, it seems to me, is the necessity to face a next and harder question, if and when we come to any conclusions about the harmlessness *or* harmfulness of *either* violence or eroticism. This is a question upon which little if any serious thought or speculation has been spent by people as intelligent as Drs. Klapper and Gerbner.

The next question is the challenging one! It consists of two words: "So what?"

While violence is a diverting subject—the reason, I suppose, that it has been about as popular as erotica with artists and dramatists and poets since ancient Greece—it behooves us to center our concerns upon the corruptive nature of erotic communications, even if, indeed, this corruption turns out to be nothing more than a legislative convenience. At least we know that erotic communications *do something,* and this in itself should be a comfort. (We are less certain about violence!) In any and all of their forms, they seem to prepare the recipient for an act of sexual gratification, be the act masturbation, heterosexual or homosexual behavior or, possibly, an apparently unrelated quirk such as caressing shoes or sniffing worn undergarments.

We have seen that the major problem with this simplistic cause and effect relationship is simply that all erotic stimuli are not equal as they are played along the keyboards of culture, age, education, upbringing, physical condition, religion and so many other factors that they are impossible to list. In the light of a good deal of evidence (the weakest scientific, the strongest impressionistic), sex alone (male or female) is not as distortive a factor in erotic response to any given stimulus as we once thought. We know this less because of our scientific progress during the past generation than because of the death of Victorianism, which had denied the presence of all erotic feeling in females. (Well, *certain* females!) On the other hand, age, physical, hormonal and psychogenic factors probably also play a larger part in differential male and female reactions than we had once assumed. In fact, when we speak of each of these four factors we may be talking about much the same phenomenon, each caused in a different way. The nuances of culture, especially influences of the family in which one was raised, are of *critical* importance, but their dynamics remained tangled somewhere in the depths of the eternal nature-nurture controversy which infuses contemporary behavioral science with so much vitality that I hope it is not settled for a long, long time.

Curious facts remain. In the absence of anything but opinion, I am afraid that I must play fast and loose with them, referring as best I can to the experiences of whatever informants I have been able to unearth who work and live in the domains of contemporary erotica. My observations, therefore, will not only be culture- and time-bound, they will all reflect other imperfect mechanisms inherent in the vanity we call "objective research."

1. Cross-media difference in erotica are roughly analogous to cross-media difference in transfers of other types of content. Methods of communication are each different one from another. (This truism in no way substantiates one sentence of Professor McLuhan's silliness.)

2. I have heard much erotica recorded in the sound medium and have

observed others responding to such erotica particularly during the "golden age of phonograph records." A steady and considerable market of erotic sound tapes—mostly recordings of sex acts performed or simulated by actors in studios—exists, and it includes material directed at many types of markets, most of it apparently male-oriented, but some seemingly directed to women as well, particularly tender lesbian dialogues. There are, therefore, descriptive tapes, homosexual and heterosexual tapes, incest tapes, and tapes that I am sure I have not been able to track down.

Despite grunts and groans, "oos" and "ahs" and sound effects, these stimuli are largely verbal and serve as extensions of dirty talk, limericks, dirty jokes and erotic conversation, any and all of which may arouse certain people under certain conditions. Like radio drama for some, recorded erotica may be particularly potent in that sound is a strangely *visual* medium that stirs the human imagination to perfections and performances impossible to achieve in the flesh, photographed or real. The same may be said of printed erotica, naturally, but my feeling is that sound is a better stimulus for most people than cold print—which is a difficult and hesitant generalization. If various reports are true, many individuals have been stimulated to unbelievable heights of sexual arousal (as I have) simply by having been caught by accident in a poorly soundproofed hotel or motel room next to a copulating couple—a devilish fate, because it is equally as hard to run away from it as it is to press one's ear against the wall, with or without James Bond's water glass to amplify the sound! At this point, the individual is trapped between imagined reality (what he *knows* is going on) and fantasy (what he *thinks* is going on) and what the tryst actually looks like, *especially* if he or she has *not* seen the participants beforehand. It is exactly this wicked tension that commercial erotic recordings attempt—and usually fail—to emulate.

3. That most of man's eroticism has been spread by means of the written or printed word is a matter that has resulted entirely from the sequential history of communications technology. Because it is the most ubiquitous form, pornography of the page probably remains the most popular type of erotic communication—and I include here the nearly lost art of writing love letters. But popularity is invariably the servant of convenience. It says nothing about power or psychological preference. For instance, I have spent far more hours reading pornographic literature in preparation of this volume than listening to records, watching films and/or live shows or whatever other medium my snooping has discovered. A porno novel could accompany me in my suitcase on a weekend's academic consultancy, sometimes causing blushes on the faces of the sweet young things who examine attache cases at various airports. Extensive experience was thus inexpensively and easily gained. I needed to be no more diffident about what I read in airplanes than about my porn library at home.

Even the worst print pornography requires literacy, some degree of concentration and an ability to fantasize. All reading—even being read to—is a highly abstract enterprise and, speaking affectively only, apparently an emotionally powerful mechanism of human communication. On the other hand, one's abstractive mechanism appears to be quite malleable, and the business of *meaning,* as Ogden and Richards noted long ago, remains a psychological enigma. The first draft of this book, for instance, was typed by a fine and loyal lady who claims not to have read a word of it, except that her non-reading has not prevented her from fixing up some of my gaucheries—misspellings, words dropped or not pluralized—as my pencil ran ahead of my thoughts. Fair enough. I cannot argue, at least, with the general tenor of her claim. Her accommodation has been to *me* and not to my subject. She is also one of the few living people who can read my handwriting. But she refuses to fantasize—probably because I have not provided her with satisfactory material for her types of fantasy. (I wish I could cite prudery as the reason, but the lady is far from a prude!)

Suffice it to say that the long history of printed pornography attests to the fact that it *works*—and it works in many different keys for, apparently, many different types of people.

4. The reason I shall lump *all* pictorial erotica together has to do fundamentally with the dynamics of prurience—the source of the itch. In a book that has recently been re-issued in paperback called *Lucifer With a Book,* the gifted young writer (an early suicide), John Horne Burns, noted how magnificently art captures the idealistic essence of carnality while eschewing entirely the unsavory aspects of its reality: noises, smells, squeaks, sweat, abrasions and even, and possibly most important, the grit and grime of human personality taken alone or as it interacts with others. I find this quality the fundamental dynamic of all pictorial eroticism, whether it is drawn, painted, still or in motion, in color or in black and white. Starting with the crudest pornographic drawing and continuing to the most sophisticated color film I have seen, one person's eye has always selected *from* reality *its own* idealistic vision of what was seen (or might be seen) and hurled that segment of nature alone into what college catalogues like to call "the communication process."

One of the joys of looking at pictures is their paradoxical nature, an irony that was amusingly summed up for me some time ago by a television commercial for a film company. "Are your pictures of your family up-to-date?" it asked. "Do your children look the way they *were* or the way they *are?* Get a role of X-Brand film. . . ." The copywriter probably could not comprehend the fact that *all* photographs—even Polaroids—show us the way we *were,* not the way we *are.* Possibly the Moslems, who regard a photographer as an individual who takes a little "something" from an individual each time he snaps his or her picture, best comprehend this fundamental principle of all pictorial art.

Part of the *enjoyment* of looking at a picture is the knowledge that "something" has been taken away from nature: a few lines in a scene designer's notebook, a caricature by the superb Hirschfeld, a photograph by

Bourke-White or a foot of film that sees reality the way Martin Scorsese does. Part of it is the knowledge that the "something" is not "everything" but only a selected part of it. To date, thank the Lord, 360-degree motion picture photography shown at fairs and carnivals in no manner replicates reality; it merely expands, for short term delight, a number of things that a cameraman selects for projection. One's affective reaction does not for a moment eliminate the theatrical "suspension of disbelief" necessary to enjoy any sort of picture. So the paradox remains, just as it does for the few extremely wide-screen (nearly 360 degrees) attempts at pornography I have had both the good and bad fortune to observe.

On the other hand, wall-to-wall filmic pornography creates an *embarras de choix,* whereas wall-to-wall scenery from a helicopter usually does not. Interesting for three or four minutes, such erotic films (or still pictures) destroy one's monomania or degree of concentration, which is apparently necessary for successful pornography. One definitely does *not* feel an illusion that he or she is in the midst of an orgy, because so much is going on in colored shadows all around him or her. Concentration is fractured and, possibly, some strange sort of anesthesia sets in as the stimulus becomes increasingly confusing, interferring with normal perceptions and reflexes.

In conclusion, I think pictures—all pictures—are successful mediators of prurience (and so popular) because they are so *un*like nature, as Burns indicated, rather than because they provide literal representations of it. When the imaginative stimulation found in the natural world is idealized in just the proper way by an artist, we talk about a "truth beyond reality," a silly phrase semantically but quite useful critically. We are talking about the nearly indefinable balance between reality and idealism which remains the hallmark of art. The achievement of prurience via pictures requires a similar sort of balance, and the ultimate value in erotic art or photography of any kind lies more in the manner and degree to which it is unreal than in its reality, I think.

(Note that the average audience—if such exists—of serious porn-film followers seems most attentive to sex when it is most fancifully presented: beautiful girls raping a man, attractive twins performing lesbian acts with a dildo, a girl sucking on an unseen man's prick in a race to achieve orgasm within sixty seconds, a couple screwing on a glass table that is suspended by wires, a beautiful blonde woman whose breasts, cunt and ass are sucked simultaneously by four attractive women costumed in black priestly robes—all of which provide scope for enormous prurience as I recollect while I write—even at my age!)

5. The nature and power of "live sex" performances presents an enigma, one that is not easy to parse. Possibly the generation of city dwellers (now decaying) who spent their youths in the burlesque houses of yesterday have lived through experiences that cannot be compared to todays so-called "sex circuses" or "all-live shows." Memory may play

tricks on one. The erotic climate of old-time burlesque may well be duplicated today for some in certain London or Paris nightclubs or in Copenhagen or Amsterdam, where the gaudy aura of circus and the "real tinsel" keeps pace with idealized adolescent sexuality. At any rate, I both shudder and laugh at the heights of stimulation to which the strippers of yesteryear could raise their jaded audiences at New York's *Minsky's*, not necessarily because of blatant sexuality, but because of idealism, intention, attitude and, for the lack of a better word, talent. Gone, at any rate, are Ann Corio (as I remember her), Georgia Southern, Margie Hart and company; their replacements are shallow imitators indeed, though they are not at fault really.

Interviewing one of these old-time female eroticists a few years ago, I was told that the cleverest among them achieve extraordinary command of an audience because nobody knows *what* article of clothing is going to be removed next, *when* it will be removed or *how*. The explanation, as an exposé of a performer's tricks, is far too facile. It has, however, been my experience that live sexual communication—other than direct interpersonal stimulation—achieves its end to the degree that it, like photographed sex, stimulates and gratifies fantasies rather than replicates realities. Once again, the problem is one of balance.

At present, most live exhibitions of real or simulated intercourse that I have managed to find in the United States are grimy, unstimulating displays that are more interesting in anticipation than in fact. Nudity alone means little in this day and age, and the endless sequence of "strippers" who populate today's excuse for burlesque shows are, nine out of ten, not interesting enough to wake up the sleepy (or zonked) audience. The occasional one who *is* interesting usually deals somehow with pantomimed fantasy—a little naughty masturbation, a glimpse or two of an actual orifice (not too long or much), possibly a provocative drop of a bosom behind the eyeglasses (somehow) of a customer in the first row or next to a runway or one of dozens of other tricks that do not come easily, I am told, to the artless.

Special exhibitions of bestiality and various perversions indeed induce highly erotic reactions in those inclined to such displays, but this is a redundancy. If the exhibitions were *not* viewed as fantastic (or fantasy), if the jaded could watch a woman copulate with a police dog every day of the week, such performances would attract few customers. These acrobatics are about as stimulating and realistic as those of the old sideshow "geek" or "Wild Man of Borneo" (still with us) who supposedly kills and eats a raw chicken for his daily quart of rot-gut.

Other types of sexual acrobatics can at times be both funny and amazing in much the same way that conventional acrobatics are, but they fare far better in films than in the flesh, one current example being the previously mentioned performer (I imagine there exist a few) who sucks his own penis to orgasm. Live audiences find him rather embarrassing to watch, except with morbid fascination, but his presence in one porno film (among the damned in a Hell of sorts) was both meaningful and provocative. Live exhibitions of urinary and scatological fun and games are, for most people, peurile and morbid—except to the well-stoned. On film, they may serve special purposes, being bleached of the tensions of reality.

Certainly a well-framed, stylized sex show—like the long running, slick, essentially effeminate *Casino de Paris* in London—may be both arousing and entertaining. But theatrical talent is required for costuming, staging, lighting and performing. Theatrical technology must be artfully employed to idealize the action, whatever it is. Theatricality does not preclude an occasional moment of badinage—or actual contact—with members of the audience, providing that the the players are skilled enough to introduce the audience member into the "show" on his or her terms in much the same way that magicians use spectators as assistants.

I am not claiming that live sexual performances must all necessarily be lavish, expensively mounted or depend upon extraordinary special effects. Theatre can occur in many places. What I am talking about, I think, is theatrical illusion. For this, all one needs if four floor boards and a passion. Nor is there any substitute for talent. Several years ago, I witnessed a young strip-tease artist (of whom I never heard again) start a near riot in a Chicago burlesque house that had been as quiet as a tomb during the ten or twelve acts that preceded her. She was not particularly beautiful, nor was she gifted with a stylized sexy physique. Yet her effect from stage was electric—possibly more than she herself could handle in her subsequent career. Every man in the theatre, I suppose, was able to fantasize, as I was, the kind of carnal partner she *might* be—which was probably *sheer* fantasy, although, most of us would never know for sure. Neither the erudite philosophy professor with whom I attended this performance nor I were able to explain sensibly this girl's appeal, nor, I realize now, was there any reason why we should have.

Are the effects of the effects of erotica more or less uniform in their dynamics? Do they, at least, closely parallel each other from person to person? This is a question that will never, in my time I think, be answered; it is similar to the question of whether five people all experience the color yellow in the same way. I am dubious about the use of the male erection as an indicator of the effect of eroticism, simply because I calculate (and have no reason *not* to believe) that a good share of hard-ons the human male experiences in his lifetime are by force of circumstance or lethargy gratuitous—that is, more or less unrelated to a present or future conscious stimulation and/or orgasm. Female lubrication and vaginal tension are likewise interesting phenomena, as interesting as the extremely attractive coed in one of my large classes last term who invariably swung her top-crossed leg back and forth (thereby creating some sort of vaginal commotion) whenever I was talking. She would stop when I stopped! Interesting, yes, but hardly productive under the circumstances, because of role-playing (student and teacher), pressure of circumstances (the fact that we met three hours a week and personal interviews were scheduled like clockwork) and various other conditions of civilization that withhold promises before they are investigated or make them too delicate to explore (her recent husband; my not-so-recent wife!).

Such cues are reflexive both for males and females and smack too strongly of Pavlovian mechanics to be important to the careful observer of the curiosities of erotic communications. Effective and powerful eroticism may in certain instances seem totally irrelevant to the neat stimulus–response nexus: Effects may be long-term. Effects may be latent. Effects may be subsumed into whatever parts of existence we label all too easily "the subconscious." Effects may be mediated so harshly by cultural taboos that they result in irrelevant neuroses. A father may be strongly attracted for a moment to his daughter. He may therefore scream that she is wearing too much lipstick or spending too much money on clothes. A son and his mother may fight like Trojans over the amount of his laundry in the bin or his attitude toward school as a by-product of a strong and devious sexual attraction between the two that culture sublimates but does not enervate. Effects may be mediated so intensively with cultural or situational flak (like guilt and frustration) that only in the wildest constructions of a psychoanalyst may they (apparently) be connected to their proper stimuli.

Custom, literature and even contemporary psychology (or certain schools of it) tell us that we may expect these irrationalities—that is, to expect the unexpected—more often from women than from men. This I strongly doubt on the basis of what little evidence we possess and some modest experimentation of my own. In fact, the opposite may be the case. Cyclic deviations from normal behavior in women, especially those keenly aware of their erotic feelings, conform to more or less perceptible and regular patterns, usually, of course, monthly. While it has been shown that such patterns are also present in male emotional swings and rhythms possibly to as great (or greater) a degree, attention is not called to their periodicity by menstruation or any other discreet organic phenomenon. They thus *seem* more arbitrary while, in fact, they may be just as regular, precise and, in my rough judgment, dramatic, particularly as men begin to feel—or think they feel—a notable decline in erotic power after about the age of forty. What they probably do feel, in fact, during this difficult period of life is less a failing of sexuality than a diminution in their ability to fantasize or to accept the fantastic as possible. Much male middle-aged depression seems to radiate in strange ways from this phenomenon, a clinical problem that has responded best at the present writing to medication rather than to talking cures like group therapy or psychoanalysis.

At what we these days call "the bottom line," there is no way to determine how the "nurture" factor in human experience influences whatever quantum of force nature has given to the human sexual drive. Complexities created by culture at the hominoid level of sexual reproduction are of such magnitude as to make most others on the other frontiers of the natural sciences seen as simple as arithmetic. For most life on this planet, reproduction is synchronous with the environment, either taking advantage of it, overcoming it or competing with disturbances in nature that occur by chance in the interest of some sort of natural selection.

Man's reproductive facility is different. It reaches full potency only after an unbelievably long period of acculturization—or civilization—and is controlled throughout his most fecund years, and vestigially thereafter, by an ever-obtrusive cultural field made up of variables that may best be called "spiritual" or "mystical" on the one side and hard and clear limitations of circumstance on the other.

"Complexity" is therefore hardly the word. To expect that relatively minor variations in the interplay of physical, psychical and cultural forces that add up to the sex life of any single human being respond easily to some sort of "corruptive" (or "therapeutic") manipulation is at best absurd. At worst, it is a peculiar act of vanity that equates judgments that *I* may make about *my* own motives—or lack of them—to *my* own behavior and assumes that these judgments apply also to *others*. We do not, for instance, even understand the most apparently simple matters: why the sex urge of one successful talented, intelligent British playwright seems directed at the opposite sex, while his identical twin, also a successful talented, intelligent British playwright, is a homosexual; each is an equally charming person and apparently a good citizen. Certainly the variables of culture are limited in this instance to their minimum and the possible variables in human acculturation are exceedingly low: as small a number as a few thousand significant ones! When, therefore, homosexuality is glibly ascribed to "parent-child relationships," or when learned discussions center upon whether or not a preference for one's own sex is a "mental illness," good brains merely spin gears that might be powering more profitable issues.

What matters most at present, I suppose, about the effects of the effects of erotica is what people *think* they are or—more precisely—how they *behave* according to what they think they are. Indeed, it is important that our courts once imprisoned publisher Ralph Ginzburg for advertising somewhat racily his wares, that they have nearly incarcerated such individuals as Al Goldstein and Harry Reems for their respective mischiefs and, beyond the limits of law, that they have indirectly caused grave physical injury to publisher Larry Flynt. All these are social tragedies—or near tragedies—that, like many tempering experiences, have left most participants wiser and maturer for their troubles. But at what cost?

The effects of these legal actions, in each of these cases has been, I believe, greater upon the society in which they occurred than upon the participants themselves. The notion of free speech is powerful, and it insists upon the intrinsic flexibility of a social order that will survive by the triumph of human rationality over barbarism, in short, according to the principle that permits citizens of a free state to go to heaven or hell on their own steam! Possibly those of us who live in fairly open societies find ourselves inflicted with a grave burden in this respect, and, possibly also, it is one that many or most of us do not wish to shoulder. Both fair play and tradition, therefore, demand from us only one thing: that we maintain sufficient faith in the flexibility of that culture to withstand an infinite number of Socrateses, all of whom may well "corrupt the young" without forcing any of them to take the hemlock, simply because his particular faith does not duplicate or pretend to follow yours or mine.

When we calculate the effects of the effects of pornography of the vilest kind as you or I may see it, we are simply drawing a line or creating an arbitrary area of influence beyond and in which we do *not* have faith in the flexibility that undergirds these notions of freedom. We say in effect, "Beyond this point, I do not believe men and women can be rational!" Let me admit that some evidence for this position is impressive. But impressive also are the absurd and irrational lengths to which people go to gather riches according to the accepted tenets of the capitalistic marketplace. Is any type of behavior *less* rational than that of "the men who moil for gold," as Robert Service called them? Saturday night in a Las Vegas whorehouse provides us with a model of decorum and sanity when held up against the floor of a modern commodity exchange, the former less steeped in superstition and wild intuition, less venal, far quieter God knows and fiscally, I think, less intrinsically dishonest!

Writers like Legman have suggested that human violence in art illustrates man's subconscious answer to his modern tendency to draw the line of faith across sexual matters, dooming them to the dank basement of repression, where, apparently sublimiated, they spill over into consciousness as rage and the desire to kill. Nature abhors a vacuum, and in this view the desire for sensual pleasure that might be filled by erotic freedom is instead satisfied by devastating dislocations in the worship of the primitive bestial satisfactions of violence.

This viewpoint has much to recommend it—in theory. But in practice it fails all tests, particularly pragmatic ones, because it does not describe man as the social animal he *is*. Rather, it deals with him as he *should be* according to selected bits of evidence. Of course, violence is intimately related to sex. But it does not play seesaw with it! Many other factors are also involved in our erotic lives. In fact, at the moment I am hard pressed to find human activities that are *not* somehow erotic in nature and were long before Freud created his personal lexicon of metaphors!

Deny any of us our erotic outlets, and we shall find *something* to replace them: exercise, scholarship, television addiction or heaven knows what. While little raw erotic emotion probably goes unappeased in one way or another in prisons—male or female—institutionalized displaced sex takes many obviously bizarre forms, only one of which may be a proclivity for violence. Considering the enormous concentration of violent men and women in any prison, most are surprisingly peaceful places! I have visited any number of so-called "bad" ones and have almost invariably been impressed with the aura of resignation that affects both the keepers and the kept, just as I have been led to bemused consideration by the apparent *uber-sanity* and worship of logic that usually pervades that segment of society we call a "psycho-ward" in a large city or state institution. These are anomalies to ponder, and in doing so one is encouraged to question all theories of sexuality that turn the erotic into a polar vector and posit any single form of human disposition as its reciprocal. Indeed, take away my toys, and I am likely to become hostile. But depending upon who I am, I am also likely to become any one of a number of other things instead!

I am sorry to report that President Nixon was well within his rights—in fact, he may have been correct—in rejecting the findings of the Commission on Pornography and Obscenity that no harm was done (to adults at least) by erotica of any variety. Common sense is kind: it tells us, as it told Nixon the politician, that as long as people think pornography is corruptive, it probably will corrupt them. This is one of the major powers of the devil: to disbelieve that he exists gives him total control over the disbeliever. Hence, the enormous quantum of devil's works one finds in this disbelieving world! Believe in the devil, and you have gone two-thirds of the way in keeping him at bay, and your advantage over the disbeliever is now notable. Nixon responded to that small degree of devil worship that still heats the blood streams of many of his constituents. His behavior bespoke the same sort of perfectly good political logic that was later to be the source of his undoing in the Watergate affair.

When we search for effects of effects, even if we grant that the Nixons of this world are correct, the shoreline of erotica recedes into a misty background as we encounter an endless ocean of forces and counter forces—"accommodations and assimilations," in Piaget's developmental terms—that occur throughout one single lifetime. Considering the magnitude of variant experiences in the life history of one average man or woman, the question of whether the young or the old, the impressionable or the impervious, the rich or the poor, the educated or the idiotic are stimulated occasionally to the illusion of corruption—or to genuine corruption by the devil himself—seems inane, pale, vapid and at times nearly senseless.

Eroticism and Technoculture

*Looking back now on the whole sexual scene we can see
that our species has remained much more loyal to its basic
biological urges than we might at first imagine. Its primate
sexual system with carnivore modifications has survived
all the fantastic technological advances remarkably well.*

—Desmond Morris

DANIEL BOORSTIN in his latest short but brilliant book on technology singles out the centennial exposition of 1876 as the moment when American
technological genius had come to full flower—when the curiosity some call
"the technological revolution" really conquered the West.[1] Among other
things, Boorstin carefully differentiates between various types of revolutions and shows us the errors we fall into when we try to use political revolutionary models for other types of social and cultural change, even as
manners of speaking. Technological revolutions, cultural revolutions, educational and economic revolutions are not socially comparable to military
or political revolutions. A. N. Whitehead has shown us, for instance, in his
study of symbolism that symbols change at a revolutionary pace in the
wake of socio-political and especially military changes—but such changes
do not seem to follow other, more metaphorical cultural changes that
occur on a revolutionary scale.[2]

Using 1879 as a marking stone is, I suppose, neither better nor worse
than using any other point to symbolize the dramatic changes that technology as a sort of foster son of science brought to the so-called "daily life of
the average man" in the developed nations of the West. Advanced technologies that had nothing to do with science as we know it, but rather

233

mystical philosophy, had already gone through their own great ages—possibly of "revolutionary" proportions—in the East, particularly in China and Korea. They subsequently turned static, which was largely the result, many assume, of the consequences of not being constantly renewed and energized by the stimulus of so constantly provocative an epistemology as that of scientific enquiry. (The point should be made here that the glories of the oriental technologies lasted between 1,500 and 2,000 years, and our own scientific technology has survived but a fraction of that time. One cannot, therefore, compare East and West in this respect with much confidence.)

I have elsewhere picked the years from 1830–1840 as modern technology's pivotal epoch, basing my assumption on the idea that the steam-operated printing press was the machine that mated the muscle of technology (the engine) with the brain of culture (the printed page) to create a novel set of conditions in the West for the physical and intellectual ferment that followed in the name of "technology." Others, like Boorstin, prefer to meld into the growth and development of the technological society its intellectual implementers, or at least some of them, such as Charles Darwin and Karl Marx; still others, such as Sigmund Freud and Henry Ford, must historically be calculated as influential vectors resulting from the societal changes modern technology had made in certain countries during the nineteenth century.

If you like, however, *modern* technology began its hegemony in the West at the very moment that the steam engine began replacing man-power, woman-power, child-power, mule power and horsepower in the semi-industrialized factories and mills of England more than a century before this nation's centennial celebration. The role of machines of one sort or another in the life of the West is expressed best as a bull market chart that rises at an astonishing rate in what has actually been a short time. I share the disenchantments of the nay-sayers, deniers and non-worshipers of technology's gods and devils on more than a few counts—particularly those of the brilliant French writer and social thinker Jacques Ellul.[3] In fact, I am perfectly willing, from a philosophical perspective only, to look at an etching of *one* steam engine operating *one* grist mill in the early nineteenth century and accept the proposition that, fundamentally, technology's basic function and therefore relationship to culture, mores, morals, material welfare, health, education and welfare has not changed an iota since 1800, nor has it revised its original—but equivocal—relationship to science in any basic way since that date to the present!

What even the most superficial analysts of modernity or devoted conservatives of former cultures, rites, rituals, faiths and gods may sanely deny is that technology has *not* changed man's social and/or living conditions in enormous and dramatic ways. In so doing, it has also deeply influenced his culture, both with a small and large "C." Finally, it may also in many ways have changed what before the age of technology (and even until quite recent times) was regarded as a universal and staple given: so-called "human nature" itself.

Nearly all forms of change in history, from the most apparently evil to the most benign, turn out in the long run to be mixed blessings, probably because neither you nor I nor historians have the vaguest idea of how to count our blessings in the first place. The technological genius of the West is one such change, and a popular one it is indeed for the diatribes of diabolists and high priests in our particular period of ecology, pollution, abortion, needless surgery, overpopulation, polio vaccine, pocket calculators and air-conditioned Pintos. As I light my twenty-fifth cigarette of the day, a consumer product cut, bound and packaged by the R.J. Reynolds Tobacco Company of Winston-Salem, N.C., 27102, USA, with my ancient Zippo lighter and inhale, roughly, the 450,000th smoke in a lifetime, I cannot afford to take the influence of technology lightly. I have considerable respect for both the Lucifers and the upstairs angels, not only of technology, but of the methodologies of scientific inquiry that technology has demanded and spawned and the broad but searing educational and propagandistic effect it has had upon us all![4]

Most of this is nothing but talk—and nearly all of it is laughably inconsistent: neo-Thoreaus extolling the ways of nature in the mass press and on national television; oil company prosodists claiming that they spend millions on species conversation and allied nonsense. Worse, cultural comics like instant so-called "folk singers" play their ditties on electronic guitars and yell similar sermons into microphones attached to ear-splitting high-fi amplifiers and speakers. Much of it indeed seems funny if viewed from a sufficient distance (like McLuhan's "global village"). But sometimes it hurts when you laugh.

Technology is terribly difficult to analyze with cogency for those of us daily immersed in it and dependent upon it for the pitch, timbre and tone of our lives. Some few have had profitable things to say in the form of useful generalizations that may help us, at least, to understand the way we are caught in our time and place by historical forces that we cannot control but can to a degree comprehend. Technology, in its evil sense, is not a "problem" to be—or that *can* be—"solved" in the way, ironically, that technological thinking implies that all human problems can be "handled." Nor is human technology, as many once thought and so preached, an extension of human evolution that, let alone, will show us how to build a stainless steel ladder from earth to heaven. On one side, technology is not science—nor is it even science fiction. They both are branches of philosophy and of our literary tradition respectively, and, while the output of both, at the hands of scientists like Oppenheimer and/or writers like Clarke, may help us understand certain aspects of technology more clearly, neither directs the destiny of technology any more than Einstein did the invention of the atomic bomb or Jules Verne the onset of submarine warfare. I find the word "tangential" geometrically perfect in this matter.

Analysts, not the least Boorstin in his short book, have, however, been of inestimable help in telling us where technology is likely to take us in the future or at least in clarifying options.

Ellul is termed "pessimistic" by literary critics who refuse to understand his humanism. To maintain, however, that technology is the enemy of humanism, transforming, in progressive stages, education into propaganda, individuality into collectivism and freedom into conformity, is the major theme of his subtle arguments. I find it difficult to deny. That democracy is impossible without freedom is, of course, self-evident. When Ellul says that in the long run the technological society is (and has always been) a tyrannical one whose seeds of destruction are what we tend to regard as its successes, he is simply explaining a good deal about cyclic illusions in man's history and giving the lie to the apparently ubiquitous faith that the present moment is somehow immune to all lessons of history.

When Arthur Koestler speaks about a "ghost in the machine," he may sound more optimistic and hopeful than Ellul, but his psychology is neither.[5] It is simply more colorfully descriptive. Should he say simply what he means: that the secular world has found its god (or its devil) in the inherent quality of a technological environment, and to this god *alone* modern man—capitalist, Marxist, nihilist or ecologist—prays by means of elaborate rites and rituals that might be the envy of a medieval Vatican council on liturgy, he would be more condemned or generally ignored than he is. Koester knows that all men have found the source of their spiritual beliefs in the pragmatic truths provided by their environments, and this is not a very fanciful or elegant message to try to communicate to people who think that they are intellectuals.

The "machine," rather all "machines," are in fact just about the only societal vehicles of truth that any of us since infancy has learned *cannot* lie to us, and I include here those aspects of technology that are not only nuts-and-bolts machines but, in Ellul's word, simply "techniques." To the most overtly godless academician, the metaphor of a "ghost" that lurks within the technique of mathematics (or statistics to the sociologist) is perfect. The technique (or machine) cannot ever be wrong, although foolish or evil men may make operational mistakes or distort truth. Nor is this enormous faith broken even when barriers of measurement are broken. Earth-bound mathematics are special cases, being limited by special circumstances: for instance, the speed of light. New mathemetics are therefore created—which are *truer* than the old true ones—to handle every possible contingency in an ever-expanding (or contracting) universe, a mathematic that describes "black holes" that cannot exist but are all the realer because of it! Cursed with a technologist's brain—and bottomless faith—Koestler's technological society is neither more nor less doomed than Elull's, nor is he more or less "gloomy." The reason, naturally, is that the human quality we call "wisdom" has very little to do either with machines or gods, nor has anyone discovered a technology that may be derived from it.[6] What technology is and is not, what it does and does not do, what it can and cannot accomplish and how it does and does not interact with scientific epistemology are central among the most profoundly and seriously misunderstood issues of our time! But this is nothing new. They were misunderstood in 1879 and, I suppose, are doomed to be forever—if anything lasts that long.

Modern Western men and women cannot (or will not) attempt to understand their own family of gods, devils and ghosts any more than they really want to comprehend the vital natural forces that coerce them into the absurd behaviors that we loosely label "sexual." The domain of modern metaphysical "reality" is both wide and strange, but it is also "real" in the sense that it is observed behavior and amenable to comprehension via that rare quality of human wisdom I mentioned above. Wisdom applied to phenomena that boil down to mysticisms, however, usually sound to the contemporary ear like irrational babbling, because it does not yield an assumption that *this* so-called "physic" must unlock the door to the comprehension of *that* so-called "physic." The two physics of such metaphysics are separated by a membrane of *uncommon* sense, in the same tentative way that meta-languages, meta-dramas and/or meta-anythings are separated and easily destroyed by parsimonious dissection. Into this nettle, however, have both technology and eroticism (at least since the eighteenth century) been thrown in the Western world with obvious consequences. Nor do I not notice anything more than superficially expressed desires to free ourselves from either on the current agenda of national priorities in Europe, America and Japan, where this diseased sort of thinking has turned into public policy!

The Impersonal Erection

I apologize.

The reason I have chosen to begin the last chapter of this section with the all-too-brief description above of several abstruse aspects of a matter of transcendent importance to modern culture is that the consideration of technology and technique as factors influencing the erotic climate in which we live today is so important. I find it far more germane to how we communicate this eroticism and what its effects are than all the experiments, studies, statistics and quantifications that have been gathered by dozens of presidential and congressional investigating task forces. Therefore, I felt some bruising had to be given to the major mystiques of technological culture—though much too little and much too weak, I am afraid.

Let me then—possibly to muddy the waters still further—turn to a notion with which I have not yet dealt at length. It is, in fact, Aristotelian in origin, going back in crude form to the *Poetics*. But Aristotle was unable to carry it far, largely because he did not live in a society of machines, nor in one with a clearly articulated notion of corruption (in today's sense) or of ghosts and/or devils. These civilities were yet to come. Nor do we have a copy of his critical essay on comedy, which was lost somewhere in an Athenian ruin or heaved out with apple cores in the garbage of a medieval Scriptorium. What does concern us in Aristotle, however, is that, whatever corruption he indeed found in the drama (or epic), it "does not touch the art of the dramatic poet, but only that of its interpreter. . . ." This was signified by a continual sense of concern in his description of the theatre of his time—particularly in those plays and entertainments he calls "vulgar"—and with the welfare of the actor or the poet as a performer.[7]

Aristotle's concern with the effects of performance upon the player is a reasonable descriptive psychology, as useful in fiction as it is frightening in reality. The haunting element of credibility gave the character Ronald Coleman played in the film *A Double Life* (1948) its eerie plausibility: an actor whose private troubles reflect those of the Othello he plays. In this age of celebrity, anomalies of this sort turn into gossip column fare and eventually into folklore. The so-called "legends" of John Barrymore, W. C. Fields and Errol Flynn are examples from the past; that of Joan Crawford of the present. Art, particularly theatrical art, and nature are separated by a razor's edge, as Elia Kazan tells us neatly in his well-crafted novel, *The Understudy*. The energy that flows from a dynamic performer of any sort—even a Janis Joplin or a Judy Garland—also flows back into each in one way or another. "An actor's tragedy begins," Leo G. Carroll once told me, "at the precise moment that he begins to believe that he is, in some reincarnation, the Duke of Gloucester." Carroll was a superb technician. The people he played affected his character no more (or less) than a talented and sane photographer's or portraitist's ability to capture his particular version of reality injures him.

Thank heaven that most performers are immune to this Aristotelian professional hazard and manage to live, as their publicists often demand, private and public lives in different keys. Most of them rarely confuse one with the other. (Of all the highly celebrated figures in show business today, I imagine that Fred Astaire has preserved this difference as scrupulously as anyone. Even after having read his autobiography, *Steps in Time,* one knows almost nothing about the private Astaire.) The celebration of performers, as noted above, creates as well other sorts of dynamics and interactions that began, I imagine, in seventeenth-century England and continues highly accelerated into this period of mass media and mass myth.

What I mean is that it usually matters not one bit in the social arena what an actor or performer's private and actual self-image is. This is largely because his public image is taken in great measure out of his hands and survives at the mercy of writers, agents, publicists and high-paid feather merchants who "create" the personalities—not all of them in show business—about whom we read in *People* and view doing whatever they are expected to do on video interview programs at the hands of exploiters like Merv, Johnnie, David, Mike and their overpaid staffs of celebrity touts. When a retired government big wheel writes a book, it behooves him well to "perform" in some manner for the enormous audience that apparently believes what it sees on the tube, just as it does for historians like Will and Ariel Durant, who, I imagine, are beyond caring. More than half of such celebrities are not talented people in any respect; they are merely famous people because they are celebrities. Many of them, I also imagine, play (for them) this not-too-serious game simply because it beats working! What the standardization for the mass public of these people as guest-show commodities means to you and me, however, is another matter.

Aristotelian corruption has here become an end in itself in that a double manipulation has occurred! First, human beings are interchangeable objects (so-called "talent" in television patois), being more or less the same from day to day on various television shows but becoming absolutely ubiquitous when they have something to *sell:* a new book, dancing lessons, a set of commemorative medallions, a new play, a film or television series, a line of clothes or cosmetics and so on. (Why does Mickey Rooney keep coming to mind? Zsa Zsa Gabor? Orson Welles?) Their appearances (which may include a short song or dance and/or an imitation of Humphrey Bogart) are trade offs: exposure and/or a few dollars in exchange for an appearance on the American midway along with other freaks! The time and distance between one such exposure and another is quite small. "Hot" celebrities clutter the airwaves at the same time on different networks and on different programs saying much the same things to different celebrity pitchmen. The individuals ostensibly responsible for these exhibitions go to few pains to keep their secrets. Their gallery of "talents" contains only depersonalized commodities, which are measured in mystical weights and measures of "audience appeal." The crocodile man is neither better nor worse than the turtle woman. Prize fighters, tap dancers, poets, magicians, sword swallowers and ex-criminals become interchangeable units. Actors are the prize freaks, because they are able to be whatever the market desires them to be—that is, if they are conventionally "smart" and listen to their press agents.

Second, an audience is being manipulated by yet another machine, and I do not mean the television set itself or radio or movie screen, because these are neutral technological media, as fundamentally impotent as an airplane without a pilot or a cannon without somebody to fire it. This is the technology of celebrity or performance *itself,* in which the *individual* personality of the artist, actor, writer or professional "guest" becomes a function of the grand technique of entertainment in its widest sense with a talent that may be no more grandiose than the ability to make innocent answers to stupid questions sound somewhat off-color—Zsa Zsa's one notable talent—or the cool nerve to say outrageously silly things with a straight face. Whatever these abilities are, it is impossible that they can be little more than essentially corruptive to the same degree that all dissembling—with the exception of intentional deceptions such as performing magic and ventriloquism—must be corruptive both for the performer and ultimately, beyond the concern of Aristotle, for the viewer or "sucker." When an individual says, on the basis of this type of celebrity exposure, "I like John Wayne but I do not like Woody Allen," they are not making even cursory critical statements. (Most people, simply and in the first place, lack wide or deep enough exposure to either man as an artist to make reasonable critical judgments of his work in reference to the theatrical traditions within which he has to operate.)

What they are doing, however, is personalizing the technology of the presentation of the "selves" of these two formidable artists by choosing the deceptive and simple device that is common to most technologies in one way or another. In this instance, they are probably confusing technique with personality. In effect, the machine of technique has been anthropomorphized, in the same manner as many of us, often without noticing it, think of our automobiles as animate, personalized objects. Remember Bill Mauldin's cartoon in *Up Front* of the cavalry officer giving the *coup de grace* to his jeep? The reason that this is such a universally pathetic and funny cartoon in technological cultures is that it is reflective of the experiences of all of us: a comic picture of a man killing Koestler's "ghost in the machine," a ghost we all recognize. When we do not recognize it—and we rarely do when the vehicle of technology is human—I fear that the outcome is more pathetic than funny and probably more ubiquitous, having been institutionalized into such conventions as the traditional chorus line of a musical show or movie, the Radio City Rockettes or in the type-casting of an otherwise talented actor whose gifts have been depersonalized and manipulated into playing stereotyped characters that prevent him from displaying his true abilities.

(The question of type-casting when it involves such superb actors as Boris Karloff, Jimmy Durante, Gracie Allen and, late in her life, ZaZu Pitts is another matter entirely that must be considered *both* in psychological and artistic terms, which are not strictly pertinent to the discussion here. In these instances, and I include men like Astaire, the performers have mastered a technology of impersonation that, in ways that I do not pretend to understand, manages to mediate to the audience what they indeed *are* as people, but it somehow becomes idealized into wide dimensions of fantasy. One good example is Karloff's superb monster in the *Frankenstein* films—a character that in no way reflected the kind, articulate, intelligent adult Karloff—a monster that he had cleverly characterized as a large, ugly and immensely powerful and amoral *baby,* an experience through which he had gone as well as obviously studied closely. The monster was indeed a "newborn infant." I can best compare the technique of a so-called "type-cast" role by a Durante, for instance, with a performance of a magician in terms of its essential honesty and lack of fundamental deception, which stems from the audience's—and performer's—knowledge that the display is "mounted simply to entertain," as my magician friend, the late John Mulholland, used to say whenever I jokingly compared him to a riverboat gambler!)

Returning directly to eroticism at last, there exists what might be called a "school of thought" that objects to eroticism of all kinds on both reflective and directive grounds. It bespeaks the claim that the erotic, of necessity, depersonalizes and manipulates individuals: both participants in media such as photographs and movies and writers of books, as well as audiences who themselves are manipulated *by* certain media machines and always *as* machines. In other words, both reflectively and directively eroticism is a vehicle of depersonalization by virtue of its isolation of sexual feeling and emotion from human personality.

Directively, one may notice this most obtrusively as he or she walks past the inviting descriptions of various "loops" on display in pornographic peep-show parlors. They mince no words! "Teen blonde makes it with red hair (authentic) chick. Hot 69. Rear action." "Black stud takes hot mama three ways," or "Suburban kink: housewife in front and rear action with well-hung twin brothers," and on and on. Reflectively, my own discovery has been that when an erotic film or book that I have over some years held in memory is given a later, repeated viewing at a point of psychic satiation (my state at the present writing!), I discover how fully I *was* exploited, not by what I saw or read, but because I was manipulated into certain inappropriate responses quite beyond my control at the time. In effect, I had fallen for fraud, notable only because poor filmmaking and/or inept writing had aroused responses in me unworthy of the stimulus. Not only were writers and performers "used," so was I!

The most brilliant exponent of this point of view with whom I am familiar is the much-published (and respected) spokesman for the Freudian right-wing—in fact, from a socio-political perspective he may *be* the Freudian right-wing—namely, the psychoanalyst and writer Ernest van den Haag.[8] His view tends to be clinical. That is, he does indeed find everything about pornography (possbily not all "eroticism" as the word is used in this book) corruptive, in that it causes to his satisfaction considerable dysfunctions among his patients. Put another way, he finds pornography injurious to the individual man's or woman's sexual lifestyle when he or she is compared to others who receive normal or reasonable erotic gratifications through life without recourse to pornography. (Other therapists, Albert Ellis for instance, maintain that the reverse is true: strictures that prevent individuals from any kind of erotic gratifications, including those of pornography, cause, they claim, sexual dysfunctions both in individuals and in society.)

In the end, I find van den Haag's combination of clinical observation and neo-Freudian theory far more reasonable regarding the so-called "outcomes" of exposure to pornography than I do the kind of experimental evidence cited in Chapter 9, though neither is entirely or even heavily convincing. But I share the view of many that experiments into certain aspects of psychology vitiate themselves by doing exactly what van den Haag claims pornography does to his patients. The experimental process, by means of epistemological magic, transforms "people" into "subjects." This metamorphosis may be quite suitable (or possible) up to a point in biomedical research but not neatly amenable to one of the most *personal* disciplines, next to philosophy, with which scientists play today—that is human sexuality. Particularly suspect is the semantic trickery that turns *both* human action and reaction into the apparently neutral term "behavior." To his credit, van den Haag is sensitive to these problems and properly wary of all instruments—including those involved in experimental social psychology—that emulate a model of technology and/or use mechanical metaphors to describe either what people do or how they feel.

On this basis then, van den Haag takes a position—in direct opposition to the generally liberal viewpoint—that also relies largely on the observation and theory which more or less follow the Freudian doctrine of repression and sublimation where sexual matters are concerned. Let me add that they do *not* necessarily follow Freud himself, who apparently objected to the frivolous nature of erotic light opera, much less pornography. Freud, however, was a Victorian in many ways until the day he died, and his personal prudery had little to do with his work. Van den Haag simply joins many liberal neo-Freudians who, following Freud's analytic ideas, expressed most clearly his familiar final essays, that alienation or anomie is the greatest by-product of contemporary technological society. These concerns have also interested hoards of psychoanalytically oriented social observers from Erich Fromm to David Reisman to Herbert Marcuse, most of whom clearly lean toward left-wing political ideologies. Van den Haag is a voice from the right, and he has centered his concerns upon what boil down largely to be technological aspects of pornography, both as given and as received by culture.

Van den Haag's point is certainly well taken, even if one wishes to regard it merely as a humanistic statement of moral idealism. Starting with an assumption, current in Western thought but obviously (and devastatingly) absent in most of the East, that human relationships are *not* subject to the same regularities as technology, and that there exists no essential technique inherent in custom or biology regarding erotic behavior, the sexual manipulation of people by other people for profit without joy or out of ignorance or under circumstances of coercion is essentially immoral. Worse than this, it is likely to be an unhealthy experience for *someone,* whether it occurs in a Park Avenue call girl's apartment, on the stage of an Amsterdam night club or in the Gestapo's slave brothels at Ravenbrueck. What is meant is that, when the human vaginal canal, mouth or rectum becomes merely a soft surface for masturbation, or when the erectile abilities of the penis are manipulated by impersonal mechanisms, both the biological and social natures of sexuality turn into exploitation, as inherently cold-blooded as a business deal between an Armenian and a Vermonter where both believe they are cheating the other! In the end, of course, neither is cheating—or kidding—anybody but themselves. No wonder, then, that those who share this viewpoint also have grave doubts about the value of *any* kind of experimental evidence employing sexual stimuli that are registered on machines neatly calibrating the strength of erections or vaginal lubrication! In these terms, it may well be argued that a motorcycle seat is inherently erotic, because it has power to arouse both prick and cunt of certain people at certain times!

Here I am reminded of one of the most famous—and possibly ubiquitous—erotic devices that has probably been part of culture since Rome, if not before. (Best descriptions are found in eighteenth-century pornography, but I have also read of the device in a number of recent homo- and heterosexual pornographic novels and have seen it used in several films, old and new.) It usually takes the form of a thin wall or curtain with a hole in it into which the "customer"—usually at a bordello—sticks his erect prick. On the other side of the partition he is manipulated by *something* to the point of orgasm: a mouth, a cunt, male, female, a dog, a slice of warmed liver—who knows what? Much to the point is the classically bizarre attraction of this device in any one of its many forms: the utter impersonality of the sexual experience, certainly more anonymous even than a rendevous with one's own hand! In fact, I think of it as a sort of Black Mass ceremony in miniature that derives its obviously strange *attraction* from exactly the same corruptive aspects of eroticism that so annoy van den Haag.

First, a metaphysic is being reduced to a simply physic; the dual aspect of the sex act has been melded into one slice, at least for the man with his cock in the hole—and I imagine for the creature on the other side as well. Second, an elaborate mysticism is being reduced to simple mechanical essentials—to a technology almost entirely devoid of personality or even personification. It is, I would say, a type of devil worship in miniature. In place of a "ghost in the machine," we discover an orgasm, a proposition highly repulsive to Dr. van den Haag on humanistic grounds, but viewed as quite harmless by others who also regard the male orgasm as a neuro-muscular response to reactions of the endocrine system stimulated by sense mechanisms in crotch and brain and points between.

There are, I think, fewer intrinsic weaknesses in van den Haag's arguments—and its variations—than its many detractors would have us believe and these do not justify the beating that van den Haag himself has taken at the hands of lawyers, psychologists, physicians, judges, social critics, artists, pornographers and others. He is concerned (following the philosopher Ortega y Gasset) about what he has seen of the many forces that undermine human health, both of mind and body. His arguments are justified by rampant trends—visible in all technological cultures—that depersonalize the unique self and impede possibilities for individual growth and uniqueness, even in one's own evaluation of oneself. It is possible to observe, therefore, in the spread of eroticism to culture at large by the mass media and by mass means of distribution, the strong threat of still one more and highly invidious invasion into the domain of human privacy, which has been already gnawed at by various mice of bureaucracy, technology and mass production—to say nothing of the tax collector.

Where I think van den Haag and others who echo his ideas go astray is in underestimating the power of the total cultural field in which the institutions of pornography are immersed, and in overestimating—or isolating—eroticism as a domain separate from and unrelated to the multitude of psychological forces that depersonalize the individual and his or her relationships to others in the technological state. Possibly these other forces are, in large measure, inevitable consequences of the mixed blessings of technology and therefore a constant factor, while mass pornography does not need to be, because it can to some degree be controlled. But, nevertheless, I tend to regard them as more or less inevitable *results* of life-styles that have turned, in Ellul's thinking, almost every human institution into a *system* dominated by technique. In a culture where one can learn the technique of making friends and influencing people, one is able, naturally, to learn also the technique of erotic virtuosity! From here it is but one step to full-blown technologies of all human relationships. For example, money will buy me friends, a superb technique that really works! Drugs or neurosurgery will influence people in certain predictable ways. Pornography will provide me with erotic pleasure. Huxley predicted devices that could accomplish all three mechanically and at the same time, and in these projections he was largely correct, mainly because his technologies of drugs and "feelies" already existed at the time he wrote about them.

The isolation of eroticism and pornography as particular instruments of depersonalization in a society dominated psychically by its own technology is therefore correct as far as it goes, but its truth is closely related to its degree of unimportance. That I personally—and obviously—find interview programs on television more degrading to performers and viewers than pornographic films and that van den Haag feels the opposite way is a reflection of our different perspectives of culture: his as a therapist, mine as an educator. We are both fundamentally concerned about exactly the same thing! In fact, we agree, except that each of us believes that the other party is getting excited about a matter of little consequence when compared to another evil that each personally understands but others do not! Once we move away from our *amours propre,* our areas of agreement widen—for instance, our feelings about the tyrannies of air travel in a culture that has made such travel a necessity for people like us, not only reducing us to pawns in an enormously complex technostructure but scaring us at times half to death!

Having looked then at the formidable quantum of sense in the charge that pornography is a serious vehicle used by technologies to depersonalize and atomize the individual and his intrinsic relationship to his natural environment, let us now consider the proposition that what seems to be a cause *may* be a result, and the possibility—however remote—that erotic communications, even as manipulated by modern media of communications, may offer us illusions that the machine has *not* disintegrated human individuality. I suppose the fundamental question boils down to whether or not the ghost in all the machines of modern technology, the ghost in the concept of the "technology of living" and the ghost in erotic communications are the same ghosts, merely kin, or unrelated one to the other.

The Erotic Classroom

What I am about to describe is in no manner a formal experiment. It is an experience. If I use some of the sterile language that often accompanies behavioral experimentalism, it is for parsimonious purposes only. As an experience, it is impressionistic, somewhat disordered in intellectual rigor, contradictory, inconsistent in parts and incapable of providing a basis for responsible generalization. In short, it is rather like experiences provided by life itself, except that an unusual set of circumstances was artificially created and apparent results were observed with, I hope, both a measure of sophistication and compassion.

To summarize, this is what happened: In the spring of 1978, I happened to be facing, in my role as college teacher, a class of fifty-five students who were more or less in my control and were under unusual circumstances. Most of them were juniors and seniors; thirty were females, and twenty-five, males. None had ever been married, except one student, a widowed Negro woman of thirty-four, who was the mother of two children and who had returned to school on a veteran's scholarship to pursue her education. The median age of the rest of the class was twenty years; the mean, twenty-one years. Of the thirty females, five were black. Of the twenty-five males, two were black. Except for impressionistic judgments of them and the fact that they all knew me personally in varying degrees of teacher-pupil intimacy, I may best characterize them as a normal cross section of college students in the suburban area where they were attending school (although five students came from areas beyond commuting distance from the university and lived on campus). A surprising number, nevertheless, also resided in the university dormitories (seven males and seventeen females), despite the fact that they lived near the university. The dorms, incidentally, were high-rise towers, some sections reserved for males, some for females and some for coed occupancy. To the best of my knowledge, the lifestyles encouraged in all of them reflected the generally liberal orientation characteristic of Long Island, the site of the university.

When I say that the class seemed "normal," I mean normal to *me* in my position as an administrator and teacher for three decades in the vicinity of New York City. A minority of students might be classified as WASPS. The rest represented various minority groups: the largest number bore Jewish surnames or versions thereof, the second largest, Italian and/or Irish, and, as mentioned above, there were seven black students in the group. Let me minimize the possible influence of race in the erotic lives of these youngsters. Without exception, the black students tended to come from much the same sort of middle-class background as the white students and, as opposed to other classes I had taught at the same institution, they did not tend to cluster socially, either in seating or in informal social groups. Nor were the black students' reactions to the sensitive issues (including matters of race) that were raised in class substantively different from those of the whites. The only sense of minority opinion I felt in the classroom concerned the issue of "women's liberation," which came up occasionally as part of the course of study. I judge this reaction to have been provoked largely by the "devil's advocate" role I played in class (that the students apparently understood) and by the measure of enjoyment I seemed to find (quite purposely) in arguing against women's rights—even the right to vote—in this context!

The subject of the course was an odd one, but it was a topic that I had been teaching off and on and in one form or another at this and other universities since roughly 1958. Called "Censorship and Communications," the title explains little, except that, ostensibly, the semester was spent reviewing the history and current practices of censorship in the realms of blasphemy, sedition and obscenity. Since its earliest days, obscenity in its many manifestations had been the topic that the students seemed most interested in, and I suppose I was too. Over the years, of course, the content of this part of the course of study had changed enormously, not only concerning changing morals and practices in the communications arts but also in terms of the legal framework within which I, as a teacher, had to work. One must remember that, in 1958, if I held up copies of Miller's *Tropic of Cancer* or Lawrence's *Lady Chatterley's Lover* (third edition) in class, I was displaying an item *illegally owned in New York State.* Counseling my students under twenty-one to read these or similar books was risky, flirting as I was then with the possibility that I might be arrested (at least) for corrupting the morals of minors or advising them to indulge in illegal behavior. I would not even have *thought* of displaying what I then considered a pornographic still photograph in class and had to content myself with nudist magazines and racy paperbacks. In fact, obtaining authentic case studies of pornography in New York City implied that I had been involved in illegal dealings of some sort, and it well behooved a relatively young professor in those days to be circumspect.

By 1978, both my youth and need for circumspection had vanished! I had, as a matter of fact, projected a print of the infamous movie *The Devil and Miss Jones* for my class the preceding year in preparation for a final examination essay question on the Burger Decision (see Chapter 11) vis-à-vis the film, only to discover that about half the class (including the girls) had already seen it (but were perfectly happy to view it again)! The tooth-grinding uncertainty through which I had gone before screening the film meant nothing—nothing, that is, except the thought of the three hundred dollar fee to rent the film.

The 1978 class seemed to present an ideal group for purposes of investigating further what I had only experienced until then in casual conversation with more or less self-selected students: young people's attitudes toward commercial pornography. I thought that I might also possibly gain some insights into how and in what way the showing of a highly erotic film in a class situation of males and females was regarded by the group. I had been impressed by the general degree of involvement in, and candor concerning, all aspects of the course until the last weeks, mindful of the fact that "Censorship" was limited (except by my permission) to juniors and seniors, that other communications courses were prerequisite to registering for it (to keep out the idly curious), and that the demands of the course (exams, term papers and such) often discouraged some interested students, particularly the requirement that every student attend one X-rated porno film *in a theatre* either in Nassau or New York County and report in writing the entire experience in detail. The latter assignment related mostly to discussion of "contemporary community standards," in particular, present problems relating to definitions of "community," especially in the various counties of New York City and Long Island (about how these standards were applied and to whom). In this regard, I assumed that students could not understand the problem of eroticism's relationship to its audiences *in vacuo* and that a trip to a porno grind house, no matter what risks were entailed to their sensitivities, limb or epidermis, was necessary to begin to comprehend vital issues in ways that the United States Supreme Court apparently could not.

Student resistance to this assignment, then four years old, had from the start been quite high, the resistance mainly due to the expense entailed in visiting a fairly clean and well-ventilated porno film theatre, which usually involved a trip to Manhattan by rail or car and an admission price of five dollars, as well as to what a number of students called the "inconvenience." Criteria for taking the course were therefore spelled out in detail in the initial session, along with admonitions to the unduly sensitive in regard to matters of race, religion, sex, deviance and so on to register for another course in place of this one—that I, as a department head, would get them into even if it were titularly "closed."

In other words, by 1978, the forty-nine or so students taking "Censorship" were typical neither of all the students at the university nor of those majoring in its Communication Arts department. As young people, however, what appeared to me to be their insistent middle-class morality—and sometimes elastic moral standards—was general liberality and tolerance, as well as an interest in subjects that young people, I assumed, should be interested in. All this gave me the general impression that I was dealing with an unusually normal group, free of "hangups" and/or "hobby horses." In addition to the dynamic or tone of the classroom—a matter that a long-toothed professor feels more in his bones than in his head—this particular class seemed exemplary in terms of candidness, apparent honesty and the kind of *esprit de corps* one finds only occasionally in "middle-class" second-to-third-rate private, suburban university college classrooms such as this one.

The film I selected for class (that took up an entire class period) was *Sometime Sweet Susan,* a fairly successful low-budget pornographic movie made in the middle seventies. I had selected it mainly because it seemed to serve the purposes of the course. Although crude, it dealt seriously with what might be a genuine problem: a schizophrenic rape victim who seems to manifest alternately two personalities. One is a sweet young thing living in fantasies of idealistic romantic eroticism, and the other is a degenerate, foul-speaking, deviant slut. In the end, the slut turns out to be the "real" girl, much to the surprise of a psychiatrist, who had been treating her in the institutional setting of the movie. The film also contained innumerable (and some insufferable) flashbacks to both the fantasies and the realities of the girl's former life as well as to the catalytic gang rape that apparently put her in the mental hospital in the first place.

The sex was explicit, but the questions raised by the film in regard to definitions of obscenity and legal criteria thereof, past and present, served the ends of the course of study almost perfectly. The movie was made in color; it contained an excellent music track of original rock compositions professionally performed; and the parts were fairly competently acted by Harry Reems, Shawn Harris and others. In general, it was a typical porno exploitation film with two critical differences between it and others similar to it, one aesthetic and one, I suppose, mechanistic.

The aesthetic difference centered upon the obvious serious intention of the film. Although a "cheap and dirty" low-budget production, a certain straightforwardness characterized the production as well as an obvious willingness on the part of the director and editor to sacrifice sensational values for the purpose of telling a coherent story. On the other hand, the sexual elements of the film (in fantasy and life) were clear and unambiguous, most of them displaying graphically the same sorts of groping, sucking and fucking that continue forever in less artistically made movies. Male-female intercourse of various types occurred largely between the psychiatrist (Reems) and his patient (in imagination) and his girl friend (in fact). The latter sexual scenes, lightheartedly played, constituted the most arousing aspect of the film to my eye, although various of my students, particularly the girls, disagreed with me and singled out one of Susan's bucolic fantasies, repeated a number of times, in which she and

Reems chase one another and eventually screw in slow motion in a wood-land setting. Considerable emphasis in the movie was placed on one lesbian sequence, rather darkly and wildly filmed but extremely explicit, in which Susan, displaying her "evil" side, seduces a buxom young nurse who joins her enthusiastically in various forms of female sex play. Susan's rape, recalled in memory, on the other hand, was not explicitly portrayed but rather filmicly suggested. The most the audience saw were short cuts of genitalia of the participants and reaction shots.

The other unusual aspect of *Susan*, immediately noticed by most of the class, was the total absence of conventional "come shots," a previously discussed convention of European and American pornography. While the male performers did indeed apparently experience orgasms, they ejaculated where they would have ejaculated in life—not for the benefit of a camera by means of interrupted coitus and a bit of masturbation but inside mouths and vaginas. Evidence of orgasm was displayed only—and realistically—by close-ups of lips or cunts after withdrawal, lubricated apparently by genuine semen.

The reason that *Susan* was exceptional in regard to these come shots (I later learned from the producer), was that the director was simply unwilling to contaminate what he felt was the realism of the film with camera shots that, when all is said and done, pander to the audience by showing them that the fucking they have seen is authentic and not simulated. The fucking in *Susan* was clearly authentic without conventional tokens of good faith. A number of my students were able to figure out the correct reason without prompting, although others, who felt that the film was poor, mentioned that it was not redeemed one bit by this effort at realism. The producer, incidentally, assured me that the absence of come shots did not hinder the business done by the film at porno box offices in the United States.

One other point: While all the performers—even the non-pornographic character actors—were good looking (with the exception of the rapists), none of them was ideally handsome or beautiful or unduly made up or artificially lit like fashion models or Hollywood's synthetic people. Even the fantasy sequences reflected more or less accurate depictions of nature, except for some hocus-pocus focusing and slow motion that in no way intruded upon the somewhat naive but earthy casting of the various parts.

Susan was by no means a superior film. It was simply a typical pornographic film that, given more time to re-shoot technically defective spots (it was made in less than a week) and given a larger budget for scenery, lighting and props, might have been an excellent, honest and serious movie. The producer, unfortunately, had overspent on the music sound track and was therefore constrained to shoot it in the same rushed and sloppy way most porno films are made.

At any rate, I felt that *Susan* suited my purposes well. It was easily available, both to show my class and to preview and study further at home. Neither my wife, my eighteen-year-old daughter nor twenty-year-old son—living with me at the time—were impressed with the film. They much preferred, correctly I think, the previous year's imaginative *Devil in Miss Jones,* although my son (at what age, I cannot imagine) had already seen *Susan* in a commercial theatre (but did not object much to viewing it again).

In attempting to bring some order to the student reactions to the film, I handed out a four-page questionnaire after it was shown, requesting that it be returned to me at each student's convenience.[9] There was no way that I could pre-test the questions, because they had to be printed before I had an opportunity to preview the film—although I had seen it three or four years before at a commercial showing. I had therefore to devise questions of sufficient generality not to reveal that I no longer remembered in detail the exact plot or sequence or individual scenes.

Returns of the questionnaire were quite interesting—possibly the most interesting part of the experience for me, largely because they produced a mystery I enjoyed solving. Despite one absence, fifty-five students viewed the film, including my student-aide, an attractive twenty-two-year old female alumna of the course, who turned out to be more than a passive agent in the episode. (The students were all familiar with her and knew that she corrected objective exams for me, kept records and performed other clerical tasks—incidentally with both objectivity and expertness. An honor student subsequently elected to Phi Beta Kappa, I had asked her to view the movie with the class in order to observe reactions with me and to help her in the eventual task of collating responses. Naively, I did not think her presence was likely to distort anyone's reaction to the film.)

I did *not* receive anything like fifty-five responses, no matter how I subsequently pleaded with the students to return them, write them on typewriters, write them with their left hands or dictate them to friends! Instead, a total of fourteen females out of thirty and seventeen males out of twenty-five responded. Although I guessed at a number of possible reasons for the low response by both sexes, I subsequently made it my business to find out why. This I discovered—unfortunately more or less impressionistically—in conversation (sometimes directed and sometimes apparently meandering) with students who had been in my other advanced classes or with those particular students who had seemed most frank and uninhibited in their classroom responses and with whom I had had, for one reason or another, relatively personal conversations in the past regarding academic and other matters. Nine such students, five males and four females, were asked to keep their ears to the ground and report to me reasons for the low response if they could discover them.

I had suspected two major reasons but did not want to assume anything without some evidence. In the largest number of cases, and particularly among the females, non-participation resulted from personal hostility toward *me,* either as a teacher or a person or, I suppose, in my role as father surrogate, which most older male teachers of young people play. In some cases the hostility was quite explicit and should have been expected, considering the backgrounds of the youngsters. "He's writing a book," one girl was quoted as having said. "Why the hell should *we* help *him* with it? Who's paying for this course?" Others were entirely convinced that I "got my kicks" from snooping into their sex lives. Still others explained (quite rationally) that *I* had done *them* no favors. Why should *they* do any for *me?* A number, quite sincerely I think, considered the questions "dumb" and/or claimed that they *could not* be answered.

Another group, though small, was made up about equally of males and females; it quite sincerely brought up the issue (mentioned, possibly unwisely, in the questionnaire) of rights of privacy and the freedom of anyone, anywhere *not* to answer personal questions of behavior or conscience unless legally directed to do so, a point upon which I had come down pretty hard a number of times in the course. In a way, I think they may have regarded the questionnaire as a test of my own willingness to accept a principle for which I obviously had spoken, despite my devil's games, quite eloquently.

A considerable number of males (including two who sought me out to explain in private) did not answer, because they were afraid my student assistant would recognize their answers and identify their questionnaires—exactly how, I am not certain. I had been quite scrupulous in determining whether the assistant had previously been sexually intimate with any of the students in the class. She had not, and was, at the time "going steady" with a pre-dental student who would not have taken a course in censorship even if he could—and he could not. These males—possibly as many as five—were simply shy! I suspect that their excuse that my attractive assistant would read their replies may have been merely a convenient alibi for their natural reticence, particularly in regard to questions about their present sexual activities (mainly masturbation).

A possibility exists that similar shyness inhibited some of the girls, although my intelligence agents, both male and female, could not discover enough to consider it worth reporting to me. In drawing a general picture of respondents versus non-respondents, my information sources (who never met together nor were identified one to the other) agreed that the "better" and "more serious" students had filled out questionnaires. "The ones who like you and understand you naturally cooperated," said one (female). *"But* remember, Dr. G., most of us are completely fed up with filling out crazy questionnaires in every sociology and psychology course we've ever taken. We've all been used as guinea pigs ever since we were in junior high school by some teacher or graduate student or testing service or another! Frankly, I wouldn't even trust my own answers myself, I'm so used to bullshitting teachers! I didn't want to do that to you. Ask somebody else your questions."

Against this colorful and dynamic background then, the following, in summary fashion, were the results of my poor survey, for what they are worth:

Of the seventeen *males:*

1. Six of them claimed to have been bored by *Sometime Sweet Susan.*
2. Eleven were interested in the film, three in the story, six *only* in the sex scenes, three *only* in the lesbian scenes and one only in the beginning sequences. (All excessive totals indicate double or triple answers.)
3. Fifteen found the film erotic; the largest number, four, singled out the lesbian scene.
4. Six students claimed to have experienced erections at some time during the film; eleven claimed they did not. (An incredible response, either resulting from dissembling or, possibly, the circumstances of the viewing. I myself experienced one or two erections during the showing of the film, both in previewing it and in showing it to the class.)
5. Eight found various scenes repulsive, mainly the rape (four), which, as I noted, was directed and edited to emphasize theatrical melodramatic values rather than explicit sex.
6. The males were nearly all erotically active individuals. Only one claimed inactivity. Five admitted to masturbation, seven to heterosexual activity, one to homosexual activity and six to unconsummated heterosexual play.
7. Twelve students claimed not to have been affected by the specific stimulus of *Susan.* Three admitted to experiencing fantasies surrounding it afterward, two to increased heterosexual activity and one simply indicated "other."
8. Sixteen of the male students did not think that *Susan* should be censored or banned, except possibly, wrote one student, for children.
9. Ten students felt they could not identify with any character in the film. Five said they did (somewhat whimsically), largely with Harry Reems, the psychiatrist.
10. Nine students said that their own fantasies were not enacted in the film. Seven said they were, with the largest number, three, citing the outdoor nude romp (in Susan's imagination) at the start of the movie and to which it returned from time to time.
11. Eleven denied that another setting would have changed their reactions. Five said it might have, two of whom perferred to view such movies alone or in a movie theatre, and three suggested a female companion.
12. Only two male students said they would pay to see *Sometime Sweet Susan.*
13. Fifteen of the males admitted to previous experiences with pornographic movies or video cassettes.
    (All other results were too ambiguous or vague to report.)

Of the fourteen *females:*

1. One-half (seven) claimed to have been bored by *Sometime Sweet Susan.*
2. Ten of the girls said that the film stimulated them sexually. Four singled out the open-air screwing, three the lesbian sequence, three a tender memory scene (imaginary) between Susan and her lover and two the sequences between Reems and his lover. All ten seemed to identify with one or another woman in the film.
3. Eight specified the presences of perceived vaginal stimulation at a wide variety of scenes, the open-air sequences being cited by two respondents. One answered that the stimulation was "consistent and remained that way for hours after."
4. Five students noted certain scenes that interfered with their erotic enjoyment, the greatest number (three) citing the classroom environment. Two were turned off by the lesbian scene, two by the "lack of feeling" that was apparent during the sex scenes, two by the rape, one by oral sex and one by the "poor quality of the film."
5. Nine found various scenes repulsive. The rape scene (despite its discretion) was mentioned three times, the lesbian scene three times, oral sex twice, and the "natural" look of the actors as well as a female masturbation sequence were mentioned once.
6. Thirteen students admitted to present sexual activity, eleven to completed heterosexual consummated acts, four to heterosexual unconsumated behavior and two to masturbation.
7. Nine of the students denied that the film had influenced their subsequent behavior in any way. Four mentioned a stimulus to heterosexual behavior (including one who "discovered a new position"), three cited masturbatory behavior, three mentioned fantasies and one recalled former homosexual tendencies. (The female answers to this question tended, as it did their responses to others, to be considerably more explicit than those of the males.)
8. All fourteen girls agreed that the film should be permitted to be exhibited to people their age. All agreed that censorship was undesirable.
9. Nine students did not identify, so they said, with any character in the film. Six others identified at one time or another with the "sweet" Susan and one noted that she identified with *any* woman who had a "tumble with Harry Reems."
10. Ten students said their own fantasies were enacted in the film. There were three mentions of the bucolic romp, three of a sex scene in a shower, two of a tender candlelight coupling of Susan and her boy friend (in imagination), two of the lesbian scene and one of the rape.
11. Five students noted that another setting in which to view the movie might have changed their reactions; eight did not feel so; one did not

answer. *All* positive answers stressed having a male companion with whom to watch the film.

12. Twelve students would not have paid to see the film in a theatre and two gave qualified positive responses.

13. In the one question in which female responses were *entirely* different from the male answers, only three out of the fourteen females said they had ever seen a hard-core porno film before (and even they presented far from clear-cut evidence). One mentioned *Emmanuel* (an X-rated French film that was recently shown on campus; it is more notable as soft-core than as hard-core pornography) and another, a short silent stag film (with which I am familiar) displaying, among other things, Linda Lovelace copulating with a dog. The student said she found it highly erotic.

What then does my little experience (or mini-experiment) prove?

Absolutely nothing. This was my expectation before I started it, and were I inclined to technicalities, I might claim my null hypothesis was confirmed.

I learned a number of things, however, or at least confirmed what I had suspected, more by virtue of what the responses did *not* say than by what they did say, and from the delightfully low rate of return, which was previously discussed.

My student assistant, unaware of the role that she was playing both in the responses and non-responses, felt that the female answers, by and large, seemed more honest, candid, specific, articulate and less inclined to braggadocio than those of the males. I agreed, but not quite as unhesitatingly as she, and over this we had a good-natured (I think) argument. At any rate, I *did* have to agree with her that the females who answered the questions seemed less disturbed by the film than the males, or seemed to display fewer uncertainties or hangups about their reactions—largely positive—to the eroticism in *Sometime Sweet Susan*. What they liked, they liked without apology. Too, their open-ended answers were generally less ambiguously written than those of the males. When I asked my assistant what *she* thought of the film, she shrugged, compared it invidiously to *The Devil in Miss Jones,* and said that she had seen better. I asked her if she had been stimulated by it, and she blushed, whatever that means, because she blushes (as I do) quite easily and frequently! She had, however, presented me with a detailed and clear analysis of the responses, which was written both frankly and objectively.

The showing of this film occurred under highly extraordinary or "contaminated" circumstances, as I have noted, and I discovered that my students—those who responded and those who did not—were not actually typical of anything, even of the socio-economic and age groups by which I would have, were I a sociologist, immediately categorized them. But I was neither writing a doctoral dissertation nor conducting a quasi-scientific experiment. I was attempting to learn.

The major point that impressed me about the experience was the uniformity in the way *all* the students—without exception—actually regarded my classroom, despite my own previous impressions to the contrary. Nearly all the students perceived *Sometime Sweet Susan* mainly in the context of their, by then, fourteen or so years of processing by the educational system in which they were involved and by the games they had played in various ways. My questionnaire was therefore—despite all sorts of admonitions to the contrary—an extension of the formal classroom and my formal role as that of a professor more than twice their age, who represented to them some degree of arbitrary and possibly dangerous authority. (This is also one facet of the many successful relationships I have had with every student assistant, including this one, in my three decades of teaching.) For many, their erotic experiences had to be reconciled with the general impression that they were taking my course only for a grade—that they somehow would be eventually marked by me on subjective final examinations and term papers. They proceeded with care, obviously not trusting my continual assurances of anonymity.[10]

The questions they later asked verbally in class (and those they asked the producer of the film, who was a guest lecturer) were all stereotyped and curiously (but not unexpectedly) impersonal. What interested them most, it seemed, was not themselves and their reactions (or lack of them) to the movie, but the motives of a porno film producer, his family problems, if any, who the actors were, what they were paid and what prompted them to fornicate and indulge in all manner of erotic behavior in such uninhibited ways before a film camera. Some seemed vaguely interested in filmmaking techniques under the pressured circumstances in which porno films are hastily shot, in their budgets, in editing and in other matters. Only one girl in the *Susan* class appeared a bit more than objectively interested in whether these performers really enjoyed their work and asked questions about them as if they were human beings. She was even so bold as to admit, under pressure, that she might herself be persuaded to appear in such a film if conditions were right. The entire class was, of course, aghast at my insistence that *all* of them would indeed appear in such movies if "conditions were right" for *them* mentioning the slave bordellos of ancient Rome and Ravensbrueck, as well as the exquisite rat torture in *1984*, a novel they all had read. In regard to this matter, the devil took quite a beating, as he always does whenever this particular issue is posed in the sterile atmosphere of the American classroom.

What the devil was attempting to do was, it seems, largely unsuccessful. I tried to convey van den Haag's notion of depersonalization to my students in a personal manner by asking them, when all was said and done, to explore their own potentials for dehumanization. I went so far as to suggest, as van den Haag does, that the conventional reaction to eroticism throughout the ages has always been impersonal—depersonalized— unless and when it is accompanied by respect and regard for what stimulates one, whatever the subject or object of arousal is. In an abstract manner, then, I was advancing the idea, caught by one or two students at most, that erotic communication without meaning in *human* terms can hardly be classified as communication at all, but is simply a type of exploitation that demeans both the exploiter and its object. By the time the devil finished, he was almost preaching a sermon, and the devil's arguments have never gained acceptance by quoting the scriptures to his advantage!

If it was a sermon, however, it fell apparently upon deaf ears. That very afternoon I noticed one of the girls from the class in the student lounge tormenting her boy friend in a ludicrous fashion; she was playing the tease in a provocative see-through blouse and a pair of short shorts. (Both had been working on the scene crew for a television production. Hence the informal costume and its ostensible propriety.) The next day the most attractive girl in the class (in my opinion—a reaction on my part that she could not help but have noticed) decided to give the old devil his due by waltzing into my office with some papers for me to sign, and, in leaning over my desk, she benevolently granted my aging eyes a clear look at her young, braless boobs for about twenty seconds, displaying a knowing cat-ate-bird smile on her gorgeous face. My inclination was to flunk her then and there! But she had judged me correctly and was honestly and highly evaluated in the course—solely on the merits of her academic accomplishments.

What else might I have expected? Depersonalization in a technological culture, I mused, is not a discrete entity any more than are the familiar demons of "anomie," "alienation" and/or "other-directedness," all of which are terms we use to describe social phenomena of which we disapprove. We reserve warmer (and less abstract) words for such activities as "museum-going," "listening to music" and attempting to reach the "higher and more spiritual values in life," all of which *may* be every bit as depersonalizing and anomic in substance as enjoying commercials on television or getting drunk or stoned or falling in love with our automobiles or enjoying pseudo-sex at pornographic movies!

Unfortunately, van den Haag's viewpoint does not lie down and die with his indictment of pornography, nor even at the psychoanalytic-psychiatric *desideratum* of adjustment to a technological culture. I grant, however, the relevance of his characterization of pornography as *one* aspect of a matter endemic to nearly all modern life.

I was also much impressed by a short passage in a book by two obvious enthusiasts for porno films, who are admirers of many of the people—as I suppose I am—who at present are experimenting with this difficult medium. Observing the shooting of a cheap porno film, they (or one of them) comment on how mundane sex becomes when viewed in the exploitative context of a New York apartment turned into a film set. They see in sexuality the very antithesis of the fantasy world the pornographic film is supposed to conjure up for its audience. They are amazed that sexual behavior seems routinized, finding it "just as hard as it is to understand how inhabitants of concentrations camps . . . could treat another of creation's alleged mysteries, death, as routine." When depersonalized, sex simply turns into "nothing special," rather like death.[11]

Possibly because of my own theatrical training and early experience, I did not react quite so dramatically to a similar experience, merely laughing to myself that professional sexploitation, no matter how much semen is spilled, is still just show business, all of a piece with so much other nonsense that gullible audiences seem to swallow whole: freak shows, horror and sci-fi films, video commercials and most other *kitsch* in today's cultural sewer! Nor could I (or can I) exclude myself from complicity, both as an exploiter and as one exploited. I think I recognized that I could no more sever myself from *this* world of disconnection with humanity than from *that* world of it! In other words, "kootch shows" on carnival midways and gas ovens in concentration camps—both of which I have personally seen too much—are simply two sides of the same coin, and the consequences of accepting one is to bear the other, I am afraid.

As Ellul says, technique *is* the god of modernity. It has replaced the old deities, who themselves employed techniques that, simply stated, were not efficient or reliable enough when they eventually had to compete with those of technology. When I consider, therefore, with Ellul, the price we have had to pay for efficiency and reliability, I am both uncomfortable and sad. Worse, whenever technique began in *all* of our schools to overwhelm the cultivation of knowledge, the understanding of humanitarian civilities and man's impulse to liberal education (in the sense that it frees one from the bondage of ignorance), Western culture started on a path from which there could be thereafter no deviation. To the degree that our universities become *useful* to society, they become *useless* for men and women. True, they now turn out their proper quota of doctors, lawyers, journalists and philosophy teachers, but each—except in extraordinary instances—is culturally replaceable by another graduate who might as well be a clone of the first. We are told that society is all the better for this change, in the face of the fact that the *major* barbarities during the sum total of man's history have occurred and are occurring during *this* great age of technology in the disguise of social controls! Aside from the death ovens of Germany before and during World War II, our inventory might merely begin with Hiroshima, Mylai, Cambodia, the stink of modern Calcutta, the labor camps of Siberia and countless other examples of our excellence in the matter of technique, of the worldwide blessings of technology.

Results of the experience? My classroom now makes me shudder in retrospect. In a way, I was, like all teachers, a pallid imitation of an SS guard at Buchenwald, except that I exercised the utter gall to introduce an imitation of life into a course from which my students expected—had learned to expect as a *right*—only technique and sterility. All of us were children together in the age of technology, expected and willing to play the game of modern education with its semester hours, credits, degrees, exams and term papers—just as long as each of us is bloodless and devoid of any honest perceptions of common humanity other than the routines of permissions for excused absences and the proper ventilation of the classroom. Nothing, absolutely nothing, seemed *less* relevant to the authentic couplings in *Sometime Sweet Susan* and the vacuous environment into which I poured the film and my silly questionnaires than the question of what the *effects* of the experience might have been upon the students who viewed it!

Any wonder, then, that the girls so often singled out for special attention a fantastic sequence of sex in the wilderness? With the special acuity of female instinct (sic), they caught clearly, I am certain, a metaphor that they could probably not explain if asked. All of us shared with the performers in the movie, and even with the producer, an unreachable vision of sex as a part of nature, not as a technique, therapy, ritual, game or habit, but rather as a sexual Eden without condoms, zippered trousers, birth-control pills, scented douches, vaginal suppositories, soft-focus crotch shots, come shots or any of the impedimenta with which man's own nature has been subdued by the countless systems that tyrannize him and by the machines that kill him.

As I have previously noted, Vance Packard once wrote of our culture as a "sexual wilderness," because he found that it burst with plural interpretations of morality, of love, of pleasure. Quite the opposite is true, I think. The Western technology of eroticism is probably one of the most advanced of all skills in the modern world! It is entirely consonant with the way we raise our children, the kind of education we provide for them and the nature of our own world view. It is also distressingly uniform, as uniform, say, as one school diploma compared to another. I fear that van den Haag is wrong mainly because he is right. He addresses his wisdom to *pornography* instead of to *all* the delinquent children of our scientific philosophy, not just to one of them—plucky little bastard that it is!

PART THREE

:: THE FUTURE

:: **11**

The Legal Pendulum

The history of this nation is studded with actions that seemed wholly practical and beneficial at the time but, with long run, left a residue of principles violated, hope defeated and tasks undone.

—James MacGregor Burns

ONE OF THE GREAT ARGUMENTS since the eighteenth century that has ramified into all the arts and sciences but is little recognized as "great"—or even any longer as an "argument"—centers on periodicity: that is, cycles.

Cyclic thinking in art, science, history or economics is based upon metaphors drawn from the world of nature. Almost all observed astronomy (on the macrocosmic level) is cyclic. So are the seasons of flora and fauna. Everything that lives is caught in a cycle of birth, death and renewal. An investor, therefore and correctly, charts the price of gold, rare coins or stocks and bonds in cycles. And in the long run he will inevitably be correct. But, "In the long run," said a non-cyclically oriented economist, "we shall all be dead!" or words to that effect. For him, as for many others, cyclic thinking is accurate as far as it goes. But it is also tendentious.

On one side, nobody has *time* for cycles—even of the most insignificant or obvious sort. Tell a freezing man that the winter will soon be over, and this means nothing to him. Quondam millionaires who did high dives on to the pavements of Wall Street in 1929 no doubt knew, many of them, that the margin calls ringing in their ears were part of a business cycle, that recovery was just around the corner. Of course it was, but so were the bill collector and bankruptcy!

On another side, all high- and low-ridged graphs even out in the long run. And there always *is* a long run, if one contrives to live to be ninety or to keep his eye on the past and future and denies the reality of the present. Such thinking is not entirely unfashionable in philosophical circles despite the recent existential thrust of so much of our so-called "best thinking" in the West. Physicists who may or may not have heard Kenneth Craik's observation, "Science is not reality. It is a way of investigating reality," have lately been muttering about the death of universes and telling us discouraging things about the finite nature of microcosms *and* macrocosms that may in tomorrow's world become new fashionable metaphors to be applied to tomorrow's arts, history or economics. Few religions—with exception of Hindu—can afford pragmatically to make much of cycles, nor may much mystical thinking or metaphysics, wherein eternal truths are just that: "eternal!" Gold bugs, coin and stamp collectors and art lovers who play their games for fun and not profit cannot afford to think cyclically. Sometimes their beneficiaries do, as they chortle over Grandma's foresightedness in keeping a trunkful of Art Deco bric-a-brac in the attic just because she liked it and despite its original worthlessness. But, true to Keynesian wisdom, Grandma is usually not around for her deserved encomia. She has been replaced by knavish grandchildren, who have suddenly discovered the art market!

In an ongoing but entirely futile battle with various mousebrains who call themselves "futurologists" and who have, for the past ten or twelve years, turned fortunetelling into a pseudo-scientific profitable pastime, I have expressed elsewhere my dissatisfaction with their various "profiles of the future." Not one of them reflects a thoughtful appreciation of the many tensions between "cycles" and "progress," however the latter is defined. The exception, I suppose, is Arthur C. Clarke, who boils down to a wise observer deeply aware of spiritual principles in human thought and is correctly humble in light of that knowledge. The rest has earned its sobriquet "Future Schlock."

My vitriol, as weak as it has been, was, I fear, directed at the wrong target. It should not have been hurled at pinheads who wrote best sellers during the late sixties and early seventies, nor at the publishers who printed them, nor at the suckers who bought them. (After all, *Star Trek* was indeed the most popular video program at the time, and what the hell did I expect? Cowboys and murder mysteries and even most espionage writing was falling into a well of trivia, and what was left *except* science fiction? Jean Le Carre had not at the time been recognized as the master of the art of the novel that he is. Strangely, his one non-espionage book, a near total flop with the public, had to be published to certify his rightful place as an important contemporary writer, which is another story I am afraid.)

What I should have been doing was storming the institutional fortresses; that is, the Rand Corporations, the Hudson Institutes and think-

tanks (some of which I was sucked into myself at the time) that were setting the agendas—amidst all too little publicity—for futures of their own
devising. My yelps would have been to no avail, I am certain, but I would
at least have centered my attack on the right targets. To what degree the
present crises in which we find ourselves in the worlds of international
commerce, energy policy, social amelioration, declining educational services and domestic economy result more or less directly from the "reports"
that such institutions have provided for private industry and government
we shall never know, but I suspect that it is a high one. And their publicly
released and printed "studies" have ranged from Alcoholism to Zoological
preservation.[1]

My point is simply that popular so-called "futurologists" like Alvin
Toffler were and are just harmless twerps. Like McLuhan and Fuller and
company, they have joined the army of the celebrated on televisions talk
shows and, thank heaven, they demonstrate about the same cultural sticking power as most other "masscom" punditry. In one ear and out the
other! If damage was done to anyone (and I believe it was, although I cannot prove it), it occurred via the heavy-gun "Centers" and "Institutes"
that printed Xerox reports such as the famous *Pentagon Papers* that are
written "For Eyes Only" of the power elite in government and industry
and even, may the Lord help us, in academia. Relieved of the risky business of making wise decisions, the amount of current policy determination
at various levels that our so-called "leaders" have dumped into the laps of
these amorphous think-tanks, no man knows. Nor, if he is smart, does he
want to know.

Paranoia? Of course! In the light of what we have recently learned—
via the opening of those "secret" documents that government agencies
have not been able to feed fast enough into their shredding machines—an
individual who is *not* paranoid in a culture fueled by its own psychopathology on every hand is in common parlance "sick." Carl Jung once said
that a society that is psychically undernourished cannot permit God to
thrive. Maybe there are exceptions, but certainly a society that is psychically irresponsible, secretive, conspiratorial and intellectually at odds with
itself cannot inspire much unwaivering faith on the part of those whose cooperation it requires for survival.

To believe, for instance, that a serious energy shortage exists in the
United States today is quite absurd, not because such a shortage is either
impossible or unlikely, but rather because both its many descriptions and
the steps taken to remediate it have been absurd—and worse, frivolous. All
of them are sanctioned and cheered on by precisely the same clowns who
are supposed to be solving a problem that they apparently do not believe
really exists! In the midst of a petroleum shortage, we have suffered from
gluts of crude oil and are nearly drowning in consumer products, hard and
soft, made from petroleum in one way or another. With electricity in short
supply, nuclear power plants are abandoned because of inevitable develop-

mental problems and the tears of a few academic ecologists and hung-over hippies, while at the same time no one *dreams* of restricting the incremental increase and advertising of domestic machines and devices that are far from essential but which swallow unnecessary voltage like a starving man at a pie-eating contest. Meanwhile, dingbats celebrate "Sun Day" with official pomp and circumstances, to what end I am uncertain. Aren't we aware that cave men used solar heating? Hasn't anyone noticed the similarity between the tides and the world's Niagaras, the source of so much potentially cheap electricity at present? The only really encouraging portent in this respect, I think, is that we have not yet celebrated "Tide Day."

The moral of all this is that I have given up fortunetelling! I still recall a thing or two about it from the perspective of the charlatan, because Tofflerism is when all is said and done old, old hat that antedates Huxley, Orwell, Bellamy, Verne and even the rascal More, a con man if ever there was one. For this reason, as we shall see, the future of erotic communications is for all practical purposes identical with the present, just as all reasonably responsible predictive statements constitute extrapolations of some aspects of the present moment. For most human affairs, there exist neither cycles nor progressive graphs drawn on an inclined plane into the future worth the trouble it takes to read them! Certainly one must plan, but Keynes' wisdom ran deep. If one plans for the present he is *mutis mutandis* planning for the future. If he plans for the future, he is only writing his own eulogy or carving his own gravestone. *Now* is the future—socially, morally and legally.

For what I consider this good reason, I have saved discussion of the current legal status of erotic communication in the West for its proper place: the chronicle of the future unrolling as we live it in an uncertain legal climate which is currently much more the business of my children than of myself, just as the present has been their future for the two decades or so since they were born.

The Ambiguous Boomerang

Some mention has been made of the so-called "Burger Decision" of 1973 in the previous section of this book. I have, however, reserved discussion of it for the present purpose of introducing us to considerations of possible futures for erotic communications in the West. The reason is simply that the case of *Miller vs. California* (Justice Burger delivering the opinion of the Supreme Court) is not as relevant to the changes it has to date wrought in the legal and moral climate created for pornography in the United States by the Warren Court as it is to two central facts that are only now emerging concerning the case itself that was decided during the summer of 1973.[2]

The first appears on face to be a puzzling one—namely that *Miller vs. California* has had surprisingly *little* effect on the legal and moral climate of pornography or on any other aspect of erotic communication of any kind in the United States during the years since the decision. At the time that the Court handed down its decision, paraphrases of Burger's words were, among other things, written in large letters in newspaper headlines. Editorialists, pundits and seers regarded *Miller* as a legal landmark, the end of an era. The lead headline of *The New York Times* of June 22, 1973 declared, both precipitously and largely incorrectly as it turned out, "SU-PREME COURT TIGHTENS RULE COVERING OBSCENITY, GIVES STATES NEW POWER; 5 Decisions by 5–4 [sic]; Burger Opinions Say Local Standards on Prurience Apply."[3] The *Times* was correct in that five cases were decided more or less together, the most important one, reflecting all the principles involved in the other four, being *Miller*. But the rest of the headline was hyperbolic, and Warren Weaver's article attached thereto displayed considerable sophisticated misunderstanding both of the issues involved and of the decision itself.

Weaver was not alone. In the editorial offices of publications such as *Screw* and among porn film producers and others growing rich from the breadth and depth of the new market for erotica, the behavior of many entrepreneurs recalled that of professional rum-runners when they heard about repeal. "What does it mean?" I asked a fairly well-known pornographer. "I don't know," he replied with good humor. "Probably that I'll have to go back to work!"

The second fact that the case illuminates—and does so far more clearly than any previous decision of the Warren Court—is that nearly everything many of us had guessed long ago about the social status of erotic discourse and its relationships to law, no matter how intended by a judicial body, has little substance and that the hypotheses I offered chapters ago (in hindsight, of course) concerning the independence of the vectors of law, morality and behavior in our time is defensible, if not upheld. I cannot question the immediate assumption made by many including me—that the Burger decision was *intended* to halt the trend in the United States toward total permissiveness in erotic communications and bring it eventually to a stop. I still think that this indeed may have been the exact objective of the five majority justices. They obviously used the wrong remedy, although possibly they thought it was the only one open to them. Having attempted it, their failure has now made it nearly impossible—or extremely difficult—for any court in the United States to attempt to find a new one.

We shall examine specifics below. In effect, the Court turned the major task of stopping America's obscenity–pornography glut to the people, to public opinion, to the consciences of all upright citizens in the fifty states and to the inherent decency of the majority of American citizens, who did not want (or so the justices believed in all innocence) an environment polluted with dirty pictures or libraries and bookstores filled with lewd novels. What was discovered was that, with amazingly few exceptions, critical values in our culture had been deeply changed during (or by) the Warren years, and that the number of citizens of influence who wanted to jeopardize the Bill of Rights by arbitrary actions against obscenity (as long as obscenity "knew its place") was pathetically small and that those who would risk social ridicule (especially from the young) by standing up for their beliefs was smaller still—almost infinitesimal. It was also discovered that this great issue of such tremendous pith to its advocates and counter-advocates was merely a small lily pad floating in an enormous pond of public indifference. In other words, more people probably reflected the thinking of Justice Douglas than of Justice Burger (if they thought at all), and the latter were willing to turn over the burden of *action* regarding obscenity censorship in the long run to majority consensus.

Nothing—not even Supreme Court decisions—happen outside of temporal frameworks, however, and one must remember that *Miller vs. California* was being adjudicated in the happy conservative sunlight of Richard M. Nixon's landslide reelection of 1972, one of the most unanimous votes of public confidence in the nation's history! This victory, it was assumed by the partisan (and even the non-partisan), echoed the voices of that mystical "silent majority" often referred to by Nixon and his Vice-President in their ritual assessments of the public's pulse. Not since the early Eisenhower years at the end of the Korean War had American conservatives been as certain—in the light of good evidence—that the nation was fed up to the back teeth with most of the social changes that had characterized the sixties, including fallout from the Vietnam War, disaffected young people, drug problems, pornography and so on, which were all thrown into the same basket. The conservatives were partially right. But revulsion at campus riots did not necessarily imply equal revulsion at the talents of Linda Lovelace or at staff photographers for *Hustler* magazine. Burger and his colleagues were fooled by exactly these assumptions (as was Warren Weaver Jr.) during that long hot summer of 1973.

Few will deny that the Burger decision was well intended. Seen now in the long run, it appears far fairer and more sensitive to the moral tone of the country than even the justices of the Court—for or against—may have dreamed at the time. It is precisely this moderation and fairness of the decision that effectively castrated its remedies as incentives for effective prohibitive action such as, for example, the Eighteenth Amendment or the various civil rights decisions of the Court before and since.

The first and most important objective of the *Miller* decision was total destruction of the "utterly without redeeming value" notion bequeathed to the Court by *Memoirs vs. Massachusetts*. This Burger did with dispatch, tracing the history (and absurdity) of the idea with considerable skill. To the relief of many liberals as well as conservatives, he wrote, "We do not adopt as a constitutional standard the *utterly* without redeeming social value test of *Memoirs;* that concept has never commanded the adherence of more than three justices at one time."

In its place Burger enunciated a number of criteria, none of them mechanically, logically, socially or artistically perfect but all certainly far better than the banal negative test in *Memoirs*. They were based on precedent and appear at first reading fairly harsh and circumscribed. In practice, however, they have turned out neither to be great departures from past thinking and practice nor unduly restrictive in the light of what appears to be the shared values of much of the American public in the seventies. Nor do they seem any more or less restrictive today than they will in a decade to come, I think. (I have also been assured by people as different one from the other as civil liberties attorneys, sociologists, pornographers, priests, law professors and college seniors that they are filled with loopholes large enough for elephants to turn around in.) Severed from the formal text of the decision, they are:

1. Whether the average person, applying contemporary community standards, would find that the work, taken as a whole, appeals to the prurient interest. (An old friend, starting with *Hicklin* and ending with *Roth,* and probably Burger's genuflection to the many unsung heroes, dead and alive, who have tried to define "obscenity." These criteria remains as useless today as they always were!)

2. Whether the work depicts or describes anything in a patently offensive way that is specifically defined by an applicable state law prohibiting it. (Note, first, the problem words "patently offensive." Second, most state censorship laws by 1973 had been found unconstitutional, bleached of their color or severly hedged. The principle as enunciated was an invitation for states to pass *new* legislation that might or might not stand judicial constitutional tests at some future date—not too inviting a prospect.)

3. Whether the work, taken as a whole, lacks serious literary, artistic, political or scientific value. (This is today known informally as the LAPS test. It sounds like a reprise of *Roth* and/or *Memoirs* but decidedly is *not*. The negative characteristics of an obscene document were described in *Miller* with some precision, inviting for a film or book at least cogent argument—up to a point. "Literary" and "artistic" values we know are equivocal matters, but, strangely, the weakest term employed here is "scientific." The basest piece of absurd scatology *may* be of scientific interest to an abnormal psychologist, a *student* of abnormal psychology or even someone with a *cursory interest* in abnormal psychology. The ambit of science, particularly the social or behavioral sciences, is never and in *no specific manner* circumscribed by taste, vulgarity or decorous behavior or, many claim, by conventional morality.)

One measure of Burger's sophistication was his faith that the people or public opinion or state or local law would deal best with the (by now) axiom that obscenity is not protected by the First Amendment and that these words are meaningless unless held against a public consensuses of some sort. Critical to the Burger decision is the following assumption, which was considered restrictive in 1973 but, because of the maelstrom of legalities into which it has since been thrown, seems far more progressive and libertarian a half-dozen years later:

> Under a national Constitution, fundamental First Amendment limitations on the powers of the States do not vary from community to community, but this does not mean that there are, or should be or can be, fixed, uniform national standards of precisely what appeals to the "prurient interest" or is "patently offensive." These are essentially questions of fact (sic), and our nation is simply too big and too diverse for this Court to reasonably expect (sic) that such standards could be articulated for all 50 States in a single formulation, even assuming the prerequisite consensus exists. When triers of fact are asked to decide whether "the average person, applying contemporary community standards" would consider certain material "prurient," it would be unrealistic to require the answer to be based upon some abstract formulation. The adversary system, with lay jurors as the usual ultimate fact finders in criminal prosecutions, has historically permitted triers of fact to draw on the standards of their community, guided always by limiting instructions on the law. To require a State to structure obscenity proceedings around evidence of a national "community standard" would be an exercise in futility.[4]

The Court's own warning did not prevent it from offering "for instances" of the kind of criteria that it expected the states to employ in good conscience when defining the limits of free speech in the context of obscenity. Seven paragraphs before the above quotation, the majority had stated: *"We emphasize that it is not our function to propose regulatory schemes for the States. That must await their concrete legislative efforts."* [5]

Here Burger and company obviously assumed that such legislative efforts would naturally be forthcoming and would be successful in one way or another. A statement like the short quote above is an encouragement to action of and by itself. But the Court went further in this exercise of "show and tell," a game that turned out to be relatively futile as years passed:

> It is possible, however, to give a few plain examples of what a state statute could define for regulation under (the above) . . . part of the standard ("patently offensive" works) announced in this opinion *supra:*
> a. Patently offensive representations or descriptions of ultimate sexual acts, normal or perverted, actual or simulated.
> b. Patently offensive representations or descriptions of masturbation, excretory functions, and lewd exhibition of the genitals.[6]

Note well that the *direction* of the Court's thinking is quite clear here. But the instances above are cited as *examples* only—an "abstract formulation" in the exact words Burger used invidiously as a criterion for determining "facts" of "prurient interest" and/or "patently offensive" communications. Once again, there remains little doubt that the five conservative justices were trying to reverse a cycle of morals, customs and laws which had for nearly a decade been gathering enormous inertia of motion by means of appeal ultimately to public opinion at the community (here the state) levels of government. Lest anyone miss the gist of his argument, Burger concluded:

> In sum, we a) reaffirm the *Roth* holding that obscene material is not protected by the First Amendment; b) hold that such material can be regulated by the States, subject to the specific safeguards enunciated above, without a showing that the material is *"utterly* without redeeming social value;" and c) hold that obscenity is to be determined by applying "contemporary community standards," not "national standards." [7]

In full cognizance of how important and delicate the Burger Court majority felt the issue of erotic communications to be, the Court was now attempting the impossible by asking for the best in the best of all possible worlds! On the one hand, it hoped for conservative *results* by turning the issue of community control back to the communities and, on the other, it wanted to preserve in statute the best rational *means* for control of obscenity even if such instruments had over the years failed for the Warren Court. (One can only imagine what chaos such a compromise, relying in the end upon state, county or local "facts," might create if the issue at hand were school segregation or fair employment practices!)

In sum total, the Court obviously lacked the courage of its convictions, all of which are now quite clear. What Burger *wanted* to say, obviously, is implicitly included in his "example" above: that smut, filth and obscenity can easily be determined by rational men. Here they are in precise fashion: "ultimate sexual acts," "masturbation," "excretory functions" portrayed in this or that way, and so on. Yet, he did *not* say it! He left the matter entirely in the lap of a "silent majority" that apparently did not and does not exist. Hence failure!

By and large, the states did not take up the challenge—nor did counties or cities. If and when they did, the looseness of the Burger decision left prosecutors with sorely chewed knuckles and nails as judges and juries rolled up their sleeves and asked serious, realistic questions about "community standards." In my old home town of New York City, for instance, the police department almost immediately attempted to close half a dozen porno theatres in one day and impounded the raunchy films they were exhibiting. Undaunted, most of the theatre managers simply reopened their doors with substitute prints or duplicates of the ones that had been hauled away by the police.

In the meantime, a municipal justice with a sense of humor upon whom the case fell for pre-trial hearing read the Burger decision, viewed the movies, and then took a leisurely walk along the streets where they had been playing and talked to local denizens, trying his best to ascertain the nature of "contemporary community standards" in the Times Square area of New York City as correctly as possible. Concluding squarely, firmly and absolutely that there was absolutely nothing at odds with "contemporary community standards" in the films he had seen (and noting that possibly they might be even a bit above the "standards" of the turf itself), he ordered the movies returned to the exhibitors and all charges dropped. *Sic transit* Burger!

Other instances of failures of the Burger decision are not quite as lighthearted as the incident above, but, by and large, all manner and sort of remedies used to stem the tide of candor in erotic communications, no matter how clever, have to date failed. Some have simply been instances of legal overkill: Porno actors have been indicted for indulging in illegal behavior at certain locations (often not even the locations where such behavior was filmed) in the hope that their convictions might stem the impetus to produce pornographic stills and movies. Most of these actions have failed, largely because it is not too difficult to prove that the same types of screwing and sucking (without benefit of clergy) that these performers indulged in before still and motion picture cameras is (and has been for a long time) fairly common behavior almost everywhere except in convents and monasteries. A guilty verdict for "fornication," say in Cambridge, Massachusetts, rendered against a porno actress just might, in the long run, create no end of problems for a male or female judge or a district attorney's daughter or the ladies and gentlemen of a jury or their friends and relatives.

Other actions have disgracefully verged upon—or actually been— sheer entrapment by zealots. That they have not resulted in more counter- suits requesting damages for harassment (at least) to their victims is an insult both to law and to common sense.

One well-known example—and one is enough—involved *Screw* publisher Al Goldstein. Aware that any action against Goldstein in states such as New York or New Jersey would almost certainly end in acquittal according to Burger criteria, certain Boy Scouts in the Justice Department picked Wichita, Kansas, as the cite for a Goldstein indictment, despite the fact that not one *Screw* subscriber lived in Witchita! Local postal inspectors took care of that problem. They subscribed to *Screw* and *Smut* themselves, both Goldstein publications, under phony names. As a result, Goldstein, who lives and works in New York, found himself indicted in Witchita under Kansas law on twelve obscenity counts.[8] After a lengthy and expensive trial involving much legal maneuvering on both sides, Goldstein was eventually acquitted.

I suppose he should consider himself fortunate that no Kansas screw- ball tried to gun him down in the manner publisher Larry Flynt was in Atlanta, Georgia, on March 6, 1978, along with Gene Reeves, Flynt's local attorney.[9] In the latter instance, because a "hot" issue had been brought into a courtroom with its inevitable publicity, attention was called to

Flynt's person, and some maniac tried to take what he thought was the "law" into his own hands. The results will probably incapacitate Flynt for the rest of his life, which he nearly lost as the result of a futile exercise in a southern courtroom to apply "contemporary community standards" to a magazine published in Columbus, Ohio, and sold not only in Atlanta but almost everywhere else in the United States.

This is not to say that the Burger decision has not had some specific effects on commerce in erotic materials. It has, but the effects are far different from those clearly intended by the Supreme Court in 1973. In fact, they contrive for the most part to work against both the spirit and nature of the actual decision itself.

Certain local communities (and some states) have exerted various controls over erotica but in an erratic, crazy, arbitrary patch-work fashion that may well derive from some sort of legal rationality but lacks much common or horse sense. In *this* small city, the sale of hard-core pornography is apparently legal. In *that* small city across the river, police action has closed three theatres showing erotic films. Young and old, therefore, in city B must drive ten minutes to city A to see a "fuck film," as they are lovingly called by the aforementioned Mr. Goldstein. So it goes from village to village, town to town, city to city and country to country, most important decisions having been made by local officials, usually cinema ignoramuses and/or prudes of every description, each one different from the others, as one crosses village, city, county and state borders. In one area sex is okay and sadism is not, even if the sadism appears in a superbly made film or is historically accurate. In another, sadism, blood and guts, Kung Fu features and dismal animalistic displays of violence are permitted but frontal photography of cunts and pricks are *verboten,* even in a film like *A Clockwork Orange,* where such scenes have been meticulously framed in a provocative and consistent filmic narrative.

True enough, as Burger has said, no *one* set of moral standards can possibly obtain for *all* citizens in the United States. By and large, people may indeed regard *many* matters differently in New England from the Northwest. But rational enforcement of regional differences in moral tonus—even *if* it could be identified—is not what has resulted from the Burger decision. Instead, neighborhoods, cities and counties have been arbitrarily sliced up into permissive and non-permissive areas, although one notes the recent tendency of an increasing number of communities to permit "adult" book shops and porno theatres to operate almost anywhere because of the difficulty in determining any standard that passes both the "contemporary" and "community" test at the same time. The mobility of so much of the American population set against recent changes in many aspects of national life are the main reasons. The grass roots ground swell to which the Supreme Court looked in 1973 simply has not occurred. Nor will it or can it. Hopes for "cleaning up" the United States by a silent majority of decent, God-fearing people, the kind Norman Rockwell used to paint, were and are entirely unrealistic; they merely represent a hankering for a moral climate that has either changed or was never there in the first place except on the covers of old *Saturday Evening Posts.*

One other side product of the Burger decision has resulted in an unsettling type of intramedia high-handedness that has received all too little attention. Various newspaper and magazine editors and publishers and others have done everything they can to interfere with free commerce in erotica of nearly every kind. This is an interesting and disturbing matter, especially because it concerns many, many newspapers and magazines that absolutely refuse to accept advertisements for any erotic films or printed materials. Their editors *quite correctly* point out that under the First Amendment they have a legal right to reject any material they do not want to print for any reason and usually end up talking about "good taste," "vulgarity" and other issues that have *not* been among the deep and classical concerns of American journalism since the first mass newspaper was printed in the 1830s—except when convenient. *In effect, therefore, the press is using its special First Amendment privilege (and privilege it is indeed) to restrict commerce in another medium that has exactly the same First Amendment privileges as the conventional press!* Grounds for the restriction upon close examination are invariably and entirely arbitrary as well!

Here is an issue quite different from the newspapers' historical refusal (in the nineteen-thirties) to print logs of radio stations because they feared competition or from their present desultory, sloppy and paltry coverage of television broadcasting, in spite of the fact that it occupies more of their readers' time than anything else they do except sleep or work!

Neither radio nor television are granted absolute First Amendment privileges directly. Films and print *are*. All warnings to journalists that the abuse of the constitutional rights of other media—whether or not publishers and editors *like* what they do—will in the end probably undermine all journalistic freedom seem addressed to deaf ears. As an editor-publisher of a good-sized local newspaper said to me recently, "It's my paper, and I'll take advertising from whom I damn well please!" His grammar is correct, and so may be his reasoning. But he is also flirting with the danger that an abuse of a freedom of any kind has invaribly been a prelude to its demise.

The chaotic results of the Burger decision have therefore been extenuated into a sort of "consumer fraud" that is little noticed, mainly because other mass media do not care to tell us about it. Sensitive to the problems of "community standards," filmmakers in particular, anxious to protect their investments, often produce quite different versions of certain porno flics. This requires double shooting of certain scenes, usually those involving explicit sex, snatch shots, come shots and the like. First, they are shot "hard core." Then they are repeated and simulated, perhaps shot from a different angle. In other words, one final version may show an explicit sequence of cock-sucking up to and beyond a male orgasm. Another version may display more or less the same thing, but no oral-genital contact actually occurs, and the cameras are so placed that all the audiences views is the back of a girl's head moving to and fro over a male pubic area. In both cases, the film is accompanied by a simulated sound track of grunts and groans that make clear what is supposed to be going on even if one shuts one's eyes.

When all is said and done, the film may even eventually appear in *three* versions. One is "hard core" and would definitely be rated X, were these films evaluated by the Motion Picture Association of America. The second is so-called "soft core," where no *explicit* sex is actually shown (or possibly even directly referred to in the dialogue except by innuendo and verbal suggestion) but the film is still fairly racy. The film might receive an R from the MPAA. Still a *third* version of the film may be constructed in the dubbing and editing rooms by softening the "soft core" simulated sex (or by excising it entirely) and bleaching the dialogue of *any* suggestion of raunch. The result might be rated PG or even G.

Different versions of said film are then exhibited in different localities, according to the degree of trouble a distributor feels he will encounter with various guardians of law and order, including local police, state laws and such, and possibly with newspaper editors who censor advertisements. What a distributor—and exhibitor—of *any* film wishes to avoid is costly trouble, particularly the expenses of a court trial. The fact that a certain film might cause only trouble in a certain locality but would, if brought to a court of law, not be found obscene according to Supreme Court or community standards is often irrelevant! Exhibiting the film *may* cause trouble, cost money and cause delay, possibly the worst enemy of exhibitors and distributors who depend upon publicity and momentary public fads and fancies for their success.

One distributor I contacted concerning this matter had voluntarily edited a fairly innocuous film to shreds—and thereby ruined it to the degree that its plot became pointless—simply because its theme and title caused trouble wherever it was shown. The movie concerned atrocities committed by the Nazi SS during World War II, including enforced prostitution and other unsavory matters, all drawn accurately from history books rather than a screen writer's imagination! While a number of police departments and district attorneys across the nation had attempted to halt the film's circulation, few had succeeded at the time the distributor decided to recut, nor were subsequent actions against the movie upheld in court anywhere. The distributor capitulated mainly because he felt the subject was timely, the film had received provocative publicity, and he feared that many exhibitors might reject a "trouble movie." Both he and the producer stood to loose money on a potentially valuable property if it were not shown as soon as possible.

From the consumer's point of view, the situation is even more confusing—and pointless. Let us assume that a film called *Naked Lust* is produced for the porno market and shot, edited and finally printed in three different versions. This means that, depending on where I am in the United States, I may in good faith walk into a motion picture theatre and see any one of *three* films, all carrying an arbitrary, self-bestowed X-rating (or triple X) and exploited in the same way. The film itself *may* be a hard-core porno movie or something as innocuous as *The Return of Lassie*. As a moviegoer (or consumer) I have no way of knowing before I see it which film I shall be watching. Even after I have seen it, there is no way that I can be certain whether other versions of the movie exist and if so, where they are being exhibited. I have been left in the wilderness of consumer fraud. Neither the law nor Mr. Nader care much that I have been conned, because I am, in their terms, spending money on sheer frivolity—as opposed, let us say, to something *they* consider serious that *is* responsive to federal laws like a bottle of soda pop, a cigar, an ice cream cone or a can of truffles! Or a pogo stick or a feather pillow! *O tempora! O mores!*

In sum then, the Burger decision has indeed been responsible for some substantive changes in our culture, but none of them has in any measure diminished the degree of candor or currency of erotic communications in the United States, even the use of minors in film "loops" and still pictures. Federal legislation has been directed against this latter practice, although in a cursory examination of the "adult" book and peep-show trade of the eastern United States last week,* I found no shortage of "kiddie porn," oriented both to homo- and heterosexual interests. Demand, apparently, makes the threat of seizure and arrest worth the risk—even in broad daylight—in stores and arcades open to the public in large cities. What the decision *has* accomplished is to test the ingenuity of erotic publishers and filmmakers.

Five Supreme Court justices could not turn back clock or calendar to the years before the decade before 1973!

The Erotic Seesaw

One of the curious aspects of the failure of the Burger decision to reach its implicit objectives is that its date coincides roughly with the failure in Denmark of legislation that may have been directed toward the same end, but which chose an entirely different means to achieve it. I have already discussed the legal aspects of this maneuver in Chapter 9. The famous "Danish experiment," now modified considerably, was based on the premise that in a healthy society if legislation were abandoned concerning erotica of all kinds (including live shows), the population would soon tire of it and the problem of obscenity as a social outrage would go away. Possibly the pornography itself would disappear too.

* October, 1978.

The Danish experiment was, for reasons that this book I hope has identified, just about as naive as the Burger majority's faith in the moral convictions of the "silent majority." Erotica as a social phenomenon does not operate in a social vacuum, nor is it unrelated to other sensitive matters in Western culture, among them the education of children, the strength of the so-called "nuclear family," habits of alcohol consumption, use of drugs, pandering and exploitation by pimps and other sycophants, the attraction and behavior of tourists (with alien cultural values) in large population centers and so on. To believe that any culture-wide "new" freedom suddenly thrust upon a technological society will not release a tremendous amount of pent-up psychic energy—to say nothing of money—and have an unsettling effect upon that population is not only naive, it is foolish. So the Danes discovered.

Before one begins to overgeneralize from the lesson of the Danish experiment, however, certain warnings must be sounded that apply to Denmark in particular. The notion that a healthy society may survive minimal regulation concerning many aspects of contemporary life is probably a valid one. It presents the problem, however, of defining, first, and locating, second, a society anywhere in the world that is indeed "healthy." Margaret Mead long ago noted that every society she ever studied has room for *some kind* of taboos of an obscene or pornographic nature. If our definition of societal "health," therefore, excludes an awareness of obscenity as a taboo, such a culture does not exist on this planet and probably never has except in the imagination of some behavioral scientists.

Even granting that such health is somehow, somewhere and someday possible, the soil of Denmark would be a poor place for its cultivation, considering that at the moment it leads the world (along with other Scandinavian countries, West Germany and the United States) in indices of psychological and social stress and strain that seem to accompany the *Weltschmerz* of technology and material progress: high alcoholism, drug addiction, suicide, murder and divorce rates, incidence of high blood pressure and other ugly statistics by which we try to measure—perhaps correctly, perhaps incorrectly—the psychic health and happiness quotients of people in groups.

The general outlines of Denmark's failure to liberate its populace from the porno plague by, in effect, fattening unto death the rats that carried it are fairly well known. Some details are not, details that are also true of similar experiments in Holland and Germany. The following concise and well-phrased news item was filed by Bernard Weinraub for *The New York Times* in 1976:

COPENHAGEN, Denmark, Jan. 25—Denmark is recoiling from its cheerful tolerance of pornography and salable sexuality, previously the greatest in Europe.

The police are busily cracking down on brothels, pornography seems on the wane and narcotics officers are stepping up their drive against smuggled drugs.

"Pornography is quieting down; it's stagnating," said Axel Frederiksen, the deputy police inspector who deals with pornography. "Some stores are closing and others say business is dropping off. We have banned live shows and we're going after the massage parlors."

In one recent week the police raided five massage parlors and charged the operators—four men and a woman—with operating houses of prostitution.

"They were nothing more than bordellos," said Mr. Frederiksen, whose vice squad has closed about a dozen massage parlors since November.

Several of the parlors have reopened, partly because the law is unclear about prostitution and partly because the Danes seem ambivalent about cracking down on vice.

"We have an attitude of live and let live," said Mr. Frederiksen. "But some people think it's gone too far."

If the Danish police and some politicians are worried about Copenhagen's free-wheeling image, this city of one million remains generally nonchalant, if slightly embarrassed, about the sex movies and pornographic shops that nestle beside automatic laundries, supermarkets and children's shops. Essentially the attitude seems to be: If pornographic books and movies aren't flaunted, then the authorities ignore them.

Each afternoon the popular tabloid *Ekstra Bladet* runs more than four columns of classified ads that hawk women, their specialities and phone numbers. Because the ads are in alphabetical order, virtually everyone's name starts with the letter A, with the hope of attracting quick attention.

What is news, however, is the stern police action against live sex shows, which once abounded in Copenhagen and massage parlors.

One of the largest parlors in the city, called Malene, was closed by the police recently.

"It was very expensive, very luxuriously arranged," Mr. Frederiksen said. "We found 3,700 names on their files—names of tourists, businessmen, diplomats, Americans, Japanese, Chinese, Arabs, all kinds of people."

Prostitution is legal in Denmark, and women can solicit unmolested in bars. If women block of streets, however, and create a nuisance, Mr. Frederiksen said, the police can ask them to move.

Living off the earnings of prostitutes is illegal, however, and massage parlors are often business establishments with employers and employees. Parlors generally operate with two to eight women each and charge anywhere from $20 to $90.

A typical operator, the police say, may collect $50 a day from each woman, regardless of what she earns.

With the crackdown on brothels, the police have stepped up their drive on narcotics dealers, who often own massage parlors or night clubs. In the first six months of last year, there were more than 400 narcotics arrests, a record here. At the same time, the Government enacted a law that stiffened to ten years from six the penalty for selling heroin.

The Danish police have become concerned in recent months about an abrupt influx of morphine tablets from Pakistan. From Denmark, the police say, the tablets and other narcotics are smuggled to other northern European countries with scant border control.

"We have had an increase in hard drugs and a decrease in hashish," said P.M. Gauguin, the deputy chief inspector for narcotics. "Five or six years ago it was hashish and morphine base, a lot of it from Lebanon. Now with the Lebanon civil war that market has dried up. We're getting morphine tablets from Pakistan.

"The tablets are small, white and very easy to smuggle in," Mr. Gauguin said. "There's enormous profit for these people. You can smuggle in hundreds of these pills, thousands of them. I have only 48 men in my unit. How can we stop this kind of thing easily?" [10]

What I find most interesting about the above dispatch from Copenhagen is that the Danes, with minor differences, were in 1976 grappling with exactly the same sort of problems as those related to our recent permissiveness in public erotic communications in the United States. While there is no *intrinsic* relationship between erotic communications and, say, drug addiction, the two seem indeed to travel hand in hand in Western culture for numerous psycho-sexual reasons. Here we may see but one index of the distance between our actual society and one that might be described as "healthy" by advocates of the progressive concept of "mental health" or exponents of the concept of cultural "mental sickness." The description of life in Copenhagen in the *Times* is not notably different from similar surface surveys of seamier parts of town in Chicago, San Francisco, Los Angeles, New York, Boston or Washington D.C. Prostitution is not legal in any of these cities. But this does not inhibit free and open advertisement of whorehouses and call girls in various specialized newspapers and other publications and, in general, a climate where punishment for selling sex in any form is minimal, haphazard and nearly impossible to enforce.

One municipal remedy for these problems—*not* necessarily the problem of pornography *per se*—has been the creation in cities like Boston of red-light districts or "combat zones," where commercial sex is supposedly confined to a limited area, ostensibly allowing the rest of the community to pursue higher standards of living untainted by the commerce of the sex jungle.

Genuine red-light districts, of course, go back to antiquity. Their establishment has usually been motivated by force of law rather than agreement, and their inhabitants, even in such anarchic cities as Aden, agree somehow to live together according to rigid standards—the expensive whores of Grant Road at one end, the cheapies at another, and various economic steps on the sexual-economic ladder designated by space and distance with exquisite complexity. In their own way, the cat houses and call girls of Nevada (the one state where prostitution is not illegal) operate according to similar rules, most of them economic or commercial in origin. They work out into a complicated class or caste system that ranges from an hour with a working casino "show girl" at the top of the ladder, through fancy "escort services" and all-night bed companions (male and female), whose favors cost into three figures per frolic, to roadside "ranches" for truck drivers and others willing to spend ten dollars for ten minutes that may include a swift screw or blow job in near assembly-line fashion with, to some tastes, stimulating impersonality. In some such bottom-rung establishments, the customer is not even allowed time to undress, and the doxies rarely wear costumes more complicated than a halter and pair of shorts!

Cordoning off urban areas as red-light districts for erotic communications seems at this writing to present many and various sorts of problems in the United States. In the first place, the law has become a poor instrument for actually zoning the physical location of porno theatres, adult book shops, peep shows and such. In some measure, it can more effectively control the placement of night clubs, live theatres, go-go bars and even massage parlors; but even these enterprises have a way of popping up in unlikely places, simply because they are sometimes most profitable when nestled in a respectable neighborhood rather than on a Tenderloin or a Times Square. New York City's most expensive and best porno film houses and massage parlors, for instance, are located in swank neighborhoods. They rub shoulders with exclusive foreign film theatres, costly boutiques, restaurants and department stores. So, as a matter of fact, do the luxury apartments of the busiest call girls (often used as working quarters) and surviving brothels, in a city where whorehouses have supposedly become obsolete. (They have not!)

I suppose that the fundamental *theoretical* reason for the inevitable failure to contain physically erotic communication conduits, including the go-go bar, live show, cinema house and bookstore, is simply that a population's general interest in the erotic cannot be segregated from its interests in everything else. Activities pursued in this connection may no more be geographically segregated than real estate or dental offices or grocery or drug stores. Copious signs and warnings indicating "FUCKING PROHIBITED ON THESE PREMISES BY LAW" would not deter bosses and secretaries from their ritual trystings one jot or tittle, any more than they would keep male students' hands out of coeds groins (or vice versa) in the clean-cut environment of the American college campus.

Houses of prostitution have historically presented a different type of challenge to the law: the desire to keep *one* type of commercial sex available in *one* community in *one* place for the mutual safety and convenience of both vendor and consumer, that safety including immunity from prosecution, protection of privacy, reasonable safeguards from veneral disease, insulation from all but well-established criminal elements, crude but realistic price controls for various services (or at least reasonably competitive prices) and various other simple but important institutional regulations that operate to everyone's advantage. Not the least important is the general public attitude that, with prostitution isolated, virtue will flourish elsewhere, as blithe and vain a hope and as poorly accomplished in modern Hong Kong as in ancient Pompeii.

Red-light districts, although they always fail in certain respects, *must* accomplish some of these objectives, and this accomplishment constitutes a workable social control. I was living in Paris in the forties when the famous whorehouses of that great aged city were closed for good. They had not been isolated into red-light districts, but they had performed many of the same civic functions for well over one hundred years. Their disappearance resulted in the inundation of the streets of Paris with titularly "free-lance" strumpets, whose pimps worked out elaborate systems of illegal "licensing" of various areas to specific girls who in each locality charged certain specific amounts (no more, no less) for their favors. The physical attractiveness of the whores, oddly, did not seem commensurate with this strange system of underworld economic "zoning," only their wardrobes did. The penalty for any girl who arbitrarily moved out of her zone into another or who undercut the price structure ran, literally, from a beating by pimps to a throat incision and burial in the Seine.

The system naturally "worked" in a manner of speaking. But the streets of Paris were thick with merchants of sex—many quite aggressive— as well as much weeping and wailing by everyone from pimps to whores to policemen to taxi drivers about the good old whorehouse days that had disappeared forever. I remember the pathetic, tearful lament of one lady of the streets: "Paris overcame the Nazi pigs, but will it overcome *this?*" [11]

Houses of prostitution are service institutions that should not be confused with other purveyors of erotic communication, either transitory or permanent. Sleazy saloons, night clubs, flea bag movie theatres, misnamed "burlesque" theatres and massage parlors may indeed tend, usually of their own accord, to congregate in clusters in large urban areas. The reasons are simple. They all require certain conditions to prosper, among them law enforcement officials who enforce as little law as possible, landlords who are not too scrupulous about the use of their premises but who must charge high rents to defray taxes and make their properties—often located on potentially valuable real estate—worth maintaining, a proper daily flow of the right part of the population and minimum interference from civic and church groups and others who object to such commerce. By clustering, they also tend to offer a sort of protection to one another. Selective "cleaning up" of such areas usually accomplishes nothing. Old establishments simply expand into places where others have vanished, or new ones are started. Urban renewal is the only solution to the so-called "blight" of these districts. But even this remedy usually impels only a change of venue for such lucrative businesses.

As I have noted, commerce in erotica transcends the physical boundaries of all these areas, because people's interest in pornography extends beyond them and many potential customers may object to their sleaziness and skid-row atmosphere. Purchasers of fine books often want to also buy erotic books. Serious and even occasional moviegoers may want to attend certain erotic films, sometimes many times. Other individuals want to enjoy the raunch of a night club sex show—or simply a sex show—in a relatively convivial atmosphere devoid of vermin, perambulating perverts and marathon masturbators. Wealthy tired businessmen—and, in certain localities, wealthy tired women—desire the erotic stimulation of a massage parlor in an odorless or scented environment where onanistic fantasies seem to come true. Such charades are not difficult to mount for a price, but such establishments cannot survive in urban districts where their clientele are uncomfortable or unsettled.

Little advantage is therefore gained for any of the parties involved by attempts at limited commerce in erotica to titular "combat zones," mainly because inducements that have classically recommended red-light prostitution districts both to customers and vendors apply selectively and weakly to books, films, theatrical shows, night clubs and even massage parlors or "swingers' clubs" that, by means of countless small evasions, avoid outright definition in both law and custom as houses of prostitution.

The latter dodges are indeed many and slight, but they add up to quite a formidable legal shield against anti-prostitution legislation today. Sex acts are *implied* in advertisements for the services rendered, and rarely specified for the price of, say, a whirlpool bath—with a nude partner as "therapist." It is also possible to receive a genuine massage in a massage parlor, albeit a rotten one!

Sexual services are never openly sold in swingers' clubs, mainly because it is impossible to tell the professionals from the amateurs. Some sexual services are genuinely equivocal or ambiguous: a nude woman may perform every act *short of* consummated fucking for a customer. He is left to achieve orgasm by his own devices—with, possibly, a bit of manual help. Other variations are numerous and naturally capricious, depending upon the hour of day or night, who the customer is, how the police and law enforcement climate seems disposed at the time and so on.[12]

All in all, one faces the inevitable conclusion that, in the last part of the eighth decade of the twentieth century in the United States, despite one's own personal attitudes toward the issue, legal remediation appears to be an almost entirely ineffective way (other than superficially) to curb or control commerce in erotic communication. Custom, as a matter of fact, without the force of law seems to work *better than law:* outraged neighborhood groups picketing movie theatres, pressure by PTAs and church organizations, stern puritanical standards of landlords who will not rent their premises to certain tenants, editorial decisions by newspaper publishers not to print certain advertisements or other non-legalistic devices that receive enough public support to sustain them *de facto.*

Few tocsins in any culture sound more ominous than the failure of law to achieve its intent, when and if that law does not have public assent to the degree that it can be enforced. During America's flirtation with the prohibition of liquor, our nation was in many subtle ways being prepared for a revolutionary thrust that nearly uprooted our capitalistic system of free enterprise during the subsequent depression that coincided with repeal and occurred at exactly the right (or wrong) psychological moment. Booze and the genius of Franklin Roosevelt's neo-Keynesian Rube Goldberg economic policies saved the United States for capitalism by the skin of its teeth. The policies would probably not have worked in an entirely sober society or in one where illegal, non-toxic alcoholic beverages were reserved for the elite. Our working men's beer may have had more to do with the success of the New Deal than we usually assume. This was a dangerous period through which we survived in that dimly remembered era—make no mistake.

The seesaw of the law has moved in its great arc, but I cannot claim that the history of the prohibition era and the subsequent depression is in any manner being repeated. I can, however, state clearly that I do smell deep dissonance in the air that may portend dangers of a different kind ahead for our nation and its institutions.

The good Professor Peckham ends his critical foray into the domains of what he regards as pornography (a fraction of erotic communications in general) by viewing obscenity in the West as an attempt at innovation not unlike science itself: a type of human "creativity," "the center of our culture and what we are proudest of. It is another name for sin." If I read him correctly, he means exactly what he says when he therefore states that "pornography may very well be the great key which has freed the energy locked into the trivial by social management. . . . Pornography, to our shame and our glory, is not peripheral to our culture; it is central," largely because of civilized man's need for "true cultural innovation," the latter being one result of pornography's "audacity and its endless invention." [13]

I may be simplifying a subtle, complex (and somewhat wearily told) liberal defense of pornography as art by a literary critic looking for consistency and value in a garbage dump where by accident and design (as we have seen) an occasional diamond, polished or in the rough, gets mixed in with discarded rhinestones. In this respect, Peckham displays considerable naiveté in facing up to the full contemporary agenda of mass culture, much of it as reverent as pornography is irreverent, but a similar garbage heap where a critic like Peckham may if he wishes discover jewels among rocks and portents of originality that will someday be salvaged and shined into fine arts and noble sciences—maybe. *Both* mass culture and pornography are people's communications, being more or less detached from established intellectual and academic values and answering mostly to untutored tastes and raw emotions that are socially viable but not culturally respectable. *Snow White and the Seven Dwarfs*, therefore, á la Disney versus á la pornographic cartoonist share many characteristics in common to the eye of a culture critic, to the degree that Disney's crude jokes seem scatological in the first version, just as the obscene gags in the second bespeak a childlike innocence—once the initial shock wears off. (Snow White and her dwarfs are a favorite porno subject in animated cartoons and live action films and in comics photographs for many obvious reasons.)

I appreciate Peckham's faith. He does indeed make much sense. Does he mean, however, that *all* societies—and especially ours during the last five hundred years or so—have required *continual* liberation from sexual bondage, restraint and deformity given to it by creative men and women who, in one way or another and in all the arts and sciences, almost *always* commit outrages analogous to those of the talented pornographer? I suppose so. The private life of the atom or DNA molecule or untapped energy sources or economic cycles or historical relationships of this to that may turn out to be as dangerous an excursion into forbidden territories as *A Night in a Turkish Harem* and eventually more shocking to established sensibilities.

One needn't be a philosopher, sociologist or psychologist to understand the degree to which all civilization with its bureaus, laws, regulations and rules tends metaphorically to castrate men and snap chastity belts onto women. The contemporary fashion of calling this old phenomenon "alienation," "anomie" or whatever only reaffirms what ancient Greek playwrights already knew: The two best answers to the shackles of hyperculture are the bawdy revel and a drunken spree. This has always been pornography's answer to the sterilities induced by social and economic cooperation—as opposed to the frantic hedonistic cooperation involved in an orgy.

Liberal social critics tend almost invariably to defend freedom of discourse in erotic communications, I think, because in sexual matters they are truly die-hard reactionaries who want to return to a halcyon culture that has never existed, where they may conceive of sex as "natural" and "unshackled" by wicked cultural impedimenta, neuroses and possibly even perversion—excluding those perversions that liberals consider unfashionable, such as sadism and necrophilia. (Homosexuality and masturbation—the latter the ultimate *sexual* perversion—are *in* fashion at the moment for heaven knows what reasons!) What their idealistic freedom really amounts to is a deeply felt magnetic pull toward *un*socialization or *anti-*civilization wrapped in cute slogans such as the now passé "Greening of America" or "Different strokes for different folks."

I suppose they are also historically correct in their own way. Sexuality *is* indeed a human vector that requires continual liberation, today mostly in the face of the multifarious intellectual, social, scientific and cultural changes that have developed in geometrically rapid strides during the past two centuries. In simple terms, the intellectual of the liberal persuasion intuits that he is becoming *too* intellectual and too civilized for his own good. As his personal ability to achieve an erection at will or at the correct "natural" stimulus declines, he realizes that things are less askew in his personal psyche than they are in culture at large, at school, in government and especially among the best people. Under these circumstances, pornography to a Morse Peckham rises as a redeemer, and erotic communication suddenly becomes a class of free speech *more* vital to societal health than *any* other form of discourse. After all, the fate of our race depends upon sexual communication more substantively than upon any other sort of activity of which he can think! (Minor modifications are necessary for female intellectuals.)

The argument is fairly sound. One does not need to be a political liberal to accept it, but I fear that it excludes as much relevant data as it includes. In the first place, despite its insistency in everyday life, neither man nor woman lives by sex alone. Second, civilization and society are mixed blessings, but their negative face is the one that the intellectual usually sees most often and clearly. Disregarding its material aspects (hardly negligible), civilization has also given us by political, economic, scientific and technological means the fairly recent blessings of both psychological and physical privacy in their widest contexts: "the right to be let alone," as a great jurist said, a right that ramifies from the physical confines of one's own bathroom to the spiritual domains of individual faith and conscience!

An entirely cogent case for the broad spectrum of human privacies that we in the West have come to expect as part of our intellectual heritage is presently difficult to defend in practical terms, except to say that without privacy not one of us will discover his or her essential self or realize anything close to our full potential for being—highly abstract, possibly mystical notions of individuality that flow in exactly the opposite direction of the liberal's unbounded faith in social cooperation and organization as mankind's salvation. Without denying the primacy of sex in our concerns, or even the necessity for the continual liberation of each generation from the sexual shackles of the previous one, the spirituality of privacy and its protection is certainly no less serious a matter than social cooperation. Or so I hope.

The dynamism of erotic communications fused to the modern mass media (and to the general nature of most mass culture) remains highly antithetical to this mystique of privacy, mostly by example but by non-stop exhortation as well. Nothing is intrinsically immoral or fattening about nude bathing beaches, and certainly nothing *can* be wrong with nudity. If nudity, however, is a functional symbol among a group—any group—that they are allowed to have *no personal secrets, no private lives* (analogies to "private parts" of the body), then very, very much is wrong with it!

To ask a beautiful girl to share freely the *sight* of her private parts with strangers may more or less inevitably lead to other more personal types of communication on her part, and nothing, I suppose, is essentially wrong with this either, *taken alone.* But *can* it be taken alone? For this young lady to ask now for privacy in matters of conscience, belief, or even bank accounts and political affiliations initiates a sequence of ludicrous inconsistencies of the sort exploited in French farces of the last century. I have previously mentioned the cute porno actress who, to Al Goldstein's amusement, refused to eat lunch with him after blowing him. I myself once knew a prostitute whose sanitary habits regarding drinking glasses were ridiculously scrupulous, although I could not locate any part of the male or female human anatomy that for a fee she would not suck ravenously with abandon, glee and skill.

Similar inconsistencies attend quite clearly the socio-political libertarian thrust for sexual freedom in the face of a desire for privacy in numerous ways. In a bitter episode in the fifties, playwright Arthur Miller learned how completely he had lost all rights to a private wedding *in a functional but quite non-legal sense,* simply because he had chosen to marry a movie star who had once posed nude for a photographer. The reporters and news photographers who intruded into a private ceremony understood what Miller in a rage did not comprehend: that privacy, like Humpty Dumpty, once shattered cannot be restored either by fair play or civility—only by fast feet running. Few are fast enough to turn the trick.

With the sacrifice of privacy, other, more profound issues arise, some of them as terrifying as a collision of religious dogma between the devout of any two hostile sects. Holding privacy up beside pornography (including much but not all erotic communication) may well place in opposition contrary mystiques that are *totally* irreconcilable. Privacy is not a major concern of this book. Eroticism is. It behooves us, therefore, to gather fragments of what we have discovered about the metaphysics of erotic communication for a final evaluation of its attendant contemporary parameters and structures, if we are able to articulate them clearly.

Once these outlines are fairly lucid, our exploration is, I believe, finished. Then, if we wish, we may also add the mystique of privacy to the large collection of societal prohibitive vectors (laws, morals, instincts, prejudices, self-delusions and so on) that other and better minds than mine had attempted and failed to measure on a scale of values that has not yet been built.

The Orgiastic Society

From the rituals of adolescent petting to the recent university experiment in which faculty wives agreed to practice onanism in front of the researchers' cameras, sexual life, particularly in America, is passing more and more into the public domain. —George Steiner

(I)t is precisely those people who have carried holiness farthest who reproach themselves with the deepest sinfulness. —Sigmund Freud

Man, proud man,
Drest in a little brief authority,
Most ignorant of what he's most assured,
His glassy essence, like an angry ape,
Plays such fantastic tricks before high Heaven
As make the angels weep; who, with our spleens,
Would all themselves laugh mortal.
—William Shakespeare
(Measure for Measure, II,2)

I SHALL SUBMIT in this chapter a number of slightly cold-blooded but nevertheless discursive hypotheses that, I believe, have been reasonably substantiated by our long, often tedious but (I hope) interesting journey. In one way or another, we have examined much of the history of erotic communications in the recent West and given consideration to the legal, moral and functional status of such communications in the United States at the present. I have also offered some possible directions (based entirely upon present data) that our current attitudes and practices regarding sexual communication in its broadest construction may be taking us.

Mine will certainly not be hypotheses in a positivistic scientific sense or even in the loose, breathless sense currently employed (in constricted language) in the behavioral and social sciences, mainly because they cannot yield to rigorous tests—some even as rigorous as we are supposed to apply to certain historical research. Should you wish to call these stabs at theory "social criticisms," I cannot object. But the establishment of categories neither adds nor detracts from the heuristic rigor of a guess or series of guesses, no matter how stupid or how enlightened. I must, accordingly, make clear that I am in no way certain of the validity of the pith of these guesses. Nor can I, in the light of the eleven chapters before this one, present them with the certitude of similar ideas offered by our present established sexual experts, both sacred and profane, from the Drs. Kronhausen, Masters and Johnson, Dr. Ellis (Albert, not Havelock) to Gerard Damiano, Hugh Hefner, Al Goldstein, his much admired antagonist Dr. van den Haag, or even Professor Peckham, who, of all the authorities above, has earned my deepest sympathies.

Secular Sin

Nietzsche was not the first philosopher in a modern key to note that God was dead. Like Bernard Shaw somewhat later and Sigmund Freud later still, he centered the praise or blame (mostly blame) for the essentially tragic nature of the human condition upon man himself. Nietzsche's vehicle was passionate exhortation; Shaw's was compassionate but often bitter humor; Freud's was despair and a tentative acceptance of the non-rational faith of religion as *the* inevitable neurosis. All three men were in their different ways waiting for a redeemer—an unborn neo-Christ—who, like Godot, would never arrive: a superman, boundless in intellect, undiminished by fears of pain and mortality, clear of eye and pure of heart, untainted by the picky ambiguities of Scholastics, Rationalists and Talmudists, uncorrupted (and uncorruptible) by socialism and capitalism as well as the hedonisms inherent in all technology and entirely free of neurotic tics. Best of all, this superman would eventually destroy both the need for and inclinations toward mankind's security blanket of so-called "spiritual comfort" (which William James, the great father figure of instrumental pragmatism, demonstrated in print only two years after Nietzsche's death) that people everywhere seemed inevitably to weave, although of different threads and into different patterns.

In various ways, each of these extraordinary figures was a Victorian in spirit, and also in his own way each looked upon sexuality as but one more albatross thrown by natural law around the human neck. Whatever manner of superman the future might produce, he would surely cast off this reprise of original sin in a metaphorical social replay of the Garden of Eden: for Nietzsche by means of the triumph of the will (A European political slogan by 1936); for Shaw by intellectual-cum-genetic hocus-pocus (as in *Back to Methuselah*) combined with a unique brand of socialism; and for Freud by a cultural psychoanalysis reborn into some sort of *Weltanschauung* that he admitted before his death he could not clearly articulate for civilized man *circa* the 1930s.[1]

In its peculiar way, eroticism, as Stephen Marcus shows, pulsed in tune with the heartbeat of Victorianism, and, unless I am entirely misled, was intimately related not only to the "secret lives" of libertines but part and parcel of the fantastic rebellions of thought, beginning with Darwin and Marx in England (or some years before with Hegel in Germany), that set the stage for the implementation of science and art into the roles they play in the technological cultures of today. A price was paid for the obvious sexual hypocrisies of the Victorians, but in modern terms it was well worth it. Victorian ideals of sexual decorum moved sexual behavior—not reproductive behavior alone—to stage center of the biological and psychological worlds; it insinuated itself into politics and economics and, possibly most important, managed to sneak almost everywhere into older notions of "free will" and "free speech" and nearly all other juridical matters that had, up to 1850 or so, been concerned almost entirely with matters irrelevant to human erotic life, as we have seen. Needless to say, corollary minor but notable rebellions were also set off like Chinese firecrackers in the world of art, including the visual arts, poetry, novels, drama, opera, and even somehow into music, particularly into whatever was called "popular" music.

As far as I know, it was Nietzsche more or less alone among these prophets who clearly understood just how completely Western man would eventually destroy his gods—the good ones like Jehovah and the bad ones (to come) like Hitler—in order to free himself of Victorianism, in itself the end product of an irrational but profound faith in reason, religion and caste systems, none of which could possibly survive the radical changes in the technology of the times. Shaw and Freud and apparently even independent thinkers like Kierkegaard (in his short, prophetic life during the first part of the nineteenth century) and certainly Darwin—all looked forward to mankind's *displacement* of God, a metamorphosis modeled upon the "transference phenomenon" in neurosis that had so amazed the young Freud in Charcot's clinic. If necessary, the superman could as long as necessary *play the role* of a god. For a good while it looked as though this view was prophetic.

A new age of the celebrity was born with this century, a technological by-product of the mass press and movies and other modern media of communications. Novel political religions seemed all to be growing more or less at the same rate and at the same time—in Italy, Germany, the new

USSR and the United States—producing for public approbation secular godheads who were more like one another than different, whether or not they wore mustaches or spoke in frenetic Italian or with the intonations of Cambridge, Massachusetts, or Eton. Mostly they shared a common and cool sophistication regarding the use of mass media as a magical socio-political control system, as they added to many languages the apt phrase, "cult of personality," and found new uses for an old word, "charisma." That they symbolized extremely various cultural values—some absolutely antithetical to others—is for me more interesting than important.

But these secular gods by displacement failed—ignominiously one and all—to fulfill their great function. They committed suicide, were hung by the heels from gas station pumps as abused corpses, were demythicized in speeches, books, films and confessions after their deaths, some in strangely sudden passings and others engulfed by despair and depression! All were publicized in effigy and chewed upon by gossips of the mass press and the sort of historians who peck like vultures at the carrion of the great in the name of "justice" or "objective history." (In general, men have always enjoyed reviling their dead minor, transient gods. At Mardi Gras time, the old king is defiled because we are certain that by the end of next year's Lent a new one will certainly be provided for a new ritual murder.)

Modern history has so far in this century been written in the wake of *failed* gods rather than *displaced* ones. The great Judeo-Christian God we strangled in the great age of technology may have disappeared into a machine, as Arthur Koestler has suggested and as we have seen, but He was certainly not neatly displaced—not by culture heroes, dictators, presidents, philosophers, sports idols, sex "goddesses," movie stars or Superman in the comic strips and cinema, nor by the entire cult of celebrity. Instead and to the amazement of all, possibly even Nietzsche's ghost, God just died!

In the technological nations of the West (and some in the East), a corner had been turned by the end of World War II from which there was no return. Jacques Ellul seems today to understand this best. His ultimate suggestion for handling what, in effect, amounts to the pan-secularization of the once Judeo-Christian world is to face the fact that God will never return. Gone with him—and forever—is the great age of reason and the philosopher's paradigm of "rational man," of man the humanist, of, in short, man made in the image of God. (I think he died somewhere near central Europe, and I think that I have visited his grave.) As Steiner who is quoted above, says, we now know that it is perfectly possible for a sensitive person to read Goethe and Rilke in the evening, to listen to Brahms and Beethoven on his phonograph and then go off to work as an administrator at Auschwitz the following morning. One of my best students some time ago (after reading Ortega) inquired of me what good a humanistic or liberal education is if all it ever seems to produce in the long run is barbarism. I stumbled through an answer, quoted Donne and was left with egg on my face. I can do no better today, years later!

Whatever changes have occurred in the erotic climate in the West during the past generation, they are inevitable side-products of many components of the technological cultures that produced them. More precisely, they are outcomes of the way that people *must* live with one another in these cultures, if they are not to be a) diminished and b) destroyed by the domestic technology around them—to say nothing of atomic bombs, chemical warfare, industrial pollution and on and on. By means of our genitalia, we find just about the only reliable and warm comfort available to us that will affirm our status as sentient animals or as human beings, whichever you please. If we find this remedy not strong enough, we will probably be hurled into the maw of technology, where we grasp at clever chemical techniques that will succeed in providing a measure of the comfort that sex has denied us! On we go—to booze, pills, drugs and, if it is our bent, to the perverse stimuli of social outrage that warms the blood of so many (probably not all) homosexuals and sadists, masochists, child molesters, fetishists and sons and daughters of Krafft-Ebing.

No, the pleasures of perversion, deviance, addiction and possibly violence are taught neither by the insipid stories or commercials of television nor by the example of prize fighters or dirty old men. They are reactive spasms, learned the way we learn that orgasms affirm our sense of identity and that strong whiskey warms the gizzard: by trial and error. In this sense, therefore, erotic communications—in fact, *all sensual communications—are functionally the most intensely practical sorts of communication in the modern world.* Until jots of human feeling may one day be stored in the molecular structure of crystals, we need not fear that computers will make man obsolete or even impotent. Quite the opposite. All computers will do for a technological culture is to enhance the ubiquity of technology and exacerbate the reactive spasms it *must* generate.

Is all of this an old story? T'was not always so! Nor is it today in those places and times where communal religions and spirituality require constant and heavy doses of mysticism to maintain themselves. As long as men and women maintain the steady faith to juggle metaphysics derived from revealed truths in their bibles, holy books and as revealed from the mouths of prophets and priests, neither eroticism, narcosis nor reversions to barbarism seem to be necessary to make a man a man: Freud's inevitable "illusion," if you wish. But identifying something as an "illusion" or "neurosis" means nothing, or next to nothing, to those who live by it. (The best immediate example of *exactly* this is the current worldwide monetary system!) But science has drained both metaphysics and mysticism from most religions, and even the concept of spirituality has been secularized. Psychologists and churchmen both talk with straight faces about a search for "spiritual experiences." And both religion and therapy have been and are being today subsumed into the grand amoeboid world of Ellul's "technique," and there exists neither a technique of metaphysics nor a technology of mysticism—so far, at any rate.

Whatever changes were required for the abolition of the old gods (with both small and capital "G") and everything they stood for did not happen overnight. And too, I am not able to place the burden of guilt or all the causes entirely at technology's doorstep. Mysticism has in recent times been meanly abused from many sides: by science, political democracy, economic theory, commerce, the arts, by the spread of what we today call "education," by the law and, mostly, by what technology has *done* to distances, to relationships between people and their urge for (and definition of) creativity and human love. I supposed many of the Victorians—including the rebels—were more sensitively tuned to what was about to happen to the civilized world than are we, their children and grandchildren who have actually lived through this change. Their ambivalence toward eroticism, both its extirpation and its cultivation on so vast a scale, provides evidence that I find convincing. They had time and luxury enough to fear for the fate of their gods, undistracted as they were by the sort of issues that concern us so deeply and almost entirely, because we intuit that they are consonant with the technocultures in which we live—diversions such as the Nazi holocaust, a B-29 over Hiroshima, Vietnam, Attica, Cambodia, starvation in India and the real value of the American dollar.

In recent years, the sharp-eyed have noticed all this, but even intelligent reactions have varied widely to it all.

Social psychiatrists have accused our time and place of rampant and endemic psychosis, insanity and worse! Waves of mysticism, most noticeable and obtrusive in the American far West, has crossed the sea from the Orient. Some mystic cults seem also to have sprung spontaneously from native soil, phenomena such as primal scream therapy, EST, Scientology, extraordinary interest in ESP and brain waves and voodoo—even hypnosis. Whatever quantum of scientific reality all these phenomena deal with (and they *must* deal with *some*), they are today most interesting and attractive because they employ black magic and offer one road among so many to quench our thirst for mysticism. Some even offer fairly coherent metaphysics that, their premises having been accepted, cause (all too) few offenses to human logic.

Inviolate in the midst of all this motion remains the sexual urge, which is essentially a device of nature's for reproducing our species, but, even in this elemental construction, presents to mind and heart unanswerable questions of enormous existential power and emotional importance. Disassociated psychically from the function of reproduction (as it is most of the time for most of us), eroticism is perhaps the only insistent avenue of mysticism that remains intact in the world we know between birth and death. Its metaphysic has grown enormous, with tentacles reaching into religion and law and almost every other significant aspect of culture. This, I suppose, has been true ever since antiquity, though it was usually in competition with other sorts of metaphysical notions that were usually subsumed (like physics itself) to the mystical all-powerfulness of a god, his churches and churchmen. In our time, however, one strand of the metaphysic in particular has been secularized and redeemed by the technologists into a family of experiences we may call "erotic communications," "sex appeal," or, when involving surrogate media, "obscenity" and/or "pornography."

We are inundated today with such an enormous galaxy of sexual communications for the most basic of reasons: they work. Snatch shots in *Hustler* may not sell breakfast cereals, but, if the truth were told, almost nobody any longer *needs* to sell breakfast cereals to anybody else—or automobiles or cigarettes or men's clothing or cooking fats! In the United States we live for the most part in a seller's market for most goods and services; the only remaining question is who gets what part of the pie, a less complicated matter than we are led to believe by those who direct the market's traffic. No, the snatch shots in *Hustler* perform a more important pragmatic function, with results possibly as great for the model, photographer, writer, publisher, editor and magazine seller as for the viewer, and possibly for both sexes equally were the stimuli equal. Borrowing a literary leaf from Henry Miller,[2] they affirm the mysticism of cunt, of erotic appetite, of warm, lubricated humanity in a cold, cold world indeed. The nude *Hustler* model of femininity, like Ernest Becker's God, shits no more or less gloriously than you and I, and she is equipped—despite stylistic male homoerotic efforts to depersonalize her—to stir us to the one most *reliable, useful* and *certain* indication of personal humanity unambiguously open to us all: the delicious urge to sin!

I say "sin" because the girl in the *Hustler* centerfold has neither been entirely sanitized by civilization nor de-sexed by photographic technology, although, in grand contradiction, she is distributed via the mass press and is almost invariably photographed against plastic and sterile settings— usually modern furniture. Her invitation to sin is vestigial modern witchcraft by means of the manipulation of mysticisms that once were intrinsic mainly to ceremony and cult. Now, in a secular setting in a secular society, her buttocks are poised, farting in the face of a Puritanism that is no longer able to counterbalance with religious fervor, brimstone or eternal damnation the fusion of my (and your) urge to godless mysticism, irreligious communion and self-affirmation as a human being. Even a gratuitous prayer to God to bless and protect all cunts is useless! What *works* is the existential joy of certain affirmation that, if I die tomorrow, I shall have not, at least, fucked in vain! A selfish reward for suffering atomization, alienation and anomie but a fitting one, I think.

When one understands this fundamental pragmatism inherent in *all* erotic communication, and that is not to reproduce the race (a minor matter and one that most of us could have taken care of, in terms of our obligations to our species, in less than three or four pleasant hours at our prime if we are male, somewhat longer and more inconveniently if we are female) but to indulge in the mysticism of obeisance of one strand of a full and somewhat powerful metaphysic, much recent cultural history and some uncertainties about our contemporary "moral revolution" are cleared up a bit.

In effect, we have left the churches and entered the bordellos, more innocently, swiftly and safely than our Victorian ancestors ever dreamed, because the bordellos these days have become symbols of freedom of speech and behavior under custom and law and been given proper blessings by our high lamas of education, mental health and political and social liberation. For the first time in history, we are able to sin in innocence *in an entirely non-theological sense,* not as a child does but as a saint does, when and if he swats and kills the mosquito that has just nipped him. Neither God nor salvation has anything any longer to do with the issue. We are attempting the least toxic and most harmless solution to our inevitable problems of alienation from our work, our families and even, thanks to the near total disappearance of the healing "arts" in favor of modern medical "technique," our own bodies.

If you or I live long enough, I grant that we shall be finally forced to reject even *this* answer to these problems in favor of a bogus return to the womb in the clever disguise of a nursing home, psychotropically induced narcosis and/or life sustaining equipment—that is, if we are *truly, deeply* and *miserably* unlucky or are cowards at heart who will not (or cannot) perform that final and most humanistic act that remains ours to perform: the taking of our own lives in favor of joining society's miserable human scrap heaps, most of them also institutional gifts of social technology.

Orgiastic Art

I am not entirely certain that erotic communications require the justification of an aesthetic relationship to what various cultures, East and West, call or have called "art." We call much ancient erotic material "art" because we have no better word to describe it. Present day books, films, photographs and drawings may invite such comparisons by virtue of forms that seem similar to expressions that do invite aesthetic evaluation. Such criticism may not only be unfair, it may also miss entirely the point of eroticism. (This may even hold true for the way in which its analysis has been attempted in certain parts of this volume by me).

Some cynical contemporary film critics recognize this implicity by the use of such rating devices as the whimsical "Peter-Meter," which takes the form of multiple penises (instead of stars), or a cock in various stages of erection, to indicate the erotic worth of a pornographic movie. If this amusing method of evaluation displays one main weakness, it is that the "Peter-Meter" rarely measures what it is supposed to measure, because one man's (or woman's) endocrine system is not the same as another's. In addition, when any reporter is called a "critic," strange things immediately happen to him, especially if he is supposed to evaluate the prurience of a motion picture. Judgments become clouded by such irrelevant matters as story lines, dialogue, acting, scenery, photography and fundamentally artistic matters that may or may not have anything to do with effective eroticism. It is true enough in theory that a well-photographed film sequence *should* convey its prurient message better than a blurred one shot out of focus. But for many reasons, this may not always be the case.

In films as well as in most other arts, aesthetic matters (literally "the philosophy of the beautiful") may have little to do with the intensity or nature of erotic content. The well-made movie, like the well-written book or well-drawn picture, may not be as satisfactory in prurience as an item that is similar but poorly done. Or—as in the case of much Oriental erotic painting and drawing—artistic criteria are so beside the point of the mystical thrust of the art that the work is truly schizoid, that is, capable of being evaluated on either of two scales, one aphrodisiac and the other artistic. This is due mainly to the fact that those works are primarily erotic communications whose obvious (to us) grace and beauty was (and is) more or less irrelevant to their function for the culture in which they were created. The same may be said of the ugliness of one of the most arousing striptease performances I have ever witnessed (years ago in a cheap Boston dive), where an ugly crone of (roughly) fifty years (or more) drove a theatre filled with drunken sailors (and me) nearly wild by means of a mad and crazy sensual performance that defies description now but which I shall never forget!

Professor Peckham is much more scrupulous than I in the mating of art and pornography, given his indefatigable desire to find somehow in obscenity the seeds of creativity, innovation and even genius. His conclusions are not irrational, and I find much about them clever indeed. I think that his major error stems from much common wisdom in the West that reflects an overly obsessive concern, manifest in many ways, with crime, punishment, policemen, detectives, laws, lawyers, courts, judges and social restraints. I am referring to the tendency, especially among political liberals, to equate the ever-increasing introduction of erotic communications into the modern mass media and/or culture at large with a form of liberation or so-called "freedom."

This assumption is anthropologically as unsound as it is historically foolish. When one builds his or her analytic premise upon such an idea, as Peckham appears to, eroticism *per se* naturally seems to connote considerable therapeutic power for both the individual and society at large—a power certainly for "heightening consciousness," for liberalizing and providing innovation in public discourse, and even for artistic, cultural and—possibly—political revolution. At least pornography (and erotic communications in general) *seems* to perform a *social* function, this tenet continues, whereby sexuality is framed and given new *importance* both to life and art, because it raises to significance much that is all too easily reduced to triviality and mitigates against the insistent boredom of much in modern life.

Even the "kinky" or perverse may be redeemed in this manner—definitely when it is treated as surrogate communication and even, up to a point, when one participates in it, because perversion is skillfully raised to the kind of normal "excitement" that occurs in most theatrical experiences. From the circus arena to plays by Tennessee Williams to Elizabethan tragedies, real life situations are raised from triviality and boredom to suspenseful drama by extenuating the commonplace. A lion tamer's act seems trivial and boring (and therefore useless) only to a person who has lived much of his life among lions, just as an exhibition of—or an attempt at—fucking a goat is only routine, trivial and boring in a society of goat fuckers.

Peckham's sensibilities are indeed keen, and I think that his theatrical insights are a good deal sharper than his erotic ones. All the above observations rest upon the assumption—no stranger, as I say, to common wisdom since World War II—that a photograph of the beast with two backs printed in a mass magazine, or even a class one, stands somehow as a liberating event, a challenge to art and a victory of sorts in the fight for freedom of speech and free will. On one side of the coin, I grant that it certainly is tempting to see recent social changes in this light, mainly because they are often accompanied by the breaking of corollary taboos, some of which are indeed freedoms from impositions of various sorts upon important art and significant ideation. On the other side, however, the same phenomena may be understood just as convincingly—more so to many—as invasions of personal freedom, privacy and domains of thought and feeling which, while similar to those of other species, alone distinguish the human being from the rest of animal life on this planet and are therefore to be cossetted. To date, this latter concept has in general not been legally or juridically attractive, simply because safeguards for all personal domains demand from law and law enforcement more negative (non-) action than positive action, more passive protection than active investigation! Yet it is precisely in this sort of language and in this spirit that our much-abused First Amendment was written!

I choose the assumption that public intrusion into the personal domain constitutes neither a step toward personal freedom, liberation or creativity, nor progress in the elimination or dimunition of triviality or boredom, nor is it therapeutic to the individual or the state, nor does it encourage rebellion or genius. Skepticism of this sort does *not* mean that I advocate throwing erotic communication to Puritans or Victorians or bluenoses of any sort, especially in a secular society like ours, where the thirst for mysticism parches the palates of all but a few atavists among us. I find it as difficult, however, to defend the aforementioned *Hustler* by exaulted encomia to human freedom, both statutory and spiritual. So did numerous other writers and critics, who, although ardent defenders of civil liberties, could not bring themselves to follow the popular reasoning that censorship of Flynt's publication was a first step in the march to cultural totalitarianism or political book burning.

In other words, I think I detect an unmistakable qualitative difference between *Ten Days That Shook the World* and *Deep Throat* that is more serious a matter than a variation in so-called "film genre" or that can be explained sensibly and entirely as a matter of creativity and art! I believe that cultural history will and must treat the two films as two quite different sorts of human experiences—or I hope it will. Nor do I think that such a viewpoint demeans the value of freedom, free speech or free will as implied in the equalitarian thrust of the Bill of Rights or in the spirit or letter of most philosophies of civil liberty. I see no good reason to defend erotic communications because they are supposed to be instruments of freedom and social therapy (both of which I doubt) any more than I find it necessary to denegrate them because they may *not* qualify as art, stimulate creativity or function as therapeutic agents either for me or for the social order in which I live.

Why, in simple terms, must we require yesterday's devil to be today's physician, when he is already so competent—and he has always been—as a *meta*physician?

The reason, I suppose, is part and parcel of the recent notion apparent in a figure of speech that equates sexual behavior with "performance" rather than with sheer "behavior" or even with a physiological human function that is wrung dry of any sort of psychological baggage, romanticism or love. Not strangely, I owe recent and fresh consideration of this curiosity entirely to my wife, who commented upon my own continually bemused considerations of the nature and evolution over the years of what I called "human sexual performance"—specifically my own! The questions she raised were both deflating and shocking. They centered on the issue of whether I regard my own erotic behavior as a type of "acting" or "dissembling," mainly because I insisted in prattling about it in "performance" terms!

What *other* types of bio-psychological behavior do we regard as a "performance"? Making a speech, participating in an athletic competition or displaying certain skills are "performances," I suppose, but not much else—certainly not cooking, eating or enjoying a meal; not most informal social (non-sexual) intercourse; and neither the enjoyment nor the creation of a work of art (though the art of interpretation, as in ballet dancing or playing a musical instrument or singing for the edification of others would be performances). For other people (that is, an audience), even hypothetical others, are indispensable for "performance." I am quite clear in my reasons for considering the sexual gyrations of an erotic dancer a "performance." But I am far less certain why I should regard my own behavior with a wife or a lover or a whore in the same terms.

Never is the idea of performance where human beings are concerned without stark connotations of skill or dissembling or acting—in short, of the display of *technique* or the appreciation of others. The technological aspect of "performance" is quite clear when we refer to the way an automobile works as its "performance." We are less likely to use the same term to describe the technology of anything that does not *display* a mastery of technique. A computer or tape recorder may "perform " well. A well-built house does not perform. Neither, as a matter of fact, does a statue, a photograph or a paperback novel. "Performances" display or show us something. They are dynamic, not static. They are exhibitions of developed or built-in techniques and display informal or formal qualities of theatricality. While they may well be spontaneous and creative, they are nevertheless delimited by certain characteristics of specific expectations, lest they turn into "spectacles" or "debacles" or worse.

"Performances" are usually social matters that by and large satisfy or disappoint audiences. What we therefore expect of ourselves and others in terms of sexual behavior has been limned for us in contemporary Western culture in terms of the acquittal of techniques, very much, it seems to me, like musical or athletic competitions. The ending of Woody Allen's film *Bananas* based its amusing premise upon exactly this figure of speech carried to absurd extremes—extremes, incidentally, that are not beyond those our culture at the moment may well accept as normative. The ABC television sports team (that had previously broadcast a political assassination) was preparing (cut off by the end title) to give a blow-by-blow description of Allen's wedding night, with announcers, cameramen, soundmen and crew all focused upon the nuptial bed and the participants therein. Without stretching credulity too far, Allen's comment upon modern erotic behavior is less fanciful, I think, than coldly descriptive.

The case *might* by made—*is* made implicitly—that when and where there is "performance," there is also the possibility of "art;" this is illustrated in the titles of such books as Fromm's famous *The Art of Loving* and many others that promise to describe the techniques (and therefore to the author, the "art") of every manner of emotional erotic behavior from hand holding to rectal coitus. Certainly the term "art" is used here as broadly and metaphorically as is the term "performance," but the fact that it is used at all illuminates the manner in which we consider eroticism and sexuality during this part of the twentieth century.

What sexual behavior of nearly every sort lacks, however, is that investiture of creativity (in any but a reproductive sense) which most so-called "performance" hankers after when human beings attempt it as so-called "art." (I am not referring here to sex acts that are intentionally theatrical.) No matter how adequately I may perform as a sexual being, the stark parameters of this behavior were delimited eons ago, I am afraid. So are the ministrations of the most highly specialized geisha, although Japanese strumpets are world famous for what are considered investitures of novelty they supposedly add to sex, a reputation they share with their counterparts in India. These reputations for speciality may be in some ways justified, but eroticism itself admits neither of genuine novelty nor of creativity, our enormous technology of vibrators, mechanical and electronic masturbators and other so-called "aids" to sexual performance notwithstanding. Should we search for art in eroticism, we shall find it as Peckham has to his own satisfaction, but only in sexuality framed by theatrical or aesthetic devices: in theatrical or ballet performance, in painting, in description—always interpreted somehow by the mirror of talent and expressed by some wider medium than person-to-person communication, even if, as in the instance of live performances, that medium is merely a living theatrical convention.

Let me suggest that the concept of sexual or erotic "performance" as somehow intrinsic to sexual behavior is fundamentally a mystical one, similar to the ancient notion of "art for art's sake" but quite different from it qualitatively. The limits of this mystical idea are quite precisely drawn in the shared metaphysic of eroticism by which we live and in the "ways of knowing" or epistemology that we accept, not only as compatible with, but ancillary to our better-known scientific-technological-pragmatic value system. These systems are energizers of our cultural and political life, our morals, our laws, our educational imperatives and our lifestyles.

In fact, we have no choice other than to "perform" or not to "perform" within the ambit of middle-class culture. Few gray areas exist between the two. Should we choose the path of "non-performance," we are probably accepting the reigning metaphysic as heartily as if we choose "performance." The difference, therefore, between the sexual dropout, be he priest or pre-psychotic, and the porno queen is not too great in a fundamental cultural sense. Long before de Sade, it was already noted by the more lucid saints that the hedonist and the anchorite are brothers—or sisters—under the skin. Both of them "perform" *in extremis,* while the rest of us affirm society's erotic espistemology (and mysticism) in more desultory manners within the tiny middle-ground territories that morals, law, custom and style permit us. Most of us "perform" with only occasional expertness and passion and choose not to "perform" in much the same way, victims, I suppose, of lesser degrees of self-delineated justifications of mission than either the rebellious whore or the smug nun. This is the price we pay for our secularized spirituality, the emotional (or neurotic) source of energy that fuels and sustains the metaphysic by which we live and that validates our concepts of personal and social adequacy.

Here we see all the more reason why the issue of freedom or free-will is in a statutory sense nearly always irrelevant to erotic communications except when and where eroticism has specific societal or political consequences. Dynasticism or monarchy are excellent examples of the latter and not quite as moribund in the modern world as egalitarian myths would have us believe. In most other instances, the liberations wrought in a political sense, for instance, by the freedom of a writer of novels to describe this or that in every scatological and anatomical detail is indeed a puny victory. He or she will write a good or bad novel—or a best seller or a cultist sleeper or an unprintable dud—according to matters that have to do with rhetorical and literary skills and powers of observations and cleverness, quite independently of how open the gates for erotic expression are in words either sacred or profane.

The social and political power of what a writer says will be more closely related by far to his or her freedom in intellectual domains than to any carte blanche to wander in the sensual vocabulary of eroticism. Nothing more clearly illustrates this principle than the uneven erotic content of many powerful writers whose political impact remains constant, while their penchant for pornography varies with time and circumstances. Jean Genet and William Faulkner come immediately to mind, probably because of Genet's unwavering sense of political and social injustice and paradox and Faulkner's occasional but irrelevant desires to explore the damaged sexuality of Temple Drake within a corpus of stories and plays that are, as I see them, in large measure social documents that could only be written in a climate of socio-political free expression.

Distracted so thoroughly as we are by imperatives of "performance" in our quiet, secret lives that are combined with the inevitable sense of inadequacy that amateurism always produces in aspiring performers, how simple it is to misconstrue and exaggerate the roles that both free speech and free choice play in our culture in one way or another. When that free choice is constricted merely to affirming one given epistemology (and metaphysic, mysticism and/or secular religion) of a certain time or place or to quitting that time or place by physical means (suicide or flight) or mental devices (madness)—boiling things down, we are really permitted very little freedom and very little choice.

Discussion of either may be fruitless. To legislate, therefore, by statute or common law that such a freedom not only exists but must be protected by the state borders on the absurd. We have already seen how the naive recognition of this absurdity provides a rationale for the near unanimous judicial agreement that obscenity (meaning erotic communications) is not (read: *cannot be*) protected by guarantees of constitutional law, at least at this moment in this particular civilization. Justice Douglas' implied insistences to the contrary—which are far from idealistic liberalism under these circumstances—appear merely to be alienated oppositions to constructions of reality permitted by the prevailing value system in our world. His consistency of argumentation, however, implies nothing at all about how his words may or will sound in the future. He may turn out to have been abnormally prescient and eerily aware of the fact that metaphysics, like physics themselves, are subject to constant revisions—and so are epistemologies.

Meaningful Relationships

We must remember that religious rituals, where and when they are generalized but authentic representations of spiritual feeling and commitment, are also considered to be "performances." In fact, when they are acted out by mere rote they qualify *better* as "performance" in a theatrical construction than when they are spontaneous! Rain dances are "performed," as are masses, funerals, rites of circumcision, marriage ceremonies and so on, and the aesthetics of the religion involved or nature of its panoply of ceremony has little to do with our construction of the term "performance." Religious mysticism—unlike the sexual sort—does, however, seem to accept philosophically the fact that acts of intimacy negate possibilities for theatricality or display or technique as "performance." The act of confession to a priest is not a "performance;" only the "performance" of a given penance is. Nor are last rites for the dying "performed" as much as they are "given," despite any display of technical virtuosity they may demand from a priest.

All religions *demand* a metaphysic. In fact, religious epistemology *must* start with some notion of the creation of the earth and some ideas about the origins of inanimate and animate beings as well as human life. These are explained invariably in physical terms even by the mystical faiths of the East that seem more concerned with the physical nature of the flow of energy called "life" than with the physical properties of "earth" or "flesh." A physic of physics is precisely where religion *begins,* and, because all constructions of reality man accepts *must* be affirmed by symbol and metaphor, all religions also find it necessary to deal in mysticism in one form or another. This preserves the integrity of their construction of reality in precisely the same way that the ontology of science (with its own "mysticism") must be reaffirmed in every experiment, theory or law that sustains the "real" physic (we assume) in the scientific method of accumulating knowledge. I know of no religion—old testament Judaism, the Quaker faith, even neo-religions like Ethical Culturism—that does not require spiritual affirmation from mystique—or from many mystiques—in order to sustain the base of its fundamental assumptions.

(I think that Freud, incidentally, objected more to the necessity for *acceptance* of spirituality and its attendant mysticisms than to the metaphysics of God beliefs themselves, because the former seemed more closely to replicate the symptoms of neurosis than did the latter. He certainly knew that belief in God, taken alone, was not unlike the quantum intellectual leap necessary to accept the apparent scientific rationale of psychoanalysis, which was itself accused quite frequently of metaphysical leanings of various sorts.)

With the death of God, all these structures collapsed, because it is always a god—called what you wish—that provides the source and pivot of the religious metaphysic. What has happened in our own time in West-

ern societies (mostly but not exclusively) is that the old God has been replaced by the biological Eros. A new metaphysic has been called upon,
therefore, to perform extremely old and probably necessary spiritual and
mystical functions in the personal and social lives to most people. If you
ask me why, I am not entirely sure, except insofar as I believe (in arguments previously made) that technology, materialism and everything that
has been given us by the intellectual advances begun in the Age of Reason
have seen new assumptions substituted for old ones, just as new assumptions have produced moral changes by filling old bottles of guilts and fears
with the new wine of an interpersonal metaphysic. What has *not* changed
is the need that men and women have for spiritual solace and mystical
recourse of some kind to face the bewildering, frustrating and absolutely
frightening nature of the human condition!

The *ideal* spiritual-mystical solution to the problem of existence remains the old religious one that served so many so well for so long. I
clearly remember my long-deceased atheistic father, a brilliant jurist and
attorney and occasional writer, counseling me when a young man: "Believe in religion, son, although it's all bullshit. It's your only hope!" He
was quite correct. But his advice was also useless, as I imagine he meant it
to be, because he could not articulate what was in his heart, being a man
who had spent his own formative youth in pre-World War I America. In
my way, I think, I have replicated the experience of millions of my contemporaries, an experience that my kind and sensitive father anticipated
that I would be forced to face. Indeed, I know what *works,* what makes
life in a technoculture bearable. But I am most of the time entirely powerless to use what I know in its most efficient forms: the old religions, East
or West, that package satisfactory solutions to the pains and fears in life
into their metaphysics, mysticisms and spiritual comfort.

Realizing what is and is not possible for us as children of modernity,
many—or most—of us have somehow or another turned to the next best
thing. We have rejected the fundamental touchstones of religion—God and
His construction reality—and chosen another metaphysic and played fast
and loose with it by means of only partially satisfying games involving a
bit of mysticism and a *bit* of spirituality, encouraged in large part by
strong but loose ideas of *freedom.* The latter fascinate us in law, push us
into wild socio-political crusades and even force us often to compromise
whatever genuinely civilized ideals we nurture by turning us, in the role of
defenders of freedom, into wartime murderers in the name of a "higher
morality" compounded of spiritual inclinations and mystical impulses in
the name (but neither in the word nor image) of God! In the end, the closest we come to a solution to our chronic discomforts—or alienation, or
anomie or whatever—has been neatly summed up in the chic phrase
"meaningful relationships."

A meaningful relationship was at one time possible for most of mankind only with God. All others were less meaningful and therefore to some

degree "meaningless." Some of the few who secularized God found these meanings (usually to their detriment) in sexual attractions or romance in the West. Heloise and Abelard, Dante and Beatrice, Romeo and Juliet and Othello and Desdemona are all examples of poor fools who courted tragedy or pathos or both by misunderstanding the true meaning of a "meaningful relationship," in other words, by confusing sexuality with Godliness. I must stress that these were exceptions rather than rules; they were almost invariably cursed to pursue horrible lives or untimely deaths, because they misconstrued the precise nature of "meaning" in the term "meaningful relationships."

The modern so-called "meaningful relationship" is quite a different matter that deals with a far less sophisticated relationship than that of Man with his Creator. It has become a peculiarly ambivalent ideal, entirely impossible to reach, as far as I can tell, that asks from (usually) two individuals an eternal balance between intellect, concern, growth and objectivity on one end of a scale with sexuality and freedom on the other. This certainly describes *no* culture's implicit notions of marriage, even where and when the dominant factor in satisfactory human symbiosis is an old-fashioned notion of "love." Nor is it, as a matter of fact, little more than an existential conceit.

Such a concept will not and cannot describe the course of a relationship through time, if for no other reason than differential biological changes in different individuals, be they of different or of the same sex. Little or nothing about the meaningful relationship ideal is consonant with scientific ontology, nor may such an ideal be even vaguely practical in a world dominated by complex materialistic economic systems, notions of nationality and social obligations, to say nothing of the political-sexual ramifications of the freedom supposedly demanded and given in such an arrangement. (I suppose the latter has been carried to its illogical conclusion by the recent fads of so-called "open marriages" and "sexual swinging"!)

The most interesting and dominant aspect of the secular meaningful relationship is inevitably erotic. It is also probably in this domain that the greatest stress is put when the relationship begins its *inevitable* implosion or explosion. Whether the relationship is or is not consummated in marriage has become an increasingly irrelevant matter, largely because just about the only remaining important issue of substance regarding marriage is its contractual nature in the eyes of God. This is a metaphysical conviction that only the Catholic church in the West (with diminishing conviction) has held onto in principle. Most other religious bodies have tempered it with exceptions enough to invalidate most of the assumptions on which it rests. The law, too, no longer regards the contract as more than a loosely binding agreement, except in economic terms, and then (increasingly) only when children's hungry mouths must be fed.

By equating some ideal, usually a hazy one, of human partnership with the *desideratum* of "meaning," the contemporary social and/or psychological therapist has created a problem of human interchange so complicated that it would provide a year's work for my sociologically inclined colleagues who draw models or matrices of what they fancy to be "communications" or "communications systems." Theirs is the wild fancy that a verbal or graphic diagram explains something or clarifies it, denying what it really accomplishes: the reduction of a point or series of ideas into worthless jots and vectors. I would enjoy seeing this Micky Mousery, however, attempted more frequently in the domain of interpersonal erotic relationships, mainly because I prize my sense of mischief. Whatever else happened, the results would be amusing. If one notes, incidentally, the general thrust of most of these sorts of models at present, they—wisely perhaps—rarely or never mention or notice the omnipresent erotic aspect of any sort of communications, which is one indication of their sterility.

What I am getting to is a modest suggestion that, as alarming as it looks at first blush, is entirely compatible with the assumptions above. It boils down mainly to the bitter observation that erotic communications are distinguished largely by and differ from other types of communications in that *they "mean" nothing or nearly nothing* when human beings use the idea of "meaning" as a component of social activity. If this is so, "meaningful relationships" in the balanced intellectual-sexual context in which we enjoy using the term today is at the outset a self-defeating ideal, a balance between an acid and a base that yields a neutral solution.

Now, how on earth can I claim that erotic communications are meaningless at the same time that so much recent research, concern, alarm, discussion and serious consideration (including my own) have been spent so freely and apparently fruitfully on the subject? My answer is, first, that meaninglessness in no manner necessitates human indifference. Human birth and death in personal terms may well be quite meaningless—in fact, what meaning *can* they have?—if we attempt to ally meaning with intellect, as if the fact (to our senses) of existence may somehow be measured against the exact nature and purpose of that existence itself. This is tautological and worse than absurd, because it measures the unknown against the unknowable. Existential artists of many kinds have shown for many years that the demonstration of the absurd is artistically satisfying, but none, to the best of my knowledge, has claimed that the absurd is *meaningful.* All they can do is demonstrate what they want to understand themselves and want us, in turn, to understand that *they* understand.

If I maintain that screwing quiets my nerves or boosts my appetite, I am indeed imbuing some aspect of erotic communication with some meaning. But I am also a self-delusive fool, in that there are better methods of sedation and appetite arousal than sexual intercourse. On the other hand, if I make these claims in the manner of a well-known popular singer who must always be sucked to orgasm by a prostitute before he makes a personal appearance in order to perform smoothly, the previously discussed

analogy to the pragmatic value of sexuality becomes quite clear. His behavior, however, tells us nothing about meaning. In other times and other
places, this singer would have bowed to a ministerial blessing, have kissed
a cross or even have rubbed a rabbit's foot instead of receiving a blow job,
and these varying mystical expedients would have worked as well for him
as they have for thousands of others.

The point, I think, is quite clear. Because of the metaphysical parameters provided by the conviction of meaningful relationships, because of
their mystical and spiritual functions, erotic communications (or those
parts of them that are interpersonally sensual) are precisely as intellectually
meaningful as any other acts of meta-intellect, metaphysics or sheer faith,
particularly those that, as I have previously noted many times, are associated with religious impulses before philosophers and priests turn them
into doctrine and law. General skepticism as well as plurality in our time
and place have reduced the once transcendent powers of formal religion to
lip service, weak tea and Sunday ritual; most of it has been secularized as
fully as an electric star on a Christmas tree. Faith remains with us, I agree,
but now it is a neutral faith, enhanced and validated, it seems to me, every
bit as effectively by transmissions of sexual emotion from person to person
as by spiritual communion with God or with his emissaries and symbols
on earth. Sartre said that hell is other people? Let me suggest that our
mod-god is also other people!

If all this translates into the unnecessary and simplistic suggestion that
erotic communications provide the framework for a not-so-new but contemporary and universal translation of the old word "religion," I cannot
object, although the elegance of what I am suggesting becomes somewhat
roughened in the reduction. (I hope nobody makes a "model" of it!)
Before I embarked upon this volume, a friend of mine, a brilliant professor
of religion, noting curiously my intense research into pornography and
allied matters (that invariably interest seekers after higher truths), asked
me, "It's all a metaphysic, isn't it?" I did not answer then, except by raising my eyebrows. I think I am prepared to do so now.

No, good friend, surrogate erotic communications in general, and
pornography specifically, are not a discrete metaphysic (or part of one) at
all. They are simply side-products of one, in much the same way that technique (or technology) *should be* (but is not) the side-product of scientific
philosophy. The parallel is excellent, because in its peculiar way erotic
communications, up to and possibly including the sex act itself, serve as a
rough analogy for technology, and they certainly involve techniques.

Nor am I delimiting the real metaphysic, that of the *meaningful relationships,* to heterosexuality alone in any sense. In our time and place,
and, let me suggest, mainly by virtue of its neurological dynamic alone,
this interpersonal metaphysic provides the basis for the epistemological
(and therefore psychological) system that includes all sorts of human transactions as well as the enormous adult's garden of verses and myths that

sexuality has generated in the Western world. I fear that I must include our multitudinous notions of perversion as well, especially and to the degree that perverse sexuality of any kind—including masturbation, if we want to consider it perverse—is understood to be a facet of "human nature," irreversible, incurable and a function, fortunate or unfortunate, of being. It just so happens that the present metaphysic of meaningful relationships assumes in large measure such a stance of predestination in much the same way as science until recently has assumed an inevitably ordered universe that must always respond to precise questions of cause and effect.

I mean also that, in the topsy-turvy vocabulary of modern therapeutics, all pornography, even the most nauseating, is in one way or another part of the technology of the metaphysical ideal of the meaningful relationship. In an age when and where criminals (including child rapists) are considered, right or wrong, to be *sick* people in need of psychotherapy and love rather than punishment, this *must be* exactly what I mean! If faith in the form of spirituality and mysticism cures all evil, as we seem to think it does, all erotic communication is a vindication of meaningfulness and part of the ceremony of celebration of mystical freedom and transcendence achieved by orgasm.

Truthfully, my friend, I fervently *wish* that pornography alone *was* indeed a metaphysical entity, because it would be easier to understand than it is. Instead, I must compare it to the ceremony or worship of mystical symbols that I find quite often impossible to explain and difficult to understand. I fear that among the ceremonies and worshipful acts and mystical rites of meaningful relationships, we discover that pornography is in the same class of experiences as Moslems prostrate toward Mecca, Jews crying at a brick wall and ministers sprinkling little babies with water—all exquisitely complex data that demand infinite amounts of inquiry and explanation.

In this light, I find that I am therefore as little impressed by Professor Peckham's argument that relates pornography to creativity, as I am with Margaret Mead's puny notion of obscenity as an ubiquitous form of reactive frivolity, as I am with the psychoanalytic idea of libidinal repression, as I am with the political thesis of pornography as freedom, as I am with the conservative doctrine of dirty pictures as instruments of corruption and depersonalization of the young, the old or both! Pornography is at the same time both more and less than any or all of these constructions—less, because it is so blatantly symptomatic of a powerful value system that seems to hold much of the contemporary world in its spell; more, because it is so intimately related to the current *Zeitgeist* of the West and, as represented by our personal qualities of understanding of this spirit, it so intimately conditions the quality of the lives we choose to live, the way we think and how we behave.

Political and corruptive matters happen to concern me most deeply at this point, however, as they have for most of this book. It is to them I must turn by way of conclusion, leaving, I fear, nobody very happy, including myself.

The Censor as Liberal

Seeds of the socio-political construction of censorship are found in John Stuart Mill's famous essay, *On Liberty,* which is probably one of the most entirely rational arguments against legal, political and religious censorship to have emerged from the Age of Reason.[3] It was written almost immediately before the last vestiges of eighteenth-century secular-political faith were blown to the four winds by Victorianism, science and the new technologies that were attracting more and more intellectual attention in England and America—even while Mill worked upon the document in the last years of the 1850s.

On Liberty is a masterpiece. It is also a deeply misunderstood masterpiece, mainly because its constructions of free speech and intellectual freedom are inevitably descriptive of manners of discourse that *had been* subject to censorship *up until* Mill wrote the essay. There existed literally *no way* that Mill might have anticipated that his arguments, directed at intellectual domains of argument having largely to do with government and religion as he knew them, would someday be interpreted as equally relevant to metaphysics entirely foreign to him and to mystical matters of faith and spirit that would have been considered aside from, or beneath, argumentation by the philosophers of the Enlightenment. In other words, the concept of erotic communications, I think, would have meant almost nothing to him—and quite beside the point of his three or four major arguments. These hinge upon assumptions that all human discourse contains ideas that are either "true" or "false," a distinction difficult—even impossible—to make at any particular moment but the major assumption upon which his discussion rests.

I find it impossible to fault Mill for not being a soothsayer. The influence of his logic has been enormous during the past century and a quarter, largely in political rather than legal or religious circles and in manners not directly apparent either from the study of his work or its uses in academia and law. Mill's major accomplishment, it seems to me, was quite intentional and proper in its time but has lost cultural relevance with increasing intensity during the past generation, a diminution that had begun almost immediately after the publication of *On Liberty.*

With the focus of censorship in Mill's time largely upon political matters, limitations upon speech were clearly reflections of conservative tempers. One hundred years of socio-political change had shaken the governmental foundations of the English-speaking world, not, let us remember, to everybody's satisfaction, and new revolutionary ideas of social progress (all of them politically oriented) were whizzing around Mill's head as he wrote. Censorship in his time meant for the most part eliminating such progressive notions from the agenda of public discourse, thus negating discussion which obviated in the end possibilities of social, cultural or political change.

The reactionary of that era had seen enough changes in these domains already and feared excesses that free speech might produce in matters such as the destruction of caste differences and the economic *status quo*. The liberal, on the other hand, for whom Mill was speaking, viewed any imposition upon freedom of speech as a brake upon the inertia of motion of the natural socio-political change that, though it had begun about a century and a half before, was all too obviously still not completed. Social perfectability was around the corner; but it could never be reached were social and politically oriented opinions—even those of the best people—silenced because they were held by some to be untrue, wrong or corruptive.

Conservatism and liberalism were both clearly articulated intellectual positions. They had little if anything to do with erotic behavior, nor had they the *slightest relevance* to the then growing but still inchoate mystique of obscenity.

At the hands of Comstocks and bluenoses from one quarter and artists, writers and later psychologists and sociologists from another, the polar positions into which pro- and anti-censorship positions had fallen were increasingly rigidified up to our modern era. In the end, approval of censorship of erotic communications *seemed* to bespeak (or replicate) the position of political and social conservatives in a vague and inarticulate sort of way. Liberals generally assumed that obscenity censorship would produce the same sort of results that the older political-social and even religious censorship had: discouragement of societal experiment, change and eventually the amelioration of cultural evils, inequalities and irrationalities.

That these conservative and liberal political positions remained so securely polarized in legal philosophy, art, behavioral science and popular culture remains something of a monumental triumph of long-term voluntarism and wishful thinking right up to our own day and age. Certainly liberal and progressive influences continue to inflame the battle of the Americal Civil Liberties Union against censorship of erotic communications. Even more certainly, fiery contemporary exponents of Comstockery like United States Attorney Larry Parrish, southern nemesis of the porno films and performers, play reactionary roles in their attempts to conserve old values by means of their noisy battles to delimit the content and flow of erotic communications. In other words, the political analogue of sexual permissiveness and wide channels of erotic communications is liberalism. The political analogue of the reverse is conservatism. *Bien entendu.*

What is most surprising is that this position has been defended as axiomatic by brilliant liberals of the Warren Court and also by brilliant conservatives, who are found less often in legal than in academic circles. Irving Kristol is an example of the latter. The fundamental proposition of this polarity has, it seems, rarely been examined closely, simply because it appears to be the natural extension of yesterday's ideas of freedom and free speech into new domains of spirit and mysticism. Old positions refer now to aspects of belief rather than what was once regarded as speech and do not yield easily either to defenses or attacks of an intellectual nature, especially when these attacks are drawn from epistemologies foreign to them. That they have been taken up as polemic by quasi- or pseudo-intellectuals such as Herbert Marcuse, Marshall McLuhan, Wilhelm Reich and their academic camp followers like James W. Carey is not surprising. It is probably inevitable.

Reasonably short and close examination of the value structure of the metaphysic of meaningful relationships to which I have referred should clarify its essentially conservative—even reactionary—nature! Because this metaphysic explains the natural world in terms of an entirely self-contained, self-justifying system (as we have seen) and emphasizes so strongly what is supposedly *given* in human nature rather than what is learned, its ideal exponent is obviously some kind of "natural man," possibly Rousseau's, possibly Edgar Rice Burroughs', who is free from the sin against God that most Western religious metaphysics agree was the double curse that caused man's expulsion from Eden: knowledge and sexuality. For this ideal man, knowledge and sexuality serve the opposite cause: blind and ultimate faith in interpersonal human meaningful relationships.

Further examination of the spiritual-metaphysical nature of erotic communications as they are today cossetted and defended demonstrates sharply that they actually *deny* the possibility of genuine human change or social progress, matters that history has shown, I submit, are invariably intellectually oriented and imply continual subtle changes in the very meaning of human relationships and the relationships of man to the natural world. If, as I contend, the pornographic mystique is essentially a matter of spirit which largely reflects human faith and feeling, it *cannot* purvey "meaning" in a socio-political sense. To encourage pornographic communications—*not* to censor them in effect—therefore moves *one step away from* social progress or everything that political liberality stands for. On the one hand, it denies the primacy of human intelligence, and on the other, it puts the neo-liberal in the position of fool (exactly where many left-leaning defenders of pornography have lately found themselves), rather like the more familiar, unthinking Krazy Kat liberal who loves mice despite the fact that they are forever throwing bricks at him (her)!

The censor's viewpoint today is even *more* idealistic—and possibly even *more* unrealistic. He does not deny the spiritual bias of erotic communications; he simply fears the reactive power that they may engender if their mysticism is somehow accepted as *more than* manifestations of spirit and faith. Should pornography perform many of the functions of secular religion—as I submit it does—such an abnegation of reason is highly likely to inhibit the social progress that usually occurs when neither mystical corruption nor spiritual depersonalization obviously and openly destroys intellectual concepts of human uniqueness and human worth. The latter are necessary for the spread of libertarianism in any of its constructions, though mainly those having to do with hopes for developing political maturity and ameliorating societal dysfunctions. In the end, the liberal places his greatest faith in *education,* a rational process that treats suspicion of intellect, superstition, mysticism and revelation with extirpation—that is with *censorship. To censor the meaningless is, for the true liberal, therefore, entirely meaningful!*

This is precisely the rationale given today by editors of such "liberal" documents as *The New York Times,* the *Los Angeles Times* and other leading newspapers in the United States in refusing to print advertisements for pornographic films and massage parlors. Kenneth MacDonald has noted in a short but trechant essay on the subject: "A newspaper has a responsibility for all the copy that appears in both its news and advertising columns and should decline copy it considers libelous, inaccurate, misleading or offensive. But passing judgment on copy is quite different from the product or service advertised *if* the product or service may be legally offered for sale to the general public."[4] Quite properly, he notes that newspaper editors understand all too well that their role as liberals, that is, as mediators of matters of meaning (often called in their circles "good taste"), necessitates that to achieve this objective they must act arbitrarily as censors whether they like it or not. And so they do, arbitrtarily and ruthlessly!

That certain sorts of people today find themselves acting like liberals while thinking like conservatives and vice versa is symptomatic merely of the enormous confusion that has flowered in our modern world regarding the cultural function of erotic communications. I suppose it is the result of an attempt to mix apples and oranges and—in the void caused by the disappearance of fixed spiritual ideals by which to guide our lives—our inclination to lump together as "software" everything that may be printed, drawn, photographed, filmed or recorded on magnetic tape, which is the consequence of the wild and wide misuse, now past redemption, of the word "media."

As I hope my reader to the bitter end long ago has understood, I oppose the censorship of erotic communications of any sort under nearly all circumstances. I think the reasons for my position have been made clear in the pages past. I also believe that my position is consistent with most of my political and social prejudices, which are by and large conservative.

I should very much like to open for discussion and unemotional discourse all the delightful diversions discussed in these pages, in much the same manner that they were handled by the British elite of the eighteenth century. Certainly problems of privacy, the depersonalization of sex and the de-idealization of love give me pause to consider the dangers inherent in my strong desire to deny the social relevance of most erotica and meet the beast—in myself, I imagine—head-on with neither guilt nor shame nor apology nor, worst of all, the urge to make sense and give meaning to an aspect of existence which, in *my* world anyway, displays damn little of either! On the other hand, I am also content (with Freud) to toss to mankind its bone of mysticism and spirituality upon which to nibble, if it amuses and does not distract people from their primary task of rediscovering the civilities of these great ages past that have apparently escaped their notice in the mad, mad, mad, mad environment of our present technoculture.

In the end, I should like to put first things first.

REFERENCE NOTES

CHAPTER 1

1. Citations of some of the excellent volumes of erotic study by Drs. Phyllis and Eberhard Kronhausen appear below. I refer to them here, because, to date, they have fought the bravest linguistic battle in this respect in the academic (or pseudo-academic) community. Of course, writers and critics in Al Goldstein's newspaper *Screw* and various obscure authors (some labeled as Ph.D.s) have, for years, produced materials written with few, if any, verbal constraints. The recent *Screw*-type authorities (who often are not bad) are, and always have been, transparent pornographers, at first (in 1968) intending to shock, but now simply to communicate. Many other bogus doctored "erotic authorities" have been mere covert pornographers—some good, some bad, mostly the latter.
2. See William H. Masters and Virginia E. Johnson, *Human Sexual Response* (Boston: Little Brown and Co., 1966), or their subsequent works.
3. See Shere Hite, *The Hite Report* (New York: Dell Publishing Co., 1976), and note stylistic differences and especially the similarities in the prose of the respondents, including both their apparent degree of candor and their vocabularies. For instance, compare, one to the other, various responses to questions about orgasms during intercourse on pp. 185–89. The stylistic similarities of most of these responses start one wondering about their reliability. The problem, in one form or another, is endemic to the entire study.
4. Morse Peckham, *Art and Pornography* (New York: Basic Books, 1969).
5. See George N. Gordon, *Persuasion: The Theory and Practice of Manipulative Communications* (New York: Hastings House, 1971), pp. 7–9. Of the 43 varieties and modes of communication listed, most are Ruesch's, but I added a few. They include numbers 42 and 43: "Sex and Pleasure Relationships" and "Procreative Sexual Relationships." Today I would certainly add more, all loosely "sexual" in nature.

6. Note Whitehead's ultimate statement on the role of education in his first essay in *The Aims of Education* (New York: Mentor Books, 1949), p. 26.

7. Is a footnote necessary at last to cite this familiar book? My worn copy is C. K. Ogden and I. A. Richards, *The Meaning of Meaning* (New York: Harcourt Brace and Co., 1953), but other editions are available.

8. Ernest Becker, *The Denial of Death* (New York: The Free Press, 1973), p. 120.

9. No, I did not make this up, nor is it the result of having read too much of this sort of literature. It is from a run-of-the-mill porno paperback: Elizabeth Watson, *A Private Lesson* (Sausalito, California: Tiburon House, 1972). The book centers on the ever-popular theme of sex relations (of many types) between pupils and teachers.

10. Note "Is There Life in a Swinger's Club" in *Time* magazine, January 16, 1978, p. 53. An intrepid reporter and female "companion" visited a public "swinger's club" in New York City. The experience is characterized as sordid, but this *sort* of experience produces different reactions in different people. Filmmakers may control every aspect of exploited privacy and create their own dream world, while real-life orgiasts must deal with the grime, smell and aesthetic disenchantments of the human state. We shall return to this problem.

11. See Kinsey *et al, Sexual Behavior in the Human Female* (Philadelphia: Saunders Publ., 1953).

12. Gordon, *op. cit.,* pp. 290–309.

13. This is the Freud, of course, who speaks to us in his two attempts to articulate (aside from his essays in the early twenties in *Group Psychology and the Analysis of the Ego*) a social psychology. I mean *Civilization and Its Discontents* and (mostly) *The Future of an Illusion,* which are both frequently republished. For those who despair at what I have said and am about to write, let me assure you that the old Puritan notion of love as "health" is alive and well itself on the American campus. Courses given by social psychologists and sociologists with titles such as "Socialization" and "Intimate Human Relations" eventually swing into positions that would cheer the heart of Bertrand Russell and find therapeutic anchors in May, Fromm, Norman O. Brown, Theodore Reik and the familiar company of yesterday's liberal apostles, Marcuse excluded, I suppose, simply because he is a political radical and not too loving.

14. Abraham W. Franzblau, "Religion and Sexuality," in B. Saddock, H. F. Kaplan and A. M. Freedman, eds., *The Sexual Experience* (Baltimore: Williams and Wilkins Co., 1976), p. 621.

15. See especially the Kronhausens' *Erotic Art,* 2 vols. (New York: Grove Press, 1968 and 1970), *Erotic Fantasies* (New York: Bell Publishing Co., 1976) and *Pornography and the Law* (New York: Ballantine Books, 1959). As erotic artists in their films, serious and frivolous, this couple is apparently not constrained by epistemological limitations, one of the reasons they may have, in recent years, seemed more interested in the production of erotic materials than in the study of it. I have only seen one of their movies, and I found it indeed erotic, if not satisfying in any other way.

16. For the non-neurologist like myself, one of the best recent books that I have come upon that makes sense to me of all this is Frank A. Geldard, *The Human Senses,* 2nd ed. (New York: John Wiley and Sons, 1972). The author wisely does not attempt to explain sexual arousal but provides the lay reader with some notion of the interactive subtleties of human sensory systems.

17. Vance Packard, *The Sexual Wilderness* (New York: David McKay Inc., 1968), p. 17.

CHAPTER 2

1. As we enter this grand new era of Orwellian "double speak," I suppose it is necessary to note that by "man" I mean "woman" too, although I do not think I mean "person," the current favored term, for obvious semantic reasons.

2. Pre-history may be written in many ways. A popular and interesting treatment of the subject for the layman is C. W. Ceram, *Gods, Graves and Scholars* (New York: Knopf, 1953). See also Ashley Montagu, *Man in Process* (New York: New American Library, 1961), pp. 15–59, 165–81, for a "shoes, ships and sealing wax" trip into the speculative world of human origins.

3. The topic is treated in Herbert Wendt, *In Search of Adam* (Boston: Houghton Mifflin Co., 1956). Excellent photographs of the Willendorf Venuses appear on unnumbered pages. See also the text on pp. 358–64.

4. The sarcasm is self-directed as well as meant for many of my colleagues of the pencil. My doctoral dissertation was largely an historical document, and nothing will protect me from the title of my last book, *The Communications Revolution: A History of Mass Media in the United States* (New York: Hastings House, 1977), except a small disclaimer in the "Introduction" denying that I am a *professional* historian. "What," asked a friend of mine, "is a 'professional historian'?" And he subsequently muttered something about a woman who claimed to be an "amateur whore."

5. Many such histories of eroticism are today freely available in bookstores and libraries, some concentrating on pictures, some words, some photographs and so on. One pictorially oriented series of five volumes available at a reasonable price is Ove Brusendorff and Paul Henningsen, *A History of Eroticism* (Copenhagen: Thaning and Appels Forlag, 1963; published in the United States in New York by Lyle Stuart). Unlike other similar documents available at discount, this collection is not an excuse for cheap reproductions and inept scholarship, the main pitfall in collecting this type of recently liberated literature.

6. Was the Yeats-Olivier *Oedipus* performed by the Old Vic thirty or so years ago, thrilling and entrancing audiences around the world, therefore inherently satire? In a *most* serious sense, it certainly was, and I personally count this performance as the single greatest theatrical occasion of my life. But why was I—like so much of the audience—emotionally devastated by the power of the verse and performances? Pity and fear? Nonsense. Catharsis? A meaningless word to Broadway sophisticates in the middle of this century. No, we had witnessed a magnificently trenchant comment by *our* culture upon *ancient* culture and the juxtaposition of the ethics and morals of both—particularly those by which we have chosen to live. When told that Olivier's favorite theatrical role was not Oedipus but Archie Rice in *The Entertainer,* I was not at all surprised. (Actor's vanity had nothing to do with it!) Archie's moral-ethical downfall is simply miles deeper into *living* hell (*our* hell) than Yeat's Grecian *Oedipus,* and Lord Olivier is nothing if not a brilliant philosopher-performer.

7. Television too? I have seen many homemade fuck films reproduced by kinescope and VTR mechanisms that date from the early fifties in the United States (probably thrown in with a "batch" of network lab work) as well as crude pornographic items recorded by kinescope on the earliest (silent) industrial vidicons and transferred to 8mm film stock. I have been *told* about previous image-orthicon studio "pornies" somehow made after closing time at early experimental video stations in the forties, but I have never seen one. (Readers knowing more about these technological oddities, please contact my publishers.)

8. McLuhan claims that communication technologies (or possibly all technologies) become "art" whenever they are "framed" or reshown by means of subsequent technologies, such as old movies shown on television or painting and statuary photographed on movie film. This notion, I think, is patent and obvious nonsense like most of Dr. McLuhan's so-called "provocative thoughts."

9. That this story, a precursor of the immaculate conception of Christ, should be so often reenacted and rewritten for the stage as a comedy seems curious only to those who do not regard comedy as serious business. In its first version (not extant), in Plautus' Roman revision, in Moliere's and Giradoux's French retelling (the latest), the comic aspects of the mechanics of the son of god's conception are emphasized, particularly the domestic side of the matter. Of the supposed thirty-eight or so theatrical versions of the story in our tradition, Henreich von Kleist's, written in the German romantic period of the nineteenth century, is the only one I know of in which the tragic implications of the incident are emphasized, although the tragedy is also domestic, and the parallel between the mysticism of Greece and that of Christianity are not treated by the author.

10. From *Le Bourgeois Gentilhomme,* Act I, Scene 1.

11. The following is taken in large part from H. Montgomery Hyde, *A History of Pornography* (New York: Dell Books, 1966), pp. 164–74.

12. In the superb magic collection of my friend Milbourne Christopher, I have seen a book apparently printed in England as late as 1702 that contained the imprimatur of the Royal Stationer's Company and included the words "printed with authority." Because this

book dealt *ostensibly* with witchcraft (it did not; it was a handbook of magic), the publisher probably thought to commit his errors on the side of caution and applied for and received the imprimatur—or possibly simply printed it without notifying anybody.

13. Hyde, *op. cit.*, p. 165.

14. Readers familiar with this sensitive period in law will notice a certain amount of inconsistency in regard to dates of the events covered here. See, for instance, Morris L. Ernst and Alan U. Schwartz, *Censorship: The Search for the Obscene* (New York: The Macmillan Co., 1964), and compare the dates with those given by Hyde and other authorities.

15. Hyde, *op. cit.*, p. 172.

CHAPTER 3

1. Note similarities between Sandwich's attack on Wilkes and recent framed obscenity prosecution against pornography publishers set in midwestern cities like Witchita, Kansas, where a few copies of a victimized publication are mailed to bogus subscribers. Wilkes' entrapment on the basis of *one-twelfth of his total press run* is a good argument for those who claim history is cyclic or that nothing ever changes.

2. I mean, here, such followers of Max Weber as Ludwig Lewisohn in *Expression in America* (New York: Harper and Bros., 1932) and others.

3. Felice Flanery Lewis, *Literature, Obscenity and Law* (Carbondale: Southern Illinois University Press, 1976), pp. 13–15.

4. In this matter, as in many others, Americans were clever at covering up their tracks during the nineteenth century, and, in great measure, they succeeded. My own personal first edition (yes) of the noted American "history" of these matters by W. W. Sanger in 1859 is peculiarly short on information about vice in the colonies of the new nation. Sanger prefers to indulge in a delightful tirade against the "downward career of fallen women" in contemporary New York. The book, quite similar to others of its sort that I have seen, is, however, a delightful cultural history of its day. It purports to survey prostitution throughout the *entire world,* in "barbarous" and "semi-civilized" nations as well as in New York, which seems to constitute, for the author, the *rest* of the world. See William W. Sanger, M.D., *The History of Prostitution: Its Extent, Causes, and Effect Throughout the World* (New York: Harper and Brothers, 1859). My copy is not for sale.

5. Citation may well be futile here, so many are the extant editions of *Fanny Hill.* The one I am using claims to be "The Unexpurgated French Edition," *copyright* 1963 (sic), published in North Hollywood, California, by Brandon House in that year. A study of all of various publications of *Fanny Hill* would require years of difficult scholarship.

6. See the Kronhousens, *Erotic Fantasies,* pp. 18–25, for liberal quotes from *Merryland* and a similar document. See also David Loth, *The Erotic in Literature* (New York: Julian Messner, Inc., 1961), pp. 103–16.

7. See Harold Greenwald, *The Call Girl* (New York: Ballantine Books, 1958), for a study by a psychoanalyst of a number of patients who worked as expensive whores in New York City and who, by self selection, were pretty pathetic and disturbed for the most part. Few, if any, are stereotypical golden-hearted strumpets. A grimier but nevertheless humanistic picture of whoredom is painted in Charles Winick and Paul McKinsie, *The Lively Commerce: Prostitution in the United States* (Chicago: Quadrangle Books, 1971), which emphasizes the profit motive in all commercial sex, that, combined with drug trade and other illegal activities, so often militates against the cultivation of much sentimentality among most doxies almost by definition. I have, nevertheless, heard little responsible sociological criticism of Jane Fonda's characterization in the film, *Klute,* in which she plays, *mirable dictu,* a whore with a cash box cunt but a heart of gold. My guess is that her characterization's apparent believability resulted neither from naturalistic writing nor integrity of dramatic concept but because of clever casting and Fonda's superb acting. The protagonist she played was simply a girl with a heart of gold *who happened to be a whore.* This kind of aberration may well occur in the movies or in novels but rarely in life. Its credibility depends upon good acting or writing or artistic talent rather than resonance with reality, a point made long ago by Zola in *Nana.*

8. Here the film was, to my eyes, a disaster, largely because Capote was dry-cleaned and characterized as a heterosexual in love with Holly. Out the window went literary *and* erotic credibility, as it did in the equally disastrous transition of Isherwood's Berlin stories, *I Am a Camera* (and the competent play and film made from them, both with superbly acted, none-too attractive or golden-hearted Julie Harris as Sally Bowles), into the musical, *Cabaret*, which was equally banal on stage and screen. Further study of the arcane topic is found in Harold Greenwald and Aron Krich, *The Prostitute in Literature* (New York: Ballantine Books, 1960). I shall return to this subject from time to time, because the last word about it has not yet been said by anyone.

9. Here Cleland seems to show considerable ignorance of the rate and nature of female secondary sexual maturation *or* purposely, like Vladimir Nabokov in *Lolita*, makes Fanny more of an immature nymphette physically than she would be in life in order to heighten the erotic content of the scene. Mature, educated males were almost exclusively the readership for whom Cleland wrote—men like himself whose fantasies often concerned nubile, almost pre-pubescent females and the violation of them in one way or another.

10. This last phrase sums up the pith of much erotic philosophy in the eighteenth century: "use and ornament." Note that one hundred years later, the strictures of Victorianism would demand that legs of sofas wear panties, those of wash basins look like claws of beasts and that "breasts" of chicken be called "white meat." "Use and ornament" had, by then, gathered for themselves completely different semantic environments—among the educated, at least.

11. The anatomy is crude here, but the analogy of cunt (and implications of the clitoris) as meeting point of ganglia of nerves—sort of a terminal box of an electric system—indicates that Clelands apparent cliche's to our eyes were, in their day, more acute than just figures of speech or symptoms of a sharp eye. Much of the sexual functionalism in Cleland's work subsequently disappeared from erotica in the English pornography that followed him, and it has only been recently rediscovered in experimental laboratories by contemporary sexologists.

12. Cleland was perfectly comfortable with male and female bi- and homosexuality, but I doubt that this reflected any extraordinary clinical sensitivity or pre-Freudian psychological acumen. Much pornography of the period is equally sophisticated and "modern" in this way. Only with Victorianism was homoeroticism, while frequently a topic of erotic discourse, held as aberrant to ideals of cultural normality that obtains to this day. In fact, in the seventeenth century, a clearly articulated psychology (or taxonomy) of inversion and perversion did not exist, largely, I suspect, because of limited interpersonal communications between classes and between social groups, both of which were subsequent custodians of normative observations regarding proper sexual habits. Even male masturbation, possibly the vilest common crime in the Victorian lexicon, was not considered harmful, sinful or unusual by the literati who read and wrote most erotica until well into the nineteenth century.

13. *Fanny Hill, op. cit.,* pp. 16–18. (Points of suspension appear in the text and do not indicate editing or omission. BUSOM is capitalized in my edition, probably because Cleland wished to emphasize his daring flirtation with linguistic bad taste to his readers. The words "tits" and "titties" and, of course, "breasts" were all available here—among others, since obsolete—for his use, but he chose not to employ these crudities.)

14. Compare the Kronhausen's excellent early *Pornography and the Law,* previously cited, with their *Erotic Fantasies,* also previously cited.

15. From Bernard Shaw's *Man and Superman* in *Nine Plays* (New York: Dodd Mead and Co., 1944), p. 618.

16. In the light of his subsequent travails in the American Midwest, I am not sure that Goldstein was entirely correct. The conversation I quote here occurred in of all places, Kalamazoo, Michigan, when Goldstein and various other obscenity "experts" participated in a loud and long radio program on an educational station, WMUK, in front of a packed studio audience. I moderated the program without much effect or success!

17. A nice dual view of this Victorian cross-hatch, from both a contemporary and an historical perspective, is found in John Fowles' novel, *The French Lieutenant's Woman* (New York: New American Library, 1969).

18. Goffman's main ideas and a lot of others, including those of Eric Berne, Hugh Duncan and Kenneth Burke right down to myself, may be found in the anthology edited by James E. Combs and Michael W. Mansfield, *Drama in Life* (New York: Hastings House,

19. 1976). My own additions aside, I think this is a fascinating and rich collection of discussions of society's theatre and the roles we all play in it.

19. Mill's rational argument and sociological observations are best summed up in his famous essay *On Liberty*, published in so many extant editions that citation is futile.

20. See G. Legman, *The Rationale of the Dirty Joke*, Vol. I (New York: Grove Press, 1968), and Vol. II, published subsequently. Legman has also done the same sort of exquisite parsing of, I suppose, all outstanding dirty limericks. (Are there any other kind?) I have not read them, my capacity for stories about "Young men from Dundee" being limited by instant ennui. Legman's exquisite scholarship far outstrips other admirers of this form of poetic eroticism (if it is poetic, and if it is erotic), such as Norman Douglas of *South Wind* fame. Legman's multi-volume output is enormous, but, in the words of John Dixon Carr, "The reader is warned!"

21. Ashbee is the subject of an analytic chapter in Steven Marcus, *The Other Victorians* (New York: Bantam Books, 1966), pp. 34–77, mentioned below.

22. *Ibid.,* p. 55.

23. The full edition of *My Secret Life* is, of course, still available, but let me recommend to the reader the considerably abbreviated version for any purpose, scholarly or prurient. Anonymous, *My Secret Life:* Abridged but Unexpurgated (New York: Grove Press Inc., 1966). Legman's "Introduction" is reprinted in full on pp. 15–57.

CHAPTER 4

1. All too little systematic research has been done upon music as a form of communication, and, accordingly, cross-cultural (and even many cultural) comments about it are any man's game, yielding chaos frequently for the music critic who must fall back upon his knowledge of only two factors: history and technique. As I say, my ear is defective, but ever since my North African experience (and a few others like it), I have been suspicious of all musicians, in my role, at any rate, as a student of communications. Let me also admit, that I have not been able to identify the cats in the caterwauling of much contemporary rock music, although I have not tried very hard. For others who are also somewhat tone deaf, let me suggest one familiar but excellent philosophical treatment of Western music's affective nature, Suzanne Langer, *Philosophy in a New Key* (New York: New American Library, 1942), pp. 165–99, as well as Roy McMullen's more hard-nosed aesthetic evaluations of our present culture, *Art, Affluence and Alienation* (New York: New American Library, 1968), pp. 54–92.

2. This is a trend that continues to this day even in Japanese erotic photographs that concentrate far more intensively upon organs involved in sex than their European equivalents and in live sex shows in which performers often hide their faces, not out of shame, but to emphasize their genitals! At any rate, their faces are often passive, as they tend to be in oriental porno films. All in all, commercial sex in modern Japan, as I understand it, reflects an ancient Japanese passion for high-degree specialism and symbolism which, for many Europeans, requires a bit of re-acculturation to appreciate as much as, say, equivalent delights in Amsterdam, Copenhagen or New York.

3. An excellent minor collection of this material that I have used as a partial source here is a quondam semi-pornographic book that has become, in the eight years since its publication, reasonably respectable—except for its verbal padding. The illustrations, however, are excellent. See James Bellah, *Anal and Oral Love*, 2 vols. (Los Angeles: Ultima Books, 1970). Note also (once again) the Kronhausen's *Erotic Art*, now published in a single volume (New York: Bell Publishing Co., 1978), one of the few bargains in coffee table books that is presently on sale from discount distributors at one-fifth the cost of the original two-volume edition, previously cited.

4. This apparent pan-human sexual adaptability has many ramifications and runs into numerous concerns, even into such special matters as homosexuality in prisons, and possibly into whatever recent successes various types of sex therapy have induced among individuals dissatisfied with their present erotic lifestyles. A provocative but conservative analysis of the possibility for diversion and change in various apparent inherent qualities of the human sex urge is Robert J. Stoller, M.D., *Perversion: The Erotic Form of Hatred*

(New York: Pantheon Books, 1975), a controversial but fascinating examination of so-called "deviance" as a human culture trait, as well as of more common beliefs that per-verse sexuality is a facet of mystical predestination or individual human nature or the works of gods and/or devils, views which prevail, in large measure, even among behav-ioral scientists at the present time. These latter notions are generally accepted by spokes-men for the cultural validity of special types of deviance, such as gay groups, more or less professional lesbians' clubs and others, simply because other etiologies of deviation admit of too many exceptions or do not make sense. A lot must still be explained, as Stoller—and lately Masters—tells us.

5. These ideas, of course, go back to Charles Horton Cooley and his "looking-glass" analo-gies of self-concept that he calls "sympathetic introspection" and that are also associated with much contemporary theory in sociology and psychology. A recent, well-presented overview of the concept is found in Floyd W. Matson, *The Idea of Man* (New York: Delacorte Press, 1976), especially pp. 20–133.

6. I am not entirely tone deaf, of course, but the crude nature of the musical distinctions permitted someone crippled as I am (a fraternity that apparently included Plato, Hume, Freud, and excluded deSade and Hitler, among others) is so simplistic as to be laughable. We can discern whether tunes are fast or slow, noisy or soft, fully orchestrated or played on a Sousaphone, but, despite countless hours, days, weeks and years of (attempted) edu-cation, we are able to tell little else, except the difference between the works of Hayden and George M. Cohan—sometimes.

7. The infamous, gutsy rascal Clifford Irving is, I suppose, a perfect living example of this principle. In his superb book, *Fake!* (New York: McGraw-Hill Book Co., 1969), the life and times of Elmyr deHory are told delightfully with copious and baffling examples of the forger's art (sic). That Irving himself tried deHory's trick in the literary genre of biog-raphy and failed so miserably says nothing about his abilities as a writer; it merely shows his blind spots in recognizing fundamental differences between painting and literature as means of communication. DeHory was exposed by accident—as many brilliant forgers are—but Irving's downfall was the inevitable result of the convergence of many, many bad judgments, *not* about the childlike gullibility of big-time publishers, a fact that Ir-ving had calculated correctly, but about the nature, largely, of literary biography.

8. A major qualification of—but not exception to—this principle would be the Aristotelian syllogistic idea that, while all fine erotic artists are not all-purpose fine artists, all all-pur-pose fine artists are probably competent to produce erotic works. Well-possibly! All fine artists are not as protean as Toulouse-Lautrec, Edvard Munch or even Gustave Doré, and we cannot judge paintings that a Turner did not, but might have, painted if he had wanted to. Nor is there really any satisfactory explanation for the peculiar talents of art-ists literally obsessed with certain forms of eroticism and little else, such as the Marquis Von Bayros, whose exotic lesbian drawings (more or less in the style of Beardsley) are wildly imaginative, sensual and exciting and survive as homage to a strange monomania. They are, however, no stranger than Degas' infatuation with ballet dancers except for the values of propriety that we bring to them. (When I was young, I knew an artist of talent who was similarly infatuated with Degas. What about *him?*)

9. See George N. Gordon, *The Languages of Communication* (New York: Hastings House, 1969), pp. 134–36.

10. My favorite history of this aspect of photography remains C. W. Ceram, *Archeology of the Cinema* (New York: Harcourt Brace and World, 1965), although any number of books (and *The Encyclopedia Britannica* in its latest edition) cover this subject well.

CHAPTER 5

1. Full citations here would lead the reader in too many directions at the same time. In-stead, see, for example, the collection edited by Gerald Mast and Marshall Cohen, *Film Theory and Film Criticism* (New York: Oxford University Press, 1974).

2. Many recent examples of this problem may be cited, but, at the time of this writing, the one that annoys me most is that the superb Italian movie, *A Special Day* (containing some of the best male-female acting and interacting since the heyday of the Lunts),

passed American box offices by virtually unnoticed, while *Close Encounters of the Third Kind* and *Annie Hall* packed them in in New York! The "hits" are few and far between; the good (enjoyable) movies (such as *The Late Show*) have even been plentiful, but their numbers now decrease. Why invest in a good movie when you can speculate on a "hit"? Shock waves from this situation in filmland reverberate almost instantly on Wall Street, which simply exacerbates the problem. Theatrical movies in America face stormy days ahead, and soon, I think.

3. Regarding rewards for patience, I recently viewed my first enema film, Gerard Damiono's *Water Power*. I doubt that it is the first theatrical film to include men giving enemas to women (or vice versa) and the consequences thereof. But it probably *is* the first such film featuring a mad rapist whose specialty is forcing his victims to take enemas! On the other hand, so-called film "loops" shown in peep-show parlors for twenty-five cents a segment are one ultra-sleazy by-product of today's porno film world. Loops are usually silent; they are made by amateurs and look it. No manner of sexual activity of which I have ever dreamed cannot be found somewhere on a loop currently in circulation. Setting oneself to the objective of seeing, on a loop, a man fuck a sheep while another man fucks the first one anally is entirely realistic, if one lives in New York, Chicago, San Francisco or some other fairly large city. Most of the so-called "porno films" that exploit juvenile sex, of course, have circulated in the demimonde of loops and are displayed in peep-show parlors.

4. I wish I knew of a definitive book on the American porno film business, but none exists to my knowledge. Two limited but amusing and accurate volumes are Kenneth Turan and Stephen E. Zito, *Sinema* (New York: Praeger Publishers, 1974) and Stephen Ziplow, *The Film Makers Guide to Pornography* (New York: Drake Publishers Inc., 1977). The latter is especially interesting, because it is written by a working porno film writer, producer and director of more than average sensitivity.

5. See Arthur Knight and Hollis Alpert, "The History of Sex in Cinema" in *Playboy* magazine, published from April, 1965, to January, 1969, in 19 (more or less) discreet articles that have not, but should be, revised, edited and published in a single volume. Stag films are treated specifically in the November, 1967, issue, pp. 154–59, 170–89. Note also the same authors' four-volume collection, *Playboy's Sex in Cinema* (Chicago: The Playboy Press, 1971, 1972, 1973, 1974), each pocket-size volume of which covers the professional erotic cinema of 1970, 1971, 1972 and 1973 and includes copious photographs in black and white and color from various films during this period as well as commentary and criticism of selected films.

6. One example is a *good book* about early pornographic movies (or stag films) that fails consistently to communicate much, either about the history or nature of these under-the-counter films from about 1915 to, roughly, 1970. It is, however, a neat conversation piece and a nice coffee table volume. See Al DiLauro and Gerald Robkin, *Dirty Movies* (New York: Chelsea House, 1976).

7. This problem is discussed in its legal context as it relates to the concept of "obscenity" in Chapter 6 on pp. 153–56.

8. See Lionel Abel, *Meta-theatre: A New View of Dramatic Form* (New York: Hill and Wang, 1963).

9. See the collection edited by Thomas R. Adkins, *Sexuality in the Movies* (Bloomington: Indiana University Press, 1975), an interesting anthology of literate essays on this general topic.

10. On April 15, 1978, I was invited to address this group at their quarterly meeting at the Waldorf-Astoria in New York after an informal luncheon. By and large, I found them a surprisingly sincere and intelligent audience and extremely interested in the topic of my talk, which concerned the attitudes of young people today—and tomorrow—toward X-rated films and the artistic and even educational potential of such cinema. In many ways, they resembled Hollywood's original filmmakers in the early days of the movies: slightly guilty because of their extraordinary financial success, uncertain about the future of their medium and deeply concerned about public attitudes toward an aspect of culture that much of the public does not understand but, in unspecified ways and without much proof, considers a dangerous form of corruption. Like the other early filmmakers, they too consider themselves to be outcasts; therefore, their drive to band together in their own common interests, as well as their unusual warmth toward a college professor who they perceived as being on their side and who treated them exactly as what they were—his peers and, in terms of common interests, his superiors by far!

11. See *Variety*, July 19, 1978, p. 28, for a report of the ceremony's second year.
12. Lawrence Becker, "Sex, Morality and Movies," in *Sexuality in the Movies, op. cit.*, pp. 98–106.
13. While I regard poor *Harry* as a morality play, I do not think it argued more effectively for ideas of "right" prevailing over those of "wrong" in personal conduct than various other films of, roughly, the same period. *They Shoot Horses Don't They?* comes immediately to mind. Moral issues do linger on one's palate in films like *Horses*, however, because they are balanced by fine performances, astute directing and editing and a remarkable musical score. *Harry in Your Pocket* might also have been a wonderfully satisfying movie had its production honestly lived up to its concept. Unfortunately the concept was all that one took out of the popcorn palace with him.

CHAPTER 6

1. This is from the *Roth* decision, quoted at the start of this chapter. An up-to-date review of these cases, somewhat cursorily presented, appears in Kenneth S. Devol, ed., *Mass Media and the Supreme Court*, 2nd ed. (New York: Hastings House, 1976), especially pp. 93–160. This quote is from Justice Brennan's opinion of the court, p. 100.
2. *Jacobellis vs. Ohio* 378 U.S. 184 (1964). (Emphasis added in text.) The entire case is fully reprised and the decision reprinted (along with selections from the argument) in Leon Friedman, ed., *Obscenity* (New York: Chelsea House Publ., 1970), pp. 143–76. The famous Stewart quote is on p. 175.
3. Anyone who has not read Thomas Szaz's various books on the semantics of so-called "insanity" is in for a treat. Most of Szaz's alarming logic applies without much modification, not only to obscenity and obscene behavior, but also to what we call "sexual deviation." Categorizing certain types of behaviors, he notes, are society's, medicine's and psychiatry's least notable talents; in fact, they are tragic failures. The more popular British therapist, R. D. Laing, seems, in the corpus of his work, to identify serious psychiatric problems with meaning, language and semantics in quite another but interesting way. In fact, his latest books are devoted almost entirely to the linguistic etiology (one assumes) of schizophrenia.
4. See Ernst and Schwartz, *op. cit.*, pp. 22–25.
5. *Queen vs. Hicklin* LR3QB (1868) in Haig A. Bosmajian, ed., *Obscenity and Freedom of Expression* (New York: Burt Franklin and Co., Inc., 1976), p. 5.
6. *Loc. cit.* (Emphasis added in text.)
7. A new and good Comstock biography is overdue, but in the meantime, see Haywood Broun and Margaret Leech, *Anthony Comstock* (New York: Albert and Charles Boni, 1927).
8. The original legislation is *Tit. 18 Crimes and Criminal Procedure*, Ch 71. *Obscenity Section* 1461 of the postal code. See *Ernst and Schwartz, op. cit.*, pp. 31–33.
9. *People vs. Muller* 96 N.Y. 408 (Ct. App. 1884). See James J. Kilpatrick, *The Smut Peddlers* (New York: Doubleday and Co., 1960), p. 48.
10. While my emotions are mixed on the subject, I am, for instance, still trying to figure out what the "abuses of presidential power" were, in specific terms and according to clear definitions, that the House Impeachment Committee so learnedly waved in front of ex-President Nixon, forcing him eventually to resign his office. The more I study the matter, the more confusing the terminological problem becomes, as does Nixon's own neatly spoken but groundless plea of "presidential immunity." I know what "treason" and "high treason" are. But the semantic legal precision of the entire affair begins and ends, I think, with the observation that we are absolutely certain that Nixon did *not* commit high treason and that he probably did not commit treason! All the rest revolves juridically around legal quibbles, moreso the deeper one gets into their complexities. Nixon is mercifully gone, but the problem—a serious one—remains, and other presidents will be forced to grapple with it.
11. Let me admit that I don't think I have ever met anyone who really *believed* he or she was "average"—or, at least, that he or she was not "more sensitive" than the average man or woman. I have heard people *refer* to themselves as average, but this is usually rhetoric. I include myself, and I, like everybody else, am firmly convinced that I am more

sensitive than the average man! This anomaly may not be as strange as it seems from a statistical perspective, considering the way "normality" and "averageness" are mixed up in common parlance today.

12. *United States vs. One Book Called "Ulysses"* 5.F. Supp. 182 (1933). The case was tried in a federal district court. See Bosmajian, *op. cit.*, p. 20.

13. *United States vs. One Book Entitled "Ulysses"* 72F 2d. 705 (1934). See *ibid.*, to p. 24.

14. *Ibid.*, p. 23. (Emphasis added in text.)

15. Kilpatrick, *op. cit.*, pp. 130–32.

16. *Ibid.*, pp. 135–37.

17. Most encyclopedias contain good material on old playing cards, and those that are well illustrated naturally make my point best. My favorite—but hard to obtain—book on the subject is Mrs. John King Van Rensselar (sic), *The Devil's Picture Books: A History of Playing Cards* (New York: Dodd, Mead and Co., 1893), which contains superb plates, in color and black and white, and is a gold mine of playing card lore.

18. *Roth vs. United States* and *Alberts vs. California* 354 U.S. 476 (1957) were treated by the Supreme Court in tandem. The full decision is reprinted in many places, including Bosmajian, *op. cit.*, pp. 67–76.

19. *Memoirs vs. Massachusetts*, 383 U.S. 413 (1966). See *ibid.*, pp. 90–103, including various notes and quotes that are superb examples of the way jurists treat the words of literary critics.

20. *Ginsburg vs. United States* 383 U.S. 463 (1966). See *ibid.*, pp. 103–14. Here the jurists' notes are as interesting as their convoluted decisions.

21. *Ibid.*, p. 68.

CHAPTER 7

1. Even the near-parenthetical mention of addiction sets us loose on a sea of semantics, quasi-legalisms and medical-therapeutic fashions. For some people, nothing is addictive if they take it regularly! A few hundred thousand heroin addicts are a miniscule number compared to the estimated ten million or so people in the United States addicted to alcohol, who are probably properly *called* "alcoholics" rather than "alcohol addicts." Opiates and alcohol are the major culturally affirmed addicting chemicals in use today in America, and the ebb and flow of laws around them seems to have little to do with either their actual use or abuse. Other drugs, such as LSD and Methadone, are unquestionably addictive, but their cultural status raises more questions than it answers. So do supposedly non-addictive mood changers such as marijuana and cocaine, as well as the ubiquitous and (usually) legal sedatives such as the barbiturates and methaqualone, as well as so-called "minor tranquilizers" such as Valium and Librium, about which few reliable studies of addiction exist to date. Nor is there any question, also, that nearly all smokers and most aspirin poppers are addicts—of a sort. See Alex Thio, *Deviant Behavior* (Boston: Little Brown and Co., 1978), pp. 293–341.

2. See Stuart Ewen, *Captains of Consciousness* (New York: McGraw-Hill Book Co., 1976), for the rueful perspective of the sad news as it relates to the development of the American merchandizing ethic (and morals pertaining to it) by a brilliant left-wing social and economic analyst.

3. See A. N. Whitehead, *Symbolism* (New York: The MacMillan Co., 1958), a small book that packs an enormous quantity. Here is Whitehead at his ripest and wisest.

4. I admire and envy the power of John Rechy's polemic in *The Sexual Outlaw* (New York: Dell Publishing Co., 1977), as well as the descriptive excellence of the narrative sections of this chilling volume. Here is a beautifully told and well-made analogy that equates homosexuality with rebellion. The reader cannot help but be impressed. What is not solved, however, is the eternal riddle of the morality of rebellion and/or the paradox that, once the law condones deviant behavior, its symbolic value as rebellion vanishes and with it therefore its reason to be in the first place. Were the proclivity for social outrage removed from deviant sex roles, the value of their deviance would be nil and, possibly, eventually non-erotic as well. To this enormous problem, we shall return.

5. See Chapter 10 for further discussion of Ellul's apparent pessimism.

6. An excellent full-dress history of the legal travails of the American cinema is Richard S. Randall, *Censorship of the Movies* (Madison: University of Wisconsin Press, 1968).
7. *Ibid.*, p. 12.
8. House of Representatives 456, 64 Congress 1st Session.
9. The case is also sometimes incorrectly referred to as the *Keystone Decision,* and states other than Ohio are drawn into its various aliases because it is confused with other legal actions at the time. See the court's full decision in *Mutual Film Corp. vs. Ohio Industrial Commission* 235 U.S. 230 (1950) in Bosmajian, *op. cit.,* pp. 151–53.
10. *Loc. cit.* (Emphasis added to text.)
11. Of books and studies making this claim, there is no shortage. Some of the most interesting are Nathan Leites and Martha Wolfenstein, *The Movies, a Psychological Study* (Glencoe, Illinois: The Free Press, 1950); I. C. Jarvie, *Movies and Society* (New York: Basic Books, 1970); Robert Sklar, *Movie-Made America* (New York: Vintage Books, 1975); Molly Haskell, *From Reverence to Rape* (New York: Holt, Rinehart and Winston, Inc., 1974).
12. This is the "history" of motion picture legislation regarding censorship that is usually emphasized in texts on "great issues" in mass communication. An excellent summary of it, in greater detail than my review below, may be found in Devol, *op. cit.,* pp. 161–98.
13. I see no reason to explain here how and why the concept of indeterminacy helped to explain the fundamental contradictions that are the inevitable by-product of the influence of scientific thought upon modern life and thought. Northrup, Whitehead, Conant and, naturally, Heisenberg explain this matter in terms that are beyond my rhetorical abilities.
14. From *Joseph Burstyn Inc. vs. Wilson* 343 U.S. 495 (1952), quoted in *ibid.,* pp. 163–65.
15. See *Kingsley International Pictures Corp. vs. Regents* 360 U.S. 684 (1959), quoted in *ibid.,* pp. 168–72, from which the following opinion and concurrences are taken. (Emphasis added to text.)
16. See 365 U.S. 43 (1961), decisions exerpted in *ibid.,* 172–78.

CHAPTER 8

1. Not that this difficulty has stopped numerous gurus in the popular press from "explaining all" to their readers or politicians from conjuring up assumptions about all manner of causes and effects for political purposes, the way men of such high moral character as Spiro Agnew did in speeches written for him by slick arbiters of culture like William Safire. I shall eventually be forced to use some of this pseudo-wisdom, printed in such journals as *Psychology Today, New York Magazine* and *Redbook,* as sources for material, however, because I lack more reliable data.
2. My reference here is largely to American "inductive" sociology rather than European "grand theory" or the newer, subtle and specialized "structural" sociology currently in vogue more in France than in other Western nations. See my comments on this whole problem of communications research in George N. Gordon, *Communications and Media* (New York: Hastings House, 1975), especially pp. 31–34.
3. *Jacobellis vs. Ohio* 378 U.S. 184 (1964). See the text of the decision, dissents and such in Bosmajian, *op. cit.,* pp. 171–76.
4. *Loc. cit.,* p. 175.
5. *Freedman vs. Maryland* 380 U.S. 51 (1965). See Devol, *op. cit.,* pp. 179–82.
6. *Loc. cit.,* p. 182.
7. See *United States vs. A Motion Picture Entitled "I Am Curious Yellow"* 404 F2d. 196 (1968) in Bosmajian, *op. cit.,* pp. 176–81.
8. For a far more generous interpretation of this sophomoric movie, defending it largely as social commentary, see David S. Lenfest, "I Am Curious Yellow: A Practical Education," in Atkins, *op. cit.,* pp. 193–99, along with some dull stills from the film.
9. This was my own experience as a so-called "expert" who gave a deposition to the Nassau County Courts of New York State concerning *Olga, She-Wolf of the S.S.* By the time the Nassau justices had decided that the District Attorney had no right to ban the film in the first place (about eighteen months after its seizure) and specifically that my written

arguments in defense of its sexual candor and brutality were essentially correct, the distributor, Cambist Films, had already re-edited the film and probably ruined its point. As the head of Cambist explained to me, what had happened in Nassau had also happened across America, and the fact that the film was often eventually found non-censorable nevertheless, from his financial viewpoint, interfered with its well-timed and publicized distribution. Although I have not seen the edited version, here may be a specific instance where capricious police actions caused a movie with tremendous (although nauseating) social value to be edited to sheer trash, well sanitized to be sure but without merit of *any* kind.

10. *Stanley vs. Georgia* 394 U.S. 557 (1969), exerpted in Devol, *op. cit.*, pp. 135–37.

11. See, for instance, Daniel Yankelovich, *The New Morality: A Profile of American Youth in the 70's* (New York: McGraw Hill Book Co., 1974).

12. Psychopathology is a kind term. Having witnessed a living exhibition of homosexual "fist" fucking, during which a man inserts his lubricated arm, well beyond the elbow, into the rectum of another male (and I presume into his entrails), I cannot understand—much less explain—this phenomenon except in terms that John Rechy uses in *The Sexual Outlaw*. What a pity that Rechy's notion of "outrage" as a result of exploiting the forbidden seems to me such weak tea. If I brew it stronger by calling it "psychotic outrage" (in terms that deSade himself, for one, recognized clearly in his own time as insane), I don't think I explain much more, except possibly to illuminate a bit the desperateness and perversity of the pleasure that a man must feel who submits to—and apparently enjoys—near unbelievable physical violation of this sort. I have searched for similar outrages performed on women by men and publicized as freely as this one is (and I am sure they exist), but the most bizarre I have come upon is that of displays of similar *vaginal* insertions in porno films, the physiology of which is quite different and not unfamiliar, under some circumstances, to certain procedures performed without anesthesia in gynocological medicine.

13. See Aristotle's *Rhetoric* and *Poetics* (New York: The Modern Library, 1954), pp. v–218. This translation by W. Rhys Roberts is not complete, but it is thorough and clear enough to illuminate the following observations.

14. See George N. Gordon, "Aristotle as a Modern Propogandist," in Eric A. Havelock and Jackson P. Hershbell, *Communication Arts in the Ancient World* (New York: Hastings House, 1978), pp. 55–62.

15. See Theodore X. Barber, *LSD, Marihuana, Yoga & Hypnosis* (Chicago: Aldine Publishing Co., 1970), pp. 113–318.

16. Bravo for aging porno actress Gloria Leonard, who told a gathering at a recent Los Angeles awards celebration (July 18, 1978): "In this business you don't have to screw to get hired. You're hired to screw." Candor is not the least disarming trait of the intelligent doxy, however rare she is. See *Variety,* July 19, 1978, p. 28.

17. The President's Commission on Obscenity and Pornography attempted, in the early seventies, to describe this market in one of its technical reports, and the result was prolix and replete with many numbers, but it suffered from the central defect of being built entirely upon available data, rather like reporting the extent and nature of the cocaine trade by studying copies of *Business Week* and *The Wall Street Journal.* This is the weakest section of the report, commissioned by President Johnson and rejected by President Nixon, to whom it was eventually submitted. See *Technical Report of the Commission on Obscenity and Pornography,* Vol. III (Washington D.C.: U.S. Government Printing Office, No. 5256-0004, n.d.). I have used some of the material in this document, where and when it refers to my argument, as well as some of the more responsible but less ambitious study of the porno market by *Time* magazine, April 6, 1976, pp. 58–63; I have also used various estimates made by personal sources who are involved in this so-called "market." The more research one does into this aspect of commerce, the more one is confused by conflicting estimates and a lack of reliable data. Most errors, it seems to me, are caused by unwise and unmerited extrapolations of unique and specific instances into broad generalities.

18. If you need to, see Harold Greenwald, *The Call Girl op. cit.,* and/or Charles Winick and Paul M. Kinsie, *The Lively Commerce op. cit.,* and/or the hyperbolic but amusing home truths of Xaveria Hollander's various "Hooker" books and articles, which were all ghost written.

19. See Robert Sam Anson, "The Last Porno Show," in *New Times,* June 24, 1977, pp.

47–56. Congress indeed called out the "experts" for an amusing—and possibly fruitless—examination of the child porno market (except that it did apparently stimulate a number of state legislatures to pass or put teeth in legislation regarding the abuse of children in general). See *Hearings Before the Subcommittee on Crime of the Committee of the Judiciary, House of Representatives, Ninety-fifth Congress, First Session on Sexual Exploitation of Children,* May 23–25, June 10 and September 20, 1977 (Serial No. 12, Washington, D.C.: U.S. Government Printing Office, 1977).

CHAPTER 9

1. See Joseph T. Klapper, *The Effects of Mass Communication* (Glencoe, Ill.: The Free Press, 1960). For all I know, this book is now entirely out of print, but when it was first published the established order in the world of mass communications made sure that it received wide circulation. I received over a dozen free copies from one source or another!

2. A number of versions of the report, suitably edited and abridged, have been printed by commercial publishers, usually minus the *Technical Reports, op. cit.* My copy is *The Report of the Commission on Obscenity and Pornography* (New York: Bantam Books, 1970).

3. See *To Establish Justice to Ensure Domestic Tranquility; The Final Report of The National Commission of the Causes and Prevention of Violence* (New York: Bantam Books, 1970), as well as the following documents involved in the same report: Hugh David Graham and Ted Robert Gurr, *Violence in America* (New York: New American Library, 1969); Robert K. Baker and Sandra J. Ball, *Mass Media and Violence* (Washington, D.C.: U.S. Government Printing Office, 1969). Note also the numerous documents surrounding the later, *Television and Growing Up: The Impact of Televised Violence; Report to the Surgeon General of the United States Public Health Service from the Surgeon General's Scientific Advisory Committee on Television and Social Behavior* (Washington, D.C.: U.S. Government Printing Office, 1972), as well as the Senate's *Hearings on the Surgeon General's Report by the Scientific Committee on Television and Social Behavior* (Washington, D.C.: U.S. Government Printing Office, March 21024, 1972), and also individual reports submitted to the Surgeon General by such fashionable behavioral scientists as Robert M. Liebert, Robert A. Baron, Seymour Fesbach, Percy Tannenbaum, Jack M. McLeod, Stephen H. Chaffee, Jack Lyle, William B. Blankenburg and George Gerbner (who has made something of a career of viewing with alarm violence on television and measuring it by means of his "violence profile"), as well as the ubiquitous Klapper. See also the reader, Otto N. Larsen, ed., *Violence and the Mass Media* (New York: Harper and Row, 1968).

4. See Garry Wills, "Measuring the Impact of Erotica," in *Psychology Today* (August 1977), pp. 30, 33–34, 74, 76. Willis is not a social scientist but a journalist, theologian and professor of humanities. The quote is from p. 30.

5. See Michal I. Goldstein and Harold S. Kant (with John J. Hartman), *Pornography and Sexual Deviance* (Berkeley: University of California Press, 1973). Consult the penultimate chapter for summarized results and the somewhat half-hearted sermon, pp. 139–53.

6. My credentials in this domain are mixed but impressive, I think. "Sex Education" was one of the topics I covered in a course I taught at a well-known (supposedly excellent) private secondary school in New York. At two universities, in both the graduate and undergraduate classes, the interests that sparked this volume were awakened in classes I taught on free speech and censorship that during the past half-dozen years were concentrated with increasing candor upon sexual aspects of human communications. I venture to guess that my course in contemporary censorship, first taught at New York University in 1958, was one of the first non-biologically oriented courses to deal with the communication of human sexuality frankly and realistically for the general university student. With generations of students now behind me, I doubt that I have helped any one of them to "solve" any single personal problem that he or she would not have solved without my intervention. I prefer to defend the classes for their value in opening up intellectual problems of new kinds that students did not know existed when they registered for these ever-popular courses. But more of this later in this and subsequent chapters.

7. Wills, *op. cit.*, pp. 34, 74, 76.
8. See Victor Bachy, "Danish 'Permissiveness' Revisited," in the *Journal of Communication* (Winter, 1976), pp. 40–42, reprising this situation and its subsequent social effects.
9. *Ibid.*, p. 42.
10. See, for example, Julia R. Heiman, "Women's Sexual Arousal," in *Psychology Today* (April, 1975), pp. 91–94. The best aspect of Heiman's pathetic matched-group experiments is that she seemed to enjoy them. She is a clinical psychologist and research associate at the State University of New York at Stony Brook, where, I have noticed, experimental psychologists seem to enjoy their work.
11. Citation of a study by Ernst and Seagle, *To the Pure . . .* (1928), p. 234, quoted and cited in Morris L. Ernst's *Amcus Curiae* brief submitted to the Supreme Court in *Roth vs. the U.S.A.*, 1957, published by the author, p. 50.
12. Lois Gould, "Pornography for Women," in *The New York Times Magazine* (March 2, 1975), pp. 10–11, 50–51, 54, 57, 60, 62.
13. *Ibid.*, p. 60.
14. Both reviews were indeed delightful, and I grant that they were probably the best—and only—therapy available to the physically broken Coward at the time. Certainly they did his withering ego no harm. The plays were *Oh Coward!* in New York and *Cowardly Custard* in London. I had the good fortune to attend them both and enjoy them equally.
15. Wills, *op. cit.*, p. 76.
16. The most recent compendium of TV violence data gathered by social scientists reported below, is also, to the best of my knowledge, the most complete. See the confusing record referred to by the authors as the "sole area of television research where this strength (a wide range of equivocal experimental methods, surveys, panels, etc.) exists." Considering the actual "findings" of the research reports they have so well reprised, I fail to see how the scientific mind might be anything but disturbed by their shallowness of objectives and arbitrariness of methods. See George Comstock, Steven Chafee, Natan Katzman, Maxwell McCombs and Donald Roberts, *Television and Human Behavior* (New York: Columbia University Press, 1978), pp. 211–50.
17. Irving D. Harris, "Is the TV Violence Issue a Red Herring?" in *The Wall Street Journal* (September 15, 1978), p. 23.

CHAPTER 10

1. Daniel Boorstin, *The Republic of Technology* (New York: Harper and Row, 1978).
2. A. N. Whitehead, *Symbolism*, cited above.
3. See particularly Jacques Ellul, *The Technological Society* (New York: Alfred A. Knopf, 1965). All of Ellul's works, even some that have not yet been translated into English, are variations on the theme of how technology distorts and modifies all other human endeavors, educational, political, historical, artistic and so on, most of them written with elegance and style.
4. Like all smokers, I suppose I am doomed to die of smoking—if not of injuries to my vascular system or cancer, then indeed of the fright and frustration that the anti-smoking propaganda and horror machines hurl at me. It takes grit, these days, either to smoke or *not* to smoke! In a sense, the nicotine habit is entirely typical of the grip that technological methodologies and customs hold on contemporary existence. No sane man who can add and divide will argue that cigarettes are any more "harmful to health" (in the Surgeon General's words) than riding in automobiles, and yet not even Ralph Nader advocates the abolition of cars or their use! Nor do I see a corollary group to *Smoke-Enders* (called, I suppose, *Drive-Enders*) on the immediate horizon. What a do-gooder like Nader wants is impossible: to have cake and eat it, similar to the pretenses of those of us who smoke. Like my friends in Winston-Salem, he asks for a *safe* automobile, just as the latter prattle about a *safe* cigarette. Caught in the grip of technocracy, the rest of us muddle along, preferring to die, possibly, as smokers rather than as non-smokers and to drive rather than walk, mainly because we know that lightning—in some form or another—will probably hit us first anyway.
5. See Arthur Koestler, *The Ghost in the Machine* (New York: The Macmillan Co., 1967).

6. Computer specialists are at present attempting in all seriousness to rectify this matter.

7. See Aristotle, *op. cit.,* pp. 223–66, especially pp. 264–65.

8. Van den Haag has testified at numerous obscenity proceedings, possibly the best known being those held in New York State against the film *Deep Throat.* See the concise reprise of his position in the anthology edited by Harold Hart, *Censorship: For and Against* (New York: Hart Publishing Co., 1971), pp. 141–63.

9. Here are the contents of the questionnaire. In the original, ample space was provided for commentary on all questions.

Questionnaire   April 20, 1978

As I explained in class, I am asking you to fill out this questionnaire as a favor to me. All I ask is that you reply to it as honestly as possible. Please take it with you and give it a bit of thought and reflection and return it to me next Tuesday, either in class or at my office. If you leave it with a secretary or student assistant, please request a gummed envelope in which to place it. (Incidentally, you have every right *not* to answer this questionnaire. Return it with the sex entry below checked, please.)

It is, of course, an entirely anonymous instrument. All I want to know is your sex. If you feel that there is a chance that I will recognize your handwriting, please type your replies or print. I promised that I would read the results in class. I shall, just as soon as I have had a chance to arrange, collate and study them.

Mostly, you have my personal thanks for what I know will be your honest, valid and thoughtful responses.   GNG

A. Check please   SEX   _____   _____

                                             Male   Female

All references below are to the film, Sometime Sweet Susan, *as shown in our classroom today.*

B. Did the film hold your attention? If so, what parts were particularly arresting? If you were bored, when and by what?

C. Did any of the explicit sex "turn you on"—that is, physically produce "the itch" as you watched? (If answer is "No," disregard the following and answer D below.)

   1. Which scenes were particularly stimulating?

   2. For how long and when during the film did you experience an erection? (Males only)

   3. What stimuli (in the film or room) diminished or eliminated your erection? (Males only)

   4. Did you experience any direct vaginal stimulation as a result of the film or the classroom experiences? Please explain. (Females only)

   5. If this experience was not more or less consistent during the period what interfered with it in the film or in the classroom environment? (Females only)

D. Did you find any parts of the film physically repulsive? (If answer is "No," disregard the following and answer E below.)

   1. Describe the scene or sections which you found repulsive.

   2. Would your reaction have been the same if you had been watching the film under other circumstances or in an altered mood ("high," "stoned," etc?)
   Please specify.

E. At present, which one (or more) of the following best describes the dominant sexual activity in your life. (check)

   _____ 1. masturbation

   _____ 2. heterosexual relations (completed)

   _____ 3. homosexual relations (completed)

   _____ 4. heterosexual relations (unconsummated)

   _____ 5. homosexual relations (unconsummated)

   _____ 6. sexually inactive

   _____ 7. other. Please explain.

F. During the three or four days after viewing the film was there any change in any of your sexual activities that you can fairly ascribe to the film, including changes in fantasies and day dreams? (If answer is "No," disregard the following and answer G below.)

   1. Which of the following do you feel were influenced by the film? In the space after each category, please indicate as best you can *how* this influence occurred. (check and explain)

      ——— a) masturbation (frequency, intensity, etc.)

      ——— b) fantasies or day dreams

      ——— c) heterosexual behavior

      ——— d) homosexual behavior

      ——— e) other behavior (not necessarily sex related)

G. Take a guess: What would have been your reaction if you had seen this film ten years ago, at whatever age you were then?

H. Do you believe that this film should be permitted exhibition in your community to people your age at present? (Forget the legal aspects of this problem.) Why?

I. Did you identify closely with any of the characters in the film? If so, which ones, why and when?

J. Were any of your own personal sexual fantasies enacted in this film? If so, what fantasies in what scenes?

K. Would you have preferred to view this film in a situation other than our classroom setting? If so, when, where, with whom, etc.?

L. Would you choose to see this film at a movie theatre, paying a reasonable admission price? Explain.

M. In addition to your assignment for COMM 104, have you ever seen an X-rated, hard-core porno film? If "Yes," indicate extent of exposure, particular films (if you remember the titles) and your motivations for seeing it. (Include 8mm "home movies," older "stag" films, videocassettes, etc.)

10. Most non-directive final examination questions over the years in this course have yielded answers that fit familiar undergraduate essay-type answers to familiar so-called "subjective" questions. Even instructions given one year to *make up their own question* about erotic print, pictures and film and answer it, sent the students, except for one or two curious exceptions, looking for "safe" models, so that their responses would display most of whatever subject matter they thought they had learned. Few—if any—ever heeded my request to forget the course material and tell me honestly what might still be worth discussing on a final exam about the censorship of obscenity. In other words, they failed completely to identify the countless questions that they, like I, must have had concerning the curiosities of eroticism (discussed so candidly, it seemed, in class) in favor of simplistic legalistic and policy statements, "good" (meaning conformist) students that they were.

11. Kenneth Turan and Stephen E. Zito, *op. cit.,* pp. 238–39.

CHAPTER 11

1. I leave zoology to its own experts, but a Rand study, published in the middle seventies and given wide press coverage, claiming that alcoholism was a "curable" disease that did not require total abstinence for reasonable recovery was an irresponsible idiocy that produced both direct and deadly effects upon some arrested alcoholics (and some drinking ones) who opted for various new behavioral "cures" and psychiatric garbage that was touted—with copious statistics—by Rand. Because these poor fools are now mostly dead or incarcerated, few naturally have complained. And who may they complain to? I am certain that the discouraging details will happily be provided to those interested by

the AA World Services, P.O. Box 459, Grand Central Station, New York, N.Y. 10017.

2. See Bosmajian, *op. cit.*, pp. 138–47, for the entire text of Burger's opinion as well as a short dissent by the Warren Court holdover, Justice Brennan, joined by old-timers Justices Stewart and Marshall. Justice Douglas submitted a longer, characteristically vigorous dissent, which is also included. The majority that upheld Burger were four Nixon appointees (Burger, Blackmun, Powell and Rehnquist), joined by Justice White. All participants—with the possible exception of Byron White—performed according to expectations along political lines.

3. *The New York Times* (June 22, 1973), p. 1.

4. Bosmajian, *op. cit.*, p. 141.

5. *Ibid.*, p. 140. (Emphasis added to text.)

6. *Loc. cit.*

7. *Ibid.*, p. 142.

8. See Ted Morgan, "United States Versus the Princes of Porn," in *The New York Times Magazine* (March 16, 1977), pp. 16–17, 26, 28, 30, 33–34, 36, 38.

9. For the gory details of this outrage—including photographs—see Ron Ridenour, "The Shooting of Larry Flynt: Conspiracy Against Truth," in *Hustler* (September, 1978), pp. 36–39, 48, 92, 94, 100–102.

10. "Danes Tighten Up on Pornography," in *The New York Times* (Jan. 26, 1976). (Page varies with editions.)

11. My information sources here have blown away with the sands of time. During this period of youth, however, I embarked upon my first scholarly production at the behest of a group of Paris hookers whose English left much to be desired. It was a short dictionary of terms translated from French to English that would, with minimum effort, permit a lady of the evening to consumate a transaction with an American or Briton on the street in a no-nonsense fashion, along with French-oriented phoetic renditions of the English phrases. Thus, a French prostitute might offer an American soldier a "blow job" or a "trip around the world" at such and such a price (an entire section was devoted to price structures), all clinched by the phrase, "You pay me first, please!"—the most important sentence in the vocabulary of the Parisian strumpet from time *in memoriam* to the present, or so I was led to believe. The scholarly work took a friend and me two days to complete. We were not paid for it (in cash) before or after, and I have never seen a copy of it in print, although its existence in France after many years has been reported to me by an ex-student who travels often to Paris. I was content at the time to offer my services for international cross-cultural amity *gratis*, considering particularly all that France had gone through during World War II. I remember that the young ladies involved in the project were quite charming, although I cannot say the same for their *maquereaux.*

12. Check the interviews, cover material and photographs in Eric Kroll, *Sex Objects* (Danbury, New Hampshire: Addison House, 1977), especially an amazing interview with Marie, a married high school librarian whose husband is a teacher in the same school and who has a lucrative part-time job as a sex masseuse. Pages are not numbered.

13. See Peckham, *op. cit.*, pp. 298, 300.

CHAPTER 12

1. On Nietzsche, I hesitate to cite references. There are so many, and they are all good. Of recent works, I prefer Walter Kaufman, *Nietzsche, Philosopher, Psychologist and Antichrist* (New York: Vintage Books, 1968), originally published in 1950. Shaw as a Victorian is discussed (poorly) in some biographies. But the plays themselves and the prefaces speak best for him, particularly *Man and Superman, Heartbreak House, Major Barbara* and the lengthy *Back to Methuselah*. His sexual attitudes are best intellectualized in *Mrs. Warren's Profession*. The Freud of whom I am speaking is the author of the final essays, *The Future of an Illusion* and *Civilization and Its Discontents*, which sum up superbly what had often been implicit in some of his former studies as early as the beginning of the twenties.

2. See Henry Miller, *Tropic of Cancer* (New York: Grove Press Inc., 1961), p. 508, for an idea of what I mean, a theme that is repeated in kind throughout many of his novels.

3. See John Stuart Mill, *On Liberty,* in any one of its many editions, but be careful not to consult an edited or digested version. My copy is published by Appleton-Century Crofts (New York, 1947).
4. Kenneth MacDonald, "Should Newspapers Be Policing Sex?" in *Columbia Journalism Review* (May-June, 1978), pp. 15–16. (Quote is from the latter page.)

INDEX